LATIN AMERICA

A Concise
Interpretive History

5th edition

E. BRADFORD BURNS
University of California, Los Angeles

PRENTICE HALL, Englewood Cliffs, New Jersey 07632

Library of Congress Cataloging-in-Publication Data

Burns, E. Bradford.
    Latin America : a concise interpretive history / E. Bradford
  Burns. -- 5th ed.
        p.   cm.
    Bibliography: p.
    Includes index.
    ISBN 0-13-526782-X
    1. Latin America--History. 2. Latin America--Social conditions.
  3. Latin America--Economic conditions.   I. Title.
  F1410.B8 1990
  980--dc20   89-31629
                                                      CIP

Editorial/production supervision
  and interior design: Virginia L. McCarthy
Cover design: Diane Saxe
Manufacturing buyer: Carol Bystrom

 © 1990, 1986, 1982, 1977, 1972 by Prentice-Hall, Inc.
A Division of Simon & Schuster
Englewood Cliffs, New Jersey 07632

Printed in the United States of America
10 9 8 7 6 5 4 3

ISBN 0-13-526782-X

Prentice-Hall International (UK) Limited, *London*
Prentice-Hall of Australia Pty. Limited, *Sydney*
Prentice-Hall Canada Inc., *Toronto*
Prentice-Hall Hispanoamericana, S.A., *Mexico*
Prentice-Hall of India Private Limited, *New Delhi*
Prentice-Hall of Japan, Inc., *Tokyo*
Simon & Schuster Asia Pte. Ltd., *Singapore*
Editora Prentice-Hall do Brasil, Ltda., *Rio de Janeiro*

*I dedicate this book to my students of History 8A,
Reform and Revolution in Latin America, at UCLA,
in order to thank them—at least partially—
for their patience, understanding, cooperation,
help, and good humor.*

Contents

LIST OF MAPS

Preface

By incorporating the most recent data and statistics, this fifth edition brings the history of Latin America up to 1990. I have added a new section, "The Rationale of Empire," to the second chapter and have reorganized the eighth chapter, replacing the section "The Rocky Road to Development" with "The Modernization of Underdevelopment" and "The City as Hope." This revision deepens the conceptualization of the challenges of economic development, puts greater emphasis on the role of rising international debts in the dependency/underdevelopment drama of twentieth-century Latin America, and intensifies the discussion of the effectiveness of political democracy. I have expanded the material on Central America, finding in the crises on the Isthmus the exemplification of problems troubling all of Latin America and of possible future trends in other regions of the hemisphere. This edition introduces material on Puerto Rico. Tightening the prose of the fifth edition permitted the insertion of new material without increasing the length of this book. These changes provide greater clarity to the major themes that characterize the Latin American past and shape its present.

Certainly by the standards of the United States and Western Europe, Latin America is economically underdeveloped. The majority of Latin Americans, that 60 percent of a population of 421 million who earn less than 18 percent of the total income, are undernourished, underemployed, undereducated, and underpaid. Paradoxically they live in poverty in a region that holds great promise of wealth. Becoming more fully aware of that promise, they want to take advantage of it, to tap their own resources for their own improvement and enrichment. In short, they yearn to improve their quality of life. Seemingly one of the major obstructions in their pursuit of improvement is a complex of institutions, patterns, and attitudes fastened on Latin America during the decades in the sixteenth century in which the Iberians were discovering, conquering, and settling the vast area. Many of those institutions, patterns, and attitudes contained vestiges from the Middle Ages, a period already well on the wane in the Iberian Peninsula. But in the New World those seeds from the past took root and flourished. Europe also transferred some aspects of its developing capitalism—commercial agriculture and mercantilism, for example—to the New World setting. The huge estate, monoculture, rigid class structures, and other such inheritances from the sixteenth century, greatly strengthened in the nineteenth, have long since proved their resiliency and revealed their injustices and iniquities—and not least of all their inefficiency—but they continue to exist today, though often hidden beneath a veneer of modernity. These dominating characteristics from the past are precisely what a growing majority of Latin Americans want to alter. To fully develop, to bring the Latin American nations into the twenty-first century, to build a new society in which Latin Americans are masters of their own destiny, it is necessary to substitute newer institutions for those discredited inheritances of the colonial past.

This desire for change engenders tension, stress, ferment, and violence in contemporary Latin America. The unrest promises to persist until the change from archaic to more rational institutions is made, until a majority both control their government and enjoy the benefits of their society. The struggle for development, then, is the major theme of contemporary Latin America. No one can hope to understand the complexity of modern Latin America without appreciating this powerful drive.

Preoccupation with the problems and goals of the United States has clouded our vision of Latin America's struggle for justice and development. Tending to interpret Latin America's struggles and problems from our own quite different experiences and perspective, we have misread the meaning of events in Latin America to such an extent that we have made it nearly impossible to understand fully either what is occurring there or its long-range significance for ourselves, our country, and our future. This has become so true that we have unjustly cast Latin America's struggle for change through development into the context of our own conflicts with the USSR, without perceiving that Latin America's struggle is much less a global duel between the ideologies of capitalism and communism than it is a local conflict between reformers and counterreformers. Confusing a struggle for change with a conflict between communism and capitalism—a dangerous misreading of events—the U.S. government has committed unfortunate international errors that have alienated many Latin Americans. Too frequently in this hemisphere, the United States has supported repressive dictatorships, governments that have tended to preserve, indeed to strengthen, those iniquitous institutions from the past that hobble Latin America's development. To the disappointment of many, the United States has not become the champion of the change and reform a majority of Latin Americans want.

The future of Latin America belongs to those intelligent enough to understand the desire for change. Identifying themselves with it and with those national elements favoring the use of reform, local resources, and technical advances to raise the majority's standard of living and quality of life, they will harness the tremendous resources of Latin America and the talents of its varied peoples. The United States will best gain the security and prosperity it desires through an alliance with the Latin Americans advocating change through development.

The intention of this concise history is to explore some of the major forces that, through time, have shaped Latin America. The emphasis is on the desires in Latin America for change and the reasons both for those desires and for their growth. I hope this book will succeed in persuading the educated public that the desires of the majority of Latin Americans for what they consider to be a more just society merit our support and encouragement.

ACKNOWLEDGMENTS

My interests in Latin American history range widely; teaching the introductory course in that subject for the past three decades at four universities and to students varying from freshmen to graduates permitted me to indulge those broad interests. This concise interpretive history reflects those many interests as well as my approach to the challenging study of the many and diverse nations with which we share this hemisphere. My reading, research, and travels provided the background information for this book, while the questions and the enthusiasm of my students certainly helped to shape its presentation. My own ideas concerning Latin American history have changed considerably over the past two decades. This fifth revision of *Latin America* reveals the extent to which those ideas have evolved during that time. I suppose—rather, I hope—they will continue to do so. This edition mirrors my present views and interpretations. I owe a debt of gratitude to many people, here, on the Iberian Peninsula, and in Latin America, who generously shared with me their insights and knowledge. Many individuals read and commented on the manuscript and earlier editions, suggesting ways to improve and revise the text. I owe them all a great debt of thanks. Henry C. Schmidt, of Texas A&M University, and Anthony M. Stevens-Arroyo, of Brooklyn College, reviewed the manuscript for this fifth edition and made helpful suggestions. I am particularly indebted to my teaching assistants and students who gave this book a very critical reading and asked pertinent questions. Seeking the answers forced me to clarify my thought and further define my historical approach. This book is for them, but it is also from them. Furthermore, it is a way of thanking those Latin Americans who shared with me their kindness and good will. I return, I hope, a little of what I have received. Of course I bear the responsibility for the content, the interpretations, and any errors.

E.B.B.

1
The Origins of a Multiracial Society

The Mayan Temple of Kukulcan at Chichén Itzá, Yucatán, Mexico

The New World provided a vast and varied stage upon which met people from three diverse and distant continents: Asia, Europe, and Africa. Representatives of the three races arrived at different times and for different reasons. They mixed, mingled, and married. From their contributions emerged the unique Latin American civilization.

AGENDA FOR DISASTER

The people of Latin America are overarmed and underfed. During the 1980s, they armed themselves to an unprecedented degree: military budgets of the Latin American nations leaped from $9 billion in 1980 to approximately $14 billion by mid-decade and continued their ascent. The latest models of rifles, machine guns, mortars, tanks, and fighter planes fill the arsenals. Moreover, these costly arms are being used. In 1982, Argentina fought Great Britain over the ownership of the Malvinas (Falkland) Islands. Civil war continues to ravage El Salvador, claiming the lives of over 75,000 since 1979. Counterrevolutionaries invaded Nicaragua from both Honduras and Costa Rica. A military response to rural unrest in Guatemala has resulted in the deaths of over 100,000 Indians in the past quarter-century. Rural violence in Mexico claimed the lives of 705 farmers between 1982 and 1987. A repressed and impoverished Chilean population challenges the entrenched military dictatorship. Guerrilla warfare intensifies in Peru, expanding from the rugged Andes into the cities by 1989. Death tolls there in the preceding decade surpassed 12,000. Colombia reels from violence. In 1986, guerrilla warfare claimed the lives of 338 soldiers, 534 peasants, and 882 guerrillas. At the same time, Colombia witnessed 11,000 homicides.

Rising military expenditures accompanied falling economic growth rates. They averaged about 5 percent per year in the 1975–80 period but tumbled to 1.5 percent in 1981, then slipped to a low of −3 percent in 1982. Slow and low growth characterized the rest of the 1980s.

Sluggish growth rates exposed a host of economic problems. In 1982, the median inflation rate registered an impressive 80 percent; in 1988, it reached the dizzying height of 180 percent. By 1989, the foreign debt of Latin American countries surpassed $410 billion. Payment of interest absorbs more than 40 percent of all export earnings. While prices of exports decline, the balance of payment deficits mount. Unemployment stands at unprecedented levels.

Chronic hunger and malnourishment are realities for half the population. Hunger riots in Brazil in 1983 injured hundreds; hunger riots in the Dominican Republic in 1984 claimed sixty lives. Malnourishment and the lack of medical attention take a distressing toll, striking infants with particular violence. In the 1970s, almost 2 million died each year before reaching the age of one. More infants died in Latin America than were born in Europe, a sobering commentary on underdevelopment. By 1988, in El Salvador, three out of every four children were undernourished; in Bolivia, one out of every three infants died during the first year of life. Even in Argentina, a country universally acknowledged to be one of Latin America's most developed, 30,000 children died each year of malnutrition and another 300,000 live in a "high-risk situation." Latin America in the late 1980s suffered the most severe economic crisis in its history.

Economic crisis and military expenditures are interrelated. While the Latin American economy has grown fitfully over the past four centuries, well-defined institutional structures have discouraged real development. Economic growth has benefited a privileged minority at the expense of the majority. In the twentieth century, that majority has become increasingly determined to initiate social, economic, and political changes in order to alter basic institutions, to solve the crisis, and to improve the quality of life. The privileged minority, the beneficiary of the inherited institutions, is just as determined to prevent any changes perceived as threatening and relies on the military to inhibit change. Money spent on the military and on internal security constitutes an unproductive economic expenditure, and it contributes to the preservation of unjust institutions as well. In short, it deepens the crisis, thereby increasing the violence. Not surprisingly, these conditions foster political instability. As Carlos Fuentes, Mexico's foremost novelist and most revered intellectual, reminds us: "Instability in Latin America—or anywhere in the world for that matter—comes when societies cannot see themselves reflected in their institutions."

Questions of change and development are central to any understanding of Latin America. To address them, it is necessary first to know what the fundamental political and economic institutions are and how they took form, then to appreciate how they affect the lives of Latin Americans, and finally to analyze the twentieth-century challenges to those institutions. As the first step toward gaining an historical perspective of the present, let us look at the varied terrain of Latin America and the people who came to inhabit it.

THE LAND

Although history studies people through time, the historian cannot neglect space, or location, the habitat of those people. Thus, geography becomes a significant ingredient in the compound of history. Geography provides the setting for human activity, localizing action and influencing it to some degree.

Contemporary Latin America, a huge region of a continent and a half, stretching 7,000 miles southward from the Rio Grande to Cape Horn, varies widely in its geographic and human composition. Geopolitically the region encompasses eighteen Spanish-speaking republics, French-speaking Haiti, five English-speaking Caribbean nations, and Portuguese-speaking Brazil, a total of approximately 8 million square miles and a rapidly growing population exceeding 421 million. That population increases at the rate of over 2 percent a year. Half of that population is either Brazilian or Mexican. Still, Latin America is relatively underpopulated, although at least two small states, Haiti and El Salvador, do suffer the effects of an overcrowded population. The area is more than twice the size of Europe with less population than Europe. It occupies 19 percent of the world's land but contains only 7 percent of the world's population. Table 1-1, Population Comparisons by World Regions, puts Latin America in a global perspective.

Most of Latin America lies within the tropics. In fact, only one country, Uruguay, has no territory in the tropics. South America reaches its widest point, 3,200 miles, just a few degrees south of the equator, unlike North America, which narrows rapidly as it approaches the equator. The concept of an enervating climate is a false one. The cold Pacific Ocean currents refresh much of the west coast of Latin America, and the altitudes of the mountains and highlands offer a wide range of temperatures that belie the latitude. For centuries, and certainly long before the Europeans arrived, many of the region's most advanced civilizations flourished in the mountain plateaus and valleys. Today many of Latin America's largest cities are in the mountains or on mountain plateaus: Mexico City, Guatemala City, Bogotá, Quito, La Paz, and São Paulo, to mention only a few.

TABLE 1-1   Population Comparisons by World Regions (in millions)

AREA	POPULA-TION 1987	CRUDE BIRTH-RATE	POPULATION PROJECTED TO 2020	PERCENTAGE OF POPULA-TION UNDER AGE 15/ OLDER THAN 65	PERCENTAGE OF URBAN POPULATION
Latin America	421	30	712	38/4	67
Africa	601	44	1,479	45/3	30
Asia	2,930	28	4,584	34/5	32
United States	270	15	326	22/12	74
Soviet Union	284	19	355	26/9	65
Europe	495	13	502	21/13	73

Source: Population Reference Bureau, 1987.

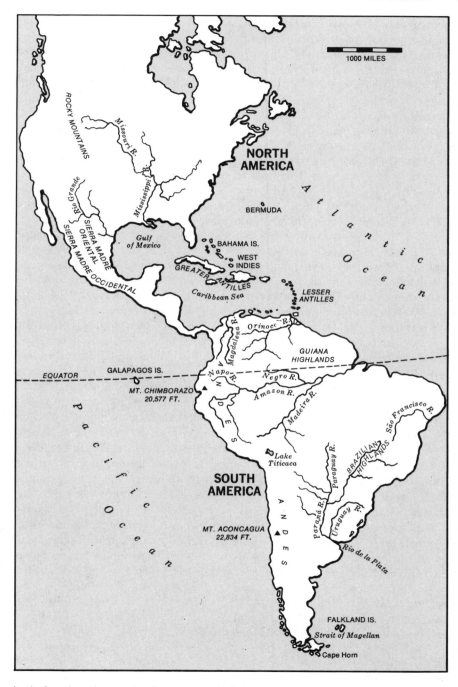

Latin America: the outstanding geographic features

Much of Latin America's population, particularly in Middle America and along the west coast of South America, concentrates in the highland areas.

In Mexico and Central America, the highlands create a rugged backbone that runs through the center of most of the countries, leaving coastal plains on either side. Part of that mountain system emerges in the Greater Antilles to shape the geography of the major Caribbean islands. In South America, unlike Middle America, the mountains closely rim the Pacific coast, while the highlands skirt much of the Atlantic coast, making penetration into the flatter interior of the continent difficult. The Andes predominate. The world's longest continuous mountain barrier, it runs 4,000 miles down the west coast and fluctuates in width between 100 and 400 miles. Aconcagua, the highest mountain in the hemisphere, rises to a majestic 22,834 feet along the Chilean–Argentine frontier. The formidable Andes have been a severe obstacle to exploration and settlement of the South American interior from the west. Along the east coast, the older Guiana and Brazilian Highlands average 2,600 feet in altitude and rarely reach 9,000 feet. Running southward from the Caribbean and frequently fronting on the ocean, they disappear in the extreme south of Brazil. Like the Andes, they too have inhibited penetration of the interior. The largest cities on the Atlantic side are all on the coast or, like São Paulo, within a very short distance of the ocean. In contrast to the west coast, the east boasts of some extraordinary natural harbors of which Todos os Santos Bay and Guanabara Bay, on which are located respectively the cities of Salvador and Rio de Janeiro, are excellent examples.

Four major river networks, the Magdalena, Orinoco, Amazon, and La Plata, flow into the Caribbean or Atlantic, providing an access into the interior missing on the west coast. The Amazon ranks as one of the world's most impressive river systems. Aptly referred to in Portuguese as the "river-sea," it is the largest river in volume in the world. Its volume exceeds that of the Mississippi by fourteen times. In places it is impossible to see from shore to shore, and over a good part of its course the river averages 100 feet in depth. Running eastward from its source 18,000 feet up in the Andes, it is joined from both the north and south by more than 200 tributaries. Together this imposing river and its tributaries provide 25,000 miles of navigable water. The magnitude of the river always has excited the imaginations of those who traveled on it. William Lewis Herndon, who sailed down the river in the mid-nineteenth century, marveled, as many had before and would after: "The march of the great river in its silent grandeur was sublime, but in the untamed might of its turbid waters, as they cut away its banks and tore down the gigantic denizens of the forest it was awful. I was reminded of our Mississippi at its topmost flood."

Farther to the south, the Plata network flows through some of the world's richest soil, the Pampas, a vast flat area shared by Argentina, Uruguay, and Brazil. The river system includes the Uruguay, Paraguay, and

Paraná rivers, but it gets its name from the Río de la Plata, a 180-mile-long estuary separating Uruguay and the Argentine province of Buenos Aires. The system drains a basin of over 1.5 million square miles. Shallow in depth, it still provides a vital communication and transportation link between the Atlantic coast and the southern interior of the continent.

No single country better illustrates the kaleidoscopic variety of Latin American geography than Chile, that long, lean land clinging to the Pacific shore for 2,600 miles. One of the world's bleakest and most forbidding deserts in the north gives way to rugged mountains with forests and alpine pastures. The Central Valley combines a Mediterranean climate with fertile plains, the heartland of Chile's agriculture and population. Moving southward, the traveler encounters dense, mixed forests; heavy rainfall; and a cold climate, a warning of the glaciers and rugged coasts that lie beyond. Snow remains permanently in most of Tierra del Fuego.

Chile may offer a dazzling array of extremes, but many of the other nations offer just about as much variety. Latin Americans have always been aware of the impact of their environment. Their novelists frequently have emphasized its influence on life styles and development. Visiting the harsh, arid interior of Northeastern Brazil for the first time, Euclydes da Cunha marveled in his *Rebellion in the Backlands* (*Os Sertões*, 1902) at how the land had shaped a different people and created a civilization that contrasted sharply with that of the coast: "Here was an absolute and radical break between the coastal cities and the clay huts of the interior, one that so disturbed the rhythm of our evolutionary development and which was so deplorable a stumbling block to national unity. They were in a strange country now, with other customs, other scenes, a different kind of people. Another language even, spoken with an original and picturesque drawl. They had, precisely, the feelings of going to war in another land. They felt that they were outside Brazil." Across the continent in Peru, Ciro Alegría depicted life in the tropical rain forest dominated by the presence of a great river, the upper reaches of the Amazon. One of the characters of his novel *The Golden Serpent* (*La Serpente de Oro*, 1935) gazes at the Amazon's tributary and exclaims, "The river, yes, the river. I never thought of it. It is so large, so masterful, and it has made all this, hasn't it?"

Latin American films, too, often assign nature the role of a major protagonist. Certainly in the Argentine classic *Prisoners of the Earth* (*Prisioneros de la Tierra*, 1939), the forests and rivers of the northeast overpower the outsider. Nature even forces the local people to bend before her rather than conquer her. Another Argentine film, *The Islanders* (*Los Isleros*, 1951), dramatizes the power of the Paraná River over those who live on her shores. Nature thus enforces some characteristics on the people of Latin America. The towering Andes, the vast Amazon, the unbroken Pampas, the lush rain forests provide an impressive setting for an equally powerful human drama.

THE INDIAN

The continents of Asia, Europe, and Africa contributed to the peopling of the Western Hemisphere, and consequently, a greater racial mixing has resulted there than in any other part of the world. From Asia came the first migrants in various waves between 20,000 and 40,000 years ago. Anthropologists generally believe that they crossed from one continent to the other at the Bering Strait in pursuit of game animals. Moving slowly southward, they dispersed throughout North and South America. Over the millennia, at an uneven rate, some advanced through hunting and fishing cultures to take up agriculture. At the same time they fragmented into many linguistic (estimates range up to 2,200 different languages) and cultural groups, although they maintained certain general physical features in common: straight black hair, dark eyes, copper-colored skin, and short stature.

Varied as the early American cultures were, a majority of them shared enough traits to permit a few generalizations. The family or clan units served as the basic social organization. All displayed a profound faith in supernatural forces that they believed shaped, influenced, and guided their lives. For that reason, the *shamans,* those intimate with the supernatural, played important roles in the indigenous societies. They provided the contact between the mortal and the immortal, between the human and the spirit. In most rituals and celebrations, the participants danced, sang, beat drums, shook rattles, and possibly played flutes. Common to the oral literature of most of the groups were stories of the cultural hero, the ancestor who taught the early members of the tribe their way of life, and the prankster whose exploits aroused both mirth and admiration. Few of the early Americans possessed a sense of private ownership of land. More often than not, like the air they breathed, the land belonged to all. Game roamed and ate off the land. Further, the land furnished fruits, berries, nuts, and roots. Tilling the soil produced other foods, corn and potatoes, for example. The Indians revered the earth as sacred, not to be destroyed or mutilated but to be preserved for the use of future generations. Many artifacts, instruments, and implements were similar from Alaska to Cape Horn. For example, spears, bows and arrows, and clubs were the common weapons of warfare or for the hunt. Although these similarities are significant, the differences among the many cultures were enormous and impressive. By the end of the fifteenth century, there were between 15 million and 100 million inhabitants of the Western Hemisphere. Scholars still heatedly debate the figures, and one can find forceful arguments favoring each extreme.

Mistaking the New World for Asia, Christopher Columbus called the inhabitants he met "Indians," a name that has remained to cause endless confusion. Exploration later indicated that the "Indians" of the New World belonged to a large number of cultural groups of which the most important were the Aztecs and Mayas of Mexico and Central America; the Carib of the Caribbean area; the Chibcha of Colombia; the Inca of Ecuador, Peru, and Bolivia; the Araucanian of Chile; the Guaraní of Paraguay; and the Tupí of Brazil. Of these, the Aztec, Maya, and Inca exemplify the most complex cultural achievements.

Two distinct periods, the Classic and the Late, mark the history of Mayan civilization. During the Classic period, from the fourth to the tenth centuries A.D., the Mayas lived in Guatemala; then they suddenly migrated to Yucatán, beginning the Late period, which lasted until the Spanish conquest. The exodus baffles anthropologists, who most often suggest that the exhaustion of the soil in Guatemala limited the corn harvests and forced the Mayas to move in order to survive. Corn provided the basis for the Mayan civilization. The Mayan account of creation revolves around corn. The gods "began to talk about the creation and the making of our first mother and father; of yellow corn and of white corn they made their flesh; of cornmeal dough they made the arms and the legs of man," relates the *Popul Vuh,* the sacred book of the Mayas. All human activity, all religion centered on the planting, growing, and harvesting of corn. New archaeological evidence uncovered in the late 1970s and early 1980s indicates that the Mayas dug a much more extensive network of canals and water-control ditches than previously was known, an implication that they practiced a more technical and extensive agriculture than had been assumed. Efficient agricultural methods produced corn surpluses and hence the leisure for a large priestly class to dedicate its talents to religion and scientific study. Extraordinary intellectual achievements resulted. The Mayas progressed from the pictograph to the ideograph and thus invented a type of writing, the only Indians in the hemisphere to do so. Sophisticated in mathematics, they invented the zero and devised numeration by position. Astute observers of the heavens, they applied their mathematical skills to astronomy. Their careful studies of the heavens enabled them to predict eclipses, follow the path of the planet Venus, and prepare a calendar more accurate than that used in Europe. As the ruins of Copán, Tikal, Palenque, Chichén Itzá, Mayapán, and Uxmal testify, the Mayas built magnificent temples. One of the most striking features of that architecture is its extremely elaborate carving and sculpture.

To the west of the Mayas, another native civilization, the Aztecs, expanded and flourished in the fifteenth century. The Aztecs had migrated from the north in the early thirteenth century into the central valley of Mexico where they encountered and conquered some prosperous and highly advanced city-states. In 1325, they founded Tenochtitlán, their beautiful capital, and from that religious and political center they radiated outward to absorb other cultures until they controlled all of Central Mexico. The constant conquests gave prominence to the warriors, and, not surprisingly, among the multiple divinities the god of war and the sun predominated. To propitiate him, as well as other gods, required human sacrifices on a grand scale. The Aztecs devised the pictograph, an accurate calendar, an impressive architecture, and an elaborate and effective system of government.

Largest, oldest, and best organized of the Indian civilizations was the Incan, which flowered in the harsh environment of the Andes. By conquest, the empire extended in all directions from Cuzco, regarded as the center of the universe. It stretched nearly 3,000 miles from Ecuador into Chile, and its maximum width measured 400 miles. Few empires have been more rigidly regimented or more highly centralized, a real miracle when one realizes that it was run without the benefit—or hindrance—of written accounts or records. The only accounting system was the *quipu*, cords upon which knots were made to indicate specific mathematical units. (Some scholars now claim the Incas wove some sort of code into the threads.) The highly effective government rapidly assimilated newly conquered peoples into the empire. Entire populations were moved around the empire when security suggested that such relocations would be wise. Every subject was required to speak Quechua, the language of the court. In weaving, pottery, medicine, and agriculture, the achievements of the Incans were magnificent. They excelled particularly in agriculture. Challenged by a stingy soil, they developed systems of drainage, terracing, and irrigation and learned the value of fertilizing their fields.

The Incan women played significant economic roles. In addition to their domestic duties, they planted and harvested crops, tended the llamas, made ceramics, wove textiles, and ran much of the local, market commerce. They also exercised a voice in community political assemblies, the *camachico*, although they could not hold office.

Many differences separated these three high Indian civilizations, but at the same time some impressive similarities existed. Society was highly structured. The hierarchy of nobles, priests, warriors, artisans, farmers, and slaves was ordinarily inflexible, although occasionally some mobility did occur. At the pinnacle of that hierarchy stood the omnipotent emperor, the object of the greatest respect and veneration. The sixteenth-century chronicler Cieza de León, in his own charming style, illustrated the awe in which the people held the Inca: "Thus the kings were so feared that, when they traveled over the provinces, and permitted a piece of the cloth to be raised which hung round their litter, so as to allow their vassals to behold them, there was such an outcry that the birds fell from the upper air where they were flying, insomuch that they could be caught in men's hands. All men so feared the king, that they did not dare to speak evil of his shadow." Little or no distinction existed between civil and religious authority, so that for all intents and purposes church and state were one. The Incan and Aztec emperors both were regarded as representatives of the sun on earth and thus as deities, a position probably held by the rulers of the Mayan city-states as well.

Royal judges impartially administered the laws of the empires and apparently enjoyed a reputation for fairness. The sixteenth-century chroniclers who saw the judicial systems functioning invariably praised them. Cieza de León, for one, noted, "It was felt to be certain that those who did evil would receive punishment without fail and that neither prayers nor bribes would avert it." These civilizations rested on a firm rural base. Cities were rare, although a few existed with populations exceeding 100,000. They were centers of commerce, government, and religion. Eyewitness accounts as well as the ruins that remain leave no doubt that some of the cities were well-organized and contained impressive architecture. The sixteenth-century chronicles reveal that some of the cities astonished the first Spaniards who saw them. Bernal Díaz del Castillo, who accompanied Hernán Cortés into Tenochtitlán in 1519, gasped, "And when we saw all those cities and villages built in the water, and other great towns on dry land, and that straight and level causeway leading to Mexico [City], we were astounded. These great towns and cities and buildings rising from the water, all made of stone, seemed like an enchanted vision from the tale of Amadis. Indeed, some of our soldiers asked whether it was not a dream!" The productivity of the land made possible an opulent court life and complex religious ceremonies.

The vast majority of the population worked in agriculture. The farmers grew corn, beans, squash, pumpkins, manioc root, and potatoes, as well as other crops. Communal lands, the famed *ejido* of Mexico and the *ayllu* of Peru, were cultivated for the benefit of the state, religion, and community. The state thoroughly organized and directed the rural labor force. Advanced as these Indian civilizations were, however, not one learned the use of iron or used the wheel. However, the Indians had learned to work gold, silver, copper, tin, and bronze. Artifacts that have survived in those metals testify to fine skills.

The spectacular achievements of these advanced farming cultures contrast sharply with the more elementary evolution of the hunting, gathering, and fishing cultures and the intermediate farming cultures among the Latin American Indians. The Tupí tribes, the single most important native element contributing to the early formation of Brazil, illustrate the status of the many intermediate farming cultures found throughout Latin America.

The Tupí tribes tended to be very loosely organized. The small, temporary villages, often surrounded by a crude wooden stockade, were, when possible, located along a river bank. The Indians lived communally in large thatched huts in which they strung their hammocks in extended family or lineage groups of as many as 100 persons. Most of the tribes had at least a nominal chief, although some seemed to recognize a leader only in time of war and a few seemed to have no concept of a leader. More often than not, the *shaman,* or medicine man, was the most important and powerful tribal figure. He communed with the spirits, proffered advice, and prescribed medicines. The religions abounded with good and evil spirits.

The men spent considerable time preparing for and participating in tribal wars. They hunted monkeys, tapirs, armadillos, and birds. They also fished, trapping the fish with funnel-shaped baskets, poisoning the water and collecting the fish, or shooting the fish with arrows. They cleared away the forest to plant crops. Nearly every year during the dry season, the men cut down trees, bushes, and vines, waited until they had dried, and then burned them, a method used throughout Latin America, then as well as now. The burning destroyed the thin humus and the soil was quickly exhausted. Hence, it was necessary constantly to clear new land and eventually the village moved in order to be near virgin soil. In general, although not exclusively, the women took charge of planting and harvesting crops and of collecting and preparing the food. Manioc was the principal cultivated crop. Maize, beans, yams, peppers, squash, sweet potatoes, tobacco, pineapples, and occasionally cotton were the other cultivated crops. Forest fruits were collected.

To the first Europeans who observed them, these Indians seemed to live an idyllic life. The tropics required little or no clothing. Generally nude, the Tupí developed the art of body ornamentation and painted elaborate and ornate geometric designs on themselves. Into their noses, lips, and ears they inserted stone and wooden artifacts. Feathers from the colorful forest birds provided an additional decorative touch. Their gay nude appearance prompted the Europeans to think of them as innocent children of nature. The first chronicler of Brazil, Pero Vaz de Caminha, marveled to the king of Portugal, "Sire, the innocence of Adam himself was not greater than these people's." In the beginning, the Europeans overlooked the grim affinity of the Indians for fighting and for at least ceremonial cannibalism to emphasize their inclinations to dance and sing. More extensive contact with the Indians caused later chroniclers to tell quite a different tale, one in which the Indians emerged as wicked villains, brutes who desperately needed the civilizing hand of Europe.

The Tupí, like many similar or simpler cultures, never achieved more than a rudimentary civilization, in no way comparable to the remarkable civilizations of their contemporaries, the Aztecs, the Mayas, or the Incas.

The European romantics who thought they saw a utopia in Indian life obviously exaggerated. The Indians by no means had found the perfect life. Misunderstanding, if not outright ignorance, has always characterized outsiders' perceptions of the Indians. Even today it remains difficult to pull back the veil of myth to glimpse reality. We have yet to focus accurately on the Indians' well-developed world vision and philosophy that put them into enviable harmony with nature. We have yet to appreciate the Indians' excellent sense of community feeling and obligation that stressed cooperation over competition. The Indians adapated in an exemplary fashion to their environments, whether the difficult craggy Andes or the lush tropics. They had much to teach the European invaders about the utilization of the land, its rivers, and products.

THE EUROPEAN

As the sixteenth century approached, the European invader was not far off. Europe, on the eve of a commercial revolution, searched for new trade and new lands. Merchants dreamed of breaking the Arab and Italian monopolies of trade with Asia, thereby sharing the lucrative profits from the spices, precious stones, pearls, dyes, silks, tapestries, porcelains, and rugs coveted by wealthy Europeans. Portugal led the quest for those new trade routes.

Like the neighboring kingdoms in Spain, Portugal had been the crossroads of many peoples—Iberians, Celts, Phoenicians, Greeks, Carthaginians, Romans, Visigoths, and Moslems—and had blended their cultures together. The last of the many invaders of the peninsula, the Moslems, had begun their conquest of Iberia in 711. The Christians initiated their crusade to reconquer the peninsula in 732 at the Battle of Tours and intermittently continued it until Granada fell in 1492.

Portugal, to assert its independence, had to free itself both of Moslem control and Castilian claims. In 1139, Afonso Henriques of the House of Burgundy used for the first time the title "King of Portugal," a title officially recognized four decades later by the Pope, then arbiter of such matters. The new state struggled to expel the Moslems and finally succeeded in driving their remaining armies from the Algarve, the far south, in 1250. Neighboring Castile, deeply involved in its own campaign against the Moors, reluctantly recognized the existence of Portugal. The task of consolidating the new state fell to King Denis, whose long reign, bridging the thirteenth and fourteenth centuries, marked the emergence of Europe's first modern national state.

Portugal became for a time Europe's foremost sea power. Its location, perched on the westernmost tip of continental Europe, was well suited for that role. Most of the sparse population, less than a million in the fifteenth century, inhabited the coastal area. They faced the great, gray, open sea and nearby Africa. At peace at home and with no imminent foreign threats to prepare for, Portugal could turn its attention outward. In a society dominated by the Roman Catholic Church, religious motives for expansion played at least a superficially important role. The Lusitanians hoped to defeat the enemies of their faith in Africa and to carry the word of God to the continent. Thus it was in Africa that the Portuguese initiated their overseas expansion in 1415 with the conquest of strategic Ceuta, guardian of the opening to the Mediterranean. However, the commercial reasons for expansion probably outweighed the religious ones. Lisbon as the entrepôt of Asian merchandise created a vision of wealth that dazzled those of all classes.

The first to appreciate fully that the ocean was not a barrier but a vast highway of commerce was Prince Henry (1394–1460), known as "the Navigator" to English writers although he was a confirmed landlubber. Listening to the expert advice of his day, he defined Portugal's policy of exploration: systematic voyages outward, each based on the intelligence collected from the former voyager and each traveling beyond its predecessor. The improvements in geographic, astronomical, and navigational knowledge that characterized a century of accelerating seaborne activity facilitated the task of the men of Sagres Peninsula, the westernmost tip of Portugal. In a moment of great maritime triumph, the Portuguese launched the *caravel,* a ship that could tack and, thus, sail against the wind. As a direct consequence of these improvements and with the encouragement of Prince Henry, the Lusitanians sailed farther and farther out to sea away from their base. At the time of the death of the prince, they were sailing the Gulf of Guinea, some 3,000 miles down the African coast. Then, three decades later, in 1488, Bartolomeu Dias rounded the Cape of Good Hope and pointed the way to a water route to India.

News from Christopher Columbus that he had reached India by sailing west in 1492 momentarily disturbed the Portuguese, who were on the verge of reaching the Orient by circumnavigating Africa. Unlike Portugal, Spain had earned little reputation for maritime prowess. In the last quarter of the fifteenth century, some Spanish expeditions plied the African coast, and one of them laid Spanish claims to the Canary Islands. Most Spanish energy, however, had been expended internally on the struggle against the Moors and on the effort of unification. The marriage of Isabel of Castile to Ferdinand of Aragon in 1469 forged the major link in Spanish unity. Thereafter, first the external and then the internal policies of Castile and Aragon harmonized. Those two monarchs increased the power of the crown by humbling both the nobility and the municipal governments. Equating religious with political unification, they expelled those Jews and Moors who refused to embrace the Roman Catholic faith. The infamous inquisition sternly enforced religious conformity. When Isabel died in 1504, Ferdinand ruled as king of Aragon and regent of Castile.

While the two monarchs were unifying Spain, they accelerated the struggle to expel the Moors. In 1492, Granada, the last Moorish domain on the Iberian Peninsula, fell. Providentially, in that same year, Columbus opened a new horizon for the Spaniards. The energy, talent, and drive that previously had gone into the reconquest, that holy and political campaign allying cross and sword for eight centuries, were invested immediately in overseas expansion. The Spaniards carried with them many of the ideas— religious intolerance and fervor, suspicion of foreigners, more prestige for the soldier than the farmer—as well as many of the institutions—viceroyalty, captaincy-general, the posts of *visitador* and *adelantado*—developed during the long reconquest.

The return of Columbus from his first voyage intensified rivalry between Spain and Portugal, both of which sought to guard their own sea lanes and prohibit the incursion of the other. War threatened until diplomacy triumphed. At Tordesillas in 1494, representatives of the two monarchs agreed to divide the world. An imaginary line running pole to pole 370 leagues west of the Cape Verde Islands gave Portugal everything discovered for 180 degrees east and Spain everything for 180 degrees west. With the exception of an interest in the Philippines, Spain concentrated its attention on the Western Hemisphere. Within the half of the world reserved for Portugal, Vasco da Gama discovered the long-sought water route to India. His protracted voyage in 1497–99 joined East and West by sea for the first time. Subsequent voyages by Columbus in 1493–96, 1498–1500 and 1502–4, suggested the extent of the lands he had discovered but proved that in fact he had not reached India. Portugal, at least for the moment, monopolized the only sea lanes to India, and that monopoly promised to enrich the realm. The cargo Vasco da Gama brought back to Lisbon repaid sixty times over the original cost of the expedition. For the time being, the Portuguese maritime routes were proving to be far more lucrative than those of the Spaniards. The kings of Portugal became rich merchants and the Portuguese turned to the sea as never before. Pedro Alvares Cabral received command of the fleet being prepared to follow up the exploit of da Gama. While sailing to India in 1500, the fleet veered off course and Cabral discovered and claimed Brazil, which later was found to fall within the half of the world the Tordesillas treaty had allocated to Portugal. Along the coasts of South America, Africa, and Asia, the Portuguese eagerly established their commercial—not colonial—empire. The Chief Cosmographer of the Realm boasted, "The Portuguese discovered new islands, new lands, new seas, new people; and what is more, new sky and new stars." It was a glorious age for Portugal, and one of the great epic poets of all times, Luís de Camões, composed *The Lusiads* to commemorate the achievements.

The discovery of the Americas was an accident, the unforeseen by-product of an Iberian search for new maritime routes and desire for direct trade with the East. At first, the discovery did not seem particularly rewarding. The Western Hemisphere loomed up as an undesirable barrier to a direct water route to Asia. Furthermore, the native inhabitants displayed scant interest in trading with the Iberian merchants.

CONFRONTATION AND CONQUEST

The discoveries of Columbus and Cabral brought the Iberians face to face with the Indians of the New World. The confrontation puzzled each side and awoke a great deal of mutual curiosity. The Iberians referred back to Biblical and classical literature in an effort to explain to themselves who the Indians were; for their part, at least two Indian societies, the Aztec and Chibcha, identified the Europeans with prophecies. The Aztecs expected a bearded white man to emerge one day from the ocean, while a Chibcha legend spoke of the arrival of the "children of the sun," for whom the Chibchas mistook the Spanish conquerors.

Since commerce had motivated the oceanic explorations that resulted in the discoveries, the Iberians hoped to trade with the inhabitants they encountered. The peoples of the simple societies of the Caribbean and along the coast of eastern South America showed scant inclination for such commercial intercourse. In fact, they had little to offer the Iberians and required even less from them. The Portuguese soon found along the coast rich stands of brazilwood, a wood that gave the newly discovered land its name and furnished an excellent red dye much in demand by the new European textile industries. The crown established a monopoly over its exploitation and eagerly sold rights to merchants. Fernão de Noronha was the first to buy the contract, and in 1503 he dispatched ships to fetch the dyewood. The ship captains bartered with the Indians, exchanging trinkets for the brazilwood they cut. A lucrative trade in the wood developed during the sixteenth century. In addition to its limited economic role, Brazil served strategically for many decades as the guardian of the western flank of the prized trade route to the Orient. So long as Portugal held a monopoly over that seaborne trade, Brazil received only minimal attention.

On the other hand, for three decades after Columbus's discovery, Spain searched the eastern coast of the New World for a westward passage, a route other European states began to seek as well. Columbus made three long voyages touching the largest Caribbean islands and coasting along the shores of northern South America and Central America. In 1513, Juan Ponce de León reconnoitered the coast of Florida and that same year Vasco Núñez de Balboa marching across Panama came upon the Pacific Ocean, which he promptly claimed for his monarch. The desire to get to that ocean by some water route intensified.

At the same time the Spaniards began to settle some of the major Caribbean islands. On his second voyage Columbus transported men and supplies to establish the first such colony. On the northern coast of Hispaniola, he marked out a grid pattern for a town, set up a municipal government, divided up the land among the colonists, and assigned Indians to each settler to work their land. He thereby established a pattern of colonization faithfully imitated in the succeeding decades wherever the Spaniards went in the New World. Many of the new arrivals searched hopefully for gold, and the islands yielded enough to excite speculations about even greater discoveries. Others turned to agriculture. The monarchs encouraged the migration of artisans and farmers to the New World. In his instructions to one governor departing for the Indies in 1513, the Spanish king ordered him to take "farmers so that they may attempt to plant the soil." Similar orders were repeated frequently. Sugar cane was planted as early as 1493. By 1520, it was a profitable industry with at least twenty-eight sugar mills operating on Hispaniola. Domestic animals imported onto the islands multiplied rapidly. Ships returning to Spain carried sugar and hides. The monarch and merchants of Spain sought to encourage such trade. In 1503, Ferdinand sanctioned the establishment of the Casa de Contratación in Seville to oversee the commerce between Spain and the New World. Nonetheless, much of the agricultural production in Spanish America, at least during the first century and a half, went to feed the colonists and to provide supplies for conquest, expansion, and further settlement.

The Spanish pattern of exploration and settlement changed after 1521, a year marking the circumnavigation of the globe by Ferdinand Magellan and the conquest of central Mexico by Hernán Cortés. The long voyage begun by Magellan in 1519 but concluded by Juan Sebastián del Cano in 1521, after Magellan was killed by natives in the Philippine Islands, proved—at last—the possibility of reaching Asia by sailing west. His expedition had found the way around the barrier of North and South America, but it also had proven that the westward passage was longer and more difficult than the African route used by the Portuguese. At the same time Spain realized it did not need the route to India. Conquered Mexico revealed that the New World held far more wealth in the form of the coveted gold and silver than the Spaniards could hope to reap from trade with Asia. Spanish opinion changed from deprecating the New World as an obstacle to the East to considering it a rich treasure chest. No longer considered simply a way station on the route to Asia, America became the center of Spanish attention.

History provides few epics of conquest more remarkable than Cortés's sweep through Mexico. His capture of the opulent Aztec empire initiated a period of conquest during which Spain defeated the major Indian nations and made their inhabitants subject to the Castilian monarch. Generally these conquests were private undertakings, the result of contract, known as a *capitulación,* signed between the monarch and the aspiring conquistador, who was given the title of *adelantado.* The adelantados by no means wandered around the Americas unchecked by the monarchs. Royal officials accompanied all the private expeditions to insure respect for the crown's interests and fulfillment of the capitulación.

Diverse motives propelled the adelantados. By subjugating new peoples to the crown, they hoped to win royal titles, preferments, and positions. By introducing heathens to Christianity, they sought to assure God's favor now as well as guarantee for themselves a fitting place in the life hereafter. Conquest, exploration, and settlement offered opportunities for some marginal or impoverished men to ascend socially and economically. The enterprises required risks whose rewards could be substantial. The adelantados raised capital to finance their undertakings, promising rich returns to investors. Doubtless visions of gold eased the task of soliciting funds and loosened many purse strings. Some adelantados earned fortunes and repaid their investors. They leaped from obscurity to fame. History, for example, treats generously the once impoverished and minor noble, Hernán Cortés, and the illegitimate and modestly prepared Francisco Pizarro. However, most adelantados failed.

The conquest of large empires by a relatively few Spaniards proved to be surprisingly easy. Steel, the crossbow, and effective military tactics—a contrast to the ritualized warfare of many Indian groups—facilitated the European victories. Gunpowder and the horse, both of which startled the Indians, were tremendous tactical advantages, at least initially. Furthermore, the Spaniards found the Indians divided among themselves. In Mexico, the tribes subjugated by the Aztecs were only too happy to join with the Spaniards to defeat their Indian enemies. In the Incan empire, rivalry between two claimants to the crown already had split the empire. The introduction of European diseases decimated the ranks of the Indians, who lacked immunity to them. In the regions of great pre-Columbian civilizations in both Mexico and Peru, population declined more than 90 percent during the first century after contact with the Europeans, falling from approximately 35 million to less than 2 million. No group remained untouched by the ravages of the new diseases. In some local areas entire populations, including whole culture groups, were completely obliterated. For these reasons, Spanish conquest spread rapidly after Cortés's victory. Central America fell to the Spaniards by 1525. Yucatán put up a bitter resistance, and the coastal portions of the peninsula surrendered to the invaders in 1545. Between 1513 and 1543, the Spaniards explored and claimed the territory in North America between the Carolinas and Oregon. In fact, two-thirds of the territory of the continental United States was at one time claimed by Spain. By the time George Washington was inaugurated as president, Spain had established colonies over a far greater area, ranging from San Francisco to Santa Fé to San Antonio to St. Augustine, than that encompassed by the original thirteen states.

Spain's expansion into South America was equally prodigious. Once again the adelantados knew little or nothing of the lands they invaded. Yet they were ready to face anything, and they triumphed over everything. Inspired by the success of Cortés and excited by rumors of a wealthy kingdom along the west coast of South America, Francisco Pizarro sailed south from Panama to initiate Spanish conquest of that continent. Only on his third attempt, in 1531–32, did he succeed in penetrating the Incan heartland, but it was still not until 1535 that Pizarro completed his conquest of the Incan empire. The wealth he encountered surpassed that which Cortés had found in Mexico. From Peru, other expeditions fanned out into South America: Sebastián de Benalcázar seized Ecuador in 1533, Pedro de Valdivia conquered the central valley of Chile in 1540–41, and Gonzalo Pizarro crossed the Andes to explore the upper Amazon in 1539. From that expedition Francisco de Orellana and a small band of men floated down the Amazon, reaching the Atlantic Ocean in 1542.

Spanish attention in South America focused on Peru, and most of the other explorations, conquests, and settlements of South America radiated from that center. Two exceptions were the Caribbean coast and the Plata region. Settlement of the northern coast began from the Caribbean. Charles V granted a large section of the Venezuelan coast to the Welsers of Augsburg in 1528 in return for financial aid, but that banking house failed to colonize it successfully, and in 1546 the grant was rescinded. Several small settlements were made along the Colombian coast, and in 1536 Gonzalo Jiménez de Quesada set out to conquer the Chibcha Indians in the mountainous interior, and he brought that highly civilized Indian kingdom within the Spanish empire. The Río de la Plata attracted some interest first as a possible westward passage to the Orient and later as a possible route to the mines of Peru. Pedro de Mendoza searched in 1535–36 to open such a route, and the early settlements in the Platine basin date from his efforts.

Spanish dominion of the New World expanded with amazing rapidity. Within half a century after Columbus's discovery, Spanish adelantados had explored and conquered or claimed the territory from approximately 40 degrees north—Oregon, Colorado, and the Carolinas—to 40 degrees south—mid-Chile and Argentina—with the exception of the Brazilian coast. Spanish settlers had colonized in scattered nuclei an impressive share of that territory. Reflecting the Spanish preference for urban living, the settlers already had founded many of Latin America's major cities: Havana, 1519; Mexico City, 1521; Quito, 1534; Lima, 1535; Buenos Aires, 1536 (refounded in 1580); Asunción, 1537; Bogotá, 1538; and Santiago, 1541. The Spaniards built Mexico City and Bogotá where Indian cities had long existed, not an uncommon practice. The rich silver and gold mines of Mexico, Colombia, and Peru stimulated the economy, but the economy enjoyed a sounder base than that. Although gold and silver were preferred exports, agriculture provided the basis for exploration, expansion, and trade. Wherever the Spaniards settled they introduced domesticated animals and new crops. Stock raising turned once unproductive lands into profitable grazing areas, and the introduction of the plow made it possible to exploit land unmanageable under the hoe culture of the Indians. The crown encouraged agriculture by sending seeds, plants, animals, tools, and technical experts to the New World.

The opening of mines, the establishment of agriculture, and the trade between the Iberian motherlands and their American colonies did not go unnoticed in other Western European capitals. The commercial successes of Spain and Portugal whetted the already hungry appetites of the English, Dutch, and French. Brazil attracted both the French and Dutch. The French operated a colony very near Rio de Janeiro between 1555 and 1567. The Dutch enjoyed far greater success. They controlled as much as one-third of Brazil for a time in the seventeenth century (1630–54). From their thriving capital of Recife, they shipped convoys of sugar to European markets. The Brazilian expulsion of the Dutch from the Northeast prompted the renewed attention of the Dutch to the Caribbean.

Indeed, the Caribbean, with its proximity to Europe, its important sea lane for Spanish silver shipments, and its increasingly attractive tropical products, already had aroused the interest not only of the Dutch but of the English and French as well. European monarchs applauded the pirate plundering of Spanish commerce. Merchants yearned to participate in the growing trade. Between 1595 and 1620, the English, French, and Dutch attempted to establish colonies in the Guianas. The Dutch were the most successful, but the other two nations also eventually succeeded. In 1624 the English colonized some small islands in the Lesser Antilles, while between 1630 and 1640 the Dutch expanded into the Caribbean. By the mid-seventeenth century the French had established their Caribbean presence with settlements in Martinique and Guadeloupe.

The late European arrivals hoped to disrupt Spanish trade, but primarily their interest lay in furnishing European goods to the entire Middle America region and in growing tropical products for export. Usually tobacco supplied the first cash crop. After the expulsion of the Dutch from Brazil, attention focused on sugar production. Sugar sold well and profitably in the Old World. The Europeans introduced new production techniques, and their efficiency soon threatened markets once dominated by Portuguese America, thus depressing Brazil's sugar trade. Confronted with the problems of labor, the new European colonizers quickly imported Africans to work the plantations. A few white masters oversaw the work of armies of black slaves.

Before the end of the seventeenth century, Spain lost its monopoly in the Caribbean. The European governments employed a variety of colonial policies in the area, but their objectives were one: to work the colonies profitably for the metropolis (see "A Glossary of Concepts and Terms"). Land patterns, the plantations, were similar; labor patterns, slavery, were also alike.

European influence on the New World and its inhabitants was immediately visible. The Europeans transplanted their social, economic, and political institutions across the ocean. They required the Indians to swear allegiance to a new king, worship a new God, speak a new language, and alter their work habits. In the process of exploiting the Indians, the Europeans also deculturated and disorganized them, forcing them into the role of subservient workers. Their labor they were forced to give, but their loyalty they held in reserve. The gulf between the master and the laborer has seldom been bridged in Latin America.

In the confrontation of the New and Old Worlds, the Americas also influenced the course of events in Europe. The abundance of gold and silver shipped from Mexico, Peru, and Brazil caused prices to rise in Europe and helped to finance industrialization. Introduced into Europe were new products: tobacco, rubber, cacao, and cotton (today's commercial cottons derive principally from those cultivated by the American Indians); new plants: potatoes and corn, two of the four most important food crops of the world; and drugs: quinine, coca used in cocaine and novocaine, curare used in anesthetics, datura used in pain relievers, and cascara used in laxatives. The Americas forced upon European scholars new geographic, botanical, and zoological information, much of which contradicted the classical writers. As one result, scholars questioned hoary concepts. These contradictions came at about the same time Copernicus published his heliocentric theory (1543) and thus helped to usher in the age of modern science. The vast extension of empire in the New World strengthened the European monarchs, who derived wealth and thus independence from their overseas domains and generally exercised greater power overseas than at home. Such great empires required innovation and revision of governmental institutions. The struggles over boundaries in the New World agitated the European courts and more than once threw European diplomacy into a crisis. Art, music, and literature sooner or later expressed Indian themes. It has been estimated that nearly 50,000 Indian words were incorporated into Spanish, Portuguese, English, and French. The New World was not simply the passive recipient of European civilization; rather, it modified and changed Europe's civilization and contributed to the development of the Old World.

To adapt to their new environment, the European settlers depended heavily on the Indians and were not reluctant to learn from the conquered. During the early decades of conquest and colonization more European males than females arrived in the New World. The conquerors regarded the Indian women as part of their conquest and freely sought sexual pleasure with them. Concubinage and casual intercourse were common, but so was marriage between Europeans and Indians. Intermarriage was permitted by the Spanish monarch in 1501 and often encouraged for reasons of state, as in Brazil during the years that Pombal directed the Portuguese Empire (1750–77). As a result there appeared almost at once a "new race," the *mestizo,* a blend of European and Indian well adpated physically and psychologically to the land. Borrowing the essential from the diverse cultures of both parents, the mestizos accelerated the amalgamation of two cultures. However, the Indians provided more than sexual gratification. They showed the Europeans the best methods to hunt and fish, the value of the drugs the forests offered, the quickest way to clear the lands, and how to cultivate the crops of the New World. When necessary, the Europeans adopted the light boats skillfully navigated by the Indians on the inland waters and copied the methods used by the Indians to build simple, serviceable structures. As a concession to the tropics, the Europeans adopted the

Indian hammock—as did the navies of the world. One early arrival to Brazil noted his delight with the hamnmock in these words: "Would you believe that man could sleep suspended in a net in the air like a bunch of hanging grapes? Here this is the common thing. I slept on a mattress but my doctor advised me to sleep in a net. I tried it, and I will never again be able to sleep in a bed, so comfortable is the rest one gets in the net." In truth, the Europeans depended heavily on the Indians during the early decades of settlement in order to accommodate to the novel conditions. Thomas Turner, an Englishman who lived in Brazil for two years at the end of the sixteenth century, summed up that dependence in his observation. "The Indian is a fish in the sea and a fox in the woods, and without them a Christian is neither for pleasure or profit fit for life or living."

The Indian at first was the principal source of labor. Reluctant to engage in manual work, the conquerors and the settlers who followed them persisted in coercing others to do it for them. The Europeans forced the natives to paddle their canoes; to guide them through the interior; to plant, tend, and harvest their sugar, wheat, tobacco, and cotton; to guard their cattle and sheep; to mine their gold and silver; and to wait upon them in their homes. In short, the Indians were the instruments by which wealth was created in the new colonies and as such were indispensable to the Europeans.

When the Indians proved inadequate or where their numbers were insufficient, particularly in the Caribbean and Brazil, the colonists began to look elsewhere for their labor supply. Their attention focused on Africa. At that moment the black was introduced into the New World.

THE AFRICAN

Africa, the second largest continent, offers extremes of contrasts: mountains and savannas, deserts and jungles. Three impressive river networks, the Nile, the Congo, and the Zambesi, add to the variety. The relatively small population contributes further to the diversity. Divided into hundreds of tribes, African cultures range from the primitive to the sophisticated. The improving quality and greater quantity of studies of the African past reveal that many groups developed highly complex societies. The base of the social structure was the family. Many of the societies were rigidly hierarchical. The political units varied from village tribes to extensive empires. The economy was agricultural, but many artistic and mechanical skills were well developed: woodcarving, bronzework, basketry, goldsmithing, weaving, and ironworking. One early European visitor to the Gambia Coast marveled, "The blacksmiths make all sorts of tools and instruments for tillage, etc. as also weapons and armour, being indifferent skillful at hardening of iron, and whetting it on common stones." Trade was carried on in organized markets.

Indeed, commerce was well developed on local and regional levels and in some instances reached transcontinental proportions.

Repeated invasions by the Phoenicians, Greeks, Romans, and Arabs brought foreigners to Africa as early as 100 B.C. The fall of Ceuta in A.D. 1415 heralded new European incursions. Africa's commercial potential— gold, ivory, cotton, and spices—attracted the Europeans, who soon enough discovered that the blacks themselves were the continent's most valuable export. Between 1441 and 1443, the Portuguese began to transport blacks to Europe for sale. The intercontinental slave trade initiated and for centuries carried on by the European marks one of the most inhumane chapters of world history.

From the very beginning, some blacks from the Iberian Peninsula participated in the exploration and conquest of the Americas. It is believed that the first African slaves reached the New World as early as 1502. Later, the slave trade, carried on with the sanction of the Iberian monarchs, transported large numbers of blacks directly from Africa to the New World. Probably the first shipments of slaves arrived in Cuba in 1512 and in Brazil in 1538, and they continued until Brazil abolished its slave trade in 1850 and Spain finally terminated the slave trade to Cuba in 1866. As the American colonies grew, accommodated themselves to European demands, and developed plantation economies, the rhythm of slave importation accelerated. A majority of the 3 million slaves sold into Spanish America and the 5 million sold into Brazil over a period of approximately three centuries came from the west coast of Africa between the Ivory Coast and South Africa, a stretch of territory exceeding 3,000 miles. These numbers do not reflect the millions of Africans killed in the process of transportation and "seasoning," a genocide of dismal proportions. Blacks could be found in all parts of Latin America and formed a large part of the population. They quickly became and remained the major work force in the Caribbean and Brazil. Their presence dominated the plantations that they worked, and their influence spread quickly to the "big house" where African women served as cooks, wet nurses, and companions of the woman of the house, while black children romped with white children.

Male slaves outnumbered females by a ratio of almost two to one. The plantation owners preferred men and paid more for them because they considered them better field hands and hence more profitable. But the women worked hard too. Indeed, traditionally they were regarded more as laborers than mothers. Their owners discouraged large-scale reproduction as uneconomical. Thus, the Latin American slave system was seldom self-sustaining and required constant replacement through the slave trade. African influence also permeated the cities where the blacks worked as domestic servants, peddlers, mechanics, and artisans. In the sixteenth century, blacks outnumbered whites in Lima, Mexico City, and Salvador da Bahia, the three principal cities of the Western Hemisphere. The sex ratio among slaves seems to have been more equal in the cities, where women played particularly active roles as domestic servants, street vendors, prostitutes, and mistresses. The urban records seem to indicate that more freedwomen than freedmen existed. The city apparently offered the black woman more opportunity to change her status, partly because of her skills as vendor and her appeal as prostitute and mistress, partly because her sale price was lower than a man's, and partly because of her economic acumen.

Handicapped by the removal of all their possessions when taken into captivity, the Africans, uprooted and brutalized, still contributed handsomely to the formation of a unique civilization in the New World. First and foremost were the blacks themselves: their strength, skill, and intelligence. They utilized their former skills, and their intelligence permitted them to master new ones quickly. In fact, they soon exercised—and in some cases perfected—all the trades and crafts of the Europeans. Visitors to the Caribbean and Brazil remarked on the diversity of skills mastered and practiced by the blacks. They were masons, carpenters, smiths, lithographers, sculptors, artists, locksmiths, cabinetmakers, jewelers, and cobblers. Around the plantations and in the cities, these black crafts people, artisans, and mechanics became an indispensable ingredient in New World society.

Herdsmen in Africa, the blacks mounted horses to become cowboys in the New World. They followed the cattle into the Brazilian hinterlands and helped to occupy the rich platine pampas. In these as well as other ways they participated in the conquest and settlement of the interior. In Brazil, after the discovery of gold, the blacks were transported into Minas Gerais to mine the gold that created the Luso-Brazilian prosperity of the eighteenth century. From the plantations and mines, they helped to transport the raw products of the land to the ports where other blacks loaded the wealth of Latin America into ships that carried it to the markets of Europe. The blacks were even expected to defend the system that exploited them. In doing so, they sacrificed their blood to protect the Luso-Spanish empires at Havana, San Juan, Cartagena, Recife, Salvador, Rio de Janeiro, and elsewhere. The first black historian of Brazil, Manuel Querino (1851–1923), reviewed the great contributions of the Africans in these words:

> Whoever takes a look at the history of this country will verify the value and contribution of the Negro to the defense of national territory, to agriculture, to mining, to the exploitation of the interior, to the movement for independence, to family life and to the development of the nation through the many and varied tasks he performed. Upon his well-muscled back rested the social, cultural, and material development. . . . The black is still the principal producer of the nation's wealth, but many are the contributions of that long suffering and persecuted race which has left imperishable proofs of its singular valor. History in all its justice has to respect and praise the valuable services which the black has given to this nation for more than three centuries. In truth it was the black who developed Brazil.

The blacks possessed a leadership talent that the slave system never fully tapped. It became evident when the runaway slaves organized their own communities, known variously as *palenques* or *cumbes* in Spanish America and *quilombos* in Brazil, or when slaves revolted against their masters. The extent of slave rebellions is still unknown and awaits the careful investigation of scholars. An authority on the blacks in Mexico points out that black slave revolts occurred there in 1537, 1546, 1570, 1608, 1609, 1611, 1612, and 1670. One viceroy informed his monarch that the blacks in New Spain sought "to buy their liberty with the lives of their masters." According to our present knowledge, most of the slave revolts in Brazil took place in the early nineteenth century. Between 1807 and 1835, there were nine revolts or attempted revolts. Brilliant black leadership directed the slaves to freedom in Haiti; we will consider this story later along with the other independence movements. The blacks repeatedly protested their enslavement by running away, rebelling, and killing their masters. Many women practiced abortion to avoid bringing children into such a horrible life.

Mixing with both European and Indian, the Africans contributed their blood to the increasing racial mixture of the New World. Mulattoes, the cross of white and black, and myriad other interracial types resulting from the combination of the mixed descendants of white, black, and Indian appeared immediately after the introduction of the African slaves. Illustrative of the extent of the mixture of white and black was the population of Salvador da Bahia at the end of the colonial period. In 1803, the city boasted of a population of approximately 100,000, of which 40,000 were black, 30,000 white, and another 30,000 mulatto. Most Brazilians, in fact, could claim at least some African ancestry.

It would be difficult to think of any activity concerned with the formation and development of society in Latin America in which blacks did not participate. The blacks helped to smooth away the asceticism of churchgoing by enlivening some of the religious festivals. They drew them out into the streets and enhanced them with folkplays, dances, and music. Much of their contribution was rooted in the syncretism by which they sought to fuse their own beliefs with those of the Roman Catholic Church. They did, in fact, develop a syncretized religion, still very visible in Cuba, Haiti, and Brazil. Wherever the Africans went in the New World, they modified the culinary and dietary habits of those around them. Many of the rice and bean dishes so common in Latin America have African origins. Yams, okra, cola nuts, and palm oil are but a few of the contributions of the African cooks. The Africans introduced thousands of words into the Spanish and Portuguese languages and helped to soften the pronunciation of both. Their proverbs, riddles, tales, and myths mixed with those of Europeans and Indians to form the richly varied folklore of Latin America. The music, whether classical or popular, bears the imprint of African melodies. The blacks continued to sing the songs they remembered from their homelands, and to accompany themselves they introduced a wide range of percussion instruments. With the music went dances. The samba, frevo, and merengue descend from African imports.

With the forced migration of the blacks to the New World, the racial triptych—Mongoloid, Caucasian, and Negroid—was complete. Each contributed to the formation of a unique civilization representing a blend of the three. Overlaying that civilization were powerful institutions imported unchanged from the Iberian Peninsula.

2

The Institutions
of Empire

The cathedral San Juan de Dios, the municipal government building, and the
Indian marketplace in Quezaltenango, Guatemala, 1875

The American domains of the Iberian crowns (Spain and Portugal) furnished increasing amounts of wealth. The rapid discovery of fabulous deposits of gold and silver in Spanish America was the exact reward the Spanish crown coveted. For its part, Portuguese Brazil proved by the mid-sixteenth century that a plantation economy distant from Europe could still be lucrative. Sugar profits more than made up for high transportation costs.

The potential and then realization of wealth conferred a new importance on the New World for the Iberians. To administer the lands and to promote their wealth, the crowns extended their governments across the Atlantic. The cross as well as the scepter swayed over western continents. The Church busied itself converting the Indians and the African slaves and in the process helped to implant Iberian civilization. From the imperial point of view, the Iberians succeeded brilliantly. They converted millions to Christianity and incorporated most of them within the two empires; they explored, conquered, and settled millions of square miles; they produced an incalculable wealth; they constructed architectural gems and founded flourishing cities; and what was truly impressive, they ruled an area many times the size of the motherlands for over three centuries. Of course they did so within a political and economic framework that subordinated the well-being of the distant colonies to the demands of the Europeans.

MINING

The Iberians had not set off on voyages of conquest and settlement. They had sought a much more modest goal: trade. Their encounter with the New World rather than China or India forced a drastic change of plans.

The Americas, at first anyway, frustrated the Iberians. The Indians of the Caribbean and the Brazilian coast, the first known to the Europeans, showed no inclination for or interest in transoceanic trade. The Portuguese contented themselves for three decades with exporting the brazilwood found growing close to the coast. The Spaniards lacked even that product to stimulate commerce in the Caribbean. With minimal trade and little readily visible wealth available, the disappointed Spaniards could only hope either to extract what tribute they could from the bewildered Indians—golden trinkets, tobacco, corn, and so on—or to use the Indians to create some form of wealth.

With less than vigorous trade in sight, the Iberians focused attention on the search for a very desirable item: gold. It offered three immediate and highly attractive advantages: easy shipment, imperishability, and extreme value. The Portuguese encountered very little of it among the Brazilian Indians and had to content themselves with beguiling rumors of gold hidden somewhere in the vague hinterlands. The first Spaniards, however, came into limited but tantalizing contact with the prized metal almost at once. The Indians displayed some golden ornaments to the delight of their visitors. Further, the Indians spoke of the existence of gold on various Caribbean islands, causing the Spaniards to initiate a search for deposits at once. In 1494, they discovered gold on the south side of Española (an area that later became the Dominican Republic). Other discoveries followed. Between 1501 and 1519 the Caribbean produced approximately 8 million pesos of gold.

After the conquest of Mexico and Peru, gold production shifted to the mainland, where silver also was discovered and mined. The Spaniards discovered in 1545 at Potosí, a remote area in mountainous Upper Peru (later Bolivia), one of the richest silver mines the world was ever to see. Other rich silver strikes in the Viceroyalty of Peru exported precious metals valued at about 85 million pesos to Spain between 1533 and 1560. During the era of greatest production (1579–1635), annual shipments sometimes surpassed 7 million pesos. Mexico, too, witnessed rich silver strikes: Taxco (1534), Zacatecas (1546), Guanajuato (1550), and San Luis Potosí (1592). In the sixteenth century, Mexico shipped more than 35 million pesos worth of precious metals to Spain. It became Spanish America's leading producer toward the end of the seventeenth century, and, in fact, over the course of the entire colonial period, the Viceroyalty of New Spain produced half of the New World's mineral wealth.

The principal source of gold in Spanish America was New Granada (Colombia), which, by 1600, had exported more than 4 million ounces of gold. Most of that gold came from placer deposits worked by slave labor. Production of gold in New Granada grew each century, eighteenth-century production nearly tripling that of the sixteenth. In total, it supplied the motherland with something like 30 million ounces of gold.

Gold discoveries in Brazil came late in the colonial period. The hardy *bandeirantes* (explorers) found gold for the first time in 1695 in the interior of Minas Gerais; other rich strikes occurred in 1721 in Mato Grosso and in 1726 in Goiás. Such discoveries were powerful incentives to open the vast southern interior of Brazil to settlement. Each discovery precipitated a wild rush of humanity to find fortune. The boom characteristic of all gold rushes was reenacted many times. Each ship arriving at Brazil's shores brought Portuguese and other foreigners destined for the mines. From every city and hamlet, from the coast as well as the interior, whites, blacks, Indians, mulattoes, and mestizos descended on the gold region. Rich and poor, young and old, men and women, none of whom had the slightest knowledge of prospecting techniques, scurried to find fortune. The boom not only caused a notable population growth in eighteenth-century Brazil but also caused a population shift from the older sugar-producing region of the Northeast to the newly opened regions of the Southeast. Gold production mounted there until 1760, when a decline set in. During the eighteenth century, Brazil produced 32 million ounces of gold, a majority of the world's gold supply.

The Iberian crowns maintained a lively interest in all mining operations and carefully collected their *quinto,* or one-fifth, of the precious metals mined. They employed large bureaucracies to oversee the mining of the metals and the collection of the quinto. The Spanish monarchs were particularly effective in encouraging the use of the latest mining techniques in their colonies. They employed European mining engineers when necessary. In the mid-sixteenth century, the Spaniards adopted the *patio* process of separating silver from ore by means of quicksilver (mercury), a far more efficient process than smelting. The crown established a mining school in Mexico that enjoyed an international reputation for excellence. For their part, the Portuguese lagged far behind the Spaniards in mining techniques. The prospectors sought out the alluvial gold in riverbeds or secondarily worked the riverbanks and shallow deposits in the neighboring hillsides. Subterranean mining was rare. With the price of slaves rising, the miners had few excess funds to spend on the needed equipment, which they would not have known how to use even if they had the funds. The government in Lisbon enacted a mining code but failed to recruit any mining experts to bring order and efficiency to the careless miners of Brazil's interior.

Mining brought a certain "prosperity." It momentarily filled the royal treasuries. Cities grew up wherever precious metals appeared, and some of them became major urban centers. Potosí, with 160,000 inhabitants in 1670, was the largest city in the New World. Ouro Prêto, Brazil, boasted a population of 100,000 by 1750. Farming and livestock raising followed the miners to supply food demands. The search for precious metals encouraged exploration and conquest, so mining became a major means of opening the interior of Latin America to European settlement and influence. However, it is easy to exaggerate the importance of gold and silver.

Many emphasize the negative aspects of mining. For one thing, the search for and flow of gold and silver sparked serious inflation both in Europe and in the Americas. For another, besides the legacy of some glorious architecture, it would be difficult to enumerate the benefits the New World enjoyed from its rich mines. Only a residue of the wealth produced remained in the New World. One Bolivian lamented that all Bolivia got from centuries of silver mining at Potosí was a hole in the ground. The wealth slipped not only through local fingers but eventually through those of the Iberians as well. The gold and silver only paused in the motherlands before falling into the hands of the northern Europeans, particularly the English, who sold manufactured goods to Portugal and Spain. There is some truth to the Brazilian observation that Brazilian gold mined by African slaves financed the English industrial revolution. Certainly mining contributed to the well-established pattern of wealth flowing from the Americas to the

Iberian peninsula and then on to Northern Europe, which industrialized while the Iberian empires rusticated.

Gold and silver were dramatic sources of wealth that easily captivated the imagination. They certainly provided compelling motives for exploration, conquest, and settlement. Yet mining produced less wealth than agriculture, which, in the final analysis, contributed more to the welfare of the American populace than did precious metals. A comparison of incomes from gold and sugar in eighteenth-century Brazil illustrates this point, even though gold was in ascendency and sugar in decline during that period: the average per-capita income from the sugar industry was considerably higher than that from mining. Because agriculture and livestock raising produced more wealth continuously, one can readily understand that the land and labor systems as they evolved were of greater importance to both the Iberian crowns and the American populations. In fact, they set the economic and social patterns—and shaped the political patterns—of the future, still weighing heavily on all Latin America at the end of the twentieth century. Rightly they deserve more of our attention.

LAND AND LABOR

Seeing their conquest of the New World as a kind of continuation of their reconquest of the Iberian Peninsula, the Spaniards transferred intact many institutions which they had used during the peninsular crusade. One such institution was the *encomienda*, literally "the entrustment," which made its appearance in the Caribbean soon after discovery. Once used for the control and exploitation of the Moors, the adelantados and their lieutenants employed it in the Americas as a means to both Christianize and exploit the Indians. The institution required the Spanish *encomendero* to instruct the Indians entrusted to him in the Christian religion and the elements of European civilization and to defend and protect them. In return he could demand tribute and labor from the Indians.

The crown hesitated to approve the transfer of the encomienda to the Caribbean. After all, the monarchs had just unified Spain and were in the process of strengthening their powers in the peninsula. They were reluctant therefore to nourish in the New World a class of encomenderos who could impose their will between the monarchs and their new Indian subjects. It smacked too much of feudalism for royal tastes. In accordance with her desires to centralize authority in the crown, Isabel ordered in 1501 that the governor of the Indies free the Indians from the encomiendas. When that experiment resulted in the flight of all Indians from the plantations and their refusal to work for the Spaniards, the queen changed her mind. By royal *cédula*, or edict, in 1503 she in effect legalized and institutionalized the encomienda in the New World:

> As we are informed that because of the excessive liberty enjoyed by the Indians they avoid contact and community with the Spaniards to such an extent that they will not even work for wages, but wander about idle, and cannot be had by the Christians to convert to the Holy Catholic faith. . . I order you, our Governor, that beginning from the day you receive my letter you will compel and force the Indians to associate with the Christians of the island and to work on their buildings, and to gather and mine the gold and other metals, and to till the fields and produce food for the Christian inhabitants and dwellers of the island.

This 1503 cédula, like those that preceded and followed it, expressed sincere concern over the welfare of the Indian subjects and admonished the Spaniards to treat them well, but it also sanctioned a labor system that would permit many abuses. The colonists also widely misapplied royal authorization to enslave Indians who made "unjust" wars on the Europeans. They so frequently claimed to royal officials that their enslaved Indians were captives in a "just" war that the crown eventually had to forbid enslavement for any cause.

The encomienda system spread rapidly across the West Indies and contributed significantly to the mounting death rate of the natives. Not so much by its overwork and mistreatment as by concentrating the Indians, it facilitated the spread of European diseases, smallpox, typhus, measles, and influenza, which proved lethal to the indigenous populations. It is estimated that between 1519 and 1650 about six-sevenths of the Indian population of Middle America were wiped out. Other areas of the Americas suffered proportional decreases. The accelerating deaths, the abuses, and the enslavement enraged the church members, particularly the Dominicans, who forcefully reminded the king of his obligations.

The papal approval of Iberian territorial claims made it clear that the monarchs must Christianize, civilize, and protect the Indians, a responsibility the kings took very seriously. At great expense, the monarchs dispatched missionaries to convert them. The lot of the early missionaries was extremely difficult. Not only did they have to master the Indian languages, win the Indians' confidence, and persuade them to embrace Catholicism, but they also had to fight against the planters and miners who feared religious interference with their labor system. They had every cause for the fear. Alarmed by the declining numbers of their charges, the church members raised their voices to defend their neophytes, to protest the practices of the colonists, and to prod the royal conscience. In their anger and concern, they took the Indians' case directly to the monarchs to whom they vividly reported the mistreatment and enslavement of their American subjects.

These prods to King Ferdinand's conscience coupled with his own political misgivings about the increasing power of the encomendero class prompted him to take action to control the encomiendas. In 1512, he promulgated the Laws of Burgos, the first general code for the government and instruction of the Indians. Its purpose was to regulate Spanish-Indian relations and insure the fair, humane treatment of the Indians. By so doing, the crown would limit and supervise the power of the encomenderos over the Indians. The theory as pronounced in Madrid sounded fine—it amply demonstrated the noble intention of the king to protect his Indian subjects—but the royal officers in the Indies found it difficult if not impossible to translate theory into practice. They faced the protests, threats, and power of the angry encomenderos who needed Indian labor.

Cortés immediately and successfully transplanted the institution to Mexico where he liberally divided up the Indians among his followers. For himself, he allotted an encomienda of 100,000 Indians. The others were considerably smaller. Although royal officials in Santo Domingo approved his action, the crown by 1519 was reluctant to see the encomienda spread. In fact, in 1520, Charles V abolished the institution. By then, however, it was too firmly entrenched in the New World to be so summarily eradicated. The encomenderos refused to acknowledge the abolition, and royal officials did not enforce the law. As is evident, the crown in Spain and the royal officials in the New World did not always act in harmony.

The encomenderos actively pressed their case before the monarch. They dispatched their own representatives to Madrid who emphasized the "barbarian" nature of the Indians, their indolence and ignorance. Without force, they emphasized, the Indians simply would not work. Their labors here on earth, the argument ran, were but small compensation for the eternal salvation offered by the Roman Catholic faith to which the Europeans introduced them. Further, they pointed out, the civilizing hand of Europe taught the natives how to better care for and feed themselves. In the final analysis, the encomenderos regarded their charges as a just reward for their participation in conquest or for some service rendered the crown. They adamantly refused to do the menial labor themselves; the encomienda provided the means to get work done. Their powerful lobby at court persuaded Charles to modify his position.

Still the king's mind would not rest; he realized that in the encomenderos he had a strong rival for power in the New World. The conquest of highly disciplined, sedentary Indian empires in the highlands of Middle and South America increased the strength of the encomenderos who controlled the Indians. The growing potential of a challenge from the encomendero class determined the monarch to take action. As in the past, the king's jealousy over his power in the New World coincided with religious concern over the welfare of the Indians.

Religious pressures had been mounting again. The strongest voice raised in defense of the Indians was that of Bartolomé de las Casas, a Dominican missionary and later bishop. Indignant, he returned to Spain from the Caribbean in 1515 to plead before Ferdinand the cause of the Indians. For the next half-century he pressed their case. Las Casas sternly reminded the monarch that the Pope had granted him territory in the New World solely for the purpose of converting the heathen. Thus, he argued, Spain had no right to use the natives for secular goals. He requested that all Spaniards except the missionaries be recalled. Foremost among those who opposed Las Casas was Juan Ginés de Sepúlveda, who relied heavily on Aristotelian theory for his arguments. Because of the intellectual superiority of the Europeans, Sepúlveda reasoned, the Indians should be subjected to them in a kind of natural servitude, which would permit the Indians to improve themselves by observing a better example of virtue, devotion, and industry. Las Casas won the debates. Pope Paul III indicated his support of the cause of Las Casas by a bull in 1537 declaring that the Indians were fully capable of receiving the faith of Christ, that is, that they possessed souls and should not be deprived of their liberty and property.

In response to both his fear and conscience, Charles promulgated the New Laws in 1542. They forbade the enslavement of the Indians, their compulsory pesonal service, the granting of new encomiendas, and the inheritance of encomiendas. More positively they declared the Indians to be free persons, vassals of the crown, and possessed of their own free will. The colonists protested vehemently. Rebellion threatened Mexico; in Peru encomenderos rose up to defy the law. Once again under extreme pressure, the monarch modified some of the laws and revoked others. Still, although the encomienda would continue for some time in parts of the sprawling American empire, the king had checked it. After the mid-sixteenth century the institution waned. The state exerted even greater control over the declining Indian population.

Replacing the encomienda as the major labor institution in Spanish America was the *repartimiento*, the temporary allotment of Indian workers for a given task. Significantly, under this institution royal authorities controlled and parceled out the Indians. The Spanish colonist in need of laborers applied to a royal official explaining both the work to be done and the time it would take and requesting a specific number of Indians to do it. In theory, the crown officials looked after the welfare of the Indians to insure that the payment was fair and the working conditions satisfactory; in practice, abuse of the repartimiento system abounded. Planters and miners constantly badgered royal officials to bend the system to better fit local needs. The institution flourished in the last half of the sixteenth century and in the first half of the seventeenth, and in fact some vestige of the institution probably has never died out in those areas where the Indian populations are still heaviest. A traveler to Guatemala in the mid-nineteenth century described the operation of the repartimiento in the northern province of Verapaz in words that could have been written three centuries earlier. In the twentieth century, the government of Jorge Ubico (1931–44) imposed a work law on the Guatemalan Indians all too reminiscent of the aims of the repartimiento.

In addition to furnishing an agricultural labor force, the repartimiento system also provided the major share of the workers for the mines in Spanish America. The state paid close attention to the labor situation in the mines, which furnished the single most important source of its income. In the Viceroyalty of Peru, the Spaniards devised the burdensome *mita* of Potosí, a special type of repartimiento, to work that rich lode. All adult male Indians of the Peruvian Andes were subject to serve in the mita for one year out of every seven. Far from his home, the Indian miner worked under the most dangerous conditions and earned a wage that did not suffice for half of his own and his family's expenses. Members of the family had to work in order to make up the difference.

As in Spanish America, the landowners in Brazil relied in part (at least in the sixteenth century along the coast and for several more centuries in the interior and in the north) on the Indians as a source of labor. Some employed Indian labor from the *aldeias,* the villages. The crown and the religious orders working together did their best to concentrate the nomadic Indians into villages, first organized and administered by the religious orders but after 1757 administered by the crown. Protected within the village, the Indians were introduced to Christianity and European civilization. In return, they gave a portion of their labor to the Church and state. This part of the aldeia system resembled the encomienda. In addition, planters could apply to the aldeia administrators for paid Indian workers to perform a specific task for a specified period of time. In this respect, the aldeia system approximated the repartimiento. The aldeia system included only a small percentage of the Brazilian Indians. The rest the planters hunted to enslave, always explaining to questioning church members or crown officials that they had captured their Indian slaves in a "just" war.

After their arrival in 1549, the Jesuits spoke out to protect the Indians. In the sixteenth and seventeenth centuries, three notable Jesuits, Manuel da Nóbrega, José de Anchieta, and Antônio Vieira, who had influence both in Brazil and at court, vigorously defended the Indians. They reminded the Portuguese monarch of his obligataions. On the other hand, the planters sent their own representatives to court to present their point of view. The high death rate among the Indians exposed to European demands and diseases, their retreat into the interior, their amalgamation into the new Brazilian society through miscegenation, and the increasing importation of Africans to supply the growing labor needs of the colony did more to solve the complex question of Indian-European relations than did all the altruistic but impractical or ignored legislation of the Portuguese kings.

Already by the mid-sixteenth century there were virtually no Indians left in the West Indies, with the result that the importation of African slaves rose markedly, and the work force in the Caribbean became almost totally black. In Brazil, too, the diminishing number of Indians caused the planters to seek ever larger numbers of African slaves, who by the end of the sixteenth century furnished the most productive labor in Brazil. In the highland areas of Spanish America, the blacks never replaced the Indians.

Growing agricultural and export demands and a limited population base intensified competition among the landowners for workers, prompting them to devise a new method to insure a more dependable labor system: they contracted the Indians as wage laborers. The crown approved the development as a progressive step, the creation of a large wage-earning class. To the monarch it seemed to verify that the Indians had been assimilated at last into the empire, that they had been in effect Europeanized. However, the system proved to be one more device of the landowners to exploit the labor of the Indians. Contract wage labor became debt peonage. It tied the Indians and their descendants, the rural working class in the agricultural society of the New World, to the landowner by debt. The *hacendados* made deceptively friendly loans to the Indians, loans that were to be repaid with labor. However, the wages paid for such labor never sufficed to liquidate the debt. Fathers passed the debts on to sons; through this system, which lasts in parts of Latin America today, the landowners hoped to assure themselves of a ready labor supply. However, the very scarcity of labor provided the Indians with at least some minimal maneuverability in their relations with the landowners. When possible, the workers gravitated toward employers who promised better salaries or working conditions.

It is obvious that the search for a viable labor system in Latin America was long and convoluted. In the Caribbean and in Brazil the Indians were enslaved or held in encomiendas and aldeias. Their numbers declined rapidly. The Brazilian and Caribbean planters eventually solved their labor shortages by importing African slaves. In the highland regions of Spanish America, the effort to solve the labor problem evolved through three stages: encomienda, repartimiento, and debt peonage. The three systems often overlapped. In parts of the vast Spanish American empire they existed simultaneously. Although presented above in an overly schematized version, there was, nonetheless, a discernible general trend that reflected a gradual progression through the three labor systems.

After their initial adjustment to the New World, the Iberians coveted the land as much as they did the Indians. Ownership of land became a basis for wealth and prestige. It conveyed power. From the beginning the adelantados had distributed land among their followers as a reward for services rendered. The officers separately received large shares of land as well as grants of Indians. The common soldiers received appropriate quantities of land but usually were not granted any Indians.

In 1532, Martim Afonso, when he founded the first permanent settlement in Brazil at São Vicente, near the present-day Santos, distributed the land with a lavish hand to his followers. In his generosity he established a pattern of land distribution quite contrary to the prevailing custom in Portugal. Since 1375, the Portuguese kings had sparingly parceled out the *sesmarias,* the traditional land grants, so that no one person received more than could be effectively cultivated. Sensing the immensity of the territory in front of him, Martim Afonso ignored such a precaution. As a consequence, the good coastal land was quickly divided into immense sugar plantations, and not many more decades elapsed before the huge sesmarias in the interior for cattle ranches put much of the backlands under claims as well.

Over the generations many of the original grants of land grew to gigantic proportions. The more astute landowners bought out their neighbors or simply encroached upon other lands. The declining Indian population freed more and more land, which the Iberians rapidly grabbed up as their awareness of its value increased. A series of legal devices confused the Indian and favored the Spaniard in acquiring land: the *congregación, denuncia,* and *composición.* The congregación concentrated the Indians in villages and thereby opened land for seizure; the denuncia required the Indians to show legal claim and title to their property—a legality for which their ancient laws had not prepared them—and failure to do so meant that the land could be seized; the composición was a means of claiming land through legal surveys, a concept once again for which the Indians had little preparation. By these, as well as other means, the Spanish landowners steadily pushed the remaining Indians, whom they had not incorporated into their estates as peons, up the mountainsides and onto arid soils, in short, into the marginal lands. Coupled with the many ways the Spaniards had of acquiring land were the entailment and primogeniture laws that protected the land and prohibited its division. The Spanish crown tolerated, if it did not encourage, the large landholdings in its American possessions.

For their part, the Portuguese monarchs, critical of the inefficiency of the large *fazendas,* most of whose land lay fallow and hence unproductive, belatedly tried to reverse the course that was already well underway in Brazil. Repeatedly, promulgated decrees tried to limit the size of the estates: in 1695, single sesmarias were limited to four-by-one leagues in size; in 1697, they were reduced to three by one; and in 1699, all land not under cultivation was to be expropriated, and so on throughout the eighteenth century. One of the viceroys late in the eighteenth century, the Marquis of Lavradio, complained bitterly that the huge estates, poorly managed and often only partially cultivated, retarded the development of Brazil. He pointed to the unused fields held by their owners as symbols of prestige, while at the same time he noted that farmers petitioned him for land to till. Some of the regions had to import food that they were perfectly capable of producing themselves. Nonetheless, the *latifundia* that originated at the birth of the colony remained as dominant a characteristic of Brazil as it did of Spanish America.

Some of the haciendas and fazendas achieved princely proportions. There were instances of haciendas in Mexico exceeding 1 million acres. In Brazil the unmeasurable ranch of Diaz d'Avila by all accounts surpassed most European states in size. Begun in the late sixteenth century in northern Bahia, it centered on the São Francisco River and extended far into the interior. The huge estates were worlds in themselves.

The Luso-Brazilians quickly developed the prototype of the plantation economy, thanks to the ready and profitable market they found in Europe for sugar, a crop that grew exceedingly well along the coast. By 1550, Pernambuco, the richest and most important of the sixteenth-century captaincies, produced enough sugar in its fifty mills to load annually forty or fifty ships for Europe. The Brazilian sugar plantations flourished during the last half of the sixteenth and first half of the seventeenth centuries, as the mills busily ground the cane into sugar for the international market. The economic pattern of a single crop for international trade was fastened onto Brazil early. In Spanish America, for a long time the haciendas produced for local markets. One of their chief responsibilities was to feed the mining towns. Only as the eighteenth century neared did the haciendas enter into international trade on a scale comparable to that of the Brazilian plantations.

The type of life exemplified by the hacienda or fazenda often has been termed *feudal,* a term that carries a strong emotional overtone connoting exploitation. Certainly the classical feudalism of medieval society did not appear in the New World. Weak though his power might have been in some of the remoter areas, the king never relinquished the prerogatives of sovereignty to the landlords. Royal law prevailed. Nor does the self-sufficient manorial system properly describe the large estates, because for all their self-sufficiency they were closely tied by their one major cash crop to the capitalistic economy. Perhaps the *patrimonialism* defined by Max Weber comes closest to describing the system. Under patrimonialism, the landowner exerts authority over his followers as one aspect of his property ownership. Those who live on his land fall under his control. He uses armed force arbitrarily to enforce his authority within the bounds of his estate. With such authority, he administers his estate in a highly personal manner according to his own whims and without any set table of organization. Finally he controls all trade between his estate and the outside world. Patrimonialism seems to describe best the hacienda and fazenda systems as they developed in colonial Latin America.

The plantations, ranches, and mines provided a rich and varied source of income for the Iberian monarchs, capitalists, and merchants. Sugar, tobacco, cacao, indigo, woods, cotton, gold, silver, diamonds, and hides were some of the natural products the American colonies offered to the Old World. The Iberian Peninsula depended on the New World for its prosperity. Both Lisbon and Madrid relied heavily on its raw products for their foreign trade. For example, for many years the products of Brazil constituted approximately two-thirds of Portugal's export trade. Curiously, Latin America enriched Europe while impoverishing itself.

The abundance of economic possibilities in the New World may well have been more a curse than a blessing since it permitted, indeed, encouraged, an economic dilettantism that handicapped orderly development. Despite a dazzling potential, the regional economies of colonial Latin America seldom diversified. They relied for their well-being on a single natural product whose sale abroad dictated the course of colonial prosperity. If a particular product sold well, an entire region prospered; if not, stagnation and misery engulfed that region. External demand dictated the colonial well-being, a dependence exaggerated by stubborn reliance on one export. The colonies had no control over their own economic destiny. Nor did the Iberians ever achieve notable efficienty in the exploitation of those natural products with which a generous nature endowed their lands. More often than not, haphazard, old-fashioned, and inefficient methods characterized their exploitation. The case of sugar is an excellent example. The Portuguese held almost a monopoloy on the production of that lucrative export for well over a century. Between 1650 and 1715, the Dutch, English, and French increased production of sugar in the Caribbean, employing efficient organization, new equipment, and their extensive financial resources and enjoying a favorable geographic position closer to the European markets than Brazil and many of the Spanish-American producers. The result was that the sugar economies of the three European rivals of Portugal prospered, while the economy of the traditional producer languished. In mining, the Spaniards made an effort to introduce new methods and to establish schools of mining, but often even in that vital economic activity they were slower to modernize than they might have been. With quick and large profits as its goal, the economy of Latin America was largely speculative and hence subject to wide variations. The patrimonial system of land and labor contributed to economic fluctuations and inefficiency. In sum, the economy of Latin America was not geared to its own best interests but to the making of immediate profits for the Iberian metropolises and for a small, New World planter-trader elite, almost exclusively of European origin.

Economic dilettantism achieved just enough success to lull the Iberians into complacency. Continuity triumphed over change. Meanwhile, during the seventeenth century, England began to industrialize, to experiment with commercial innovations, and to expand its trade. The English were pioneering a new path to economic prosperity that the Iberians showed slight interest in following.

THE STATE

Spain and Portugal ruled their American empires for more than three centuries, a remarkable longevity that places them among the great imperial powers of all time. Both can rightly claim considerable political success for maintaining such vast empires for so long. They owed that success to quite different concepts of imperial organization. The Spanish colonial administration was relatively well organized, the hierarchical ranks were well defined, and the chain of command was easy to recognize. Not so in the Portuguese empire. It was loosely organized, the institutions less well defined and more transitory. Although the overlapping of duties, on the one hand, and the failure to assign responsibility, on the other, characterized some of the Spanish imperial administration, these were much more pronounced characteristics of the Portuguese government. In the eighteenth century, the Portuguese began to regularize and better define their imperial administration.

The concept of government markedly differed from concepts discussed in contemporary courses on political theory. Few of the political subtleties we must reckon with today had yet developed. Neither division of power nor distinction between branches of government existed. Church and state were practically one, and although secular and ecclesiastical officials bickered and squabbled among themselves, the two institutions buttressed each other, together preserving order and stability in the empires for centuries. All power rested in the hands of the monarch, who was the state. He made, executed, and judged the laws. On the one hand, he formulated the general concepts that governed the empires, and, on the other, he decreed a staggering array of minutely detailed laws such as setting of prices in the marketplaces or ordering the type of clothing the Indians would wear. He protected and governed the Church within his vast domains. Indeed, he ruled by divine right. The king was the unquestioned authority in whom all power rested and from whom all power emanated. That power was great, and yet tradition as well as natural and divine law imposed some limitations on its exercise. Still, the mystique and tradition of the monarchy gave the institution such force that no one questioned the king's right to rule or refused his loyalty to the crown. In all matters the king spoke the final world.

The monarchs jealously guarded their powers. Both the Portuguese and Spanish rulers made the initial error of delegating too much authority to subordinates in the New World. We have seen already that the Spanish monarchs, regretting the grant of so much power to the adelantados and encomenderos, reversed themselves in order to restore that authority to the crown. The Portuguese monarch had made an identical error. In 1532–34, in order to colonize Brazil without reaching into the royal coffers, he had distributed Brazil in the form of large captaincies to twelve donataries who were to enjoy broad powers in return for colonizing the American domains. By 1548, John III reversed that decision and began to reassert his authority over the captaincies so recently bestowed with a lavish hand on court favorites. Once they had decided to assert absolute control over the American

THE INSTITUTIONS OF EMPIRE

colonies, the monarchs never ceased their efforts to centralize power in their hands.

The great distance between the Iberian Peninsula and the New World and the slowness of communication and travel worked to confer considerable local autonomy on officials in the New World and to permit some irregularities. What it meant in practice was that the kings could only hope to dictate the broad outlines of policy, leaving much of the interpretataion and implementation to colonial and local officials. *Obedezco pero no cumplo* ("I obey but I do not fulfill") became the accepted way for New World officials to manifest their loyalty to the Spanish crown while bending the laws to suit local situations. The philosophy of acknowledging the king's authority without enforcing his will—as common in Brazil as in Spanish America—accounts, at least in part, for the longevity of the empires. It permitted a certain flexibility in the laws that could accommodate many interests, the monarch's as well as the colonist's. The many laws and edicts emanating from Iberia represented the wishes of the crowns, but complex and powerful pressures in the New World influenced the colonial administrators to consider the diverse local desires and needs. The results were legal and governmental systems that probably pleased neither the crowns nor their representatives in the Americas, but the system that resulted from the compromises did work surprisingly well.

To keep their royal officials and their subjects in check, the Iberian monarchs had at their disposal many useful instruments. They sent out to the New World only officials of unquestioned loyalty. At best they suspected that the colonies increased in everyone "the spirit of ambition and the relaxation of virtues." For that reason they hesitated to appoint many Americans to the highest colonial posts. They frankly suspected their loyalty. The Portuguese monarchs were more prone to appoint Brazilians to high office than were the Spanish monarchs willing to name Americans to elevated offices in the New World. Americans, however, occupied many of the minor posts, and as the empires matured they increasingly held influential ecclesiastical, military, and political positions. Despite royal frowns, the Iberian officials at times married into distinguished American families, and marriage thereby provided a link between the local and Iberian elite. Since so many of the officials had direct access to royal ears, there was considerable reporting and "tattling," which made all overseas personnel cautious. The kings encouraged it. Furthermore, officials might receive at any time a *visita,* an on-the-spot investigation to which all subordinates could be subjected. At the end of all terms of office, each administrator could expect a *residencia,* a judicial inquiry into his public behavior. All these checks required an immense amount of paperwork, a characteristic abundantly evident in all Iberian bureaucracy. A multitude of lawyers, scribes, and notaries in all the major cities testified to the fascination with and importance of legal and bureaucratic matters. Thanks to that legal obsession elaborate law codes were drawn up in the Old World to govern the New. A monument to Spanish legalism was the famed Recopilación de Leyes de las Indias, which in 1681 brought together many scattered laws, enactments, and decrees governing the New World. It served as a supplementary code for Spanish law. Portugal too had its monumental law codes. Frequently amended and supplemented, they uniformly governed the entire Portuguese empire regardless of their applicability or lack of it. The concern with law and legalities among the Iberians helped to make the monarchs' task of ruling far-flung empires easier.

Considering the size of the American colonies, the scant number of small and scattered garrisons, the few soldiers, and the handful of royal officials, almost all of whom resided in the most populous cities, the extent of metropolitan control over the American colonies was nothing short of remarkable. It must be concluded then that the crowns maintained their authority and control principally through the power of legitimacy. The Americans accepted the system, rarely questioned it, and seldom challenged it. When they did question or challenge the system prior to the end of the eighteenth century, they quickly and easily acceded to the forceful imposition of the royal will. Popular uprisings, mostly motivated by economic discontent, did break out periodically. The populace reacted to specific greivances rather than adhered to any philosophical current advocating change. For their part, the American elites, feeling they had more to gain through cooperation with the metropolises, lent their considerable authority to the maintenance of the imperial system. They eyed change with caution if not outright suspicion.

Although the power rested in the hands of the kings, no one person, regardless of how gifted that person might have been, could have ruled the immense empires to which the Iberian monarchs held claim. They required administrative assistance, and in seeking it they developed the administrative machinery for their empires.

Brazil constituted only one portion, albeit an immense one, of the global Portuguese empire. Because of the profits first from sugar and later from gold, it emerged as Portugal's most valuable overseas possession. Still, until the royal house of Braganza moved its court from Lisbon to Rio de Janeiro in 1807, Brazil was governed by no special laws or institutions that would have distinguished it as a separate, distinct, or privileged entity within the larger empire. Reviewing colonial Brazil's political evolution—its continuous advance from a simple to a complex state—over the course of three centuries, two general characteristics stand out. First, governmental control over Brazil grew stronger, even though that process might have been erratic at times. By 1807, the king, his viceroy, and his governors exercised more power more effectively than at any time previously. Second, the political status of Brazil slowly improved throughout the course of three centuries. A central government under a governor-general began to exercise authority in 1549 to bring some order and justice to the unhappy and generally ineffective rule of the donataries in their captaincies. In 1646, the king elevated Brazil to the status of a principality, and thereafter the heir to the throne was known as the Prince of Brazil. After 1720, all the chiefs of government of Brazil bore the title of viceroy. Although no document exists to show the exact date of its elevation, Brazil was in effect a viceroyalty thereafter. Finally, Prince-Regent John raised Brazil to a kingdom in 1815, thus, at least in theory, putting it on an equal footing with Portugal.

Portugal was well into the sixteenth century before the rulers made any distinction between home and overseas affairs. Never did the crown authorize a special body to handle exclusively Brazilian matters. Local administrators did become adept, however, in adapting the general imperial codes and fiats to suit the local scene. They had to. The third governor-general of Brazil, Mem de Sá, confided to the king, "This land ought not and cannot be ruled by the laws and customs of Portugal; if Your Highness was not quick to pardon, it would be difficult to colonize Brazil."

The king could not rule his vast domains unaided. A variety of administrative organs that, in the practice of the times, exercised a combination of consultative, executive, judicial, and fiscal functions assisted him. One of the most important of those bodies was the Overseas Council (*Conselho Ultramarino*) created by John IV in 1642. It was the evolutionary result of considerable experience. The president, secretary, and three councilors of the Overseas Council usually had served in the colonies, and during its history the council included many who had resided in Brazil. The council divided itself into standing committees to treat the various military, administrative, judicial, and ecclesiastical matters. Its primary duty was to advise the king. Increasingly it showed greater concern for commercial matters.

Other governmental organs continued to have dual metropolitan and colonial responsibilities. A Treasury Council (*Conselho da Fazenda*) created in 1591 to replace the Treasury Supervisors (*Vedores da Fazenda*) administered public finances and the treasury. A Board of Conscience and Religious Orders (*Mesa de Consciência e Ordens*) established in 1532 advised the Crown on Indian matters. Finally a Casa da Suplicação served as a supreme court for many colonial judicial disputes.

A royal secretary or secretary of state, who, after 1736, bore the title of Minister of Navy and Overseas, also assisted the monarchs in their imperial rule. These ministers became increasingly important in the last half of the eighteenth century. The ministers, as well as other close advisers to the crown, were selected because of loyal and often meritorious service and enjoyed unqualified royal confidence. They had direct access to the king's ear and were, of course, responsible to him. Together these secretaries, ministers, and organs formed the principal bureaucratic apparatus in Lisbon that enabled the monarch to rule his scattered overseas domains. Their experience and expertise made that rule more effective—at least in theory.

In Brazil, representatives of the royal government administered that colony. At the apex stood the governor-general, after 1720 called the viceroy. His effectiveness depended largely on his own strengths and weaknesses. Those viceroys who were vigorous exerted considerable influence over the colony. Those who were weak found themselves almost unable to control the capital city and their powers eroded by ambitious bishops and subordinate bureaucrats. The viceroys of the eighteenth century tended to be stronger and more effective administrators than their predecessors. The king's chief representatives in Brazil served for an average term of six and a half years in the sixteenth century, three and a half years in the seventeenth century, and slightly less than six years in the eighteenth century. Most of them were professional soldiers and members of the nobility.

Salvador da Bahia served as the first seat of the central government of Brazil. A splendid port, in the early nineteenth century it boasted a population of approximately 100,000, making it, after Lisbon, the second city of the empire. In 1763, the seat of the viceroyalty moved southward to Rio de Janeiro. A foreign challenge to the southern extreme of the colony prompted the transfer. Foreign threats to the northeastern sugar coast ended after the defeat and expulsion of the Dutch in 1654. The West Indies thereafter attracted most of the attention of the European maritime powers. However, by the end of the seventeenth century, Portuguese America faced a growing threat from the Spanish in the Plata region. In 1680, the Portuguese had founded the settlement of Colônia do Sacramento on the left bank of the Río de la Plata, across from Buenos Aires. The Spanish challenge to Portuguese claims to the region caused a century and a half of intense rivalry and frequent warfare along the Plata. The Portuguese crown felt it necessary to have the viceroy nearer the scene of military operations and so moved the capital 800 miles southward. Also, economic crises in the mining regions of the southeast suggested that it might be wise to have the viceroy closer to those vitally important economic centers. Furthermore, the shift of the capital reflected a broader population shift during the eighteenth century from the northeast to the southeast.

The governors-general and later the viceroys depended on a growing bureaucracy to carry out their primary functions of administering the colony, overseeing its military preparedness, dispensing the king's justice, and enforcing taxes. Of greatest importance was the High Court (*Relação*), the first of which was established in Bahia in 1609 under the presidency of the governor-general. A second was established in Rio de Janeiro in 1751. These courts primarily had judicial responsibilities: they functioned as the highest law tribunals in Brazil from which there was limited appeal to the Casa da Suplicação in Lisbon. They reviewed the conduct of all officials at the end of their terms of office. Secondarily they served as consultative and administrative organs. When the governor-general absented himself from the capital, the highest member of the court usually governed in his place. The governor-general often requested the advice of the legally trained judges on a host of judicial and administrative matters. Tax questions and the supervision of the treasury were the responsibility of another bureau, the Board of Revenue (*Junta da Fazenda*).

The nation we know today as Brazil was divided during most of the colonial period into two states. The state of Brazil, about which we have talked thus far, was by far the more important of the two, but it should be noted that another, very impoverished colony existed in the far north, the state of Maranhão. The government of Maranhão was similar to that of Brazil, only seemingly less well defined. Nor did the northern state ever develop the vitality of the southern one. It depended even more heavily upon Lisbon. The king appointed a governor-general and a chief justice after the state was established in 1621. A slow growth and a scanty population negated the need for a high court and none was ever authorized. In 1751, the capital was transferred from São Luís to Belém, a smaller although an increasingly more active port that for some time had been the effective center of the state. In recognition of the growing importance of the Amazon, the king created in 1755 the Captaincy of São José do Rio Negro (the present-day Amazonas), subordinate to the Captaincy of Pará.

Captaincies were the principal territorial subdivisions of the two states. Representatives and appointees of the king, the governors or captains-general of those captaincies carried out the same responsibilities on a regional level as the governor-general or viceroy did on a broader scale. The governor-general was charged with overseeing, coordinating, and harmonizing their efforts. Here, as in so many instances, theory and practice diverged. Distance, the varying effectiveness of personalities, intrigue, and vagueness of the law often meant that the governor-general was only first among equals and sometimes unable to exert any authority in the captaincies. In times of crisis, particularly those brought about by fear of a foreign attack on a coastal city or Spanish expansion into southern Brazil, the military authority of the governor-general or viceroy increased. His martial powers may well have been his strongest. However, more often than not, the lines of communication ran from the capital of each captaincy directly to the king, seldom passing through the colonial capital. In truth, the governor-general and his later successor, the viceroy, never exercised the same degree of control or authority as their counterparts in Spanish America.

The municipal government was the one with which most Brazilians came into contact and the only one in which they participated to any degree. Governing much more than just the town and its environs, the municipality extended out to meet equidistant the boundaries of the next. In sparsely settled Brazil, the municipalities contained hundreds, often thousands of square miles. European countries seemed dwarfs compared to some of these municipal giants.

The most important institution of local government was the *senado da câmara,* the municipal council. A restricted suffrage of the *homens bons,* which is to say the propertied class, elected two justices of the peace, three aldermen, and a procurator to office every three years. At first the presiding officer was selected by the other councilmen, but by the end of the seventeenth century, the crown was appointing a presiding officer in the most important towns and cities. The duties of the council varied. Meeting twice weekly, it meted out local justice, handled routine municipal business and local administration, and passed the necessary laws and regulations. The procurator executed those laws. In cooperation with the church, the senado helped to oversee local charities. The municipality enjoyed its own source of income: rents from city property, license fees for tradesmen, taxes on certain foodstuffs, charges for diverse services such as the verification of weights and measures, and fines. The senado of São Luís during the seventeenth century was particularly ambitious. So often did it summon the governor to appear before it that the king in 1677 ordered it to desist forthwith, reminding the councilors that the governor represented the crown and could not be ordered around. Sometimes the senados and governors engaged in power struggles. At times the senados dared to challenge the crown itself. To protect their interests, the larger cities maintained a representative at the court in Lisbon as a sort of lobbyist.

As Brazil's foremost historian of the colonial period, João Capistrano de Abreu, has pointed out, the senado frequently served as an arena—the first one—for the struggles between the *mazombos,* the whites born in Brazil, and the *reinóis,* the whites born in Portugal. The Portuguese officials, occupying all levels of government except the municipal, enforced the universal law of the empire. Their point of view was global. They saw Brazil as one part of a larger empire that existed for the grandeur of Portugal. The mazombos sitting on the municipal councils cared only for the local scene; their vision was restricted. It was, in short, Brazilian. They wanted to enforce those aspects of the laws beneficial to them, to their community, and, to a lesser extent, to Brazil. These different perspectives gave rise to repeated clashes in which the mazombos did not always give ground to the reinóis. In times of crises, the senado da câmara amplified its membership to become a *conselho geral,* a general council. On those occasions local military, judicial, and ecclesiastical authorities as well as representatives of the people met with the senado to discuss the emergency at hand.

A second institution of local government deserves mention because of its influence on subsequent Brazilian events: regional militias. In them the principal figure of prestige and power in an area, usually the largest landowner, bore the rank of *capitão-mor,* equivalent to colonel. The majority of them seem to have been born in the colony. In the absence of regularly

constituted governmental officials in the hinterlands, the capitães-mor per-
formed a variety of administrative and even judicial tasks. Obviously it was
to their own interest to enforce law and order in their region, which they
did to the benefit of local tranquility. Their power varied widely and as in
so many cases depended mainly on their own abilities and strengths, since
the distant government could do little to help or hinder them. They often
became the local strongmen or *caudilhos*, the precursors of the later *coroneis*,
who control rural Brazil.

Stronger in organization and authority than governmental institutions were the patriarchal plantation families. These large, cohesive family
units appeared at the inception of the sugar industry, and the two grew
together. The paterfamilias dominated the household and the plantation,
ruling family, slaves, and tenants with unquestioned authority. He and
other males of the household liberally expanded the basic family unit
through their polygamous activities to include hosts of mestizo and mulatto
children. In fact, it was in and around the plantation house that European,
Indian, and African cultures blended together the most perfectly to create
a Brazilian civilization. The traditional godparent relationship (*compadrio*)
further ramified and reinforced the family structure. Certain ideal models
were set for the behavior of the women of the patriarch's family, who were
destined either for matrimony or religious orders. They were to remain
virgins until their marriage and to live separated from all men except their
fathers, husbands, and sons. A high value was placed on their duties as
wives and mothers. Although women of other economic strata could not
follow such an elitist model, they were certainly influenced by it. Profoundly Christian and emphatically patriarchal, these family units set the
social tone and pattern for the entire colony. The strongest of the families
formed a landed aristocracy, which in the colonial period dominated the
senados and later, in the imperial period, the newly independent national
government.

Brazil by the close of the eighteenth century was widely if thinly settled. Its steady expansion from a narrow coastal band to subcontinental size
represents one of the most dramatic and dynamic themes of the colonial
period. As the colonists grew in number and strength in the sixteenth
century, they gradually began to fill in the voids between São Vicente in the
south and Olinda in the north. Foreign threats from the English, French,
and Dutch hastened Portuguese occupation of the coast in order to defend
it. Slowly the colonization moved northward from Olinda to conquer the
north coast and finally the mouth of the Amazon. With the coast conquered
by 1616, the Luso-Brazilians, disregarding the papal Tordesillas line, began
to penetrate the interior with increasing boldness in search of slaves and
gold. They carried the banner of Portugal to the Andes in the west and to
the Plata River in the south. Daring *bandeirantes* (explorers) claimed thousands of square miles for the Portuguese crown. Too late Spain realized

what had happened, and in the Treaty of Madrid (1750) the Castilian crown was forced to recognize its rival's conquest of the heartland of South America. Although the boundaries between Spanish and Portuguese America were altered slightly therafter—particularly in the Plata area—Portugal successfully retained its claims to half of South America.

Population growth did not keep up with territorial expansion. Growing at a rate estimated at 1.9 percent annually, the population at the end of the eighteenth century numbered about 2.3 million with Minas Gerais, Bahia, Pernambuco, Rio de Janeiro, and São Paulo being the most populous captaincies in that order. The majority lived along the coast or in the rich river valleys. The trend to migrate to the interior accelerated by the discovery of gold had been stemmed, and in many cases reversed with some return of the population to the coast. Obviously hollow frontiers still characterized the settlement.

It was possible to distinguish five different regions of settlement. The far north, which included the vast Amazon valley, was scantily settled, a few villages dotting the river banks and coast. The Indian predominated. The economy depended on the extraction of forest products and cattle raising in the interior and the cultivation of sugar and coffee along the coast. The cattle lands of the *sertão*, the arid interior, stretching from Maranhão to Minas Gerais were the domain of the mestizos. The dry land and light vegetation grudgingly supported cattle, some horses, and a few sheep and goats. Ranches and hamlets were scattered over that vast interior with little concentration of settlement. The lush sugar coast extending from Maranhão to São Vicente included excellent ports and the largest cities in Brazil; blacks prevailed in that more concentrated settlement. The mining regions of Minas Gerais, Goiás, and Mato Grosso exported their gold and diamonds but retained enough of the wealth to create a few prosperous towns. Stock raising, sugar cane, and agriculture played a secondary economic role in the region. The far south boasted of excellent agricultural and pastoral lands. Immigrants, Europeans from the Azores, settled the coastal region. Their small family farms grew grapes, wheat, and olives. Bandeirantes migrated overland from São Paulo to colonize the interior of the south. There one encountered patriarchal cattle ranches and a profitable business in mule and horse raising.

Unlike Portugal, Spain possessed few overseas domains outside the Americas. Consequently, the colonial system the Spanish devised was to govern principally their vast territories in the New World. Two administrative bodies aided the king in his rule of Spanish America. The first created was the Casa de Contratación, and, as previously mentioned, it served to regulate and develop commerce with the New World. The second, the Council of the Indies (*Consejo de las Indias*), established in 1524, advised the king on all American affairs. It prepared most of the laws for governing the Americas, saw that the laws were executed, and then sat as a high court to judge cases involving the fracture or interpretation of the laws. Ecclesiastical matters fell within its jurisdiction as well. In the beginning, the king favored the appointment of clergymen as councilors; later he tended to select lawyers of noble blood for these positions. Always the council counted among its members some naval and military officers. Upon their return to Spain, successful administrators in the New World often sat on the council.

The viceroy served as the king's principal representative in the New World. Columbus bore the title of viceroy of any new lands he might discover when he left Spain in 1492. The crown appointed Antonio de Mendoza, a member of one of Spain's foremost families and a trusted diplomat of Charles V, as the first Viceroy of New Spain. Amid great pomp, he arrived in Mexico City in 1535 and immediately set about to restrict the authority of the adelantados and encomenderos while he strengthened and centralized the king's power in the New World. By the time he left Mexico in 1551, he had imposed law and order, humbled the landowning class, and exalted the royal powers. In short, he consolidated the conquest of New Spain. Peru became the second viceroyalty. The first viceroy arrived in 1543 to find chaos, rivalries, and civil war disrupting Spanish South America. Not until the able administration of the fifth viceroy, Francisco de Toledo (1569–81), was the king's authority firmly imposed on his unruly South American subjects. During his long administration, Viceroy Toledo tried to improve the relations between the Indians and Spaniards, promote mining, and organize the administration of justice. Like Mendoza, his major achievement was the consolidation of Spanish rule and the imposition of the king's authority.

Numerous accounts testify to the splendor and prestige surrounding the viceroys and their New World courts. They were, after all, the "shadows of the king," and many accustomed themselves to royal treatment in their American domains. For example, in his lively history of Potosí written during the early decades of the eighteenth century, Bartolomé Arzáns de Orsúa y Vela provided posterity with a vivid view of a viceregal visit to that extremely important silver-mining center in 1716. Priests, nobles, and representatives of one of the labor guilds met Viceroy don Fray Diego Morcillo Rubio de Auñón outside the city to escort him into Potosí, whose principal streets and plazas opulently displayed banners and bunting of silk, damask, and satin. Passing beneath silver-encrusted triumphal arches especially constructed for the visit, the official party approached the awaiting municipal dignitaries who stood expectantly beneath "a canopy of very rich pearl-colored cloth lined with silk." A short musical concert began, while Urbanity and Generosity (represented by two children) recited elegant verses expressive of the city's gratitude for the honor of the visit. The viceroy then accepted as gifts golden spurs and a richly decorated Chilean horse with silver stirrups. On the fine steed the viceroy, accompanied by a growing crowd of elaborately dressed worthies, marched to the principal church richly outfitted with hangings of satin, velvet, silk tapestries, and damasks and paintings of landscapes and portraits—a magnificence, the historian assured his readers, only the local women "all with their beauty, fine clothing, coiffures, jewels, and pearls" surpassed. The priests and representatives of the city's religious communities awaited His Excellency on the steps to conduct him into the service. Hours later, exiting from the lavish religious pageantry, the viceroy reviewed the troops smartly drawn up in an adjacent plaza. Finally, he retired to a local aristocrat's home "so richly and appropriately adorned so spacious and magnificent that it was worthy of lodging our king and lord Philip V himself." That observation acknowledged the stature of the viceroy.

More than a description of a visit, the account identifies which persons—and more importantly the institutions they represented—enjoyed prestige. The viceroy greeted the local elite, the city officials, the clergy, and the military. Significantly, at least some labor (guild) representatives participated in the elaborate rituals. Thus, the arrangements surrounding the hospitality accorded the viceroy in Potosí detail accurately the composition of the local ruling hierarchy in colonial Spanish America and preserve a glimpse into their relations with a distant monarch and his immediate representative.

The *audiencia* was the highest royal court and consultative council in the New World. In some instances it also prepared legislation. The Spanish audiencias had much in common with the Portuguese relação. The first audiencias were established in Santo Domingo in 1511; Mexico City, 1527; Panama City, 1535; Lima, 1542; and Guatemala, 1543. In the eighteenth century, fourteen such bodies were functioning. The number of *oidores*, or judges, sitting on the audiencia varied according to time and place. In the sixteenth century, their number fluctuated between three and four, but later it expanded to as many as fifteen. Because the tenure of the oidores exceeded that of the viceroy and overlapped each other, the oidores provided a continuity to royal administration that the viceroy's office did not have. Over the audiencias in the viceregal capitals, the viceroy himself presided. The chief executive of the political subdivisions served as president of the audiencia located within his confines.

Presidencias and captaincies-general were the major subdivisions of the viceroyalties. Theoretically the presidents and captains-general were subordinate to the viceroys, but in practice they communicated directly with Madrid and paid only the most formal homage to the viceroys. Ranking beneath the presidents and captains-general were the governors, *corregidores*, and *alcaldes mayores* who administered the municipalties and other territorial divisions. Within their localities, these minor officials possessed executive and judicial authority as well as some limited legislative powers.

Municipal government, known as the *cabildo*, provided the major opportunity for the creole, the American-born white, to hold office and to exercise some political power. From it the creoles gained most of their political experience, however limited it might have been. Also, throughout the colonial period it remained the single self-perpetuating governmental institution in Spanish America. As in Brazil, the town council governed not only the town itself but also the surrounding countryside, thus in some instances exercising power over vast administrative areas. Some of the cabildos far removed from immediate viceregal supervision, such as Buenos Aires prior to 1776 and Asunción, exercised considerable autonomy. Property-owning citizens at first elected the *regidores,* the town councilmen, although later increasing numbers purchased or inherited the office or were appointed to it by the king. As royal power grew stronger in the eighteenth century, the cabildo grew weaker, and the tendency to tighten the centralization of the empire restricted the independence of the municipal governments. The cabildo probably exercised its greatest authority in the sixteenth century.

Because the local elites tended to be very conservative in their outlook—sometimes even more so than the king—the cabildo meetings rarely raised questions of reform or change. They usually concentrated on the ordinary business of daily municipal government. A somewhat "typical" session of the cabildo of Lima on November 6, 1626, reflected that conservatism. It engaged in a land dispute, claiming encroachment on municipal lands, voted monies to repair the water system, and made three appointments. Thus, the cabildo sought to restore lands to its control, to maintain the water supply as it had been, and to appoint three officials in the prescribed manner. Such sessions reinforced a continuity pervading the imperial system. Yet, when they felt their own interests threatened, the members of the cabildo responded. Like its Brazilian counterpart, the cabildo sometimes provided the arena for local elites to voice views that lacked the wider vision of empire characteristic of the senior bureaucrats sent from Spain. In certain moments of crisis, the cabildo expanded to include all the principal citizens of the municipality, who were requested to offer their advice. That *cabildo abierto* became the agency of transition from colonial to independent government in several places in the early nineteenth century.

Spain's empire in America at the end of the eighteenth century swept southward from California and Florida, through the Caribbean, Mexico, and Central America, and down the length of South America. Approximately 16 million people inhabited the Spanish-governed domains. The empire had grown by steady expansion, rapid in the sixteenth century, more slowly thereafter. From the original settlements in the Caribbean, the central valley of Mexico, and the highlands of Peru, adelantados followed by colonists had pushed into new regions. In the older colonies, agriculture continued to progress; in the newer ones it became established and advanced rapidly. The real riches of the New World were its farms, ranches, and plantations. The silver and gold mines poured forth their treasure, but despite their glitter and attraction they remained secondary to agriculture as a source of wealth. Unfortunately very few shared in the growing wealth of the Americas.

Most of America's riches flowed to Europe north of the Pyrenees, pausing only briefly in Spain. The bustling ports of Veracruz, Havana, Portobelo, La Guaira, Callao, Valparaiso, and Buenos Aires dispatched the wealth of the New World aboard ever larger numbers of merchant ships to the markets of Europe and welcomed the merchandise and immigrants of the Old World.

To handle the lucrative trade, a small merchant class developed in Spanish America. These merchants later united into the *consulados* and obtained for themselves formidable privileges and prerogatives. The crown authorized the first such trade association for Mexico in 1592; the merchants of Lima received permission for one in 1613. Thereafter, the consulado spread to other parts of Spain's American empire, a significant indicator of increasing trade with the metropolis. Together with the consulados in Seville and Cadiz they exercised a virtual monopoly over the trade and commerce of Spanish America.

Probably no area better illustrates the growth and prosperity of Spanish America in the eighteenth century than the Plata region, particularly Buenos Aires. Today Argentina is the most prosperous Spanish-speaking nation in the world, but its beginnings were humble. Buenos Aires languished after its refounding in 1580. The Lima merchants persuaded the crown not to open that Atlantic port to trade. In theory, goods from Buenos Aires made a 3,000-mile overland trip to Lima, thence by sea to Panama to be transported by mule across the isthmus, and finally by sea again on the fleets to Spain. The *porteños*, as the inhabitants of Buenos Aires are called, argued for the opening of their port and the logical direct trade with Spain that would result. Only thus, without the tremendous transportation costs of the Lima route, could their products compete in European marketplaces. Without royal sanction for the opening of the port, Buenos Aires succumbed to the temptation of contraband. The port thus provided a natural, albeit illegal, commercial outlet for Asunción, Córdoba, and Potosí. The silver that made its way down from Peru paid for slaves, sugar, textiles, and a thousand other manufactured goods demanded by the wealthy inhabitants of the interior who found it cheaper to buy them from the merchants of Buenos Aires than from Lima.

Buenos Aires grew rapidly in the eighteenth century for strategic and commercial reasons. After the Portuguese founded Colônia do Sacramento (1680), Buenos Aires assumed a new strategic importance in the Spanish empire, and the crown gave it increasing attention so that it could counter the Luso-Brazilian threat of expansion. At the same time the pampas were giving abundant evidence of their wealth. Salted meat, hides, tallow, and wool became increasingly important exports and awakened the Spanish government to an appreciation of the natural wealth of the region. The statistics indicate the rising importance of the port: the population quadrupled in the last half of the eighteenth century from approximately 12,000 to 50,000, and royal revenue derived from import and export taxes jumped tenfold from 100,000 pesos in 1774 to 1 million pesos in 1780.

After the establishment of the Viceroyalty of the Plata in 1776 with its seat in Buenos Aires, the crown gave every encouragement to trade. The presence of the viceroy accompanied by an army of bureaucrats and officials prompted the construction of new governmental buildings, the paving of streets, the laying out of parks, and in the early 1780s the opening of a theater for the amusement of the inhabitants. The change that had overtaken Buenos Aires mirrored similar changes that had taken place throughout Latin America by the end of the eighteenth century.

While Buenos Aires began to flourish, the Spanish expanded the other extreme of their American empire. The frontier moved northward into California by means of the mission, presidio, pueblo, and rancho to settle one of Spain's last colonies and to thwart foreign, particularly Russian, claims to that distant corner of the crown's realm. Captain Gaspar de Portolá founded San Diego in 1769, and in the following decades Spanish settlement advanced up the coast as far as Sonoma, just north of San Francisco Bay. The wealthiest of the twenty-one missions established by the Franciscans in upper California was San Gabriel, founded in 1771, whose vast lands produced corn, wheat, barley, beans, and a variety of vegetables. Orchards bore fruit and the vineyards grapes. The mission Indians also raised herds of cattle.

Encouraged by the prosperity of San Gabriel Mission, Governor Felipe de Neve founded the pueblo of Los Angeles in 1781, distributing to the first eleven or twelve families lots for houses as well as fields to cultivate. By 1800, four or five large ranchos existed in the Los Angeles area. Cattle abounded and a limited but growing trade sprang up in hides and tallow. After 1800, Yankee clipper ships frequently appeared off the California coast and trade, legal or contraband, gradually increased with them. The remote colony was largely self-sufficient, an outpost to protect the empire. Like Buenos Aires at the other geographical pole, California testified to the renewed vigor of the Spanish empire after nearly three centuries of expansion.

THE CHURCH

The presence of the twelve friars accompanying Columbus on his second voyage to the New World and of six Jesuits in the retinue of Brazil's first governor-general, Tomé de Sousa, signified yet another intention of the Iberian monarchs. They resolved to Christianize the Indians in the newly discovered lands, a resolution they took very seriously. The instructions to Columbus stated that "the King and Queen, having more regard for the augmentation of the faith than for any other utility, desire nothing other than to augment the Christian religion and to bring divine worship to many simple nations." The immense task of evangelizing the Indians confronted the Church, challenging its vitality. The task involved more than simple conversion. By Christianizing the Indians, the missionaries would also be Europeanizing them: teaching the trades, manners, customs, languages, and habits of the Spanish and Portuguese.

Conversion was essential, according to Iberian thought, not only to give the Indians the true faith and eternal salvation but also to draw them within the pale of empire, that is, to make them loyal subjects to Their Most Catholic Majesties. To be Portuguese or Spanish was to be Roman Catholic. The two were intimately intertwined, and consequently Church and state appeared as one. The populace embraced the Catholic faith unquestioningly and whether understanding its dogmas or not defended it devotedly. The Iberians were born, reared, married, and buried Catholics. The Church touched every aspect of their lives. The monarchs defended the faith within their realms, in return for which the Pope conferred royal patronage upon the crown by bulls to the Spanish monarchs in 1501 and 1508 and to the Portuguese monarchs temporarily in 1515 and permanently in 1551. That royal patronage permitted the Iberian monarchs to exercise power over the Church in their empires in all but purely spiritual matters. They collected the tithe and decided how it should be spent, appointed (and at times recalled) the bishops, priests, and other ecclesiastical officials, authorized the construction of new churches, determined the boundaries of the bishoprics, and, of great significance, approved and transmitted papal messages—or refused to. The royal patronage meant, in short, that the state dominated the Church, but conversely it allowed the Church to pervade the state. If the king and his ministers had a final say in church matters, it is equally true that clerics often occupied the top administrative posts in government. Churchmen often served as ministers, captains-general, viceroys, and even regents. Cardinal Henry, after all, ruled the Portuguese empire in the sixteenth century.

To carry out its initial assignment to introduce the Indians both to Christianity and European culture, the Church depended on the effectiveness of the missionaries, who belonged to the regular clergy, that is, the religious orders as contrasted with the secular clergy who served as priests in the growing number of churches. In the sixteenth century, the missionaries displayed an unflagging zeal. They were as aggressive in their spiritual conquest as the soldiers had been in their physical conquest. The regular clergy, particularly the Dominicans, Jesuits, and Franciscans, devoted their considerable energy to their neophytes. Pedro de Gante and Juan de

Zumárraga in Mexico, Bartolomé de las Casas in the Caribbean, and Manuel da Nóbrega and José de Anchieta in Brazil exemplified the sincere concern of the Church for the Indians' welfare, its dedication to their cause, and its love for the native American.

Conversion of the sedentary, concentrated Indian groups proved much easier and quicker than conversion of the scattered, nomadic tribes. Prelates decided that the wisest course would be to gather the nomadic natives into villages, the aldeias in Brazil and the *reducciones* in Spanish America, where they could more easily be instructed, Christianized, and protected under a watchful eye. The village system permitted the maximum use of the few regular clergy: usually one or two brothers administered each village and in that way supervised many Indians. Each village centered on a church, built of course by the indigenous converts themselves. Around it were a school, living quarters, and warehouses. The ringing of church bells awoke the neophytes each day, summoning them to mass. Afterward, singing hymns along the way, they marched outside the village to cultivate the fields. The brothers taught reading, writing, and the mastering of useful trades to the young and able. Indian sculptors, painters, masons, carpenters, bakers, and locksmiths, among others, were soon practicing their trades. Many of the villages achieved a high degree of self-sufficiency, and most raised some commercial crops, such as tobacco, sugar, or wheat, for sale to outside markets. Also large cattle herds tended by the neophytes provided hides and meat for sale. Alexander von Humboldt, a German visitor to Latin America at the end of the colonial period, inspected some of the missions and noted that where once nomadic Indians roamed, "The road leads through plantations of sugar, indigo, cotton, and coffee. The regularity which we observed in the construction of the villages reminded us that they all owe their origin to monks and missions. The streets are straight and parallel; they cross each other at right angles; and the church is erected in the great square situated in the center." Although the brothers administered the missions through various Indians whom they appointed to office and invested with the customary symbols of that office, the churchmen in the final analysis rigidly controlled the lives of their charges. It was not a simple figure of speech when they spoke of the neophytes as "their children," for that was exactly how they regarded them. Under their guidance, the Indians contributed to the imperial economy, worshiped as Roman Catholics, dressed like Europeans, mastered European trades, and paid homage to the king in Lisbon or Madrid. Thus, those touched by the village system were brought into the empire by the determined hand of the missionaries.

Within the empires, the missions served a military function. The village system minimized Indian revolts and warfare, thereby freeing soldiers for other duties. The missions also helped to hold distant frontiers against foreign claims and intrusions. In the imperial schemes of defensive colonization, they played vital roles in California, Texas, the Plata, and the Amazon. Church and state expanded together.

As the missionaries enthusiastically attended to conversions, clerical organization and hierarchy were transferred from the Old World to the New, where they followed perfectly the European model. The Spanish crown authorized the first bishoprics in 1511, two in Hispaniola and one in Puerto Rico. By 1600, there were five archbishoprics and twenty-seven bishoprics in Spanish America, numbers that jumped to ten and thirty-eight respectively before the end of the colonial period. The Portuguese crown erected the Bishopric of Brazil in 1551, and in 1676 approved the creation of the Archbishopric of Brazil with its see in Salvador. Two new bishoprics, Rio de Janeiro and Pernambuco, were established at the same time. By the end of the eighteenth century there were four others. It is interesting to note that the African bishoprics of São Tomé and Angola also were suffragan, or subordinate, to the Archbishop of Bahia. The Church in Angola in every way depended heavily on Brazil. Serafim Leite, distinguished historian of the Jesuits in Brazil, has affirmed "The evangelization of Angola was in the hands of the Jesuits of Portuguese America."

Of major importance to the social and religious lives of the colonists were the lay brotherhoods, voluntary associations of the faithful. They built handsome churches, merrily celebrated the feast days of patron saints, and dutifully maintained charitable institutions such as hospitals and orphanages. Indeed, works of charity, education, and social assistance composed some of the noblest chapters of the history of the Roman Catholic Church in the New World.

The Church offered to women one alternative to family life, a choice they did not always make voluntarily. Patriarchs sometimes placed their daughters in convents to guard their virginity or to prevent marriage. A marriage could mean a huge dowry of land, property, or capital, which the father preferred to pass on intact to a son. On the other hand, widows often retired to a convent from which they administered their wealth, estates, and property. A religious life by no means meant one dominated exclusively by prayer and meditation. Nor were nunneries necessarily dreary houses of silence, service and abnegation. Through the religious orders, women operated schools, hospitals, and orphanges. In some convents, the nuns, attended by their servants, entertained, read secular literature, played musical instruments, sang, prepared epicurean delights, and enjoyed a lively and comfortable life.

One of the most remarkable intellectuals of the colonial period was a nun, Sor Juana Inés de la Cruz (1651–95), whose talent earned her fame in New Spain during her lifetime and whose complex and brilliant poetry insures her an exalted place in literature. A woman of great learning, she also wrote splendid prose. Her works, expressing ideas far advanced for her own time, reveal a complex personality. For one thing, she argued that women were as intelligent as men, a conclusion her own life amply illustrated. She also advocated education for women. The Church once gently reprimanded her and suggested she apply her intelligence to study of the Holy Scriptures. Yet the Church also expressed a certain pride in her brilliance, and for many years she enjoyed her status as a favorite in the viceregal court and among Mexican intellectuals (all male).

The Church maintained a careful vigil over its flock. Nonetheless, some examples of moral corruption among the clergy provided bawdy gossip for colonial ears. Alleged backsliders—especially Jewish converts, the New Christians—could expect to account for themselves before the Inquisition. Philip II authorized the establishment of the Holy Office in Spanish America in 1569, and it began to operate in Lima in 1570; in Mexico City in 1571; and in Cartagena in 1610. Significantly he exempted the Indians from the jurisdiction of the Inquisition "because of their ignorance and their weak minds." The Inquisition served as much a political as a religious end in its vigilant efforts to purge and purify society in order to make it unified and loyal. The considerable power of the Inquisition lasted until the last half of the eighteenth century when the winds of the Enlightenment blew across the Iberian Peninsula, causing the flames of the Holy Tribunal to flicker. As an institution it was never established in Brazil, but it operated there through the bishops and three visitations from Inquisitors. In general, the hand of the Inquisition rested lightly on Brazil.

While the Church censored books and kept one ear attuned for discussions that might criticize dogma or question the divine right of kings, it also educated Americans and fostered most of the serious scholarship in the New World. In the sixteenth century, some sensitive intellectual church members wrote excellent studies of the very Indian cultures they were helping to eradicate. To learn of the Indian past, scholars still consult Bernardino de Sahagun for the Aztecs, Diego de Landa for the Mayas, Bernabé Cobo for the Incas, and José de Anchieta for the Brazilian Indians. In order to facilitate the mastery of the Indian tongues, and thus to speed up the process of Christianization, the friars compiled dictionaries and grammars of the many Indian languages. Their work continued and in some cases even broadened as the colonial period lengthened, and one of their major scholarly contributions of the eighteenth century was to the natural sciences. Since church members composed a large share of the educated of the colonies, it was from their ranks that most of the teachers came. The Church exercised a virtual monopoly over education. Monasteries housed the first schools and taught reading, writing, arithmetic, and Catholic doctrine. Contrary to the attitude of the Portuguese crown, the Spanish monarch encouraged the founding of universities in the New World, granting the first charters in 1551 to the University of Mexico and the University of San Marcos in Lima. The clergy occupied most of the chairs. Before Harvard opened its doors in 1636, a dozen Spanish-American universities, drawing on medieval Spanish models, were offering a wide variety of courses in law, medicine, theology, and the arts, most of them taught in Latin. The universities made one major concession to the New World: they taught theological students Indian languages for their future benefit and effectiveness.

Foremost among the Church's scholars were the Jesuits, and they staffed some of the best colonial schools. Well organized and militant, they also displayed an industry and efficiency that made the order very powerful economically. Their success aroused the jealousy of other religious orders as well as the suspicion of the crown. Always protective of their powers, the Iberian kings distrusted the strong loyalty the Society of Jesus maintained toward Rome. That the Black Robes would appeal to the pope—or God—over the head of the king or take orders directly from Rome and bypass the channels through Madrid and Lisbon did not harmonize with the growing absolutism of eighteenth-century Iberia. Pombal drove the Jesuits from Portuguese domains in 1759 as one means of fortifying royal authority. Approximately 600 were forced to leave Brazil. In 1767, Charles III followed suit, expelling some 2,200 Jesuits from Spanish America.

Perhaps the relations between Church and state were not always perfect examples of harmony but they were sufficiently tranquil to allow the Church to grow wealthy in the New World. Having converted (at least superficially) the Indians in the sixteenth century, the Church turned its attention to the mundane matters of organization and amassing property and riches. Tithes, the sale of papal indulgences, and parochial fees provided a small share of the Church's income. The legacy furnished the principal source of wealth. In their wills, the affluent were expected to leave at least part of their wealth to the Mother Church in whose bosom they died. Over the decades the Church accumulated vast estates, much of which it administered wisely during the colonial period. It quickly became the largest landowner in the New World. When the Jesuits were expelled from Brazil, it was discovered that the Jesuits were by far the largest single property owner in the colony. Financial transactions further filled ecclesiastical coffers. Banks were extremely rare and the elite possessed little capital. When the landowners or merchants needed to borrow money, they usually applied to the more provident monasteries, which had capital to loan for a fee and at established interest rates.

The Church wealth was by no means evenly distributed. In cities such as Lima, Salvador da Bahia, Ouro Prêto, Quito, Antigua, and Mexico City, ostentatiously imposing churches crowded one another, while "shocking poverty" characterized hundreds of humble parish churches, dotting the countryside. While some of the higher clergy lived on incomes surpassing those of many of the sovereign princes of Germany, impoverished clerics administered to the needs of the faithful in remote villages. Maldistributed the Church's treasure might have been, but no one seriously doubted the awesome extent of it. To its collection, multiplication, and management, the Church eventually came to devote much of its time. Security and comfort supplanted the zeal and concern characteristic of the Church during the century it dedicated to the conversion of the Indians.

The wealth reinforced the conservative inclinations of the Iberian Church. After the initial phase of evangelizing, it too exploited the Indians, as well as the African slaves, to till Church lands or to erect larger and more opulent edifices. To the masses it preached resignation. If God had made them poor, it would be a sin to question why. Poverty was to have its reward in the next life. It was not from the masses that the Church drew its leadership. Generally the sons of the wealthy and/or noble became bishops and archbishops, positions in the New World dominated by the European-born. Thus, the highest ranks of the clergy, like those in the military and civil service, were associated with and filled by the elite. In wealth, power, prestige, and monopoly of education, the Roman Catholic Church by the end of the eighteenth century ranked as an omnipotent institution in the Western Hemisphere. Its influence weighed heavily, not only in the social and religious life of the community but in politics and economics as well.

THE BAROQUE CITY

The foundation of cities in Spanish America coincided with a period when urban planning was changing in Iberia, indeed in all of Europe. The medieval walled city with narrow, winding streets gave way to the monumental city of open space, order, and harmony. Those concepts of the city suited Spanish goals in the Americas well, not so much perhaps because they coincided with the foundation of towns and cities, though it seems logical that new urban settlement might draw on new urban-planning ideas, but more probably because they reflected the new order of a unified Spain, the new power of a consolidated monarchy, and the vigor of emerging capitalism. The Spanish monarchy assigned the city a fundamental role. A symbol of the age of empire, it was the primary instrument of imperial control.

In the city resided the makers, executioners, enforcers, and judges of the king's law. There the tax collector gathered monies owed the king; a treasury stored the taxes; a mint changed precious metals into negotiable specie. From the urban cathedrals, the bishops watched over dispersed flocks of the faithful and directed affairs of the parishes scattered throughout the dioceses. The merchants directed local trade and participated in imperial commerce. State, Church, and business blended together in the urban environment to control the vast hinterlands. The city radiated power, ultimately the king's power. The Ordinance for Town Planning promulgated in Mexico City in 1573 frankly proclaimed the city as symbol of that power. It advised the Spanish colonists to build imposing houses to impress the numerous indigeneous population, to the end that the Indians would be "filled with admiration and will realize that the Spaniards are settling there permanently and not temporarily. They will consequently fear the Spaniards so much that they will not dare to offend them and will respect them and desire their friendship. . . ."

Those new cities were eminently baroque. The concept of the baroque city embraced two seemingly contradictory elements: order and extravagance. Both characterized Latin American cities throughout the colonial period. The Spanish-American cities followed a rigidly prescribed geometrical design. The Laws of the Indies, first written in 1523, codified those standards. They dictated the size and location of the main plaza, width of the streets, location of public buildings, subdivision of the land into lots, and so forth. The notable feature of these planned cities was the grid pattern of streets and a central plaza. The great buildings, secular and religious, grouped around the central plaza, had a most serious symbolic purpose. Their size, magnificence, and imposing presence bespoke the power of Church and State: they reminded one of all of the wealth and power of monarch and God.

Baroque extravagance was clearly visible in the facades, paintings, and sculpture, as well as in the behavioral patterns of the people and in the intricate official rituals. Ostentation, glitter, and expensive visual titillations pervaded public life. The reception given the viceroy in Potosí, described earlier in this chapter, well illustrates the propensity to display. But the well-choreographed reception also enacted homage to the monarch in the person of the viceroy. Thus, baroque extravagance served an important purpose: it reinforced hierarchy. The elites, florid in speech, manners, and dress, enjoyed fancy amusements in the city. Some fiestas lasted days and even weeks, merry events of carousing and conviviality. The masses enjoyed cock fights, bull fights, tourneys, and parades. One of the commonest types of public spectacle was the *mascarada,* a parade of people wearing imaginative costumes and masks and of floats of an allegorical nature. Often the mascaradas employed a theme. For example, in Mexico City in 1621, one such parade featured the familiar figures of the romances of chivalry still very much in vogue. On other occasions, those mascaradas satirized political events or poked fun at public officials. Roman Catholicism provided limitless opportunities for both solemn and joyous festivals. The churches' services often spilled out into the streets in the form of elaborate processions attracting the attention and participation of rich and poor alike. Again those extravagances served imperial purposes, whether it was to provide relief from monotony and a valve to vent social frustration or to emphasize the unity and grandeur of the empire.

During the colonial period, Mexico City and Lima, viceregal capitals, ranked as the principal cities of Spanish America and perfectly exemplified the order and extravagance of the baroque. In 1600, Mexico City boasted a population exceeding 100,000, making it a major world metropolis. It was the seat of the viceroy, audiencia, and Inquisitor General as well as an episcopal seat. Its university dominated the educational and cultural life of Middle America. Printing presses flourished. An impressive cathedral and imposing governmental buildings surrounded the ample central plaza, the location also of an important market. Grandeur, comfort, and elegance mixed with squalor, poverty, and disease, highlighting the contradictions and anomalies of that busy and important city.

Lima left similar impressions on its visitors. In the second half of the seventeenth century, François Correal described Lima in approving terms: "The streets are beautiful and perfectly straight, but the houses have only one story, seldom two, because of the earthquake. Moreover, they are beautiful (at least those which are near the Plaza), their fronts ornamented with long galleries. . . . Trees have been planted round the houses to protect them from the heat of the sun. They regain in width and depth what they have lost in height." He also commented at length on the "very beautiful" Plaza Real with its impressive bronze fountain and well-designed public buildings. Around 1740, a later visitor, Antonio de Ulloa, wrote an informative account of Lima, which described in detail the richness, beauty, and pageantry of the city. The traveler concluded, "The magnificence of its inhabitants and of its public solemnities are proportional, and displayed with a dignity peculiar to minds inflamed with a desire of honor, and who value themselves on celebrating the principal solemnities in a manner which distinguishes Lima from the other cities of its kingdom."

The Brazilian cities were baroque too, but it was expressed in quite a different way. The Portuguese felt the need for closed, defensive cities along the Brazilian coast. Salvador, founded in 1549 as the first capital, was a walled city atop an escarpment fronting a vast bay with the rear protection of a lake. Within the walled confines of the capital, narrow streets meandered in every direction and unexpectedly converged on a handsome esplanade or an impressive plaza. Although the Portuguese broke with the urban medieval form much later, the baroque spirit nonetheless characterized Brazilian cities, where extravagance dominated but differed from the Spanish-American expression. Often somber exterior architecture gave way to wildly ornate interiors. The city certainly manifested the royal presence, serving as a vital link of control and unity in Portugal's far-flung global empire.

The baroque city in its extravagance and order symbolized throughout the Americas the ideal of empire. It gathered together Iberian and creole, African and Indian, impressing on all the omnipotence of the monarch. For three centuries, the city served the empire well. Yet, inevitably, the city's role altered. As the eighteenth century waned, it served increasingly as a focal point for criticism and agitation. It gradually rejected the empire to better serve its own, more local needs. The city played its inevitable role as a catalyst for change.

THE RATIONALE OF EMPIRE

Spain and Portugal had played key roles in European expansion during the sixteenth century. Thanks to their vast empires, both participated vigorously in a trade that enhanced the rise of the nation-state and capitalism in Europe. In doing so, both subscribed to a body of economic doctrines and practices known as *mercantilism*. Mercantilist ideas, in turn, promoted European expansion and contributed to the rise of commercial capitalism.

An impetus to empire, mercantilism rationalized that colonies existed to enrich the European metropolises. Consequently, any policies originating in Lisbon or Madrid sprang from the determination that the American colonies would strengthen Portugal and Spain within the emerging European concert of nations. Mercantilism dictated imperial trade policies. To increase their wealth, nations like Portugal and Spain subscribed to mercantilist policies that exhorted exportation over importation, the desired "commercial balance." The possession of bullion supposedly distinguished a successful mercantilist program, but the discovery of great quantities of gold and silver in the Western Hemisphere in reality disguised the weaknesses in Iberian mercantilist policies. Those precious metals enriched the Iberian treasuries only momentarily. The monarchs wasted them, ignoring their potential to develop Portugal and Spain economically. Not exclusively as a supplier of bullion but in every way, the New World colonies were expected to be a source of wealth to the motherlands. Royal officials looked upon them as a great "milch cow," to be drained dry. The brilliant Brazilian satirical poet and social commentator of the seventeenth century, Gregorio de Matos, scoffed that the Brazilians worked endlessly to support Portuguese idleness.

Spanish mercantilist policies rigorously controlled trade with the New World. All commerce fell under the direction of the Casa de Contratación, aided by the *consulados,* trade associations of merchants, at home and overseas. The Casa authorized Cadiz and Seville as the only Spanish ports to trade with Spanish America, and Vera Cruz and Portobelo as their counterparts in the Americas. Under the protective guns of the royal navy, two fleets sailed each year, one to Vera Cruz, the other to Portobelo. These two fleets returned bearing the products of Spanish Middle and South America. Carefully as the restrictions on trade were enforced, contraband still flourished—to which the slow but constant growth of Buenos Aires, after it was reestablished in 1580, testified. The English, French, and Dutch were only too eager to enter the markets of the New World, and from time to time European wars and diplomacy forced the Spaniards to legalize one or another aspect of that contraband trade. A later device to eliminate contraband trade as well as to encourage the development of neglected regions was the formation in Spain of monopolistic companies with exclusive rights in the New World. The crown itself exercised many monopolies including salt, pepper, quicksilver, gunpowder, and stamped paper.

Under the Bourbon kings of the eighteenth century, particularly Charles III (1759–88), Spain reformed its imperial structure, always with the goal of increasing administrative efficiency, political control, and profits. The power of the Council of the Indies waned as the ministers of the king took over many of its former duties. In the eighteenth century, the chief responsibility for the government of Spanish America rested in the hands of the Minister of the Indies. The Casa de Contratación also felt the weight of Bourbon reforms. The king's ministers absorbed so many of its powers that it became useless and was abolished in 1790. As the population grew and spread and as the economy grew, the crown thought it wise to redivide territorially Spanish-American government so that the king's representatives could more intensely care for the territories under their authority. Two new viceroyalties were created: New Granada in 1717 (it was abolished in 1724 only to be recreated again in 1739) and La Plata in 1776. Likewise, the crown authorized new captaincies-general: Venezuela, 1731; Louisiana, 1763; Cuba, 1777; and Chile, 1778.

The most radical innovation was the establishment of the intendancy system, an administrative unit used by the Bourbons in France and copied by their relatives on the Spanish throne. It was another important measure of the Bourbons to centralize authority and thereby increase their power. The intendants, royal officials of Spanish birth, with extensive judicial, administrative, and financial powers, were to supplant the numerous governors, corregidores, and alcaldes mayores in the hope that a more efficient and uniform administration would increase the king's revenue and bring an end to numerous bureaucratic abuses and corruption. In financial affairs, the intendants reported directly to the crown. In religious, judicial, and administrative matters, they were subject to the viceroy and were to respect his military prerogatives. In 1764, Cuba became the first intendancy, and by 1790 the system extended to all the Spanish-American colonies. The new administrative system seemed to augur well, but no comprehensive judgment can be rendered since the outbreak of the Napoleonic wars in Europe followed by the struggles for independence in Latin America allowed such a short time for it to function.

As another reform measure, Charles III in the 1760s created a colonial militia with creole officers in order to shift some of the burden of the defense of his distant domains onto the Americans themselves. The soldier always had played an important role in the history of the Americas. He conquered, defended, and extended the empire. Great prestige accompanied high rank. Many, if not most, of the viceroys held exalted military rank

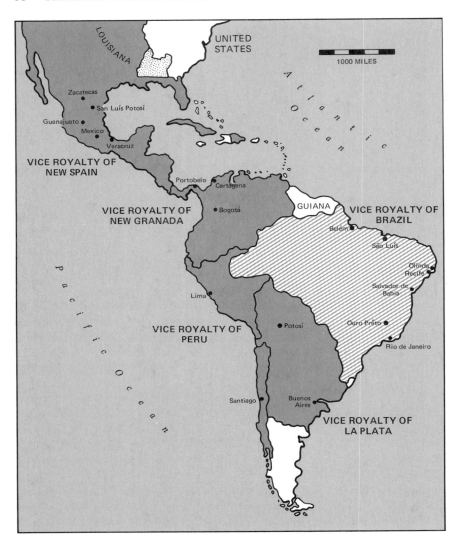

The viceroyalties in Latin America at the end of the eighteenth century

at the time of their appointment, and their military experience enhanced their authority in the New World. The granting of military commissions to the creoles afforded them a new prestige. Usually the high ranks were reserved for—or bought by—wealthy members of the local aristocracy, and as a consequence many desired them as a means of identifying with the rich and the powerful, in short, the elite, of the colonies. Hence, a close identification developed between high military rank and the upper class. Further, the creole officers enjoyed a most practical advantage, the *fuero militar,* a special military privilege, that exempted them from civil law. In effect, it established the military as a special class above the law, the effects of which would be increasingly disruptive for Latin American society.

The Bourbon kings, in particular Charles III, infused a new and more liberal economic spirit into the empire. They hoped to strengthen Spain by liberalizing trade, expanding agriculture, and reviving mining in the Americas. They dispatched European engineers and mining technicians to the New World to encourage the adoption of the latest mining techniques. The crown authorized the establishment of a College of Mining in Mexico, a visit to which prompted Baron von Humboldt to remark: "No city of the new continent, without excepting those of the United States, can show scientific establishments as fine or as well established as the capital of Mexico." Trade policies became more practical in the eighteenth century. Cadiz lost its old commercial monopoly when the king permitted other Spanish ports to trade with the Americas. The fleet system gradually disappeared. After 1740, Spanish ships commonly rounded Cape Horn to trade with Peru and slowly abandoned the old isthmian trade route. In the 1770s Charles lifted the restrictions on intercolonial commerce. These reforms were enacted with imperial motives in mind, for the benefit more of the metropolis than the colonies. The Americans did not favor all of the reforms, while, on the other hand, they did not think that some of them went far enough.

Portuguese mercantilism was never as effective as that of its neighbor, particularly before 1750. Attempts were made sporadically to organize annual fleets to and from Brazil protected by men-of-war, but the highly decentralized Portuguese trade patterns and a shortage of merchant and war ships caused innumerable difficulties. Between the mid-seventeenth and mid-eighteenth centuries, the crown partially succeeded in instituting a fleet system for the protection of Brazilian shipping. Still, it never functioned as well as the Spanish convoys. Economic companies fared little better. The crown licensed four. In general they were unpopular with the residents of Brazil and the merchants, both in Portugal and Brazil. The Brazilians criticized them for abusing their monopolies and raising prices with impunity. The merchants disapproved of the monopolies, which eliminated them from much trade, and accused the companies of charging outlandish freight rates. All sides bombarded the companies with charges of inefficiency. Crown monopolies—such as brazilwood, salt, tobacco, slaves, and diamonds—flourished.

Royal control over Brazil tightened during the eighteenth century. The plantations produced their major crops for export, demand dictated incomes, and incomes regulated production. While Lisbon encouraged the capitalist trends toward higher production, it continued to prevent direct trade with European markets, much to the increasing frustration of the

Brazilian elites. Their desire to enter the capitalist marketplace of the North Atlantic and the imperial, mercantilist, and monopolistic policies of the Portuguese crown charted a course of conflict that prompted the exercise of greater royal control.

The absolutist tendencies noticeable during the long reign of John V, 1706–50, found their instrument of perfection in the person of the Marquis of Pombal, who ruled through the weak Joseph I, 1750–77. An ardent nationalist, Pombal hoped to strengthen his economically moribund country through better and fuller utilization of its colonies, the foremost of which unquestionably was Brazil. To better exploit Portuguese America, he centralized and standardized its government. He abolished the state of Maranhão in 1772, and incorporated it into the state of Brazil, creating for the first time (at least in theory) a single, unified Portuguese colony in the New World. After the unification of the two states, Pombal encouraged trade between them so that commerce would further cement political integration. An impatient enemy of the hereditary captaincies, the prime minister dissolved the remaining ones, with one minor exception, and brought them under direct royal control. As a further measure to fortify royal authority, Pombal expelled the Company of Jesus from the empire in 1759. He accused that powerful order of challenging the secular government and of interposing itself between the king and his Indian subjects. Pombal strengthened the government's hand in both the education and care of the Indians. For good or for bad, he ended the isolation enforced upon them by the church-controlled aldeias. By requiring the Indians to speak Portuguese, dress like Europeans, and adopt useful trades and crafts, and by encouraging whites to intermarry with them, he attempted to bring them within the Luso-Brazilian community. Finally, he tried to restrict some of the independence of the municipal governments, and although it is true that these local governments exercised less freedom than they had in their heyday, the seventeenth century, they still continued to be active and important centers for local politics.

To the end of the colonial period, the metropolises feared their American colonies might relax their efforts to grow the crops, to raise the herds, or to mine the minerals Europe demanded. Responding to another fear, royal officials kept sharp eyes peeled for any unnecessary diversification of the American economies. They forbad Brazil or Spanish America to produce anything that the Iberian nations already produced or could furnish. For example, in 1590, the crown prohibited grape cultivation in Brazil because Portugal already produced a surplus of wines. With few exceptions the colonies were not encouraged to manufacture. The motherlands wanted to supply all the needed manufactured goods and earn for themselves the profits for doing so. Fear that an incipient industry might develop to the detriment of its mercantilist goals prompted the Portuguese monarch to promulgate a long series of decrees, from that of 1578 forbidding the blacksmith Bartolomeu Fernandes of São Vicente to teach his profession to that of 1785 prohibiting all manufacturing in Portuguese America. Spain was less inclined to enforce its restrictions. A healthy textile industry developed that provided cotton and woolen cloth for the lower classes. Flourishing artisans produced furniture, glassware, shoes, tiles, and tools.

Not all mercantilist policy was negative. Within the confines of their policies, the two crowns tried to encourage the production of new crops that would find a ready market in the metropolises or in Europe. Though meeting with frequent frustrations, the Marquis of Lavradio diversified the Brazilian economy by promoting the production of indigo, rice, and wheat. Captain General Matías de Gálvez, with the full encouragement of the Bourbon monarchy, did all he could to increase Central America's indigo exports. With lack of imagination on the part of the two governments, the merchants—both in the Americas and in Europe—and the local farmers probably did as much to hinder economic diversification and growth as did stern mercantile decrees.

The relationships between metropolis and colony remained relatively constant across three centuries. While officials in the metropolis believed they provided necessary services and protection to the colony, they never deviated from the idea that the colony existed to serve the motherland. On the other hand, the attitudes of some Latin Americans, in particular the elites, underwent change across time. By the last half of the eighteenth century, they began to question their role in the imperial relationship. They concluded that their own best interests were not being served by Iberian mercantilism.

3

Independence

Juan O'Gorman, "Mexican Independence Mural"

During the long colonial period, the psychology of the Latin Americans, particularly the elite, changed significantly. A feeling of inferiority before the Iberian-born gave way to a feeling of equality and then to superiority. At the same time, nativism, a devotion to one's locality, matured into feelings of nationalism, a group consciousness attributing supreme value to the land of one's birth and pledging unswerving dedication to it. These changing attitudes resulted partly from the Latin American's greater appreciation of and pride in the regions where they were born and raised and partly from a fuller understanding that their own interests could be better served if they, not distant monarchs, made the fundamental economic and political decisions. Greater self-awareness intensified the Latin Americans' resentment of the authority, control, and direction of the Iberian metropolises. Inspired by the North American example and encouraged by the changes wrought in Napoleonic Europe, they declared their independence in order to realize their potential and chart their own future. In all cases, except in Haiti and during the early stages of the Mexican revolution, the creole and mazombo elites directed the movements toward independence, broke the ties with the former mother countries, and exercised the powers once reserved for the Iberians. Paraguay, as we soon will see, stands as a curious exception to the Latin American experience. There, a member of the elite led a genuine populist revolution that benefited the majority for at least half a century. The major historical questions for consideration during this period encompassing the end of the eighteenth century and the opening of the nineteenth are why the Latin Americans pursued independence, how they achieved it, and what they intended to do with it. Who benefited and who lost as a result of the political change from colony to nation?

A CHANGING MENTALITY BEGETS NEW ATTITUDES AND ACTION

Reasoning, questioning, and inquiry characterized the attitude of the European intellectuals in the seventeenth and particularly in the eighteenth centuries. Under the influence of the Enlightenment, people became increasingly concerned with life here on earth, rather than with the metaphysics of celestial existence. As one result, they set about to study, explore, and improve their temporal life.

Before the end of the first century of Iberian colonization, the inhabitants of the New World began to reflect on themselves, their surroundings, and their relations to the rest of the world. They spoke and wrote for the first time in introspective terms. Juan de Cárdenas, although born in Spain, testified in his *Problemas y Secretas Maravillosos de las Indias* (The Marvellous Problems and Secrets of the Indies), published in 1591, that in Mexico the creole surpasses the peninsular (the Iberian) in wit and intelligence. Evincing a strong devotion to New Spain, Bernardo de Balbuena penned his *La Grandeza Mexicana* (The Grandeur of Mexico) in 1604 in praise of all things Mexican. He implied that for beauty, interest, charm, life in Mexico City equaled—or surpassed—that in most Spanish cities. In 1618, Ambrósio Fernandes Brandão made the first attempt to define or interpret Brazil in his *Diálogos das Grandezas do Brasil* (Dialogues of the Greatness of Brazil). In doing so, he exhibited his devotion to the colony, chiding those Portuguese who came to Brazil solely to exploit it and return wealthy to the peninsula. Poets, historians, and essayists reflected on the natural beauty of a generous nature. They took up with renewed vigor the theme extolled in the early sixteenth century that the New World was an earthly paradise. A climax of sorts was reached in the early nineteenth century when the Brazilian poet Francisco de São Carlos depicted paradise in his long poem *A Assunção* in terms that made it sound strikingly similar to Brazil. A few distinguished visitors who glimpsed the Iberian colonies spoke with awe of the beauty and potential they beheld. Exemplary of their observations was the remark of Alexander von Humboldt that "The vast kingdom of New Spain, if cultivated with care, would alone produce what the rest of the world produces, sugar, cochineal, cacao, cotton, coffee, wheat, hemp, linen, silk, oil, wine. It would supply all the metals, without excluding mercury." Physically Iberian America impressed native and foreigner alike to be a privileged region, an idea that had prompted the colonial Brazilian intellectual Sebastião da Rocha Pita to remark, "The sun now rises in the West."

Concentrating ever more earnestly on themselves and their surroundings, the elite in the New World searched for ways of improving their conditions. The intensification of that search coincided with the sweep of the Enlightenment across Latin America. As manifested in that part of the world, the Enlightenment became primarily a search for and then promotion of useful knowledge, a selective search. The Latin American intellectuals drew from the enlightened ideologies those practical examples that best suited their goals. Principal attention focused on science, economics, commerce, agriculture, and education. Political matters received secondary attention and religion, at least for the time being, little at all. The American intellectuals read Smith, Locke, Benito Feijóo, António Vernei, Voltaire, Rousseau, Diderot, Raynal, and Montesquieu. Nor did they neglect ideas emanating from the United States, whose declaration of and struggle for independence and resultant federal republic fascinated the Ibero-American elite. In every region of Latin America, at least a few intellectuals had read Thomas Paine, Thomas Jefferson, or Benjamin Franklin. Copies of the Declaration of Independence, the Federalist Papers, the Constitution of 1787, and Washington's Farewell Address circulated.

The new ideas entered Latin America with minimal difficulty. The frown of neither the Inquisitor nor the customs officer could stem the intellectual tides. A French visitor to Brazil during the waning years of the colonial period commented on the ease with which the censor's prohibitions on book imports could be evaded. Inventories exist of private libraries from disparate parts of the Iberian-American empire—Francisco de Miranda's in Havana, Antonio Nariño's in Bogotá, Francisco de Ortega's in Buenos Aires, and Luís Vieira's in Mariana—representative of the local preference for the enlightened writers and philosophers of the eighteenth century. The owners seemingly read the books in their libraries. The intellectuals delighted in quoting from European authors.

The pressures of the British and French on the Iberian monarchs for greater trade with their American empires, burgeoning European contraband in the Americas, and the more liberal commercial code promulgated by Spain in 1778 brought Latin America into close contact with Europe and with European ideas. Foreigners visited the Americas, many of them on scientific missions. Foreigners likewise helped to introduce the latest thought into eighteenth-century Brazil, a colony always more accessible than Spanish America. The Portuguese monarchs also dispatched to Brazil various and varied scientific expeditions, many of whose members were foreigners. Occasionally foreign ships visited Brazilian ports. For example, in 1759, both French and English squadrons dropped anchor in Salvador.

Representatives of the American elite traveled in Europe, and American students went to Iberian universities and at times beyond to French and English universities. Miranda, Simón Bolívar, Manuel Belgrano, Bernardo O'Higgins, José de San Martín, and José Bonifácio all studied and traveled in Europe. All espoused ideas of the Enlightenment, and it is probably no coincidence that together they freed South America. These travelers made contact with foreign academies and maintained their contact through correspondence.

Once admitted, the new ideas diffused rapidly throughout the colonies. The universities of Spanish America, of which twenty-three existed at the opening of the nineteenth century, contributed to their spread. Professors and students alike challenged the hoary theories of Aristotle and the scholastic tradition. Lectures covered the ideas of Descartes, Newton, Leibniz, and Locke. In at least one instance, the ideas of the French naturalist Lamarck on the theory of evolution were being discussed in a New World classroom within a year of their publication. Other centers in Spanish America for the diffusion of the latest European knowledge were the Economic Societies of the Friends of the Country (*Sociedades Económicas de Amigos del País*), which had developed in Spain and spread to the New World by the 1780s. In general the societies showed a strong tendency to emphasize the natural and physical sciences, agriculture, commerce, and education, as well as to give some attention to political and social questions. Portuguese America had not a single university, but its counterpart of the Spanish economic societies was the literary and scientific academies of which there were six, all established between 1724 and 1794 in either Salvador or Rio de Janeiro. Each had a short but apparently active life. The printing presses in Spanish America—Lisbon rigidly prohibited the setting up of a press in its American possessions—contributed significantly to spreading ideas. Among their many publications numbered several outstanding newspapers, all fonts of enlightened ideas and nativism. Their pages were replete with references to, quotations from, and translations of the major authors of the European Enlightenment.

Considerable evidence testifies that the Latin Americans drank deeply from the heady intellectual wines of the Enlightenment. The minutes of the meetings of the Economic Societies and the academies, the discussions in clandestine Masonic lodges, and writings, both private and published, indicate that some of the ideas most prevalent among the intellectuals were the equality of all men before the law, the need to open the ports to world trade, the hardships worked by monopolies and restrictions on trade and production, the desirability of expanding educational facilities and opportunities, the benefits of a free press, and the necessity of establishing justice as an independent branch of government. Upon some of these ideas, liberals concentrated their attention throughout the nineteenth century. Concerning the role of ideas in the mounting tensions between the Old World and the New, the Argentine statesman and historian Bartolomé Mitre observed, "There can be no revolution until the ideas of men become the conscience of the masses, and until the passions of men become a public force. . . ." A fascination with these ideas, an inclination to experiment, and the urge to reason all weakened a former blind respect for authority and tradition.

The privileged classes in the New World desired most to reform commerce and trade. The American merchants and planters chafed under monopolies and restrictions, and the reforms in the eighteenth century were not all welcome. The thrust of the reforms was to accelerate centralism and thus to increase the effective political and economic powers of the crowns. The Americans felt more heavily than before the weight of royal authority, a closer supervision and contact that multiplied tensions between the colonies and the metropolises.

Physiocrat doctrine—the ideas that wealth derived from nature (agriculture and mining) and multiplied under minimal governmental direction—gained support among Brazilian intellectuals. Timidly at first they began to suggest some changes. Bishop José Joaquim da Cunha de Azeredo Coutinho argued against a higher tax on sugar in 1791 and three years later pointed out the inconveniences of several crown restrictions and monopolies. Other Brazilians spoke out in favor of reducing or abolishing taxes and duties and soon were advocating a greater freedom of trade. From Bahia, João Rodrigues de Brito boldly called for full liberty for the Brazilian farmers to grow whatever crops they wanted, to construct whatever works or factories were necessary for the good of their crops, to sell in any place, by any means, and through whatever agent they wished to choose without heavy taxes or burdensome bureaucracy, to sell to the highest bidder, and to sell their products at any time when it best suited them. Similar complaints and demands reverberated throughout the Spanish-American empire. Chileans wanted to break down their economic isolation. Reflecting on the potential wealth of Chile and the lingering poverty of its inhabitants, José de Cos Iriberri, a contemporary of the Bahian Rodrigues de Brito, concluded, "Crops cannot yield wealth unless they are produced in quantity and obtain a good price; and for this they need sound methods of cultivation, large consumption, and access to foreign markets." Manuel de Salas agreed and insisted that free trade was the natural means to wealth. And Anselmo de la Cruz asked a question being heard with greater frequency throughout the colonies, "What better method could be adopted to develop the agriculture, industry, and trade of our kingdom than to allow it to export its natural products to all the nations of the world without exception?"

As the American colonies grew in population and activity and as Spain became increasingly involved in European wars in the eighteenth century, breaches appeared in the mercantilistic walls Spain had carefully constructed around its American empire. British merchants audaciously assailed those walls and when and where possible widened the breaches. For their part, the Spanish Bourbons tried hard to introduce economic reforms that would reinforce Spain's monopolistic economic control. They authorized and encouraged a series of monopolistic companies. Doubtless, the Guipúzcoa Company best illustrates the effects of these monopolies and certainly the protests they elicited from a jealous native merchant class.

By the end of the seventeenth century, Venezuela exported a variety of natural products, most important of which were tobacco, cacao, and salt, to Spain, Spanish America, and some foreign islands in the Caribbean. This trade expanded to England, France, and the United States during the early years of the eighteenth century. Commerce enjoyed a reputation as an honest and respectable profession in that Spanish colony. A small, prosperous—and increasingly influential—merchant class emerged. The liberator of northern South America, Simón Bolívar, descended from one of the most successful of these native merchant families. The creation of the Guipúzcoa Company in 1728 to insure that Venezuela traded within the imperial markets and to eliminate commercial intercourse with foreigners evoked sharp protest from the merchants, who readily foresaw the impending injury to their welfare. They complained that the company infringed upon their interests, threatened their economic well-being, shut off their profitable trade with other Europeans, and failed to supply all their needs. Spain, after all, they quickly pointed out, could not absorb all of Venezuela's agricultural exports, whereas an eager market in the West Indies and northern Europe offered to buy them. Finally, exasperated with the monopoly and discouraged from expecting any results from their complaints, the merchants fostered an armed revolt against the company in 1749, a revolt that took Spain four years to quell. The struggle against the company was both armed and verbal, and it fostered a hostile feeling toward the crown, which was committed to support the unpopular company. The friction between the local merchants, business people, landowners, and population on the one hand and the Guipúzcoa Company and crown on the other continued throughout the rest of the century. The merchants' belief that freer trade would fatten their profits was more than satisfactorily proven when Spain, after 1779, entered the war against England with the consequent interruption caused by the English fleet in the trade between Venezuela and Spain. The merchants took immediate advantage of the situation to trade directly and openly with the English islands in the Caribbean. Their profits soared.

Two new institutions soon organized the protests and activities of the disaffected Venezuelans. The Consulado de Caracas, authorized in 1785 and established in 1793, brought together merchants and plantation owners, and it soon became a focal point for local dissatisfaction and agitation. Then in 1797 the merchants formed a militia company to protect the coast from any foreign attack. That responsibility intensified their nativism, or, at that stage, patriotism. Nurtured by such local institutions, the complaints against the monopoly, burdensome taxes, and restrictions mounted in direct proportion to the increasing popularity of the idea of free trade. As one merchant expressed it, "Commerce ought to be as free as air." Popular songs at the end of the eighteenth century also expressed the economic protests:

> All our rights
> We see usurped
> And with taxes and tributes
> We are bent down
>
> If anyone wants to know
> Why I go shirtless
> It's because the taxes
> Of the king denude me
>
> With much enthusiasm
> The Intendents aid the Tyrant
> To drink the blood
> Of the American people

One of the results of these intensifying complaints was the series of armed uprisings in 1795, 1797, and 1799. Great Britain continued to encourage these and other protests against Spain's system of commercial monopoly. Clearly English interests coincided with those of the creole elite who thought in terms of free trade.

Economic dissatisfaction extended beyond the narrow confines of the colonial elite. Many popular elements protested the burdensome taxes and expressed hope for improvements. In fact, a wider segment of the population probably understood and appreciated the economic motivations for independence more than they did the political ones. Popular antitax demonstrations rocked many cities in both Spanish and Portuguese America in the eighteenth century. Oppressive economic conditions helped to spark two potentially serious popular uprisings, the Tupac Amaru Revolt in Peru in 1780 and the Comunero Revolt in New Granada (Colombia) in 1781, and to foment the Bahian Conspiracy in Brazil in 1798.

Taking the name Tupac Amaru II and considering himself the rightful heir to the Incan throne, the mestizo José Gabriel Condorcanqui Noguera led a revolt—mainly of Indians, but at least in the beginning with the support of mestizos as well as some creoles—that broke out in November 1780, to protest the most distressing abuses of the Spanish colonial system. Excessive taxation, economic exploitation, and forced labor constituted some of the bitterest complaints of the followers of the Incan pretender. Much blood flowed before a well-armed militia checked the Indians, captured their leader, and suppressed the revolt in 1781. Later that same year a leading Lima intellectual, José Baquíjano y Carillo, expounded before the newly arrived viceroy the injustices Spain had perpetrated on the Indians. His emotional discourse rang with ideas from the French philosophers. He subtly questioned not just the abuses of royal power but royal power itself.

Protesting an increase in taxes and burdensome monopolies, creoles and mestizos in New Granada rose up to nullify unpopular Spanish laws. The revolt spread spontaneously through New Granada in 1781. Faced with the growing success of the rebels, the Spanish authorities capitulated to their demands for economic reforms. However, once the *communeros* dispersed, satisfied with their apparent success, the viceroy abrogated former agreements and arrested the leaders, who were executed in 1782 and 1783.

Across the continent in Bahia, another popular conspiracy, this one against the Portuguese metropolis, came to a head in 1798. It exemplified the penetration of the ideas of the Enlightenment into the masses, which, in this case, thought in terms of economic, social, and political reforms, even of independence. The conspirators were simple folk: soldiers, artisans, mechanics, workers, and so large a number of tailors that the movement sometimes bears the title of the "Conspiracy of the Tailors." All were young (under thirty years old), and all were mulattoes. The conspirators spoke in vague but eloquent terms of free trade, which they felt would bring prosperity to their port, and of equality for all men without distinctions of race or color. They denounced excessive taxation and oppressive restrictions. The plot, after it was uncovered by the colonial officials, caused one Portuguese minister to lament that the Bahians "for some unexplained madness and because they did not understand their own best interests, had become infected with the abominable French ideas and shown great affection for the absurd French Constitution."

Dissatisfaction thus pervaded many classes. Its increase during the eighteenth century coincided with many reforms enacted by the Iberian crowns. Perhaps this situation further substantiates the conclusion of the historian Crane Brinton that revolutions stem from hope, not despair, from the promise of progress rather than from continuous oppression. The Latin Americans came to realize that in order to effect the reforms they desired they themselves would have to wield political power.

The enlightenment of the elite (and to a much lesser degree of a small portion of the masses); the growing feeling of nativism, which indicated a greater self-confidence on the part of the Latin Americans and certainly a psychological change that diminished former feelings of inferiority; concern among the Latin Americans with the mighty potential of their region coupled with frustration because the potential went unrealized; resentment of the overseas metropolitan exploitation of the colonies; and growing complaints of excessive taxes, restrictions, and monopolies all widened the gap between the colonials and the Iberians. The resentment was very noticeable on the highest level, between the creoles and mazombos on the one hand and the peninsulares and reinóis on the other. Those born in Latin America seldom received the preferment, positions, or promotions that the crowns lavished on the Iberian born. Of the 170 viceroys, only 4 were creoles—and they were the sons of Spanish officials. Of the 602 captains-general, governors, and presidents in Spanish America, only 14 had been creoles; of the 606 bishops and archbishops, 105 were born in the New World. Such preference aroused bitter resentment among the creoles. In his early seventeenth-century travels, Thomas Gage witnessed and discussed the bitterness arising from creole-peninsular rivalry. One distinguished representative of the creoles, Simón Bolívar, stated in 1815, "The hatred that the Peninsular has inspired in us is greater than the ocean which separates us." The Iberian suspicion of the New World elite in effect questioned both their ability and loyalty. One high Portuguese official remarked of Brazil, "That country increases in everyone the spirit of ambition and the relaxation of virtues." A distinguished Chilean, advising the king that all would be better served if the crown would make use of the creoles, concluded, "The status of the creoles has thus become an enigma: they are neither foreigners nor nationals . . . and are honorable but hopeless, loyal but disinherited. . . ." Further, the New World inhabitants resented the flow of wealth into the pockets of the peninsulares and reinóis who came to the Americas to exploit the wealth and return to Iberia to spend their hastily gained riches. A *visitador* to New Spain, José de Gálvez, expressed to the crown an oft-repeated creole grievance: "Spaniards not only don't allow us to share the government of our country, but they carry away all our money."

Obviously the points of view of the Iberian and the American varied. The first came to the New World with a metropolitan outlook. He saw the empire as a unit and catered to the well-being of the metropolis. The latter had a regional bias. His prestige, power, and wealth rested on his lands. Whatever political base he had was the municipal government, whose limited authority and responsibility reinforced his parochial outlook. In short, he thought mainly in terms of his region and ignored the wider imperial views.

During the last half of the eighteenth century, a new position, once again of local significance, was opened to the Latin Americans when the crowns created the colonial militias. The obligation to defend the colonies from foreign attack intensified nativism. Further, the high militia ranks conferred new prestige on creoles and mazombos alike and encouraged their ambitions. They awaited with growing impatience an opportunity to improve their status. The Napoleonic wars provided that opportunity.

Napoleon rocked the foundations of both Iberian monarchies. In 1807, his armies crossed Spain, invaded Portugal, and captured Lisbon. The Portuguese Braganzas, however, did not fall prisoner to the conquering French armies. Prince-Regent John packed the government aboard a fleet and under the protecting guns of English men-of-war sailed from Lisbon for Rio de Janeiro just as the French reached the outskirts of the capital. The transfer of a European crown to one of its colonies was unique. The Braganzas were the only European royalty to visit their possessions in the New World during the colonial period. They set up their court among the surprised but delighted Brazilians and ruled the empire from Rio de Janeiro for thirteen years.

After seizing control of the Portuguese metropolis, Napoleon immediately turned his attention to Spain. He swept first Charles IV and then Ferdinand VII off the Spanish throne in order to crown his brother Joseph king. The Spaniards detested the Bonaparte puppet and renewed allegiance to Ferdinand, a prisoner in France. Rising up against Napoleon, they created a series of juntas to govern the empire in the name of the captive king. Spanish-Americans reacted with equal repugnance to the usurper. Various juntas appeared in the New World to govern in Ferdinand's name. In effect, this step toward self-government constituted an irreparable break with Spain. By abducting the king, Napoleon had broken the major link between Spain and the Americas. The break once made was widened by the many grievances of the Latin Americans against the metropolis.

Most of Latin America achieved its independence during a period of two decades, between the proud declaration of Haiti's independence in 1804 and the Spanish defeat at Ayacucho in 1824. Nearly 20 million inhabitants of Latin America severed their allegiance to France or to the Iberian monarchs.

Every class and condition of people in Latin America participated at one time or another, at one place or another, in the protracted movement. Four distinct aspects of the movement stand out: the slave uprising in Haiti, the autonomous revolution of Paraguay, the popular revolt in Mexico, and the elitist defiance in most of the rest of Latin America.

THE SLAVES DECLARE HAITI'S INDEPENDENCE

Saint Domingue, the western third of the island of Hispaniola, witnessed the only completely successful slave rebellion in the New World. Long, bloody, devastating, it expelled or killed the white masters, terminated French rule, and left the blacks free to govern themselves.

Sugar profits soared in the eighteenth century as the French planters exploited the good soil of the island, adopted the latest techniques for growing and grinding the cane, and imported ever larger numbers of African slaves to work the land and to process the crop. The motherland smiled with satisfaction on its rich Caribbean treasure. A multiracial society had developed, a divided society, which by 1789 counted 40,000 whites and half a million blacks with approximately 25,000 mulattoes. The Code Noir, promulgated in 1685, regulated slavery. Theoretically it provided some protection to the black slave, facilitated manumission, and admitted the freed slave to full rights in society. In reality, the European code but slightly ameliorated the slave's dreadful state. In general, slavery on the lucrative plantataions was harsh. To meet the demand for sugar, the plantation owner callously overworked his blacks, and to reduce overhead he frequently underfed them. An astonishingly high death rate testified to the brutality of the system.

The distant cry of "Liberty, equality, fraternity" echoed in the Caribbean in 1789. Each segment of the tense colony interpreted it differently. The white planters demanded and received from the Paris National Assembly a large measure of local autonomy. Then the Assembly extended the vote to all free persons, a move favoring the mulattoes. The planters' demand for the repeal of that law precipitated a struggle between them and the mulattoes. Then on August 22, 1791, the slaves demanding their own liberty rebelled in northern Saint Domingue. Over 100,000 arose under the leadership of the educated slave Toussaint L'Ouverture, son of African slave parents. In pursuit of his constant goal of liberating his fellow blacks, he fought for the following decade against—depending on the time and circumstances—the French, British, Spaniards, and various mulatto groups. Victory rewarded his extraordinary leadership and the courage of the blacks. By 1801, L'Ouverture commanded the entire island of Hispaniola. In that year Napoleon resolved to intervene to return the island to its former role as a profitable sugar producer. A huge army invaded Saint Domingue and the French induced L'Ouverture to a meeting only to seize him treacherously. Imprisoned in Europe, he died in 1803. His two lieutenants, Jean-Jacques Dessalines and Henri Christophe took up the leadership. A combination of black strength and yellow fever defeated the massive French effort. On January 1, 1804, Dessalines proclaimed the independence of the western part of Hispaniola, giving it the name of Haiti. Haiti emerged as the second independent nation of the Western Hemisphere, the first in Latin America. For the exploited blacks of the New World, it represented hope; into the hemisphere's plantation owners, it instilled a chilling fear.

The African-born Dessalines acclaimed himself Emperor Jacques I in October of 1804. His brief reign collapsed two years later when mulattoes who had risen up against his regime ambushed and killed him. The nation split. Christophe, an illiterate, Caribbean-born black ruled the north; he crowned himself King Henri I in 1811. Alexandre Pétion, a mulatto educated in Paris, governed the south as president until his death in 1818. Paralyzed by a stroke and confronted with rebellion in 1820, King Henri committed suicide. Their deaths paved the way for the reunification of Haiti. Jean-Pierre Boyer, the French-educated mulatto who succeeded Pétion, not only united the north and south but also subdued the eastern two-thirds of Hispaniola (later to be known as the Dominican Republic) and by early 1822 brought the entire island under his control in Port-au-Prince, the capital.

PARAGUAY'S AUTONOMOUS REVOLUTION

Napoleon's imprisonment of King Ferdinand VII intensified the political unrest in the Plata region. In the resultant political vacuum, the Paraguayans in 1810–11, asserted their independence, not only from Spain but also from the Viceroyalty of La Plata. Their defeat of the Argentine army sent from Buenos Aires confirmed their determination to chart their own independence. Later a popular congress comprised of more than 1,100 delegates, proportionately representing the nation's 150,000 inhabitants, conferred the title and powers of *Dictador* on José Gaspar Rodríguez de Francia, who governed until his death in 1840. During these decades the Paraguayans radically restructured their social, economic, and political institutions. These profound changes distinguish Paraguay as the first autonomous revolution in the Americas.

The standard history texts always have castigated Dr. Francia. One describes him as "cruel beyond description"; another characterizes him as "cunning," "neurotic," and "misanthropic"; while yet a third adds "distrustful, unyielding, and vengeful." No more generous than their North American counterparts, Brazilian, Argentine, and even many Paraguayan historians habitually have maligned Francia as a "modern Nero" or a "hypochondriatic and atrabilious genius." Yet, a minority current within Paraguayan historiography, and some very recent revisionist studies, have put the events of nineteenth-century Paraguay into a more realistic perspective. Offered are some challenging interpretations of a nation forced into semi-isolation by the aggressions of its large neighbors, Argentina and Brazil. These studies reveal that along with the removal of both the Spanish and creole elites from their traditional positions of dominance, the Francia government enacted a radical land reform and the nation embarked upon a successful program of economic development without any foreign financing. Examined from this perspective, Paraguay's independence movement constitutes a radical and autonomous revolution, one inspired and carried out by the Paraguayans themselves.

Austere in dress and customs, Francia manifested a modesty, honesty, and efficiency that set him apart as a singular leader. First as lawyer and later as chief of state, the radical Doctor of Theology championed the dispossessed against the privileged. As the Scottish adventurer-merchant John Parish Robertson, who spent four years in Paraguay, observed, "His fearless integrity gained him the respect of all parties. He never would defend an unjust cause; while he was ever ready to take the part of the poor and the weak against the rich and the strong."

Together with a clear vision of a self-sufficient and independent Paraguay, which he made every effort to realize, Francia's nationalism provided the fundamental principles of his radical administration. Nearly isolated from contacts with the outside world, the landlocked nation changed and developed under the leadership of Dr. Francia to emerge as the most egalitarian society yet known in the Western Hemisphere. Contrary to the backward despotism imputed to it by traditional historians, Paraguay offered a better life to more of its citizens than any of the other American nations.

Throughout the colonial period, the people—a highly miscegenated society comprised of many mestizos and Guaraní Indians as well as a few Spaniards—had lived simple, rustic lives. Compared with other parts of the Spanish-American empire, the province's relatively small and weak elite lived modestly. While concentrating his efforts to improve the conditions of the masses, Francia further reduced the elite's numbers and comforts.

In possession of the great majority of the nation's land, which it acquired by inheriting the crown's land, nullifying the royal land grants, and confiscating the Church's property as well as much of the elite's holdings, the government established scores of prosperous state ranches and rented the rest for a nominal fee to anyone willing to till the soil. With no large estates dominating the economy, a rarity in Latin America, Paraguay became self-sufficient in the production of food. New information indicates that a rudimentary educational system, satisfactory for the needs of a simple agrarian society, practically eliminated illiteracy.

In order to strengthen the state as well as to further its egalitarian goals, Francia nationalized the Roman Catholic Church, confiscating its temporal goods, abolishing the tithe, and decreeing religious freedom. Thus, the government not only eliminated a potential rival but avoided the church-state conflicts that eroded national harmony in most of the Latin American nations.

While the establishment of a state iron works and state textile and livestock industries provided employment for thousands of Paraguayans, small handicraft industries further augmented national production, thereby meeting the basic needs of the people. Forced to develop a new overland trade route due to the blockade of the Río de la Plata by hostile Argentine forces, the young nation conducted an active international trade during the latter half of Francia's administration. It provided the Paraguayans with manufactured goods that they were unable to produce themselves. Through a strictly enforced system of trade licenses and its own massive participation, the state prevented the growth of a native or foreign commercial class; no foreign interests were permitted to penetrate the economy; nor did foreign debts, loans, or interest rates hobble it. Paraguay enjoyed economic as well as political independence, thus escaping for a long period the neocolonial dependency that characterized the history of nineteenth-century Latin America.

AN UNSUCCESSFUL POPULAR REVOLUTION IN MEXICO

Taking advantage of the political vacuum in Spain in 1808, the creoles of New Spain maneuvered to form a local junta to govern the viceroyalty, a move calculated to shift political power from the Spaniards to the Mexican elite. Alarmed by the maneuvering, the peninsulars feared the loss of their traditional, preferred positions. They acted swiftly to form their own junta and thus shoved the creoles aside. The creoles plotted to seize power, but in September 1810, the peninsulars discovered the plan and jailed the leaders. One plotter, Father Miguel Hidalgo, a parish priest in the impoverished town of Dolores, escaped detection. Well educated, indeed, profoundly influenced by the Enlightenment, he professed advanced social ideas. He believed that the Church had a social mission to perform and a duty to improve the lot of the downtrodden Indians. Personally he bore numerous grievances against peninsulars and the Spanish government.

Hidalgo resolved to carry out the exposed plan. Ringing his church bell on September 16, 1810, he summoned his humble parishioners, most of whom were mestizos and Indians, to exhort them to expel the peninsulars from office and to establish a better government. In so doing, Hidalgo unleashed new forces. Unlike the creoles who simply wanted to substitute themselves for the peninsulars in power, the mestizo and Indian masses desired far-reaching social and economic changes. The popularity of the revolution, as well as the fury of the masses, amazed the benign churchman. The ranks of his army swelled overnight to awesome numbers. With little difficulty, Hidalgo's forces swept through Guanajuato and Guadalajara and advanced on Mexico City. A swath of massacred peninsulars as well as many creoles lay behind them. With energies released after three centuries of repression, the Indians and mestizos struck out at all they hated. The creoles became as frightened as the peninsulars, and the two rival factions united before the threat from the masses.

Hidalgo did little to discipline the people under him. Indeed, his control of them proved minimal. His ideas were disorganized, vague, at times contradictory. While voicing his loyalty to Ferdinand, he denounced the abuses of the viceregal government—later he declared Mexico free and independent. He threatened the peninsulars with death; he abolished slavery. Poised before Mexico City, he hesitated, then ordered a withdrawal, an action that cost him much of the allegiance of the masses. The Spanish army regained its confidence and struck out in pursuit of the ragtag rebels. It captured Hidalgo and in mid-1811, a firing squad executed him. To Hidalgo goes the credit for initiating Mexico's revolution for independence.

Father José María Morelos, a mestizo parish priest, took command of the revolutionary movement. He defined his program: establish the independence of Mexico; create a republican government in which the Mexican people would participate with the exclusion of the former wealthy, nobility, and entrenched officeholders; abolish slavery; affirm the equality of all people; terminate the special privileges of the Church as well as the compulsory tithe; and partition the large estates so that all farmers could own land. At Chilpancingo, he declared that Mexico's sovereignty resided in the people who could alter the government according to their will. He called forth pride in the Mexican—not the Spanish—past. His program contained the seeds of a real social, economic, and political revolution and thereby repulsed peninsular and creole alike. He ably led his small, disciplined army in central Mexico for more than four years. In 1815, the Spaniards captured and executed him. The royalists immediately gained the ascendancy in Mexico and dashed the hopes of the mestizos and Indians for social and economic changes. New Spain returned momentarily to its colonial slumbers.

The conservative elite consummated Mexican independence. The peninsulars enjoyed their comfortable privileges in Mexico so much that they, allied with the creoles, were willing to free themselves from Spain in order to perpetuate them. Spain in 1820 smacked of a liberalism far too extreme for their tastes. A revolt in that year restored constitutional government to Madrid. A current of liberal and anticlerical sentiment characterized the high Spanish officials, much to the annoyance of the peninsulars and creoles in New Spain, who rejected Spanish liberalism just as they earlier had turned away from Mexican liberalism. In their reaction to the events in Spain, they decided to free themselves and thus chart their own destiny. The ecclesiastical hierarchy, fearful of the loss of property and of secular restrictions if the liberals in control of Spain had their way, converted to the independence movement, buttressing it with the Church's prestige and power. The peninsulars and creoles selected a pompous creole army officer, Augustín de Iturbide, who had fought against Hidalgo and Morelos, first as their instrument to effect independence and then as their emperor. The most conservative forces of New Spain ushered in Mexican independence in 1821. They advocated neither social nor economic changes. They sought to preserve— or enhance if possible—their privileges. The only innovation was political: a creole emperor replaced the Spanish king, which was symbolic of the wider replacement of the peninsulars by the creoles in government. The events harmonized little with the concepts of Hidalgo and Morelos but suited creole desires. The Mexican struggle for independence began as a major social, economic, and political revolution but ended as a conservative coup d'état. The only immediate victors were the creole elite.

ELITIST REVOLTS

The triumph of the Mexican creole elite paralleled similar victories in other parts of Latin America, where the local aristocrats, occasionally in alliance with some peninsulars, took advantage of the disgust with Iberian rule, the changing events in Europe, the example of the United States of America, and the desires for reform, to declare the independence of their locality and assume power. The actual consummation of independence in Latin America only affected a minority of the area's inhabitants. The masses, composed primarily of Indians, blacks, mestizos, and mulattoes, played an ambiguous role, at times fighting for their Iberian leaders and at other times filling the ranks of the American armies. Their loyalty often depended upon a variety of local factors as well as the abilities, promises, and persuasiveness of rival generals. With the major exceptions of Haiti, and Paraguay, and of Mexico during the early years of the wars of independence, the masses gained little. At best there were vague and contradictory promises of change that might improve their lot.

The issues at stake revolved mainly around control of the government and trade policies and as such affected almost exclusively the local aristocracy. The successful urban merchants and rural planters stood to gain the most from independence. The landed gentry enjoyed considerable power and social prestige because of their huge estates and their influence over local government. They identified more closely with local conditions than with either of the distant Iberian metropolises. They favored independence in order to expand their own power and to assure a greater freedom of access to international markets. Conservative by nature, they advocated few structural reforms. An influential Brazilian journalist of the period summed up their viewpoint when he pleaded, "Let us have no excesses. We want a constitution, not a revolution." The cities brought together the planters to discuss their common problems and aspirations, while at the same time within the cities a small but vocal class of free persons appeared, neither plantation owners nor slaves nor peasants, an unstable class anxious to improve its status. Most influential of the urban dwellers were the merchants who saw in independence an opportunity to better control their own destiny and hence to increase trade and business. The cities had previously been focal points of discontent and agitation. In them, the waves of nativism crested. Frequently the municipal councils served as the forum of debate and the instrument for action by which the cause of independence was furthered.

Representatives of the privileged classes led the hastily recruited American armies, whose ranks of patriots as well as adventurers expanded or contracted depending on the forcefulness of the generals and their successes in battle. The wars for independence in South America—in many areas, protracted, bloody, devastating—have been reduced largely to a chronicle of the exploits and brilliance of a handful of able generals: Simón Bolívar, Bernardo O'Higgins, José de San Martín, and Antonio José de Sucre, to cite those most often mentioned. The narrative and glorification of the biographies of single elitist leaders evolved into a marked characteristic of Latin American historiography. In Brazil, the Visconde de Pôrto Alegre once announced, "To know the biographies of all the outstanding men of a period is to know the history of those times." The Peruvian historian Francisco Garcia Calderón later echoed that observation: "The history of the South American Republics may be reduced to the biographies of their representative men." Such an outlook obviously eliminated the study of the actions and thoughts of the common people. Increasingly, attention focused on the exploits of two extraordinary representatives of the creole elite, General José de San Martín of Argentina and General Simón Bolívar of Venezuela, who between them led courageous armies through a grand pincers movement that defeated the Spaniards in South America.

In 1810, the movements for independence got underway simultaneously in opposite ends of South America, Venezuela and Argentina. The Argentine movement went practically unchecked, while in the north the Venezuelans battled heroically, although not always victoriously. The struggle for Spanish America's independence fell into three rather well-defined periods: the initial thrust and expansion of the movement between 1810 and 1814; the faltering of the patriotic armies and the resurgence of royalist domination, from 1814 to 1816; and the consummation of independence between 1817 and 1826. The actual fighting was limited to a few areas, principally Mexico and Venezuela. In large sections of Latin America—Central America, Paraguay, Argentina, and Brazil—no major battles occurred.

In both Venezuela and Argentina some leaders understood that their declarations would be meaningless and their aspirations thwarted so long as a Spanish army remained anywhere on the South American continent. For that reason they expanded their struggle from the regional to the continental stage. From Argentina, the army of San Martín crossed the Andes to contribute in 1817 to Chile's struggle against the Spaniards and then in 1820 invaded Peru, stronghold of Spanish royalism. In the north, Bolívar's army moved back and forth between Venezuela and Colombia before penetrating southward into Ecuador, Peru, and Bolivia. Although the independence of Spanish South America was virtually guaranteed by Sucre's decisive victory at Ayacucho in late 1824, the wars of liberation really only ended in early 1826 when the Spanish garrison occupying Callao, Peru's principal port, surrendered. Long before then, the new nations of Latin America had declared their independence. In most cases either a specially assembled congress or a local assembly—always dominated by the creoles—issued the declaration. Some, as in the case of Peru, Uruguay, Mexico, Brazil, Colombia, and Venezuela, did so before de facto independence was achieved; and others, Argentina, Bolivia, Central America, Haiti, Paraguay, and Chile, afterward.

The prolonged struggle for independence had some social and economic consequences for the new nations. Class and color lines blurred slightly. None of the newly independent nations continued the legal disabilities once restricting mestizos. In spite of some creole desires, it was impossible. In Mexico, for example, the clergy no longer kept the minute records of caste in their parochial books. In fact, some mestizo army officers quickly rose to power in the new nations. Mentally they tended to identify with the creoles. In a few areas, the governments abolished slavery or began the process of gradual emancipation. Contacts with Europe north of the Pyrenees multiplied with the resultant influx of new ideas. Economically the revolutions brought disaster to many areas. Normal trade and communication routes were interrupted; mines were flooded and equipment destroyed; herds of livestock were slaughtered, confiscated, or dispersed; currency manipulation, depreciation, inflation, the flight of capital, forced loans, confiscation of property, and capricious taxation brought financial ruin; and part of the work force was scattered, maimed, or killed. On the other hand, the ports of Latin America opened to the world and trade policies liberalized, although these changes were not without their disadvantages. Iberian mercantilist policies were abandoned, but in the new order, Great Britain came to exercise the economic hegemony once held by Spain and Portugal. The complex taxation system of the colonial past gave way to a reliance on customs duties as the principal source of national income.

Portuguese America achieved its independence during the same tumultuous years. Like its republican neighbors, Argentina and Paraguay, Brazil entered into nationhood almost bloodlessly, and following the trend evident in Spanish America, the mazombos clamored for the positions of the reinóis, although their ascendancy was more gradual than that of the creoles. The difference lay in the way Brazil achieved its independence.

Under the guidance of John VI, Brazil's position within the Portuguese empire improved rapidly. He opened the ports to world trade, authorized and encouraged industry, and raised Brazil's status to that of a kingdom, the equal of Portugal itself within the empire. Rio de Janeiro changed from a quiet viceregal capital to the thriving center of a far-flung world empire. The psychological impact on Brazilians was momentous. Foreigners who knew Brazil during the first decade of the monarch's residence there commented on the beneficial effect the presence of the crown exercised on the spirit of Brazilians. Ignácio José de Macedo typified the optimism of his fellow Brazilians when he predicted, "The unexpected transference of the Monarchy brought a brilliant dawn to these dark horizons, as spectacular as that on the day of its discovery. The new day of regeneration, an omen of brighter destinies, will bring long centuries of prosperity and glory."

When the royal court returned to Lisbon in 1821, after thirteen years of residence in Brazil, John left behind the Braganza heir, Prince Pedro, as regent. The young prince took up his duties with enthusiasm, only to find himself caught between two powerful and opposing forces. On the one side, the newly convened parliament, the Côrtes, in Lisbon, annoyed with and jealous of the importance Brazil had assumed within the empire during the previous decade and a half, sought to reduce Brazil to its previous colonial subservience; on the other, Brazilian patriots thought in terms of national independence. As the Côrtes made obvious its intent to strip Brazil of previous privileges as well as to restrict the authority of its prince-regent, Pedro listened more attentively to the mazombo views. He appointed the learned and nationalistic mazombo José Bonifácio de Andrada e Silva to his cabinet, the first Brazilian to hold such a high post. Bonifácio was instrumental in persuading Pedro to defy the humiliating orders of the Côrtes and to heed mazombo opinion, which refused to allow Lisbon to dictate policies for Brazil. Princess Leopoldina, although Austrian by birth, had dedicated her energies and devotion to Brazil after she arrived in Rio de Janeiro in 1817 to marry Pedro. She too urged him to defy Portugal. She wrote him as he traveled to São Paulo in September 1822: "Brazil under your guidance will be a great country. Brazil wants you as its monarch. . . . Pedro, this is the most important moment of your life. . . . You have the support of all Brazil. . . ." On September 7, 1822, convinced of the strength of Brazilian nationalism, Pedro declared the independence of Latin America's largest nation, and several months later in a splendid ceremony he was crowned "Constitutional Emperor and Perpetual Defender of Brazil." The evolutionary course upon which Brazil had embarked provided a stability and unity that no other former viceroyalty of the New World could boast. But Brazilian independence, similar to that in most of the Latin America, really only affected and benefited the elite.

4

National Consolidation

A nineteenth-century country home outside Asunción, Paraguay

Most of Latin America had crossed the threshold to independence by the end of the first quarter of the nineteenth century. The protracted struggle elevated to power a small, privileged elite who, with few exceptions, had enjoyed many benefits from the Spanish and Portuguese colonial systems and reaped even larger rewards during the early decades of nationhood. The independence of the new nations proved almost at once to be nominal, since the ruling elites remained spiritually linked to Iberia, culturally dependent on France, and economically subservient to Great Britain. The impetus to build a nation-state came from "above." In the apt judgment of José Martí, a Cuban intellectual acknowledged as one of Latin America's foremost nineteenth-century thinkers, the elites created "theoretical republics." They tended to confuse their own well-being and desires with those of the nation at large, an erroneous identification since they represented less than 5 percent of the total population. That minority, in spite of some efforts by the majority to impose their preferences, set the course upon which Latin America has continued to the present.

In any examination of the decades immediately following independence, fundamental questions arise: How do people inexperienced in self-government create governments and what types of government should they forge? How does economic poverty influence the exercise of sovereignty? Should past social patterns be abandoned or enhanced? These and other questions challenged the new nations and their citizens.

THE CONSEQUENCES OF THE ENLIGHTENMENT

The Enlightenment bequeathed to Latin America a complex legacy. An inherent and obvious danger resided in the fact that most of the ideas the Latin Americans associated with the Enlightenment originated in Europe north of the Pyrenees and thus reflected experiences alien to those of Indo-Ibero-Afro-America. Political ideas associated with the Enlightenment encouraged the urge for independence and nationhood. Affirming that each people should enjoy its own right to self-government, the Enlightenment prescribed the form and content of those governments. The notion that each people should enjoy the fruits of its own resources and labor was another powerful concept, which convinced the Latin Americans to deregulate commerce, experiment with free trade, and to embrace the practice of "competitive advantage," whereby they willingly entered a commercial relationship to sell agrarian and mineral products and to purchase manufactured goods. They professed an attachment to experimentation, one which dictated the adoption of European technology, increasingly regarded as the explanation for Northern European prosperity. Education—European education, because the elites wanted to duplicate European society in the New World—was emphatically regarded as the portal through which any nation or person must pass to achieve happiness, success, and wealth. Latin American faith in the redeeming virtues of a European education remained unshakable. Obviously the Latin Americans ignored other aspects of the many-sided Enlightenment.

Although the precise political labels adopted by the elites in the nineteenth century varied, they tended to group themselves under the headings of liberals and conservatives. Those labels confused rather than clarified because the elites had much more in common than in opposition. They tended to gravitate toward what (in the broadest terms of the Enlightenment) was considered to be liberal for the early nineteenth century: a written constitution, which defined the office of the chief executive, who shared power with a legislature and judiciary; a limitation if not outright abolition of trade restrictions; public education; and formal equality before the law.

The ideology of progress that emerged from the elites' flirtation with the Enlightenment was nowhere better expressed than by Argentina's Generation of 1837, an exceptionally articulate group of liberal intellectuals. Their ideas and actions reached far beyond the Argentine frontiers to shape much of the thinking of modern Latin America. Impressive unity and urgency were achieved by those intellectuals because they believed they faced a powerful alternative to their preferences in the figure of the popular caudillo Juan Manuel de Rosas, who dominated Argentina from 1829 until 1852. The Generation of 1837 regarded their conflict with Rosas as a struggle between "civilization" and "barbarism," a dialectic repeatedly invoked by intellectuals throughout the century. In defining civilization, the Generation of 1837 identified the Argentina they intended to create—and in fact did create—as a copy of Europe.

Associated with the port of Buenos Aires, the intellectuals looked with horror on the rest of the nation as a vast desert in need of the civilizing hand of Europe. Buenos Aires would serve, according to their blueprint, as a funnel through which European culture would pass on its civilizing mission to redeem the countryside—if it was redeemable. Many of the elite finally concluded it was not and advocated European immigration as the best means to "save" their country. They aspired to govern Argentina by means of a highly restrictive democracy. Esteban Echeverría summed up that aspiration in his influential *Dogma Socialista* (1838): men of reason should govern rationally to avoid the despotism of the masses. Nothing extraordinary resided in that nineteenth-century concept of the few governing the many, but it could prove devastating if the few challenged or changed, intentionally or not, the preferred life styles of the many and/or if by miscalculating the few lowered the quality of life of the majority. Domingo Faustino Sarmiento forcefully set forth the dialectic in his *Civilization and Barbarism* (1845): the conflict was between the progress of the Europeanized city versus the ignorance, barbarism, and primitivism of the country-

A political map of contemporary Latin America

side. The best-known Argentine novel of that century, *Amalia* (1855), further propagated the attitudes of the Generation of 1837. The author, José Mármol, characterized Rosas as a tyrant, the representative of rural barbarity. An open racism pervaded the novel: the persecuted elite of the capital was white, thus of pure European lineage and obviously "civilized"; the supporters of Rosas were a cruel collection of "mongrels," mulatto and mestizo, equated with inferiority and barbarism. *Amalia*, like *Civilization and Barbarism* and *Dogma Socialista*, represented the outlook of a generation instrumental in the shaping of Argentina in the nineteenth century. Indeed, two participants in that movement, Bartolomé Mitre and Sarmiento, served successively as presidents of Argentina (1862–68 and 1868–74) during crucial years in the formation of that nation.

The ideology of progress pursued by the dominant elites extolled a type of liberty and democracy sanctioning individualism, competition, and the unchecked pursuit of profit. That ideology tended to be abstract, exclusive, and dependent on authority.

The elites spoke constantly of "progress," perhaps the most sacred word in their political vocabulary. It defied facile definition. Later generations of scholars substituted the word "modernization," but that replacement did little to clarify the concept. Both words, used interchangeably hereafter, implied an admiration for the latest ideas, modes, inventions, and styles of Europe and the United States and a desire to adopt—rarely to adapt—them. The elites believed that "to progress" meant to recreate their nations as closely as possible in the shape of their European and North American models. Believing that they would benefit from such a recreation, they assumed by extension that their nations would benefit as well. They always identified (and confused) class well-being with national welfare.

The economic system that the elites obviously associated with progress was capitalism. It could not be otherwise when their primary models were England, France, and the United States. The constitutions, laws, and political practices they put into effect complemented the penetration and growth of capitalism. They abandoned the protective but restrictive neocapitalism and mercantilism of the Iberian empires to try their fortunes with the dominant capitalist nations of the century. In nineteenth-century practice, the landowners produced their crops on as large a scale as possible for sale in an external market from which they expected a satisfactory profit. Foreign exploitation of natural resources was approved by politicians, who hoped that some residue of the wealth created would enrich them. The wealth from the countryside and mines—shared increasingly with middlemen in the ports—also brought landowners and politicians prestige, and the combination of both conferred power. The growing merchant class, dependent firstly on the flow of primary products from the countryside and mines and secondly on the ability of the landed gentry and political leaders to afford costly European imports, exhibited scant inclination to challenge a system that also benefited them.

Progress was always measurable in quantitative terms—at least according to the elite, politicians, and scholars. It could be measured in the number of miles of railroad tracks or telegraph lines built, no matter where they went or what ends they served. The expansion of port facilities was equated with development, just as were rising exports. Capital cities vied with each other for the coveted title of "The Paris of Latin America," and to the extent they approximated their model, historians classified them as "cultured," "civilized," or "progressive." The arrival of increasing numbers of European immigrants signified the continuation—indeed, the acceleration—of the progress cherished by the elites, since the newcomers brought with them tastes and skills their American counterparts lacked or only knew secondhand.

Nineteenth-century historians chose the "progress" of Latin America as a major theme for their studies and based their judgments on the quantitative evidence of the presence or absence of that "progress." A city that adopted the outward manifestations of Europe was to be praised, while an Indian village that remained loyal to its indigenous past could readily and pejoratively be categorized as "primitive." Any Latin American politician who spoke with the rhetoric of the Enlightenment emerged in the history books as a statesman, but a political leader who appealed to local customs and the American past either was ignored by the scholars or castigated as a "barbarian." The historical dichotomy became as simplistic as it was universal. Latin American historiography, with only occasional but noteworthy exceptions, lauds the liberal laws and constitutions despite the fact that they obviously spoke to a small minority and more often than not were used as a means to intensify the concentration of political and economic power. Satisfaction with quantitative evidence of progress overshadows questions of quality of life for the majority.

Competitive social intercourse demanded by the ideology of progress obviously favored the strong, wealthy, and resourceful minority over the huge but weakened majority. In fact, the values the elites placed on abstract liberties and democracy conflicted with the values and experiences of most of the population, who understood little of European theories and nothing of the European experiences that gave rise to them. Their own experiences were rooted in the New World, and they drew from a past of interdependence, cooperation, solidarity, and a harmony contrary to the theories of individuality and competition. Not prepared for the values imposed by the elites, the masses could not hope to gain much from them. In fact, they did not. Liberty and democracy as they took form in nineteenth-century Latin America quickly became a superficial rationale excusing or disguising the exploitation of the many by the few. As one Argentine historian, Hector Iñigo Carrera, graphically expressed it, "Liberalism promised a theoretical garden of happiness which historically became a jungle of poverty."

The masses often repudiated the values imposed on them and attempted to express their own. What distinguished the folk was their adherence to ideas and values formulated by the American experience over centuries. Because the folk drew cautiously and slowly from European sources, carefully mediating those outside influences, they did not embrace the values and ideology emanating from Europe—and later the United States—with the same enthusiasm and rapidity that generally characterized the welcome extended by the elite, wealthy, and aspiring middle class.

Folk culture, a common way of life shared by ordinary people, was based on common language, heritage, beliefs, and means of facing daily life. It instilled a feeling of unity, loyalty, and tradition within the folk, more intuitive than codified, although folk wisdom, poetry, and tales gave insight into them. Throughout much of that century, the common folk cultures bound people together into intradependent, intimate, and largely self-sufficient folk societies, with a well-defined moral order in which each person knew both his own role and his interrelationship with other individuals. The folk held more to fixed laws of behavior and human existence. A unity of feeling and action accompanied a sense of harmony with the environment to satisfy inner needs.

Education within those folk societies emphasized the individual's relationship to the group and inculcated in children a moral behavior honored by the community. Education provided continuity by passing on and maintaining tradition.

The incentives to work and to trade originated in tradition, moral dictates, community obligations, and kinship relations. In those essentially nonmaterialistic cultures, economic decisions took second place to social considerations. The system worked sufficiently well to provide the folk with employment, food, housing, community spirit, and reasonable satisfaction. Life styles were simple; hardships were common; the disadvantages were obvious, at least to the outsider. Such life styles repulsed the Europeanized elites of the cities. Indeed, the behavior of the folk could be neither understood nor explained within the framework of Western thought. It did not evolve exclusively from the Iberian experience, nor did it acknowledge the influence of the liberal ideology of the Enlightenment or the French Revolution. Within their own experience, however, the folk societies seem to have provided adequately for their members.

In the face of the elites' Europeanized "official" culture, one function that Latin American folk culture assumed, consciously or not, was protest. Folk values readily reveal how limited was the "universality" of the official culture. To comprehend this, one can juxtapose official rhetoric, such as "Equality before the law," with popular proverbs such as "The rich man eats, while the poor man works." The limits of official culture can be understood in the life styles of at least that part of the masses that refused to accept the "universal" values. Large numbers of Indian groups tenaciously held and still hold their own beliefs and culture in the face of strong pressure from the official culture. Their own manner of dress is a direct challenge to the official consumer ideology that each person must dress differently, own a variety of clothes, and change styles frequently. Throughout Latin America viable folk cultures existed—and still exist—that either challenged the official cultures, or adapted to it, or evolved parallel, albeit subordinate, to it.

In making any assessments of the success or failure of folk cultures and especially of liberal "progress," one confronts a major semantic confusion: the equating of growth with development. The failure to distinguish between these two concepts creates innumerable difficulties. They are quite distinct. *Growth* indicates simply and only numerical accumulation, and it in no way indicates how change occurred or whom, if anyone, it benefited. Latin America in the nineteenth century grew wealthier through exports, but the wealth was increasingly concentrated in fewer hands. One could argue convincingly that such growth was detrimental. *Development,* on the other hand, signifies the maximum use of a nation's potential for the greatest benefit of the largest number of inhabitants. Development can imply or include growth, although it is conceivable that a nation can develop without growing. Involved in these assessments are considerations of quantity (statistical matters rather easily resolved) and of quality of life (more subjective and consequently more controversial).

THE TRANSFER AND LEGITIMIZATION OF POWER

Who would govern and how they would govern were fundamental questions facing the newly independent Latin Americans. They were questions previously unasked. For centuries all authority and power had been concentrated in the Iberian kings who ruled the New World in accordance with an ancient body of laws and customs and by "divine right." For nearly three centuries the inhabitants of the New World had accepted their rule. The monarchies provided their own continuity. The declarations of independence created a novel political vacuum. The Latin Americans experienced anguish, bloodshed, and chaos in their uncertain and contradictory efforts to fill it.

Brazil alone easily resolved the questions, mainly because of the presence of the royal family in Portuguese America. On hand to lend legitimacy to the rapid, peaceful political transition of Brazil from viceroyalty to kingdom to empire were first King John VI and then his son, Prince Pedro, heir to the throne, who severed the ties between Portugal and Brazil, and wore the new imperial crown. The mazombo elite supported the concept of monarchical government and thereby avoided the acrimonious debates between republicans and monarchists that split much of Spanish America. Obviously facilitating their decision was the convenient presence of a sympathetic prince, a Braganza who had declared Brazil's independence. By his birth and inheritance as well as through the concurrence of the Brazilian elite, Pedro's position and power were at once legitimate. As a Braganza, he inherited his authority. All the symbols of power surrounded him and enhanced his status. Historical precedent strengthened his position. The throne legitimately occupied by a Braganza proved to be the perfect unifier of the new and immense empire.

If there was a genuine consensus as to who would rule, the question remained open as to how he would rule. The emperor and the elite agreed that there should be a constitution, but the contents and limits of that projected document sparked a debate that in turn generated the first major crisis in the Brazilian empire. Elections were held for an assembly that would exercise both constituent and legislative functions. The group that convened on May 3, 1823, composed of lawyers, judges, priests, military officers, doctors, landowners, and public officials, clearly represented the privileged classes of the realm. They came from the ranks of the old landed aristocracy and the new urban elite, neither of which at that time was totally divorced from the other. With few exceptions, they lacked legislative experience. Almost at once, the legislature and the executive clashed, each suspicious that the other infringed on its prerogatives. Furthermore, the legislators manifested rabid anti-Portuguese sentiments and thus by implication a hostility to the person of the young emperor born in Lisbon. Convinced that the assembly not only lacked discipline but also scattered the seeds of revolution, Pedro decided to dissolve it. On November 11, 1823, troops closed the assembly hall, and the principal legislative leaders fled into exile.

Despite the dissolution of the assembly, Pedro intended to keep his word and rule under a constitution. He appointed a committee of ten Brazilians to write the document and then submitted it to the municipal councils throughout Brazil for their ratification. After most of them signified their approval, Pedro promulgated the new constitution on March 25, 1824. It provided for a highly centralized government with a vigorous executive. Although power was divided among four branches—executive, legislative, judiciary, and moderative—the lion's share rested in the hands of the emperor. Assisted by a Council of State and a ministry, the emperor exercised the functions of chief executive, a function enhanced by the novel moderative power. That power made him responsible for the maintenance of the independence of the nation as well as the equilibrium and harmony of the other powers and the twenty provinces. The emperor was given and expected to use broad powers to insure harmony in a far-flung empire whose wide geographic and human diversity challenged the existence of the state. In the last analysis, the crown was the one, pervasive, national institution that could and did represent all Brazilians. The General Assembly was divided into a senate, whose members were appointed by the emperor for life, and a chamber of deputies periodically and indirectly elected by a highly restricted suffrage. The constitution afforded broad individual freedom and equality before the law. Considering the time, place, and circumstances, it seems safe to conclude that the constitution was a liberal document. Proof of the viability of the constitution lay in its longevity: it lasted sixty-five years, until the monarchy fell in 1889. It has proven to be Brazil's most durable constitution and one of Latin America's longest lived.

The Brazilians gradually took control of their own government. At first, Pedro disappointed them by surrounding himself with Portuguese advisers, ministers, and prelates. The Brazilians had their independence but were tacitly barred from exercising the highest offices in their own empire. Pedro had been born in Portugal (although he came as a boy to Brazil and always displayed a deep devotion to it), and soon the mazombos accused him of paying more attention to affairs in the former metropolis than to those of the new empire. Indeed, after the death of John VI in 1826, the young emperor became increasingly involved in Portuguese dynastic struggles. Meanwhile, as the Brazilians demanded access to the highest offices of their land, the currents of anti-Portuguese sentiments swelled. Pedro's failure to understand those nationalistic sentiments and to appoint Brazilians to top positions was a primary cause of the discontent leading to his abdication in 1831. After his departure for Europe, members of the elite with their roots firmly in the plantation economy replaced the Portuguese-born who monopolized the high posts of the First Empire. In 1840, when Pedro II ascended the throne, a Brazilian— for the adolescent emperor had been born and raised in the New World— even occupied that exalted position. Thus, the mazombo ascendency was much more gradual than the creole. It began in 1808 when the royal court arrived in Rio de Janeiro and reached its climax in 1840 when a Brazilian-born emperor took the scepter.

Unlike Brazil, Spanish America experienced a difficult transfer and legitimization of power. The political vacuum stirred winds of disorder and ambition that blew forcefully for many decades. The question of what form the new governments should take absorbed considerable energy and aroused heated debates, particularly over the issues of federalism versus centralism and a republic versus a monarchy. Monarchy harmonized with the past and with the hierarchical, aristocratic structure of Spanish-American society. However, a desire to repudiate at least the outward symbols of the Spanish past, an infatuation with the political doctrines of the Enlightenment, and the successful example of the United States strengthened the arguments of the partisans of a republic. Only in Mexico did the monarchists carry the day, but, unable to persuade a European prince to accept the new Aztec scepter, the creoles crowned one of their own, Augustín de Iturbide, whose brief reign lasted from May of 1822 until February of 1823. Still, since Mexico at that time included the territory from Oregon to Panama, it meant that together with Brazil, a majority of Latin America in late 1822 and early 1823 fell under monarchical sway. Iturbide's reign was not a happy one. Like Pedro I, he could not agree with his constituent assembly. Consequently he dictated his own constitution. His power rested firmly on the army and hence on the whims of jealous generals. Unlike Pedro, he enjoyed scant popular and minimal elitist support and none of the tradition that legitimized the Brazilian emperor's position. Falling prices for exports, economic stagnation, and an empty treasury complicated Iturbide's reign. Tired of waiting for delayed salaries, the military officers deserted their creole emperor and adhered to the republican cause, one that seemed to promise a more punctual delivery of paychecks. The army banished Iturbide in early 1823, abolished the empire, and helped to establish a liberal, federal republic. With that, the principle of republicanism triumphed, at least as an ideal, throughout Spanish America. Nonetheless, some would continue to argue the case for monarchy, and, in fact, Mexico experimented with it once again in the 1860s.

The debates over the merits of centralism and federalism reached no immediate conclusion. A reaction against the previous Spanish centralism, a host of local rivalries, and the apparent successful example of North American federalism combined to persuade many of the Latin American leaders to experiment with federalism. Most of the nations, large and small, tried it at one time or another. Indeed, an occasional experiment with it still continues, and several of the republics maintain the fiction of being federal. The experiments at best were unsuccessful, but in the case of Mexico and the United Provinces of Central America, they were a disaster that led to partial or total dismemberment of the nation. Colombia's experiment with a confederation under the Constitution of 1858 nearly dissolved the nation, and only the emergence of a strong caudillo, Tomás Cipriano de Mosquera, restored unity. The centrifugal propensity in the huge, underpopulated, and poorly integrated nations cautioned against further experiments with federalism and eventually led to the abandonment of the idea in most of the nations.

The question of who should govern posed yet another problem for the new states to solve. The immediate answer was to turn the reins of authority over to independence heroes, and therefore the first chiefs of state in many lands were the very men who had declared and fought for the independence of these nations. Thus, Bolívar served as president of Gran Colombia (the modern states of Colombia, Venezuela, Panama, and Ecuador); O'Higgins governed Chile; Sucre became the first constitutional president of Bolivia; San Martín ruled as "Protector of Peru"; Iturbide wore the crown of Mexico; and so forth. The Latin Americans found it more difficult to select successors to the independence heroes—most of whom were turned out of office as their popularity faded and the nations showed themselves less grateful for past services rendered. Efforts to fill presidential chairs unleashed bitter power struggles among various factions of the elite, struggles conducive to despotism.

The contending factions all too often sought simply to seize, hold, and exercise power for its own sake and its own reward. Only secondarily did the leaders cloak their power with some cloth of legality, a cloth usually of exotic and impractical fabric. During the early decades of independence, elections seldom were held and even more rarely were they honest. Consequently the various factions resorted to violence as the path to power. Once in office, they usually exerted more violence in maintaning themselves in power than they had in achieving it.

As the question of who was going to rule was never properly answered in most of the republics during the first decades after independence—at best satisfactory *ad hoc* solutions were provided—so too did the problem of how the nations should be governed remain largely unsolved. Almost without exception the elite, as well as most of the caudillos, imbued with a long legalistic tradition, desired a written constitution, even though, in most cases, the document proved to be more theoretical than practical. The elite and their political representatives espoused an idealism, thanks to their flirtation with the Enlightenment, far removed from local realities. In their compulsive writing and rewriting of their constitutions, they repeatedly eschewed local experience to import the latest ideas from abroad. Apparently the more novel the idea the better, so long as it originated in one of the nations they regarded as progressive. The most popular models for the many nineteenth-century Latin American constitutions were the North American and French constitutions as well as the Spanish Constitution of 1812, considered in the early nineteenth century as a splendid example of liberal thought. In defense of the framers of the Latin American constitutions it should be emphasized that they had minimal experience on which to draw. Lacking experience they were seduced by theories. Any desire to fundamentally alter past experience was probably superficial, an intellectual enthusiasm or exercise out of touch with reality. The creole elite found the patterns they inherited from the Spanish colonial past far too comfortable for them to want to stray too far from them in practice.

The Latin Americans promulgated and abandoned constitutions with numbing regularity. It has been estimated that in the century and a half after independence, they wrote between 180 and 190 of them, a large percentage of which were adopted during the chaotic period before 1850. Venezuela holds the record with 22 constitutions since 1811. The four major Latin American nations have a somewhat stabler constitutional record. Brazil's constitution, promulgated in 1824, lasted until 1889. After several attempts, Chile adopted a constitution in 1833 that remained in force until 1925. Argentina's Constitution of 1853 survived until 1949 but was put into force again in 1956. Mexico promulgated a constitution in 1857 that remained the basic document until 1917.

Generally the constitutions invested the chief executive with paramount powers so that both in theory and practice he exercised far greater authority than the other branches of government, which were invariably subservient to his will. In that respect, the Latin Americans reverted to their experience of the past. The presidents played the omnipotent role of past kings. Chile and Brazil experimented with parliamentary government. By the mid-nineteenth century, all the Latin American governments shared at least three general characteristics: strong executives, a high degree of centralization, and restricted suffrage (the vote invariably was limited to literate and/or propertied males). With a few notable exceptions, the new governments were by, of, and for the elite. The masses generally stood as silent witnesses to political events.

THE TENSE SOCIETIES

Tension characterized the early governments. A feeling of insecurity complicated the search for political formulas and the creation of the nation-state. The new governments felt threatened by internal challenges, aggression from their neighbors, and the possibility of European reconquest. There was the psychological insecurity of those uncertain of their new positions of power, of those pressing for class fluidity—the restive commercial class and educated mestizos—and of those apprehensive over political change and its implications for the future. The mounting tensions between those imposing Europeanization and those favoring the folk culture of the past often erupted into violence.

From the start, the fear existed that Spain or Portugal, alone or in union with other European governments, might try to recapture the former colonies in the New World. The conservative monarchies of Russia, Austria, and Prussia formed the Holy Alliance, which numbered among its goals the eradication of representative government in Europe and the prevention of its spread to areas where it was previously unknown. The Alliance boldly intervened in a number of European states to dampen the fires of liberalism. At one time, it seemed possible that the Holy Alliance might help Spain in an effort to reassert its authority over its former American colonies, a possibility as displeasing to the United States as it was to Latin Americans. National self-interest, menacing European rhetoric, and Russian settlement advancing down the western coast of North America prompted President James Monroe to issue the Monroe Doctrine in 1823, which declared that the Americas were no longer open to European colonization and that the United States would regard any intervention of a European power in the Americas as an unfriendly act against the United States. Desirous of keeping open the lucrative markets of the newly independent nations, English statesmen agreed with the substance of the defiant declaration. The doctrine received a mixed reception from the Latin Americans, some of whom had as much reason to suspect North American motives as they did those of the Europeans. The Spanish-American nations never officially recognized the doctrine nor gave it hemispheric legitimacy. At best they only tacitly accepted it. Brazil, to the contrary, always accorded the doctrine a cordial welcome.

Latin American fears of European intervention were not unfounded.

Several European governments did physically intervene in the new republics. Spain made several feeble attempts to invade Mexico and Central America in 1829 and 1832. Later, in the decade of the 1860s, Spanish imperialism threatened the former colonies again. Spain made war on Peru, seizing one of its guano-producing islands, and bombarded the Chilean port of Valparaíso. During that same decade, the Dominican Republic, a sad spectacle of chaos, invited Isabel II to accept the return of a contrite nation to the Spanish fold. Spain reasserted its authority in 1861, but the insular nation proved so unruly and expensive that Spain withdrew in 1865, leaving the Dominican Republic independent once again, the unique example of a former colony that voluntarily, if temporarily, returned to its colonial status. France and Great Britain also intervened in the New World. The French occupied Vera Cruz, Mexico, in 1838 to force Mexico to pay alleged debts; and they blockaded Buenos Aires in 1838–40, and again in 1845–48, this time in conjunction with the British, to discipline Rosas. The Argentine adventures proved to be far less successful than the Mexican one. The most brazen European intervention occurred in Mexico during the 1860s. Responding to the grandiose schemes of Napoleon III, a French army in 1862 marched into central Mexico to set the hapless Maximilian of Austria on a shaky Aztec throne. The French remained until 1866, when, defeated by geography and the determination of the troops under the command of Benito Juárez, they withdrew. These examples show that Latin American anxieties over European intervention were well founded. For half a century, these apprehensions—or, on occasion, the interventions themselves—increased local tensions as well as diverted resources and energy that could have been invested more profitably in national development.

To diminish the threat of invasion from the former mother countries as well as from other European states, the new nations sought international recognition of their independent status. The European governments hesitated to extend a hand of friendship before the former mother countries did so. Portugal, due to a family pact among the Braganzas who occupied the thrones both in Lisbon and Rio de Janiero, extended the promptest recognition, accorded to Brazil in 1825. France delayed its recognition of Haitian independence, declared in 1804, until 1825. Spanish recognition was tardiest and most complicated. The death of Ferdinand VII in 1833 ended unrealistic Spanish intransigence and opened the way for negotiations with the former colonies. In 1836, Spain and Mexico agreed "to forget forever the past differences and dissensions which unfortunately have interrupted for so long a period the friendship and harmony between two peoples." Spain then recognized Mexico, and gradually over the decades extended similar recognition to the other republics, the last being Honduras in 1894.

Unlike the European nations, the United States felt no need to consider the feelings of the Iberian monarchs before acting, although other considerations—the desire to obtain Florida from Spain, for example—did delay recognition. In 1822, the process began when the Department of State recognized Argentina, Gran Colombia, and Mexico, followed in 1823 by the recognition of Chile, and in 1824 of Brazil and Central America. The United States maintained a high degree of interest in Latin America. Of the ten legations provided for by the Department of State's budget in 1824, five were in Latin America. By 1821, commerce with the southern neighbors already accounted for over 13 percent of U.S. trade. Although formal recognition might have made the new states feel somewhat more secure and reduced by a small degree the tensions disturbing the new societies, it did not in and of itself eliminate foreign threats or even deter interventions.

The threats were by no means all external. The national unity of the new states proved to be extremely fragile, and the forces that shattered it more often than not were internal. Geography provided one major obstacle to unity and the creation of the nation-state. Vast tracts of nearly empty expanse, impenetrable jungles, mountain barriers, and lonely deserts separated and isolated population pockets among which communication was tardy and difficult and transportation often nonexistent and, where existent, hazardous and slow. The rainy season halted all communication and transportation in many regions. Such poor communications and transportation complicated the exchange of goods, services, and ideas on a national basis. It was easier and cheaper to ship a ton of goods from Guayaquil, Ecuador, to New York City via the Straits of Magellan than to send it 200 miles overland to the capital, Quito. Rio de Janiero could import flour and wheat more economically from England than from Argentina. Likewise the inhabitants of northern Brazil found it easier to import from Europe than to buy the same product from southern Brazil despite the fact that sailing vessels connected Brazil's littoral population nuclei. Most of the population lived within easy reach of the coast. To penetrate the interior, the Brazilians relied on inland waterways—in some areas generously supplied by the Amazon and Plata networks—or cattle trails. A journey from Rio de Janiero to Cuiabá, capital of the interior province of Mato Grosso, took eight months in the 1820s. The situation was comparable in Spanish America. The trip from Vera Cruz, Mexico's principal port, to Mexico City, a distance of slightly less than 300 miles, over the nation's best and most used highway took about four days of arduous travel when Frances Calderón de la Barca made the journey under the most favorable conditions in 1839. She described the road as "infamous, a succession of holes and rocks." In the 1820s a journey from Buenos Aires to Mendoza, approximately 950 miles inland at the foothills of the Andes, took a month by ox cart or two weeks by carriage, although a government courier in an emergency could make the trip in five days on horseback.

Distance, difficult geography, slow communication and transportation, and local rivalries, in part spurred by isolation, encouraged the growth of a regionalism hostile to national unity. Experiments with federalism intensified that regionalism. With the exception of Brazil, the former vice-royalties engendered few feelings of unity among their widely dispersed residents, who tended to give their loyalty to former political subdivisions—the captaincies, kingdoms, and presidencies—which seemed closer in harmony with regional realities and needs. As a result, soon after independence the former territories of the Spanish viceroyalties disintegrated. None splintered more than the Viceroyalty of New Spain. In 1823, Central America, the former Kingdom of Guatemala, seceded. In turn, in 1838–39, the United Provinces of Central America broke into five republics. Texas left the Mexican union in 1836, and during the war of 1846–48 the United States detached California, Arizona, and New Mexico. Gran Colombia failed to maintain the former unity of the Viceroyalty of New Granada: Venezuela left the union in 1829 and Ecuador followed the next year. Chile and Bolivia felt no loyalty to Lima, and consequently the Viceroyalty of Peru disbanded even before the independence period was over. In a similar fashion, Paraguay, Uruguay, and part of Bolivia denied the authority of Buenos Aires, thus spelling the end of the Viceroyalty of La Plata. By 1840, the four monolithic Spanish viceroyalties had split, giving rise to all of the Spanish-speaking republics of the New World except Cuba and Panama, which appeared in the wake of a new, aggressive North American imperialism at the end of the nineteenth and beginning of the twentieth centuries.

The maintenance of Brazilian unity while the Spanish-American vice-royalties disintegrated begs an explanation. Certainly the reasons for unity will not be found in the common language, religion, cultural heritage, and contiguous territory. On that basis, Spanish America would have remained unified too. Permissive Portuguese colonial institutions, amazingly ill-defined in contrast to those of Spain, allowed a more leisurely formation of the colony and permitted a flexibility uncommon in the more rigid Spanish bureaucracy. Apparently, unlike Spain's, they could be bent without breaking, which permitted them to change to meet new situations. Further, the presence of the Braganzas starting in 1808, with all the centralization of control and power that involved, unified Brazil during its final colonial years—at the very time when Napoleon's campaigns were breaking the bonds between Spain and its colonies, a break that came suddenly and without any preparation on the part of the creoles. Certainly, eighty-one years of highly centralized monarchy (1808–89) with, until the end, few questioning or challenging the emperor's authority, goes a long way in helping to explain Brazilian unity. Perhaps the small mazombo landholding class's constant fear of a slave rebellion in an empire with a huge slave population caused the widely dispersed elite to hold similar opinions and to advocate similar actions, a harmony that might not have characterized them had there been no common fear. Other scholars have pointed to the vast Brazilian frontier as an instrument of unity. Cattle paths and water networks crisscrossed to link the interior together, a matrix also holding the coastal population nuclei together. Of course, within that unity existed— still exists—an immense variety that the regions exemplify. There has been conflict between the forces of unity and diversity, that is, between centralism and regionalism. The scales at one time or another have tipped both ways. In the long run, however, the two forces have maintained a certain balance. The essential fact is that the Brazilian union remained intact despite stress and threat. National unity and homogeneity are achievements of which Brazilians can be justifiably proud. They stand in contrast to the fate that befell the four Spanish-American viceroyalties.

None of the eighteen new nations had clearly defined frontiers with its neighbors, a problem destined to cause war, bloodshed, and ill will ever after. In some cases, commercial rivalries added to the difficulties. Further, the rapid multiplication of new states raised hemispheric trade barriers, which in turn complicated and intensified those rivalries. In short, former colonial regional rivalries took on a nationalistic tone after independence. The resultant suspicion and distrust among the eighteen states accelerated the tensions felt within the new societies. On occasion, these tensions gave rise to war as neighbor fought neighbor in the hope of gaining a trade advantage, greater security, or additional territory.

Argentina and Brazil struggled in the Cisplatine War (1825–28) over possession of Uruguay and in an exhausted stalemate agreed to make the disputed territory independent; Chile attacked Peru and Bolivia in 1836 to prevent the federation of the two neighbors, and during the War of the Pacific (1879–83) the three fought for possession of the nitrate deposits of the Atacama Desert; the Dominican Republic battled Haiti in 1844 to regain its independence; westward expansion brought the United States into conflict with Mexico, 1846–48; and throughout the nineteenth century the five Central American republics challenged each other repeatedly on the battlefield. This catalog of conflicts is only representative, not inclusive. The major conflict of the century pitted tiny, landlocked Paraguay against the Triple Alliance—Argentina, Brazil, and Uruguay—in a clash of imperialistic pretensions in the strategic La Plata basin, one phase in a constant and continuing struggle to maintain the balance of power there. It took the allies five years, 1865–70, to subdue plucky Paraguay. That war solved two difficult problems that had troubled the region since independence. First, it definitively opened the Plata River network to international commerce and travel, a major concern of Brazil, which wanted to use the rivers to communicate with several of its interior provinces. Second, it freed the small states of Uruguay and Paraguay from further direct intervention from Argentina and Brazil, which came to understand the importance of the independence of the two small Platine states as buffer zones. The two large nations might try to sway one or both of the small nations to its side, but neither Brazil nor Argentina physically intervened again.

Relations between the new states and the Roman Catholic Church created tensions of another sort to disturb domestic tranquility in all the states. On occasion, conflict between church and state degenerated into civil war, as the history of Mexico amply illustrates. The Roman Catholic Church had penetrated every region of Latin America. Almost all Latin Americans in the early nineteenth century professed to be at least nominal Catholics.

Due to efficient organization, able administration, and the generosity of the pious, the Church continued to amass riches in the New World. At the end of the eighteenth century, the traveler Humboldt estimated that in some provinces of New Spain the Church controlled as much as 80 percent of the land. That, however, constituted only part of the Church's wealth. Lucas Alamán, a devout Catholic, leader of the clerical party in Mexico during the first half of the nineteenth century, and one of the most reputable Mexican historians of that century, revealed that although rural estates and urban properties of the Church accounted for half the total value of the nation's real estate, the Church's real wealth accrued from mortgages and the impressive sums of interest collected.

Wealth begot considerable power for the Church, but the Church's strength rested on other foundations as well. The clergy, one of the best-educated segments of society, enjoyed tremendous prestige, particularly among the masses, prestige that often made a mere suggestion carry the weight of a command. The clerics regularly entered politics, held high offices in the new governments, or endorsed political candidates. The clergy exerted its influence within the educational system; in almost all of the new countries they monopolized education from the primary school through the university. It was obvious then that in the early national period the Church wielded great influence not only in the spiritual lives of the new nations but also in economics, politics, society, and the intellectual pursuits. Alamán concluded, "The influence of the clergy was great for three reasons: respect for religion, rememberance of its great benefactions, and its abundant riches." Favorable as he was toward the Church, Alamán discerned potential danger in the authority of the clerics: abuse of their powerful influence. Under the sway of the ideas of the Enlightenment, a vociferous body of critics began to accuse the clergy of just such abuse.

Any criticism of the Church was aimed neither at religion itself nor at Dogma, but rather at the secular power and influence of the institution and its servants. Religious discontent had not been a cause for the wars of independence. Rebellion against the Church was unthinkable at the time. Indeed, the revolutionaries and their early successors offered to Catholicism recognition of its traditional position and privileges. The new constitutions respected the status of the Church. But many of the leaders of the new states quickly became apprehensive of the overwhelming power wielded by the privileged Church, which was far better organized and more efficient than the state, and, more often than not, better financed. They felt it necessary to subordinate the Church to the state by control of the patronage in a manner characteristic of the former Iberian arrangement with the Vatican. They sincerely believed that the independence of the new states could not be guaranteed if they did not exercise some temporal control over the Church. For that reason, the Latin American chiefs of state claimed the right to exercise national patronage as heirs of the former royal patronage. The Pope in turn announced that the patronage had reverted back to the papacy, its original source, with the declarations of independence. In their open sympathy with the Spanish monarchy the popes antagonized the Latin American governments. In 1824, Pope Leo XII issued an encyclical to archbishops and bishops in America to support Ferdinand VII. This confirmed to Latin American leaders that the Vatican was in league with the Holy Alliance. The new governments found it necessary to expel a number of ranking clerics who refused to swear allegiance to the new state. Such a fate befell Archbishop Ramón Casaus y Torres of Guatemala in 1830, for example.

Out of consideration for the feelings of Madrid, the Vatican for a long time refused to recognize the new American states, much to the chagrin of their governments, which were fearful that the discontent of the American Catholics with their isolation might endanger independence. Rome began to change its attitude toward the Latin American states in 1826, when the Pope announced his willingness to receive American representatives strictly as ecclesiastical delegates, in no way implying political recognition. The next year the Roman pontiff began to preconize (that is, approve) candidates presented by the American governments. With the death of Ferdinand VII in 1833, the Pope no longer felt any Spanish constraints on his policy in the New World. In 1835, the Vatican recognized New Granada and the following year accredited to Bogotá the first papal nuncio. The recognition of New Granada signified the end both of the problem over political recognition and of Spanish influence over the Vatican's diplomacy in and relations with Spanish America. However, other questions remained unsolved and for the remainder of the century the difficulties between Church and state centered on such questions as lay teaching, secularization of the cemeteries, civil marriage, the establishment of a civil register for births, marriages, and deaths, ownership of religious property, and patronage.

The religious questions rigidly separated the adherents to the two strongest political currents of nineteenth-century Latin America, liberal and conservative. On other issues the stands of the liberals and conservatives might have varied from country to country or even from region to region, but not so the Church. The conservatives invariably favored the status quo of the Church, supporting its spiritual and temporal powers, privileges, and prestige. Just as invariably, the liberals challenged the temporal powers of the Church. They uncompromisingly demanded that the state exercise patronage and thus temporal control of the Church.

The disputants often failed to settle their differences by compromise or conciliation. On more than one occasion, armies took to the field to settle them. Mexico, in particular, suffered from the conflict over the question of the proper place of the Church within the new states. The early constitutions established Roman Catholicism as the state Church but endorsed the principle of national patronage. The liberals campaigned to reduce the privileges of the Church, and, in 1833, during the brief tenure of Valentín Gómez Farías as chief of state, reforms were enacted to secularize the California missions and to confiscate their funds, to secularize public education, to abolish compulsory tithes, to give members of the religious orders the option of retracting their vows, and to strengthen the principle of national patronage. Santa Anna removed Gómez Farías from power in 1834 and annulled these reforms. Under the succeeding conservative governments, the Church regained its privileged status. During this time, Mexico expended much of its energy and resources against the rebels in Texas, to thwart French intervention, and to attempt to halt or deflect the expansion of the United States into the northern provinces. The attendant bankruptcy and disappointments paved the way to power for a new generation of liberals, an outstanding group of intelligent and honest men, the most prominent of whom was Benito Juárez, a full-blooded Indian. Never deviating from his liberal principles, he held the liberals together during a decade and a half of stress. In the Plan of Ayutla issued in 1854, the liberals called for the overthrow of Santa Anna and a new constitution. They came to power the following year but were repeatedly challenged. Of all the issues at stake, the religious question predominated.

The liberals initiated their religious reforms in 1855 with the Ley Juárez, which restricted the privileges of military and ecclesiastical courts by ending their jurisdiction in purely civil cases. In 1856, the Ley Lerdo required all corporations to sell their lands; the intention of this law was to divest the Church of all its property not strictly devoted to religious purposes. The well-intentioned law had several unfortunate consequences for Mexico. In the first place, the Church lands were more often than not the most efficiently run and productive and hence a major contributor to the national economy. Further, income from these lands supported a wide variety of essential charities. The requirement that all corporations sell their lands included the Indian *ejidos,* so therefore the liberals contributed to divesting the Indian communities of their lands. The *hacendados,* owners of the large estates, found as a result of the enforcement of the Ley Lerdo considerable new land on the markets that they snatched up to add to their already considerable holdings. The new constitution promulgated in 1857 incorporated both the Ley Juárez and the Ley Lerdo and went on to nullify compulsory observance of religious vows and to secularize education. The conservatives and the Church denounced the new laws and constitution. Pope Pius declared, "We raise our Pontifical voice in apostolic liberty . . . to condemn, to reprove, and to declare null and void the said decrees and everything else that the civil authority has done in scorn of ecclesiastical authority and of this Holy See." The clergy and military united to defend their privileges and attacked the liberals, initiating the bloody War of Reform, 1858–61. The bold challenge to the liberal government unleashed an avalanche of anticlerical laws upon the Church: the nationalization of cemeteries, civil marriage, abolition of tithes, nationalization of all real property of the Church, separation of Church and state, suppression of all monasteries, and the prohibition of novitiates in nunneries.

Defeated on the battlefields, the conservatives resolved to seek foreign intervention rather than accept the triumph of Juárez. They persuaded the ambitious Napoleon III to intervene in their favor in 1862 by supporting the restitution of the monarchy in the person of the Austrian Archduke Maximilian, who arrived in 1864. Much to the annoyance of the conservatives, Maximilian accepted the religious reforms. To oppose the French intervention and monarchical restoration, the liberals took up arms again. Napoleon found it necessary to commit 34,000 regular troops to support the unsteady throne of Maximilian. Even so, the monarchy never extended its authority over more than a fraction of Mexican territory and never enjoyed the support of more than a minority of the Mexican population. The French withdrawal in 1866 condemned the monarchy to immediate extinction. The following year the liberal army captured and shot Maximilian. Juárez returned to Mexico City and the herculean task of rebuilding a ravaged Mexico. The Church had lost considerable wealth, prestige, and power during its prolonged struggle with the state, but the battles were by no means over. They flared up later and extended well into the twentieth century.

Mexico represents an extreme in the Church-state struggles that added much to the tensions of nineteenth-century Latin America. Although such bitter warfare might not have characterized the rest of the hemisphere, no new nation entirely escaped the conflict. The struggle over patronage and to reduce the Church's powers continued throughout the nineteenth century. It complicated and strained relations between the Vatican and Latin America and gave rise to considerable national tension.

ECONOMIC STAGNATION

A major paradox has always characterized Latin America: the potential richness of the land and the abject poverty of the majority of the people who work it. The contrast between what could be and what is confounds all careful observers and begs explanation. Luís dos Santos Vilhena, a Portuguese professor of Greek who resided twelve years in Salvador da Bahia at the end of the eighteenth century, posed the sad question about Brazil, "Why is a country so fecund in natural products, so rich in potential, so vast in extent, still inhabited by such a small number of settlers, most of them poor, and many of them half-starved?" He answered his own question frankly, putting the blame for underdevelopment on slave labor, the latifundia, and inefficient or obsolete agricultural methods. Across the continent at exactly the same time, the Chilean intellectual José de Cos Iriberri asked an identical question: "Who would imagine that in the midst of the lavishness and splendor of nature the population would be so scanty and that most of it would be groaning under the oppressive yoke of poverty, misery and the vices which are their inevitable consequences?" He blamed the sad economic condition of Chile on the unequal distribution of the land, which favored a few large landowners but condemned most of the population to the role of overworked, underpaid, landless peons. What they said about Brazil and Chile could be applied to all of Latin America. As we will have ample opportunity to observe, all economic discussions of Latin America must begin with an understanding of land-ownership and -use patterns.

Independence proved no panacea for Latin America's economic ills. The trend established during the colonial period to subordinate the economy to Europe's needs continued unaltered. During the nineteenth century, Latin America's economy remained locked into commercial capitalism, more dependent than ever on foreign markets for local prosperity. Meanwhile, Europe and the United States had industrialized and moved into yet another phase of international capitalism—financial—in which financiers owned and managed the assets of large, industrial empires.

During the first half of the century, Europe and the United States entered a period of rapid population growth and accelerated industrialization and urbanization. They demanded raw products: food for the urban centers and materials for the factories. In turn, they sought markets in which to sell growing industrial surpluses. The newly independent nations of Latin America with their abundant natural wealth and limited industries were pressed into a working relationship with the burgeoning capitalist centers: they exported the raw materials required in Europe and the United States and imported the manufactured goods pouring from the factories. Latin America's exports depended upon and responded to the requirements of Europe and the United States. In catering to the caprices of an unpredictable market, the Latin Americans encouraged the growth of a reflex economy, little different, except perhaps more hazardous, than the previous colonial economy. External factors, over which the Latin Americans had little or no influence, determined whether the economies prospered or vegetated. The economic cycles of boom and collapse repeatedly reoccurred in all regions of Latin America. Responding to the needs and requirements of Europe and the United States condemned most of the area to remain on the periphery of international capitalism.

Between 1800 and 1850, world trade tripled, and Latin America participated in that growth. After recovering from the wars of independence, it shipped ever greater amounts of agricultural produce abroad. While two or three ships a year had handled trade between Chile and England in the 1815–20 period, more than 300 carried Chilean exports to England in 1847. The value of exports leaving Buenos Aires nearly tripled in a quarter of a century, 1825–50.

Improving international transportation put Europe and the United States into closer contact with Latin America. Faster sailing vessels and then the introduction of the steamship, which was being used successfully in North Atlantic crossings in the 1830s, were responsible. The steamships appeared in the waters of Brazil in 1819 and of Chile in 1822. By 1839, a steamship line connected Rio de Janiero with the northern provinces of the empire. A dramatic event in 1843 impressed the Brazilians with the importance of the steamship for their future development. In that year the puffing and chugging *Guapiassú* churned the waters of the Amazon for the first time. The steamship journeyed from Belém to Manaus, 900 miles upstream in nine days and returned in half the time, a remarkable record considering that hitherto the sailing vessels required two or three months to ascend and a month to descend. Much of Latin America was witnessing at that time the rapidity that the steamship afforded international commerce.

In 1840, the British chartered the Royal Mail Steam Packet Company to provide regular twice monthly steamship service to the entire Caribbean area. That same year, the Pacific Steam Navigation Company initiated steamship service along the western coast of South America. In 1868, the Valparaíso-Liverpool line began operations. For the Atlantic coast, the Royal Mail Steam Packet from England to Brazil began service in 1851. The English inaugurated direct steam service to the Río de la Plata soon thereafter. At the same time, the United States expanded its international steamship service, which reached Latin America in 1847 with the foundation of the Pacific Mail Company. These improved communication and transportation systems further meshed the economies of Latin America with those of the United States and Europe and most particularly with that of Great Britain.

Great Britain quickly replaced the two Iberian kingdoms as the dominant economic force in Latin America and held that primacy throughout the nineteenth century. Foreign Secretary George Canning mused in 1824, "Spanish America is free, and if we do not mismanage our affairs sadly, she is English." As soon as Portugal and Spain fell to Napoleon, eager British merchants began to move in large numbers into Latin America to capture the markets they had so long craved. By 1810, approximately 120 merchants resided in Buenos Aires alone; by 1824, the English community in that strategic port numbered 3,000. It has been estimated that by that time about 100 English commercial houses operated in Spanish American cities. The British sold more to Latin America than anyone else and in some cases almost monopolized the imports into certain countries. British firms handled the lion's share of Latin America's foreign trade, and British bottoms carried much of it to distant ports. The English government maintained men-of-war in Latin American waters to protect British commerce, to safeguard the rights of Englishmen, and on occasion to transport specie. London supplied most of the loans and investments to the new nations. Already by 1822, four Latin American loans had been floated, in 1824 five more were, and the following year saw an additional five. In the years immediately after independence, British investors readily subscribed to joint-stock companies being formed in Latin America, particularly the mining companies—almost all of which failed.

By 1850, foreigners had invested a limited amount of capital, most of which was British. The most successful investments were in trading firms. The Europeans largely invested their capital to facilitate the production and export of the products they needed most. Thus, they used their capital to shape the Latin American economy to suit their needs, not those of the Latin Americans.

The British government successfully wrested from the Latin Americans agreements and treaties favorable to its merchants, traders, and bankers. Brazil's experience was classic. The new empire provided the English merchants and manufacturers with their most lucrative Latin American market. Exports to Brazil in 1825 equaled those sold to the rest of South America and Mexico combined and totaled half those sent to the United States. Naturally the British wanted to keep their Brazilian market. In exchange for arranging Portugal's recognition of Brazilian independence in 1825, London exacted a highly advantageous commercial treaty from Pedro I. It limited the duty placed on English imports to 15 percent and bound Brazil not to concede a lower tariff to any other nation. The treaty thereby assured British manufacturers domination over the Brazilian market and postponed any Brazilian efforts to industrialize.

Captivated by foreign political ideologies that bore little relevance to local conditions, the Latin American elite also showed a penchant for economic doctrines more suitable to an industrializing Europe than to an underdeveloped New World. Adam Smith mesmerized many Latin American intellectuals who embraced free trade as a solution to their nations' economic problems. In the words of Mexico's *El Observador* in 1830, the country needed "absolute and general freedom of commerce" to promote prosperity. In reaction to the former mercantilism they had deplored, the Latin Americans adopted policies of economic liberalism that they associated with the triumph of the Enlightenment but that bore no relation to the requirements of Latin America. Consistently modest tariffs deprived the new governments of sorely needed incomes and facilitated the flood of European manufactured articles inundating the New World, to the detriment of local industrialization. Mexico, for example, opened its ports in 1821 to all foreign goods at a uniform tariff of 25 percent ad valorem. Artisan manufacturing immediately declined. A petition to the national government in 1822 from Guadalajara for protection blamed the liberal tariff for putting 2,000 artisans in that city alone out of work.

Latin America's early economic woes cannot be blamed exclusively on the flirtations of the intellectuals with European ideologies. The destruction wrought by the wars for independence in many parts of the hemisphere and unsettled conditions during the early decades of the national period inhibited economic growth. The chronic political instability so characteristic of most of the new countries did not provide the proper climate for development. Politics rather than economics absorbed most of the attention and energy of the new nations. At the same time the quality of public administration deteriorated. Many trained public administrators departed with the defeated Spanish armies or returned to Lisbon with John's court. Recruitment seldom was based on talent; rather, positions in the civil service came as a political reward, and the frequent changes of government hindered the training of a new professional civil service. The national treasuries lay bare. Public financing was precarious and the fiscal irresponsibility of the governments notorious.

Legal changes in the labor system further disturbed the precarious Latin American economies. The governments abolished Indian tribute (in theory, if not always in practice) and slowly freed the blacks. Central America and Chile ended slavery in 1823; Bolivia, in 1826; Mexico, 1829; Uruguay, 1830; Colombia, 1851; Ecuador and Argentina, 1853; and Peru and Venezuela, 1854. Brazil forbade further importation of African slaves after 1850. As usual, however, the resourceful landowners found a variety of ways of observing the letter of the law while changing but slightly the patterns of labor employment. They perfected systems of apprenticeship and debt peonage to that end.

Labor in many regions was in short supply. Since the greatest profits came from the export sector, the workers were often shifted to producing exportable crops leaving an inadequate force to grow the subsistence crops. Labor allocations tended to reinforce the patterns of Latin America's deepening dependency. Furthermore, peasants were expected not only to grow and market cheap food products but also to sell their labor—cheaply—to local landowners, particularly during periods of maximum labor demand such as planting and harvesting. That double exploitation enriched the rural elite, while leaving the peasants as poor as ever.

Mining and manufacturing suffered the most during the decades after independence. With some mines flooded and machinery destroyed during the fighting, the labor system in flux, and investments lacking, the production of the once-fabled mines plummeted. The decline continued steadily in Mexico and Peru until midcentury. The Bolivian mines did not revive until around 1875. Industry fared no better. The availability of cheap European manufactured goods reversed the industrial advances made during the final decades of Iberian rule, decimated the handicraft industries, and put local artisans out of work.

After the initial shock and decline, agriculture recovered and improved. The markets of Europe and the United States readily absorbed many of the agrarian products and some of the natural wealth of Latin America, and their sale provided the basis for any prosperity in the decades before 1850. At midcentury, the overwhelming majority of Latin Americans lived in the countryside. Fully 90 percent of Mexico's 8 million inhabitants, for example, were rural. Social indicators for that population were dismal but not unusual: literacy reached only 10 percent, life expectancy barely 24 years.

The large estates survived intact the turmoil of the independence period. In fact, many multiplied in size during those turbulent years. In northern Mexico, the Sánchez Navarro family, by a combination of astute business practices and shrewd political maneuvering, managed to preserve everything it had amassed during the colonial period. The power base the family chiefs had built in the state of Coahuila enabled them to expand significantly during the early decades of Mexican independence. Their landholdings reached a maximum between 1840 and 1848, consisting of seventeen haciendas that encompassed more than 16 million acres, the largest latifundio ever to have existed in Mexico. In Argentina, the Anchorena family, wealthy merchants in Buenos Aires, began to invest in ranches in 1818. Four decades later, they boasted of being the largest landowners in the country with 1.6 million prime, amply watered acres. Indeed, the times proved to be exceptionally propitious for the landlords to extend their holdings. The governments put the lands of the Church, Indian communities, and public domain on the market. The hacendados and fazendiros grabbed them, accelerating land concentration in the hands of the few. By 1830 in Argentina, approximately 21 million acres of public land had been acquired by 500 individuals. The elites acquired land at a rapid pace, but, while denying it to those eager to work it, they failed to exploit it efficiently.

In the national period, as in the colonial past, land retained its primary importance as the principal source of wealth, prestige, and power. The landed gentry immediately took control of the new governments. The chiefs of state owned large agricultural estates and/or were intimately connected with the landowning class. Representatives of that privileged class filled the legislatures. As far as that goes, the voting requirements of property ownership and/or literacy almost restricted the franchise to that class.

The courts represented them—from the ranks of the elite came the lawyers and judges—and invariably decided cases in their favor. Not surprisingly then, the governments acquiesced in the extension and perfection of debt peonage to ensure an adequate and docile labor force for the expanding estates. The restraints a distant king once had imposed on the landed aristocracy existed no longer. That aristocracy, after independence, ruled for its own benefit, disregarding the larger and more fundamental well-being of the nation as a whole.

The rapid consolidation of such large but often inefficient estates raised serious social and economic questions, which were occasionally addressed although more often ignored. In Mexico shortly after independence, Francisco Severo Maldonado, for one, warned that national prosperity required widespread land ownership. He advocated the establishment of a bank to buy land from those who owned large, unused parcels and to sell it "at the lowest possible price" to those without land. A serious observer of Brazil's economy, Sebastião Ferreira Soares, concluded in 1860 that if Brazil's economy were to develop, it would require that uncultivated land be put in the hands of people who would work it. An editorial in the Buenos Aires newspaper *El Río de la Plata*, September 1, 1869, lamented, "The huge fortunes have the unfortunate tendency to grow even larger, and their owners possess vast tracts of land which lie fallow and abandoned. Their greed for land does not equal their ability to use it intelligently or actively."

One inevitable result of agrarian mismanagement was the increase in the price of basic foodstuffs. In 1856, the leading newspaper of Brazil's vast Northeast, *Diário de Pernambuco*, sharply condemned large landholdings as a barrier to development. Their owners withheld land from use and/or cultivated the land inefficiently, resulting in scarce and expensive foodstuffs. Better use of the land, the newspaper editorialized, would provide more and cheaper food for local markets as well as more exports. At the same time in the southern province of Rio de Janiero, a region undergoing a boom in coffee production for export, Ferreira Soares came to similar conclusions about the distortion of the economy through land misuse and export orientation. He observed with alarm the rapid extension of the export sector accompanied by declining production of food for internal consumption, a trend he documented with convincing statistical evidence. He noted that foods that had been exported from Rio de Janeiro as late as 1850 were being imported a decade later. Prices of basic foodstuffs—beans, corn, flour—rose accordingly. By withholding most of their acreage from cultivation, the large landowners caused the spiraling costs of foodstuffs, deprived the rural inhabitants of steady employment, and consequently encouraged the unemployed or underemployed to migrate to the cities where no jobs awaited them. While the elite few became wealthy from coffee exports, the majority suffered loss of land and employment, and much resultant misery. In short, the emphasis on export crops abused the land to the detriment of Brazil's majority.

In order to better understand the Latin American economy, it is worthwhile to examine the large estate and something of its operation. The landlord was a patriarch chief who ruled family, servants, slaves, tenant farmers, sharecroppers, peasants, and even neighbors—unless they were large estate owners like himself—with absolute authority. The vastness of the estate, its isolation from the seat of government, the relative weakness of local bureaucrats, and the propensity of the government to side with the landed class all strengthened the landlord's power. Furthermore, the estate chaplain and local parish priest orbited around him like satellites, lending the prestige of the Catholic Church to augment his authority. From the comfort and security of his house, because naturally the "big house" was the focal point of the estate's activity, the patriarch administered his holdings, listened to petitions from his subordinates, dispensed justice, and in general held court. These large, strong, and sometimes well-furnished houses sat in the midst of barns, stables, carriage houses, warehouses, workshops, granaries, sheds, and a chapel. In the lowland plantations the slave quarters stood nearby; in the highlands the Indian peons lived in small villages on the estate. The estate contained fields for growing the commercial crop as well as food for the residents, orchards, pastures for pack animals, cattle, and sheep, and forests for firewood. Still, only a fraction of the extensive estates was put to use. As far as possible, the estates were self-contained. The patriarch and part of his family visited the nearest town and the nation's capital from time to time to purchase from the outside world a few luxury items for themselves and to savor the conviviality and pleasures of urban life. The wealthiest landlords maintained city homes. Often they or a member of their families served in the local municipal government.

Foreign visitors to Latin America in the nineteenth century have left us vivid accounts of the large estates. After having been a guest in numerous Mexican country homes in the early 1840s, Frances Calderón de la Barca generalized:

> As for the interior of these haciendas, they are all pretty much alike, so far as we have seen; a great stone building, which is neither farm nor countryhouse (according to our notions), but has a character peculiar to itself—solid enough to stand a siege, with floors of painted brick, large deal tables, wooden benches, painted chairs, and whitewashed walls; one or two painted or iron bedsteads, only put up when wanted; numberless empty rooms; kitchen and outhouses; the courtyard a great square, round which stand the house for boiling sugar, whose furnaces blaze day and night; the house, with machinery for extracting the juice from the cane, the refining rooms, the places where it is dried, etc., all on a large scale. If the hacienda is, as here, a coffee plantation also, then there is a great mill for separating the beans from the chaff, and sometimes also there are buildings where they make brandy. Here there are 400 men employed exclusive of boys, 100 horses, and a number of mules. The

property is generally very extensive, containing the fields of sugar cane, plains for the cattle, and the pretty plantations of coffee, so green and spring-like, this one containing upwards of 50,000 young plants, all fresh and vigorous, besides a great deal of uncultivated ground, abandoned to the deer and hares and quails, of which there are great abundance.

Included in her visits was one hacienda the awed woman described as "princely." "This beautiful hacienda . . . is 30 leagues in length and 17 in width [roughly 1,800 square miles]—containing in this great space the productions of every climate, from the fir-clad mountains on a level with the volcano of Toluca, to the fertile plains which produce corn and maize; and lower down to fields of sugar cane and other productions of the tropics."

Huge plantations dominated the Brazilian countryside as well. To all appearances, the fazendas remained the same in structure and operation as they had for hundreds of years. One observant traveler, Daniel F. Kidder, visited a fazenda at Jaraguá in the interior of São Paulo at midcentury. The estate belonged to an enterprising woman who resided most of the year in the city of São Paulo. The variety of the products grown on the fazenda impressed Kidder: sugar cane, manioc, cotton, rice and coffee. He left this description of part of it:

Around the farm-house as a centre, were situated numerous out-houses, such as quarters for negroes, store-houses for staple vegetables, and fixtures for reducing them to marketable form.

The engenho de cachassa was an establishment where the juices of the sugar-cane were expressed for distillation. On most of the sugar estates there exist distilleries, which convert the treacle drained from the sugar into a species of alcohol called cachassa. . . . The apparatus for grinding the cane was rude and clumsy in its construction, and not dissimilar to the corresponding portion of a cider-mill in the United States. It was turned by four oxen.

He then went on to describe the customs of the plantation houses and of his hosts:

Our social entertainments at Jaraguá were of no ordinary grade. Any person looking in upon the throng of human beings that filled the house when we were all gathered together, would have been at a loss to appreciate the force of a common remark of Brazilians respecting their country, viz that its greatest misfortune is a want of population. Leaving travelers and naturalists out of the question, and also the swarm of servants, waiters, and children—each of whom, whether white, black, or mulatto, seemed emulous of making a due share of noise—there were present half a dozen ladies, relatives of the Donna, who had come up from the city to enjoy the occasion. Among the gentlemen were three sons of the Donna, her son-in-law, a doctor of laws, and her chaplain, who was also a professor in the law university, and a doctor in theology. With such an interesting company the time alloted to our stay could hardly fail to be agreeably spent. . . . It is a pleasure to say, that I observed none of that seclusion and excessive restraint which some writers have set down as characteristic of Brazilian females. True, the younger members of the company seldom ventured beyond the utterance of Sim Senhor, Não Senhor, and the like; but ample amends for their bashfulness were made by the extreme sociability of Donna Gertrudes. She voluntarily detailed to me an account of her vast business concerns, showed me in person her agricultural and mineral treasures, and seemed to take the greatest satisfaction in imparting the results of her experience on all subjects.

The ownership and management of estates by women was probably not all that uncommon. Carl Scherzer encountered a female rancher in mid-nineteenth century Nicaragua: "I met with an elderly lady, the owner of an estate in Segovia, who had been to Granada with a large quantity of [hides] for sale, and was now returning with a heavy purse and twenty-one beasts lightened of their burden."

The elite tended to romanticize the large estate, one useful means of enhancing their ideology. No one better idealized the mid-nineteenth century hacienda than Jorge Isaacs in his highly acclaimed novel *Maria* (1867). The author provided a wealth of detail about a patriarchal estate in the Cauca Valley of Columbia, from which emerged his concept of the exemplary hacienda. Orderly, hierarchical, harmonious, the novel's well-run estate centered on the comfortable "big house" and patriarchal authority, which extended from the devoted slaves to the doting family. "Father" always knew best in that patrilineal setting. The novel's extreme popularity arose mainly from the ideal but tragic romance it depicted, although it must also have come from its appealing portrait of the idyllic country life where people and nature intertwined, where social roles were well defined and unquestionably accepted, where the values of human relationships took precedence over business and ambition, and where alienation apparently was unknown. Such patriarchal estates symbolized the model society to many Latin American writers, who frequently used them as backdrops for their stories. This vision complemented a system that doubtless seemed less perfect to the *campesinos* than it did to the elites.

CAUDILLOS

The violence, tension, and economic uncertainties during and after the struggles for independence gave rise to a peculiar political reality: the rule of the *caudillo*, or strong leader. The caudillos were an assorted lot. Some were popinjays who sported splendiferous uniforms and adopted sonorous titles; others lived ascetic lives, hidden from public view and attired in somber suits. All radiated mystique and charisma.

Two major groups of caudillos emerged in the nineteenth century. Both responded to Latin America's search for leadership in the political vacuum left by independence. The larger of the two groups faithfully represented the elites and thus at least paid lip service to the ideology of progress. This group receives considerable attention and frequent praise in Latin American historiography. The smaller group championed the needs of the popular majorities and hence were "popular" or "folk" caudillos.

Advocating a selective Europeanization while cautious not to disturb well-established institutions, the first group enjoyed the support of the elites. In truth, these caudillos offered a continuation of the patterns of the past: large landed estates, debt-labor systems, export-oriented economies, and highly centralized political power. Since all power, all authority emanated from the caudillo, he played, in short, the role of the "king." In practice, however, he exercised more control over his "subjects" than the Spanish monarchs ever dared to. The caudillos shared power with no one. As one remarked, "I neither want nor like ministers who think. I want only ministers who can write, because the only one who can think am I, and the only one who does think am I." Neither convictions nor principles necessarily guided the caudillo. He favored expediency, an ideological irresponsibility in which his will and whim were supreme. To rule, the caudillo employed force with impunity. Nor did his measures stop with imprisonment, confiscation, or exile. He could and did impose the death penalty as he saw fit. The general lack of restraints on his power permitted him to tax and spend as he pleased, a situation conducive to financial abuse, if not outright dishonesty.

To balance the picture, it should be noted that many of the "elite" caudillos bestowed some benefits on the nations they governed. Those disturbed by the chaos, or anarchy, of the early decades of independence, welcomed the order and stability characteristic of *caudillismo.* The early caudillos unified some of the nations, and there can be no doubt that their great strength in several notable cases prevented a national disintegration. Later caudillos liked to cast themselves as modernizers and in that role bequeathed material improvements to the nations they governed. They built roads and imposing government buildings, lay railroad tracks, strung telegraph wires, and renovated ports. They even built schools with the intention of propagating their own virtues in them. Their favorite project was to rebuild the centers of the capital cities in accord with the latest European architectural dictates, an outward manifestation of modernization that brought great satisfaction to the elites, who could thus fancy their nations as thoroughly up to date.

Although the caudillos did not have to concern themselves with public opinion—for all intents and purposes it did not exist—they did seek the support of at least three groups, individually or in combination, to buttress their personal power: the rural aristocracy, the Roman Catholic Church, and the army. The early caudillos were more often than not members of or related to the rural landowning class, men notable for their desire to preserve their class's prestige, wealth, and power and for their opposition to land reform, extension of the suffrage, and popular government. The caudillos usually represented their interests. Despite the fact that they ruled from the capital cities (although they might spend long periods of time on their estates), they tended to suppress the influence of the more liberal urban elements. The Church as an institution was a conservative force suspicious of reforms and usually in open conflict with the liberals. Church leaders—with a few notable exceptions—rallied to endorse any caudillo who respected and protected Church interests and property.

The army, the only truly national institution, immediately emerged as a political force. Its strength revealed the weakness of the political institutions. In many countries it was the dominant political force and has so remained. Since few of the republics developed satisfactory means to select or alter governments, palace coups—in which the military always had a role—became the customary means to effect political shifts. The military then exercised the dual role of guaranteeing order on one hand and changing governments on the other. No caudillo or president would willfully alienate the military. Consequently officers enjoyed generous salaries and rapid promotions. The Latin American armies became and have remained top-heavy with brass. Thus, armies not only retarded the growth of democracy through their political meddling but also slowed down economic growth by absorbing a lion's share of the national budgets. They spent the capital needed for investment. On the average, prior to 1850, the military received over 50 percent of the national budgets. Mexico provides one of the most shocking examples: between 1821 and 1845 the military budget exceeded the total income of the government on fourteen occasions. Caudillos often arose from the ranks of the army; thus they understood and commanded the major institution for maintaining order and power. Chile was the first—and for a long time the only—Spanish-speaking nation to restrict the army to its proper role of defending the nation from foreign attack. After 1831 and until the civil war of 1891, the army kept out of Chilean politics. Few other nations could boast of a similarly well-behaved military.

Another and perhaps more complex group of caudillos also emerged. While they shared some of the characteristics of the first group, two major distinctions marked them as unique. They refused to accept unconditionally the elites' ideology of progress, exhibiting a preference for the American experience with its Indo-Afro-Iberian ingredients and consequently greater suspicion of the post-Enlightenment European model. Further, they served the folk rather than the elite.

The folk expected their leader to represent and strengthen their unity, express their soul, personify their values, and increase their harmony; in short, to be as one with the people he led. Their caudillo recognized and understood the folk's distinctive way of life and acted in harmony with it. In the eyes of the people, he inculcated the local, regional, or national values—traditional values—with which most of the people felt comfortable. He was a natural, charismatic leader of the majority, who found in him an adviser, a guide, a protector, a patriarch in whom they entrusted their interests. They surrendered power to him; he incarnated authority. The fusion of leader and people had to be nearly perfect (that is, perceived by those involved as nearly perfect), and when such an interplay existed both people and leader sensed, valued, and honored their interdependency. In his discussion of leadership and folk, José Carlos Mariátegui, ascribed to the leader the roles of "interpreter and trustee." Mariátegui concluded, "His policy is no longer determined by his personal judgment but by a group of collective interests and requirements." The leader seemingly arose from and blended with his physical and human environment. Thus identified with America, he contrasted sharply with the Europeanized leaders imposed by the elites.

Juan Bautista Alberdi, probably more than anyone else in the nineteenth century, studied the psychology of the relationship of popular caudillos with the masses, and he concluded that the people regarded a popular caudillo as "guardian of their traditions," the defender of their way of life. He insisted that such leaders constituted "the will of the popular masses . . . the immediate organ and arm of the people . . . the caudillos are democracy." He reiterated frequently in his writing the equation of the popular caudillo with democracy. If the folk obeyed unreservedly those popular leaders, the caudillos in turn bore the obligation to protect and to provide for the welfare of the people. The ruled and ruler were responsible to and for each other, a personal relationship challenged in the nineteenth century by the more impersonal capitalist concept that a growing gross national product would best provide for all. The popularity of those caudillos is undeniable. Their governments rested on a base of folk culture, drew support and inspiration from the folk, and expressed, however vaguely, their style. Under the leadership of such caudillos, the masses apparently felt far more identification with government than they ever did under the imported political solutions advocated by the intellectuals and the elite. On many occasions the folk displayed support of their caudillos by fighting tenaciously to protect them from the Europeanized elites and/or foreign invaders.

Few in number at the national level, the folk or populist caudillos had disappeared by 1870. Still, an introduction to them will remind us of a significant political current within Latin America's first half-century of independence.

Dr. Francia (discussed in Chapter 3), the early *Dictador* of Paraguay's autonomous revolution, undoubtedly ranked as the first and perhaps the foremost of the populist caudillos. His death in 1840 did not end Paraguay's experiment. His two successors, Antonio Carlos López (1840–63) and Francisco Solano López (1863–70), father and son, extended the folk

government for three more decades. Honoring the policies of their predecessor, the Lópezes constructed a modern steamship navy, railroad, a telegraph network, and Latin America's first iron foundary, all without incur-
ring one cent of foreign debt and all to serve Paraguay's own internal
needs.

Alarmed by Paraguay's national development, which comparatively
outstripped the growth of its neighbors and thereby—to them—threatened
the balance of power in the Río de la Plata, Brazil, Argentina, and their
puppet-state Uruguay joined forces in the War of the Triple Alliance
against Paraguay (1865–70). Financed in part by English loans, the allies
waged a war that resulted in the eradication—some have claimed the
genocide—of Paraguay's male population, killing a high percentage of the
males between the ages of fourteen and sixty-five. During the five years of
occupation following the war, the popular institutions of Paraguay's autonomous revolution were dismantled. It was opened to foreign capital and
reshaped in the standard mold of nineteenth-century Latin American institutions. One foreign observer noted that absentee landlords grabbed most
of the land so that "no campesino could till the soil of his own country
without paying rent to the bankers of London, New York, or Amsterdam."
Ironically, the distant *Manchester Guardian*, a newspaper that not infrequently voiced the views of expansionist capitalism, pronounced a fitting
eulogy for autonomous Paraguay. Destroying "a remarkable system of government," the allies, the newspaper concluded, had "overturned the only
South American state wherein the native Indian race showed any present
likelihood of attaining or recovering such strengths or organization as to fit
it for the task of government."

Jean-Pierre Boyer's rule (1818–43), the longest in Haitian history,
merits further study as a populist government. During those decades, Haiti
remained isolated from the world, meaning few foreign merchants, bank
loans, or investments impinged on national life, although the island constantly feared European intervention and suffered financially from a crush-
ing indemnity France had imposed on its former colony. Haitian nationality grew increasingly distinct. A unique language, a *patois* composed of
European and African languages, dominated; a singular religion, the syncretism of Roman Catholicism and African religions often termed voodoo,
pervaded the population. Boyer accelerated his predecessor Alexandre
Pétion's policy of distributing land in small plots, thus creating a peasant
class. Agricultural production diversified; the people seemed to be satisfactorily nourished; they certainly enjoyed their freedom from the demands
of an export economy. Most outsiders judged the island harshly. They
decried the absence of European influence, a situation they inevitably characterized as "a return to barbarism." Yet, they overlooked the leisure, freedom, access to land, sufficient food supply, and expression of a unique
culture that characterized the lives of the half-million Haitians.

Another already mentioned folk caudillo, Juan Manuel de Rosas, enjoyed the support of the Argentine gauchos from 1829 until his exile in 1852. He appeared in Argentine history at the exact moment that Argentina, submerged in anarchy, threatened to split apart. The old viceroyalty of La Plata had disintegrated in the early nineteenth century and Argentina itself dissolved into squabbling regions. Sharpest was the rivalry between Buenos Aires, the port and province growing prosperous through trade with Europe, and the interior provinces, impoverished and wracked by civil wars.

Buenos Aires advocated a centralized government—which it fully expected to dominate—while the interior provinces favored a federalized one that would prevent the hegemony of the port. The bitter struggle between Buenos Aires and the interior delayed Argentine unification until Rosas strode onto the political stage. He had lived and worked in *gaucho* country before being elected governor of Buenos Aires in 1829, and he judiciously pursued the federalist idea of a pastoral economy, based on the simple premise that whatever complemented the life of the interior's cattle-herding people benefited society. Understandably, the cattle breeders and the hide and meat producers supported Rosas because his economic inclinations favored them. In his full exercise of political control, however, the caudillo acted as a centralist. Suspicious of Europe, he defied on occasion both England and France, deflecting their economic penetration of Argentina. The Argentine masses were convinced that he had their interests at heart and governed for their benefit. It would appear that the gauchos enjoyed an access to land, freedom of movement, greater economic alternatives, and better living conditions during the Rosas period than at any time afterward. To stimulate occupation of the land, Rosas initiated in 1840 a program to distribute land to soldiers. Such policies contrast sharply with the trends of the last half and particularly the last quarter of the century, when quality of life for the common majority declined sharply. The masses demonstrated their identification with and loyalty to Rosas by their willingness to fight for him for nearly a quarter of a century. Their caudillo suffered defeat and exile only when the elites enlisted the Brazilian and Uruguayan armies to unite with them to overthrow him. Defeated at the Battle of Monte Caseros, Rosas left Argentina for a European exile. The fall of Rosas in 1852 opened the door to the promulgation of a liberal constitution, the growth of capitalism, a flurry of land speculation, and the commercial expansion of the cattle industry on an unprecedented scale. Argentina merged with the capitalist world and intensified its dependency in the process.

A fourth example of the caudillos who preferred local models to imported ones is Rafael Carrera who governed Guatemala from 1839 until his death in 1865. At least half Indian, Carrera negated many of the Enlightenment reforms applied by previous liberal governments and ruled at least in part for the benefit of the Indians—the vast majority of the Guatemalans. The elites regarded him as a barbarian; the Indians exalted him as their savior. Since it is the elites who have written Guatemalan history, Carrera emerges from their treatment as a "menace" to Guatemala's "progress."

Carrera led the Indian revolt of 1838–39. Among the many changes that popular rebellion signified was the refusal of the Indians to countenance any further exploitation and destruction through Europeanization. They wished to be left alone by the elites of Guatemala City so that they could live unmolested according to the dictates of their own culture. They rejected Europeanizing education, culture, economy, and laws that would integrate them into a capitalist economy centered in Europe. They chose instead to withdraw, to isolate themselves; and withdrawal was, and remains, a common reaction of the Indians to the Europeans. But, in regions where the elites depended on those Indians for labor and taxes, withdrawal signified rebellion. Carrera understood the Indian position, he sympathized with their desires, and he rose to power on their strength.

During the generation in which Rafael Carrera dominated Guatemala, he respected the native cultures, protected the Indians insofar as that was possible, and sought to incorporate them into his government. His modest successes in those efforts assume greater significance when compared to the disastrous conditions suffered by the Indian majority during the decades of liberal, Europeanized governments that preceded and followed the Carrera period. That popular caudillo, totally unschooled in foreign theories, was a practical man who knew Guatemala and its peoples well. He had traveled and lived in many parts of the nation, always among the humble folk whom he understood. He learned from and drew upon his Guatemalan experiences—a marked contrast to the elites seduced by European experiences and theories. Carrera appreciated the Indians' opposition to the Europeanization process imposed by the liberals. He regarded it as his principal duty to allow "the people to return to their customs, their habits, and their particular manner of living." The government, he affirmed, had the obligation of representing the majority of the people and of offering "a living example of virtue, equity, prudence, and justice." Those principles seem to have guided much of his long administration.

While Carrera repudiated the radical ideas of the liberals, he never rejected change. He believed it must come slowly and within the particular social context, a change acceptable to the people and not forced on them. Gradually historians have come to credit his government with respecting Indian customs and protecting rural Indians. The president held that the art of governing well sprang from the "formation of a government of the people and for the people." Accordingly, the government officially abandoned the liberals' goal to incorporate the Indians into Western civilization. One even could argue that under Carrera the government was "Indianized." Indians and particularly mestizos, all of relatively humble classes, participated directly in the government, holding, in addition to the presidency of course, such exalted offices as the vice-presidency, the heads of ministries, governorships, and high military ranks. The army became nearly an Indian institution. The Carrera government was unique to Latin America for encouraging the political ascendency of the once-conquered race. Significantly the "white" political monopoly was broken, and never again could the minute white aristocracy govern Guatemala alone.

To lift some of the economic burden from the impoverished majority, President Carrera reduced taxes on foodstuffs and abolished the head tax. Further, he excused the Indians from contributing to the loans the government levied from time to time to meet fiscal emergencies. By removing many of the taxes on the Indians, which were paid in the official currency circulating in Europeanized Guatemala, the government lessened the need for the indigenous population to enter the monetary economy, thus reducing the pressure on them to work on the estates. The Indians, then, could devote that time and energy to their own agricultural and community needs.

Of all the efforts made on behalf of the Indians none surpassed those affecting the protection of Indian lands, the return of land to Indian communities, and the settlement of land disputes in their favor. The government declared in 1845 that all who worked unclaimed lands should receive them. What was even more unusual, it enforced the decree. It was decided in 1848 and again in the following year that all pueblos without ejidos were to be granted them without cost, and, if population exceeded available lands, then lands elsewhere were to be made available to any persons who voluntarily decided to move to take advantage of them. In 1851, Carrera decreed that "the Indians are not to be dispossesed of their communal lands on any pretext of selling them," a decree strengthened a few months later by prohibiting the divestment of any pueblos of their lands for any reason. Carrera thus spoke forcefully and effectively to the most pressing problem of Latin America: the overconcentration of land in the hands of the elite and the need for the rural masses to have land to cultivate. Those decades witnessed increasing agrarian diversification, an escape from the monoculture that had characterized agriculture for so long. The intent was not so much to increase exports as to insure a plentiful supply of food in the marketplace at prices the people could afford. From the evidence at hand it would seem that the quality of life for the Indian majority improved during the Carrera years. The characteristics marking the Carrera experience as unique in Indo-America are the respect the government extended to Indian cultures and the reluctance to push the Indian population into Europeanizing themselves.

The Indian victory under Carrera proved to be as transitory as the gauchos' under Rosas. The death of Carrera in 1865 reinvigorated the elites' effort to wield power, and they succeeded under the leadership of another and different type of caudillo, Justo Rufino Barrios (1873–85). Positivist in orientation, President Barrios duly emphasized order and material progress. Under the liberal reforms of the Barrios period, capitalism made its definitive entry into Guatemala, which meant large-scale exportation of coffee with all the attendant consequences for that agrarian economy. The government rushed to import foreign technicians, ideas, and manufactured goods. It did not hesitate to contract foreign loans to pay for the Europeanization. The improvement of roads from the highland plantations to the ports and then the construction of the much-desired railroads first to the Pacific and later to the Atlantic accelerated coffee production and integrated Guatemala into the world market system more closely than ever.

Spiraling coffee production for export had several long-range, negative consequences. For one thing, it diminished the amount of land, labor, and capital available to produce food for local consumption. Wheat harvests especially declined. Monoculture again became a dominant characteristic of the economy. To create the necessary work force on the coffee *fincas,* the Indians were forced, under a burdensome system called *mandamientos* (not dissimilar to the old *repartimientos*), to become wage laborers. Meanwhile the government did not hesitate to concede to private landowners many lands on which the Indians had lived and worked for generations. By a variety of means, the large estates encroached on the Indians' communal lands. As a consequence the economic and social position of the Indian majority declined.

During the period Carrera governed Guatemala, Bolivia, another overwhelmingly Indian country, witnessed the singular leadership of its own popular caudillo, Manuel Belzu. He played an extremely complex role combining the forces of populism, nationalism, and revolution in ways that would not be used again in Latin America for over half a century. He built an effective power base of campesino and urban-artisan support, which brought him to the presidency in 1848 and sustained him until he peacefully left the presidential palace in 1855. As dispossessed and impoverished as their counterparts throughout Latin America, the artisans and campesinos rallied to Belzu probably because his novel rhetoric spoke directly to their needs and certainly because of a series of wildly popular actions he took. He encouraged the organization of the first modest labor unions, ended some free-trade practices, terminated some odious monopolies, abolished slavery, permitted the landless Indians to take over lands they worked for the latifundista elite, and praised the Indian past. Often vague, frequently unsuccessful, his varied programs nonetheless won popular support. To his credit, Belzu seemed to have understood the basic problems bedeviling Bolivia: foreign penetration and manipulation of the economy and the alienation of the Indians' land.

Under the intriguing title "To Civilize Oneself in Order to Die of Hunger," a series of articles in a weekly La Paz newspaper in 1852 highlighted a vigorous campaign denouncing free trade and favoring protectionism. The paper argued that free trade deprived Bolivian workers of jobs while enriching foreigners and importers. It advocated "protectionism" as a means to promote local industry and thereby to benefit the working class, goals that had the obvious support of the president. Indeed, free trade bore some responsibility for the nation's poor agricultural performance. A chronic imbalance of trade between 1825 and 1846 had cost Bolivia nearly $15 million pesos, much of which was spent to import food the country was perfectly capable of producing. La Paz, for example, imported beef, mutton, and potatoes, among other foods. The local producers might deserve protection from cheaper imports, but protective tariffs alone would not necessarily raise the efficiency of the notoriously inefficient latifundios.

Although taking no legal steps to reform the land structures, Belzu never opposed the Indian occupation of their former community lands. Landlords, fearful of the restive Indian masses, found it prudent to move to the safer confines of the cities, thus abandoning their estates, which the Indians promptly occupied. Two major consequences of the de facto land reforms were the greater supplies of food entering the marketplaces and the drop in food prices. Belzu further delighted the campesinos by relieving them of some taxes.

If rhetoric were the measure of government, Belzu's administration stood as revolutionary. These examples from his public speeches serve as a yardstick:

> Comrades, an insensitive throng of aristocrats has become arbiter of your wealth and your destiny; they exploit you ceaselessly and you do not observe it; they cheat you constantly and you don't sense it; they accumulate huge fortunes with your labor and blood and you are unaware of it. They divide the land, honors, jobs and privileges among themselves, leaving you only with misery, disgrace, and work, and you keep quiet. How long will you sleep? Wake up once and for all! The time has come to ask the aristocrats to show their titles and to investigate the basis for private property. Aren't you equal to other Bolivians? Aren't all people equal? Why do only a few enjoy the conditions of intellectual, moral and material development and not all of you?
>
> * * *
>
> Companions, private property is the principal source of most offenses and crimes in Bolivia; it is the cause of the permanent struggle among Bolivians; it is the basis of our present selfishness eternally condemned by universal morals. No more property! No more property owners! No more inheritances! Down with the aristocrats! Land for everyone; enough of the exploitation of man. . . . Aren't you also Bolivians? Haven't you been born to equality in this privileged land?

For the great mass of dispossessed campesinos, Belzu's heady words did not fall on idle ears. Some seized the estates. Where the landlords resisted, the followers of Belzu attacked and defeated them.

The identification of the folk with President Belzu and vice versa established the harmony and integration between caudillo and people that conferred sweeping power on the former. The president cultivated that identification. From the balcony of the presidential palace, Belzu assured his listeners, "I am one of you, poor and humble, a disinherited son of the people. For that reason, the aristocrats and the rich hate me and are ashamed to be under my authority." The president frequently reminded his followers that all power originated in the people who had conferred it on him. He simply acted on behalf of the people and their interests. Belzu correctly claimed that new elements of order and stability supported his government: "The popular masses have made themselves heard and played their role spontaneously; they have put down rebellions and fought for the constitutional government. The rise to power of this formidable force is a social reality of undeniable transcendence."

In the last analysis, Belzu was too Europeanized to feel comfortable for long as a folk caudillo, for he insisted on codifying his government within the confines of a Europeanized constitution. His political reforms and Constitution of 1851 reduced the presidential term to a specific period and prohibited reelection. Elections in 1855, classified by one Bolivian historian as "the cleanest ever held," brought a constitutional end to the Belzu presidency, awarding the office to the president's preferred candidate, but a man unequal to the tumultuous task. In August of 1855, at the height of his power, Belzu stepped down—unwilling to follow the well-established precedent of *continuismo*—turned over the presidency to his elected successor, and temporarily left Bolivia. To the Indian masses he remained their "tata Belzu," friend and protector, whose short, unique government had benefited them.

The Indians had every reason to be apprehensive of the electoral process in which they had played no role. With Belzu in Europe, the old elites quickly seized power. At the same time, they took possession of their former lands and returned the campesinos to subservience. In the years that followed, the Indians often revolted with cries of "Viva Belzu!" on their lips, but as the elites became increasingly integrated into international trade and consequently strengthened, they were not about to repeat the previous political errors that had permitted a popular caudillo to govern. When, for example, the Huaichu Indians of Lake Titicaca rebelled in 1869 to regain communal lands, President Mariano Melgarejo dispatched the army to massacre them.

The populist caudillos constitute an intriguing if seldom-studied chapter in nineteenth-century Latin American history. They appeared and disappeared within a sixty-year period. Yet, in 1850, four caudillos ruled at the same time: Carrera, Belzu, López, and Rosas. Three of those nations had large Indian populations with well-defined cultures, while the Argentine gauchos boasted an equally well-defined folk culture. The popular caudillos identified with the majority and vice versa. In all cases (Haiti under Boyer included) foreign investments were comparatively low or practically nonexistent; the governments and majority expressed strong views against foreigners and shunned foreign influences. At the same time, land became available for the majority and/or pressures on the peasants diminished. Subsistence agriculture dominated export agriculture. More food was available for popular consumption. Although those folk governments obviously appealed to large elements of society that customarily had been neglected, we cannot lose sight of the fact that they were few in number and had disappeared by 1870—or at least those operating on a national scale. The elites succeeded in imposing their will on the folk and on Latin America. Nonetheless, those few folk governments that did arise serve as useful reminders of alternatives to the Europeanized governments that the elites imposed. If, indeed, the people enjoyed a more satisfactory quality of life under the folk caudillos, those governments then suggest possible roads to development that were denegrated and/or ignored after 1870.

The continuity between the thirty years after independence and the colonial period is remarkable. Economic changes were few. Agriculture and the large estate retained their prominence, and the new nations became as subservient to British economic policies as they once had been to those of Spain and Portugal. The wars of independence had shaken and weakened some of the foundation stones of society but the edifice stood pretty much intact. A small, privileged elite ruled over muted although sometimes restless masses. Less than one in ten Latin Americans could read and less than one in twenty earned enough to live in even modest comfort. Land remained the principal source of wealth, prestige, and power, and only a few owned the land.

The continuity, however, was not perfect. Two major political changes marked the early national period. The first and most obvious was the transmission of power from the Iberians to the creole and mazombo elites. Political power no longer emanated from Europe; it had a local source. The second was the emergence of the military in Spanish America as an important political institution destined to play a decisive role in Latin American history. The military were the elite's only guarantee of order and initially they provided prestigious employment for some sons of the rich as well as one means of upward mobility for talented and ambitious plebians. Early in the national period, the liberals challenged the status of the military, thus alienating the officers and driving them into the welcoming embrace of the conservatives. The remarkable early stability of both Brazil and Chile can be explained in part by the close identification and harmony between conservatives and the military.

5

The Emergence
of the
Modern State

Rio de Janiero in the early twentieth century

The many problems faced by the new nations after independence found no easy solution—indeed, no nation yet, after a century and a half of effort, has succeeded in solving all of them. Still, by the mid-nineteenth century it was possible to see that some of the nations, of which Brazil and Chile served as outstanding examples, were moving toward political stability and economic prosperity. Foreign threats had diminished; the republican principle had triumphed everywhere but in Brazil; centralized government had been gradually accepted. Nationalism became a better-defined force as more and more citizens in the various states expressed greater pride in their homeland, appreciated its uniqueness, and sought its progress. Positivist ideology dominated governmental circles and complemented foreign investment and capitalist expansion. Although official histories dwell on political stability and economic prosperity, large numbers of the population questioned, even protested "progress." They felt it marginalized or threatened them. Consequently, beneath a surface of apparent tranquility, currents of protest and violence flowed.

To understand the successes, failures, and challenges of the last half of the nineteenth century, the historian must question the type of economic growth that occurred and who benefited from it.

If political change and instability had marked the first half of the nineteenth century, economic and social innovations as well as political stability characterized the last half. An accelerating prosperity—at least for the favored classes—encouraged material growth and attracted a wave of immigrants, particularly to Argentina, Brazil, and Chile. The combination of stability and prosperity helped to accelerate three trends, industrialization, urbanization, and modernization, which in turn threatened to alter some of the established patterns inherited from the colonial past.

POLITICAL STABILITY

With civil disorder on the wane, the chiefs of state consolidated and extended their authority. They governed supremely with few if any checks from the congresses and the courts, which they customarily dominated. In some cases, they selected their own successors who were assured of impressive electoral victories. Nonetheless, a greater respect for legal forms prevailed, and some caudillos even appeared to be more legally conscious and circumspect than their predecessors. At any rate, they paid more lip service to constitutional formalities and some even showed an occasional indication of heeding the constitution. In somber frock coats, representatives of the elite discussed and debated the political issues of the day. The term "elite" can be hard to define. First, one must recognize that no single elite existed in any of the Latin American nations. Rather, a plurality of elites combined in various ways to dominate each nation. At best, elite is a shorthand expression signifying those in social, economic, and political control. Because of their economic power, wealth, prestige, knowledge of Europe and the ideas originating there, skills, influence, and/or importance, the small but varied elites one way or another exerted authority over a society whose formal institutions were of European inspiration. They made the major decisions affecting the economic and political life of their nations.

The earlier division of political proclivities into conservative and liberal prevailed. Those of liberal suasion often flirted with federalist schemes, maintained a theoretical interest in the rights of man, demanded an end to the Church's temporal powers, embraced laissez-faire economic doctrine, and professed a willingness to experiment with new ideas and methods. The conservatives, on the other hand, lauded centralism, defended a hierarchical society, approved the privileges and prerogatives of the Church, and felt more comfortable with a controlled or regulated economic system. Neither political division expressed any desire to tamper with the major land, labor, and social systems. The latifundia and debt peonage continued. Indeed, in most cases they grew. Nor did either party become seriously concerned with extending the suffrage. Consequently, on many fundamental issues the two major political divisions harmonized rather than diverged. In Brazil, the Visconde de Albuquerque wryly remarked, "There is nothing quite so much like a Conservative as a Liberal in office." More distinctive than party labels were the personalities. The individual, rather than a vague catalog of political ideas, attracted or repelled support. The politician as a man, as a leader, exercised far more strength than the more abstract institution, the party.

In some countries, the formalization of political beliefs into two major divisions did contribute to political stabilization. The parties helped to train young men for politics, and they provided the means for nominating and electing men to office. The contributions of parties to political regularization were very noticeable in Chile and Brazil, two major countries where the landed aristocracy drew together after independence and enforced stability. On the other hand, examples exist in which the division of political beliefs into conservative and liberal created not two debating societies but two war camps. Nicaragua provided the perfect example. The Liberals centered in León, while the Conservatives concentrated in Granada. They fought back and forth throughout the nineteenth century. The victory trophy was the presidency. Colombia furnished a similar example. The tumult encouraged by party strife in Colombia and Nicaragua contrasted vividly with the more tranquil experiences of party politics in Chile and Brazil.

Brazil had enjoyed stability during the First Empire (1822–31); but during the regency established after the abdication of Pedro I, centrifugal forces began tugging at the huge empire. One province after another, from the far north to the far south, rebelled against the government in Rio de Janeiro. To save national unity, the Brazilians proclaimed the young Pedro

II emperor in 1840, four years before he was legally of age to ascend the throne. As expected, the monarchy, the only truly effective national institution in Brazil, provided the ideal instrument to impose unity on the disintegrating nation. Brazil's nearly disastrous experiment with federalism ended when Pedro II reimposed a high degree of centralism on the nation. The Brazilian-born emperor succeeded in restoring order and stability to his badly shaken realm. The last rebellion broke out in 1848. After midcentury, the opposition no longer resorted to violence but relied on constituted and orderly channels to voice disagreement. Before the end of the 1840s Pedro was more than a figurehead; he was tightly controlling the reigns of government. As the constitution prescribed, he functioned on a plane above politics as the grand manipulator of all the instruments of government. He ruled benevolently but firmly. As the years of his reign lengthened, he preferred to exercise power more indirectly, but nonetheless his presence was always felt. During most of his reign, Pedro enjoyed the devotion and respect of his subjects. In manner he was calm, deliberate, and serious, eschewing military uniforms for somber black suits and preferring books and study to the active life of the outdoors. He practiced a morality in both private and public life that few could equal and thereby imposed a Victorian morality on the court and government in an otherwise relaxed nation. In 1847, the emperor created the post of President of the Council of Ministers, and a type of parliamentary system developed. The emperor saw to it that the two political parties, the Liberals and the Conservatives, alternated in power. Guided by the emperor, the parties accepted the give-and-take of politics in a manner rare on the continent.

The fall of a Liberal ministry in 1868 divided the political history of the Second Empire. The Liberals blamed the heavy hand of the emperor for their loss of power, which was in their opinion nothing short of a coup d'état. As a result, the following year the Liberals issued a reform manifesto calling for the abolition of the moderating power, the Council of State (they regarded it as the stronghold of conservatism), the National Guard (they denounced the privileges of the officers), and slavery and favoring the establishment of direct elections, expansion of suffrage, periodical elections for senators for a limited term of office, popular election of provincial presidents, an independent judiciary, more educational institutions, and other reforms. If enacted, their program would have weakened the government in Rio de Janeiro because in effect what the Liberals envisaged was federalization with its consequent decentralization. At the same time, the Federal Republican Party emerged, and in a manifesto issued in December of 1870 it denounced the monarchy and called for a federal republic. By 1870, some major structural reforms—of which the abolition of slavery, the substitution of a republic for a monarchy and federalism for centralism, and the expansion of the political base were the most significant—had been suggested, injecting into politics more substantial issues than was usually the case. Some of these reforms were enacted during the following decades.

The foundations of the monarchy slowly weakened. In the early 1870s, a display of royal anger annoyed many church members. It began when the Bishop of Olinda carried out a papal order, unapproved by the emperor, to expel Masons from the lay brotherhoods of the Roman Catholic Church. Pedro II ordered the bishop to remove the penalty. His refusal to comply challenged the emperor. The government arrested and jailed the churchman along with another bishop, both of whom the royal courts found guilty of disobedience of civil law. That controversy with the Church and the resultant imprisonment of the bishops created religious enemies for the crown. In a mood of sullen resentment the once-devoted Church cooled toward the monarchy. The manumission of the slaves in 1888 without any compensation to the owners distressed part of the landowning class, which also turned its back on the emperor. Emancipation had been brought about largely by urban groups. They did not identify closely with the monarchy, which they felt did not represent their interests. They viewed the aging emperor as a symbol of the past, an anathema to the modernization they preached. It was among these urban groups that republican doctrine spread. That doctrine, as well as the urban mentality, pervaded the army officer corps. Pedro had ignored the military officers, an increasingly restless group in the 1880s. In them, the disgruntled clergy, landowners, and urban dwellers—as well as the coffee planters—found their instrument for political change. The republican cause won many military converts, particularly among the junior officers who equated a republic with progress and modernization. The fate of the monarchy was sealed when the principal military leader, Marshal Deodoro da Fonseca, switched his allegiance and proclaimed himself in favor of a republic. Under his leadership on November 15, 1889, the army surrounded the royal palace, occupied the important governmental buildings, and silenced Rio de Janeiro. The military overthrew the monarchy and declared Brazil to be a republic. Brazil's foremost novelist of the period, Machado de Assis, ably caught the mood of the times, a great ambivalence, in his brilliant novel, *Jacob and Esau*. The old emperor abdicated and, like his father before him, sailed into European exile. There was no turmoil. The transition was bloodless. A new constitution, presidential, federal, democratic, and republican, was promulgated on February 24, 1891.

Chile, too, found its stability early. In fact, by 1830, Chile's search for national order was over. The small and powerful landowning class consolidated quickly, and from the ranks of the conservatives emerged one of Chile's ablest leaders of the nineteenth century, Diego Portales. Through his force, efficiency, and skill, he imposed conservative rule in 1830, and it lasted until 1861. He never served as president, although he held various ministerial portfolios, Interior, Foreign Relations, War, and Navy, until his assassination in 1837. Matters of power, discipline, stability, and order concerned him, not social or economic reforms. In sharp contrast to what was happening in the rest of Spanish America, he succeeded in subordinating the army to a civilian government and thereby removing the military from nineteenth-century politics. He also framed the Constitution of 1833, which lasted until 1925. It guaranteed aristocratic influence for nearly a century.

Presidential mandates in Chile lasted five years and could be renewed for an additional five. Three conservative leaders each held the office for ten years, enforcing the remarkable stability imposed by Portales. Manuel Montt, who served from 1851 to 1861, accepted a moderate, José Joaquín Pérez, to succeed him. The thirty years, 1861–91, were a period of liberal rule tempered by conservative opposition, in direct contrast to the preceding three decades. The major reforms enacted by the liberals indicated the direction and degree of change they advocated: private liberty of worship in houses and schools, the establishment of cemeteries for nonCatholics, the abolition of the privileged Church courts, civil marriage, freedom of the press, no reelection of the president, a modification of the electoral-reform law to substitute a literacy test for property qualifications, greater autonomy for municipal governments, and the power of congress to override a presidential veto. As is obvious, none of these altered the power structure in Chile, none attempted to shift the social and economic imbalance of the country. Chile's record of stability and order encouraged economic prosperity and a high degree of material progress.

One useful, if fictional, insight into nineteenth-century Chilean political life came from the satirical pen of Luis Orrego Luco. His *Casa Grande* (1908) cast a nostalgic glance at the rural patriarchal past. One of the principal characters of the novel, Leonidas Sandoval, represented that patriarchal type linking the rural estate with national politics. After a rudimentary education, Sandoval toured Europe with a priest chaperone. Returning to Chile, he married a woman of his own social status and settled down to administering the family estate. Then, with obvious glee, Orrego Luco revealed the connection between the landowning elite and politics:

> It wasn't long before honors and political fortune came to him. He became deputy in congress, where he constantly voted with the majority and accepted as articles of faith the opinions and caprices of the President of the Republic on whom depended both rain and sunshine. He spoke two or three times before the august assembly requesting protection for national industries or a higher tariff on Argentine beef. For him, the very reason for politics was to serve his own personal interest whether it was to enact taxes that favored him, to push for the construction of a railroad, bridge or road in his province, or to create a new job useful for some relative. What is more, for the members of the government Don Leonidas was the perfect friend. Although a man personally honorable, he voted without question the most shamelessly phony powers

to the friends of the cabinet ministers and ardently defended the ministers in all their maneuvers. With such a social background and with a gentle appearance accented by a huge moustache, a serious yet relaxed air, a tranquil walk, discreet tone, and a certain reputation for being wealthy, he soon assumed a cabinet portfolio himself, which was a splendid accomplishment in those times when ministries lasted for years, not just months as they do now.

In a similar satirical vein, Orrego Luco introduced his readers to other representatives of the rural ruling class, and none was more affable than Senator Peñalver, whose ancestral credentials were as impeccable as his visible means of support dubious. In one memorable statement the old gentleman confessed, "I have realized the political-economic ideal: I live in the best possible style possible with the least amount of effort. I live off the country." Picaresque as those rural aristocrats might appear, they seemed harmless eccentrics alongside the wheeling and dealing of the corrupt, immoral urban elite populating the novel. On both the rural and urban levels, Orrego Luco succeeded in demonstrating that the immediate best interests of the dominant elites shaped national political life.

Argentina and Mexico experienced greater difficulty than Chile and Brazil in their search for political stability. After Rosas fell in 1852, the city and province of Buenos Aires refused to adhere to the new Argentine union, fearful that they would have to surrender too much power. The old struggle between the port and the provinces continued until 1862, when the prestigious and powerful Governor of Buenos Aires, Bartolomé Mitre, was able to impose his will on the entire nation. His force and ability reunited the nation. A succession of able presidents, each of whom served for six years, followed him. These presidents wielded almost total power. In 1880 the thorny question of the city and province of Buenos Aires was finally solved. New legislation separated the city from the province, federalized the city, and declared it the national capital, a role it had previously played. The rich province then went its own way with a new capital, La Plata. Meanwhile, the nation was investing the energy once given to political struggles into economic growth.

Mexico's search for stability was one of the most difficult in Latin America, complicated by questions of federalism and the position of the Church in the new nation. The bloodshed and drama that began in 1810 lasted well over half a century and exhausted the nation. Finally a mestizo strongman, Profirio Díaz, who had risen through the military ranks to become general and in the process had fought against Santa Anna, the French, and Maximilian, brought peace to Mexico in 1876—an iron peace, as it turned out. For the next thirty-four years, he imposed a conservative, centralized government on Mexico while ruling under the liberal, federal Constitution of 1857. His government brought order and stability to a degree unknown since the colonial period. The strength and political longevity of Díaz rested on the powerful supporting alliance he created. The Church, the army, foreign capitalists, and the great landowners found it beneficial to back his regime, and they reaped substantial material rewards for their allegiance. On the other hand, the wily Díaz manipulated them at will for his own ends. Under his guidance, Mexico made outstanding material progress and witnessed a prosperity surpassing the best years of colonial mining.

The supporting alliance Díaz formed proved to be the most effective combination of forces to buttress political stability. To varying degrees the chiefs of states of other nations made use of similar combinations to buttress their power. The two key groups obviously were the army and the landowners.

Where the elites were generally in concurrence and worked in harmony—as, for example, in Chile and Brazil—order came early in the national life; where the elites found it more difficult to concur—Argentina and Mexico are examples—order was delayed. Of course, there were nations in nineteenth-century Latin America—Bolivia, Uruguay, and Nicaragua, for example—in which no concurrence at all was reached with the consequence that order and stability eluded them throughout the century. Peru, once the opulent center of Spain's South American empire, floundered in the nineteenth century. Already in severe economic straits when San Martín's army from the south and Bolívar's from the north imposed independence from the outside, Peru entered nationhood amid economic depression, civil strife, and military control. Ramón Castilla dominated the country from 1845 to 1862 and managed the insure unity and provide a welcome relief from warfare, civil and external. But that caudillo afforded only an interlude of peace and stability. Peru's problems remained unsolved, and its military and elite showed no ability throughout the century to come to grips with them. Those nations where political order was imposed, however, moved into a period of lively economic activity and much needed prosperity.

ECONOMIC PROSPERITY

Political stability and economic prosperity were linked; each contributed to the maintenance of the other. Stability also encouraged foreign investment, and much of the prosperity grew from the influx of such investments and the increasing volume of exports.

The demands of the industrialized nations for raw products continued to rise throughout the last half of the nineteenth century. Not only was there a rapidly increasing number of consumers in Western Europe and the United States but also their per capita purchasing power was ever greater. During that half-century the United States emerged as the principal industri-

The central plaza of La Paz, Bolivia, 1863

alized nation of the world and as the foremost consumer of Latin America's exports. As the industrial centers bought more agricultural and mineral products from Latin America, the region's trade underwent a dramatic expansion. Plantation owners and miners produced larger amounts of grain, coffee, sugar, cotton, cacao, bananas, livestock, copper, silver, tin, lead, zinc, and nitrates for export. The natural products—such as palm oils, nuts, woods, rubber, and medicinal plants—also found a ready market abroad, and their exportation rose sharply.

Similar to well-established patterns of the colonial past, the export sector of the economy remained the most active, the dynamic focus of investment, technological improvement, and official concern. More often than not, foreigners, with their own agendas, dominated that sector. Following the colonial pattern, the economy in general depended to a large degree on the export sector for its growth and prosperity. Dependency has become a widely used (and frequently abused) concept to describe Latin America's economy. Definitions of that concept vary. A frequently cited one holds dependency to be a situation in which the economy of one nation is conditioned by the development and/or growth of the economy of a second nation to which the former is subordinated. This book will adopt that definition.

Foreign observers marveled at the rapid rate of increase of Latin American trade in the last half of the nineteenth century. An official U.S. report in 1890 called attention to the fact that Latin America's foreign commerce exceeded 1 billion dollars per year and had increased roughly 43 percent between 1870 and 1884. By comparison, during the same period British trade increased by 27.2 percent. The five principal areas engaged in foreign commerce were Brazil, Argentina, Cuba, Chile, and Mexico, which together accounted for more than three-quarters of Latin America's trade. With the exception of Argentina, they exported more than they imported. Trade statistics for the individual nations were impressive. Argentine exports jumped sevenfold between 1853 and 1873 and doubled again by 1893. Mexican exports quadrupled between 1877 and 1900. The smaller nations benefited too. Exports of coffee from Costa Rica increased fourfold between 1855 and 1915, and tin shipments from Bolivia quadrupled during a four-year period, 1897–1900, and tripled again by 1913.

In Brazil, the value of foreign trade increased by six to seven times between 1833 and 1889, a record made possible by coffee, a relatively new export. At the time of independence, coffee accounted for only about a fifth of Brazil's exports, a figure that rose to two-thirds by the time of the fall of the monarchy, 1889. These figures indicate an increase from 190,000 to 5,586,000 in the number of sacks of coffee beans shipped to world coffee markets in a sixty-seven-year period. The value of the coffee sold during these years equaled that of all the exports during the entire colonial period. The coffee industry flourished first in the Paraíba Valley in the province of Rio de Janeiro from where it spread into the neighboring provinces of Minas Gerais and São Paulo.

A number of inventions, among them the railroad, barbed wire, the canning process, and the refrigerator ship, facilitated the exploitation of Argentina's hitherto untamed pampas, potentially one of the world's most fertile regions. The sailing of the first primitive refrigerator ship from Buenos Aires to Europe in 1876 changed the course of Argentine economic history. The successful voyage proved that chilled and frozen beef could be sold in lucrative European markets. Measures were taken at once to improve the quality of the beef. By 1900, 278 refrigerator ships plied between Great Britain and Argentina. During the decade of the 1870s, Argentina also made its first wheat shipments to Europe, a modest 21 tons in 1876. In 1900, wheat exports reached 2,250,000 tons. During the same period, the cultivated acreage on the pampas jumped fifteen times. Exports rose fivefold from 30 million gold pesos in 1870 to 150 million by 1900. This extraordinary economic boom made Argentina the most prosperous nation in Latin America.

Chile offers an excellent but by no means exceptional example of the development of a mineral-exporting economy. Already in the first decades of independence it exported increasing amounts of silver and copper. By midcentury, Chile enjoyed a well-balanced program of exports divided between various minerals and agricultural products. That diversification ended after 1878 when the new nitrate exports grew increasingly important until, within a few years, they dominated the export sector. Dependent on the world's need for nitrates, the Chilean economy declined or prospered according to demand and price for one product. The vulnerability of the economy was obvious.

Most governmental leaders paid far more attention to the international economy than to the national, domestic economy. The export sector of the Latin American economy grew more rapidly than the domestic sector, and income from foreign trade contributed an unusually high percentage of the gross national product. Foreign trade emphatically did not mean commerce among the Latin American states. They were total strangers in each other's marketplaces. Their economies complemented the demands of the distant major capitalistic economies in Western Europe and the United States.

Mounting foreign investments also characterized the Latin American economy in the last half of the nineteenth century. Europe generously sent capital, technology, and technicians to Latin America to assure the increased agricultural and mineral production its factories and urban populations required. The more pronounced stability of Latin America engendered greater confidence and generosity among foreign investors. The politicians of Latin America discovered the advantages of foreign investment. It created new wealth, which caudillos, politicians, and elite alike enjoyed. In a pattern being well established throughout the hemisphere, Porfirio Díaz meticulously paid off Mexico's foreign debts and decreed laws favorable to foreign investors. Foreign investment poured into Mexico. As investments rose, profit remittances flowed out of Latin America. The foreign capitalists might have invested in part to obtain the raw products they needed, but they also expected a rich return in the form of profits, interest payments, patent fees, and commissions.

To handle the new flow of money, banks, both national and foreign, sprang up with amazing rapidity in the major Latin American cities. Only one bank existed in Brazil in 1845, but in the following twelve years, twelve new banks were founded as the Brazilians began to rapidly expand their banking system. Foreign banks made their appearance in Brazil for the first time with the inauguration of the London and Brazil Bank in Rio de Janeiro in 1862. In that same year, the Bank of London and the River Plate was established in Buenos Aires. The London Bank of Mexico and South America opened in Mexico City in 1864. Spanish, Portuguese, Italian, French, German, and North American banks followed. The banks facilitated international trade and investment. They also brought to an end most of the personal financial transactions characteristic of the decades after independence. Impersonal institutions of growing resources, they multiplied the power and importance of the city and conversely diminished the prestige of the landowners, whose debts to the urban banks increased.

By the eve of World War I, foreign investments totaled $8.5 billion. The English invested the heaviest, $5 billion, or 20 percent of British overseas investment. The French were second with $1.7 billion, followed very closely by the United States with $1.6 billion. Germany was fourth with somewhat less than $1 billion. The largest share of the money went to Argentina, Brazil, and Mexico, and the most popular investments were railroads, public utilities, and mining. British investments predominated in South America; those of United States capitalists dominated in Mexico and the Caribbean area.

With sources of capital, markets, and headquarters abroad, the foreign investors and business people identified neither with their host countries nor with local needs. Their ability to direct capital investment, their hostility to tariffs, and their preference for free-trade policies exerted an unfavorable influence on Latin America's economic development.

During the last half of the century, the larger and stabler nations began to industrialize in order to meet growing internal demands for manufactured goods, to develop more balanced economies, and to protect the national economies from extremes of fluctuation in international trade. Some farsighted statesmen believed that without that industrialization the Latin Americans would be doomed to economic dependency and backwardness. The Chilean Manuel Camilo Vial, Minister of Finance during the administration of Manuel Bulnes (1841–51), preached, "Any nation in which agriculture dominates everything, in which slavery or feudalism shows its odious face, follows the march of humanity among the stragglers. . . . That future threatens us also, if we do not promote industry with a firm hand and a constant will." The governments raised the tariffs, particularly during the final decades of the century, to encourage and protect the new industries and from time to time promulgated other legislation such as tax incentives and permission to import machinery duty-free to give further impetus to the process. Despite such disadvantages as limited capital, unskilled labor, low labor productivity, lack of coal, limited markets, and a mentality emphasizing the continued reliance on the exploitation of mineral and agricultural possibilities, industrialization grew gradually in the last decades of the nineteenth century.

In the beginning, industrialization was primarily concerned with the processing of natural products for local consumption or export. Flour mills, sugar refineries, meat-packaging plants, tanning factories, lumber mills, wineries, and breweries developed wherever the requisite resources were at hand. Then service industries appeared: gas and electric utilities, repair shops and foundaries, and construction enterprises. Finally, protected industries began to manufacture other goods for home consumption, principally, textiles or processed food.

In Brazil, the textile industry was by far the most important. The 9 cotton mills in 1865 multiplied into 100 before the fall of the empire. The new republican government that came to power in 1889 visualized an industrial expansion for the nation. Symbolic of their ambitions, the Republicans changed the name of the Ministry of Agriculture to the Ministry of Industry. As further encouragement, they promulgated a protective tariff in 1890, raising to 60 percent the duty on 300 items, principally textiles and food products, that competed with nationally produced goods. Conversely they lowered the duty on primary goods used in national manufacturing. The tariff rose again in 1896 and still higher in 1900. Fundamental to any industrialization, the government established four new engineering schools in the 1890s.

The Argentine government began to turn its attention seriously to the encouragement of industrialization during the 1870s. In 1876, it enacted a high protective tariff. Industrialization concentrated in and around Buenos Aires, which by 1889 counted some 400 industrial establishments employing approximately 11,000 workers. During the last decade of the century, larger factories appeared and industry began to penetrate other regions, although Buenos Aires would always remain the focal point. The census of 1895 listed the number of factories and workshops as 23,000 with 170,000 employees (small workshops employing fewer than ten workers were by far the most common); the next census, 1914, raised the number of factories and workshops to 49,000 and the number of employees to 410,000. By that time, Argentina manufactured 37 percent of the processed foods its inhabitants consumed, 17 percent of the clothing they wore, and 12 percent of the metals and machinery they used.

Other nations, certainly with Chile and Mexico foremost among them, followed the industrial leadership of Argentina and Brazil. The process of industrialization not only challenged and changed timeworn economic structures but also brought in its wake some political and social innovations.

POSITIVISM AND PROGRESS

The Latin American elites intensified their awareness of the material progress being made in Great Britain, France, Germany, and the United States. Many of them had mastered French, the second language of the elite, and a few had a knowledge of English or German, so that they had direct access to the information and literature from the nations whose progress impressed them. The newspapers carried full accounts of what was happening in the leading nations of the Western world, and the programs of the learned societies featured discussions of the technical advances of the industrializing nations. Many members of the elite traveled abroad and were exposed to the innovations firsthand. They returned to their quieter capitals in the New World with a nostalgia for Paris and the irrepressible desire to ape everything they had seen there. Of course, the imports bore testimony to larger segments of the population of the manufacturing skill and ingenuity of those technically advanced societies.

The elites closely followed the intellectual trends of Europe. In fact, they could more readily discuss the novels of Émile Zola or Gustave Flaubert than those of Jorge Isaacs or Machado de Assis, and they paused to admire European painters while they ignored the canvases of their compatriots. Not surprisingly, some members of the elite became knowledgeable about the new philosophy of Positivism, formulated in Europe during the second quarter of the nineteenth century by Auguste Comte. They eventually imported it into Latin America, where governments warmly welcomed it.

Many of the ideas on progress that the Latin Americans extracted from the Enlightenment, Charles Darwin, Herbert Spencer, as well as from other sources, seemed to converge in the form Auguste Comte's Positivism assumed in Latin America during the last decade of the century. To Comte, progress was attainable through the acceptance of scientific social laws codified by Positivism. Outward manifestations of progress—railroads and industrialization were prime examples—assumed great importance in Positivism and emphatically so among the Latin Americans, whether they acknowledged Comte or not.

With its emphasis on material growth and well-being, Positivism ideally suited the trends of the last half of the century. It favored a capitalist mentality, regarding private wealth as sacred. Indeed, private accumulation of wealth was a sign of progress as well as an instrument for progress. Because of the weakness of domestic, private institutions, the state had to assume the role of directing progress. Of course, to promote capitalism and to direct progress, the state, according to Positivist doctrine, had to maintain order and impose stability. With its special emphasis on order and progress, Positivism reached the height of its influence between 1880 and 1900. It became almost an official doctrine of the Díaz regime in Mexico; some of his principal ministers, who, very significantly, were known as the *científicos,* had imbibed deeply of Comte's doctrines and tried to offer a scientific solution to the problems of organizing national life.

In Venezuela, President Antonio Guzmán Blanco governed directly or indirectly from 1870 to 1888 under the influence of Positivism. First he imposed order and then set out in pursuit of elusive progress. Order meant the consolidation of the past and admitted minimal social change, while progress signified the adoption of the outward manifestations of European civilization. Aping the reconstruction of his beloved Paris, Guzmán Blanco laid out wide boulevards for Caracas and constructed an opera house as well as a pantheon for national heroes. New railroads and expanded port facilities speeded Venezuela's exports to European markets to pay for the material progress.

Positivism also attracted many adherents in Brazil, particularly among the new graduates of the technical and military schools, members of the fledgling middle class. They favored the abolition of slavery, the establishment of a republic (albeit not a democratic one), and the separation of Church and state, changes that did occur in Brazil between 1888 and 1891. Material progress absorbed much of their concern. Interestingly enough the flag of the Brazilian republic created in 1889 bears to the present the Positivist motto "Order and Progress." The Positivists assume significance because their ideology indicated the direction in which the intellectual elite was moving in the last quarter of the nineteenth century. They unwittingly synthesized the transformation overtaking urban Brazil. Most of the other Latin American nations had their disciples of Comte who preached the new method of achieving national progress and prosperity.

Where political stability and economic prosperity existed, material progress was most notable. It is not surprising therefore that Brazil and Chile were among the first Latin American nations to experiment with the inventions and innovations offered by Europe and the United States and correlated with progress. The steam engine made an early appearance in these two nations. In 1815, Bahia boasted its first steam-driven sugar mill. Two years later Pernambuco also possessed one. By 1834, there were 64 of them in operation, a number that rose to 144 by 1852 and then increased rapidly thereafter. At the same time, the coffee processors were beginning to acquire steam-driven machinery. In Chile, the first steam-powered flour mill went into operation in 1839. By 1863, Chile counted 132 steam engines used in sawmills, distilleries, blower furnaces, flour mills, and coal mines.

None of the innovations had more impact than the railroads. Its steel rails had the potential of helping to bind together nations, an effective agent to counteract the centrifugal propensities always at work in the larger Latin American nations. It could serve an equally vital economic function. Penetrating distant regions, the railroads tapped new sources of economic propserity. Bulky and perishable products could be rushed over long distances to eager markets.

Cuba can boast of the first railroad in Latin America. The line from Havana to Güines, approximately 30 miles, began operation in 1838. Chile initiated its first railroad in 1852 and a decade later had laid 543 miles of track. A new Brazilian law in 1852 provided favorable conditions for any entrepreneur who would undertake to construct a railroad. The capitalist Viscount Mauá accepted the challenge and in 1854 inaugurated a line of 10 miles. By 1874, there were approximately 800 miles of track. After 1875, construction increased rapidly: from 1875 to 1884, 2,200 miles were laid; from 1885 to 1889, 2,500 more miles. By 1889, then, trackage totaled approximately 6,000 miles. Argentina's railroad era began in 1857 with the inauguration of a 7-mile line. The government offered a variety of inducements to encourage its expansion: the duty-free entry of materials and equipment, interest guarantees, and land grants. British capital readily responded and dominated rail construction. Britain supplied technicians and engineers as well and then sold English coal to the railroad companies to run the steam engines. In 1914, Argentina boasted the most extensive railroad network in Latin America and the eighth largest in the world. In total, South America's railroad mileage grew from 2,000 miles in 1870 to 59,000 in 1900.

Mexico began its railroad construction very slowly. When Díaz took power in 1876, only 400 miles had been laid. He pushed rail construction with the result that approximately 15,000 miles of rail were put down during his long regime. At first glance the extensive railroad network might seem to have served as a unifier of the large and diverse nation. If, indeed, it served such a worthy end, that was only secondary in the plans of those who financed and built it. Foreign commercial objectives predominated, and they were dictated by market not political considerations, by external not internal requirements. The railroads tapped new minerals for export. Before the railroads, Mexico sold only silver abroad. The railroads made it possible to export zinc, lead, and copper and thus intensify the flow of Mexico's natural resources to the industrialized nations. It is noteworthy that Mexican exports increased eight and a half times between 1877 and 1910, coinciding with the period of intensive railroad construction. U.S. interests completed the line linking the border with Mexico City so that in May of 1880 it was possible to travel by rail from Chicago to Mexico City for the first time. The economic and political implications for Mexico were momentous and soon realized. Mexico, Argentina, Chile, Cuba, and Uruguay developed a reasonably extensive network of railroads covering much of the effective national territory, but in the rest of Latin America the railways were short, feeder lines for seaports, unconnected and unrelated with each other.

Along the newly laid rail lines, at rail junctions, and at railheads sprang up villages and towns. Older settlements took on a new life. The railroad brought the countryside and the city into closer contact and as a result the neofeudalistic and paternalistic aspects of plantation and hacienda life were challenged as never before. The railroads opened new markets for the incipient industries of the large cities and brought into the hinterlands a greater variety of goods than these populations had hitherto seen. Railroads thus helped to promote the fledgling industries. They also provided some amusement during their early years. When the railroad finally reached Guatemala City in the 1880s, it became a custom for the capital's inhabitants of all social levels to congregate at the railroad station for the semiweekly arrivals and departures of the train. On those occasions, the National Band played in the plaza in front of the station for the further entertainment of the crowd.

While railroads perfectly illustrated Latin America's urge to progress, they exerted a negative influence on development. It was ironic. The railroads accomplished the opposite ends they were meant to achieve. They deepened Latin American's dependency, strengthened the neocolonial in-

The central railroad station and urban transportation center, Santiago, Chile, circa 1908

stitutions, and impoverished the governments. The primary explanation for those adverse effects lay in the fact that more often than not foreigners built and owned them, and did so where they would best complement the North Atlantic economies rather than Latin America's. In Argentina, as but one example, English-financed, -built, -equipped, and -administered railroads carried the resources of the rich pampas to the port of Buenos Aires for their inevitable export. As this example aptly suggests, the railroads served export markets by lowering transportation costs of bulky items, incorporating new regions into commercial agriculture, and opening up new lands and mines to exploitation. More often than not, the railroads expanded and strengthened the latifundia wherever the rails reached, since they often conferred considerable value on lands once considered marginal. Whereas previously peasants had been tolerated on that marginal land, its new value caused the landlords first to push the peasants off the land and then to incorporate them into the estate's labor force. Commercial agriculture, much of it destined for export, replaced subsistence agriculture, and the numbers and size of small landholdings declined. Indian landholdings in particular suffered incursions in those areas touched by railroads. Mexico proved perfectly the equation of railroad expansion to increased exports, growth of the latifundia, and disappearance of small farms.

Bolivia provided a sobering example of the contribution of railroads both to dependency on a single export and to the reduction of food production for local markets. By the end of the nineteenth century, rails connecting the highlands with Pacific ports accelerated tin-ore exports. The rail cars descended the Andes loaded with the ore. In order to fill the otherwise empty cars on their return, the trains carried agricultural products imported from Peru, Chile, and the United States. The importation of food wrought havoc on the agrarian economy of the fertile Santa Cruz region, depriving it of its national market. Production declined sharply. Bolivia became locked into a double dependency status: dependent on foreign markets for its single export and on foreign producers for a part of its food supply.

Costa Rica illustrated in a slightly different but even more disastrous way the effects of railroads on the economy of a small nation. In the case of Costa Rica, the pursuit of modernization allowed foreigners to take control of the national economy. To market larger quantities of coffee and thus earn the money to modernize, the government encouraged the construction of a railroad (1870–90) that stretched from the highlands where the coffee grew to Puerto Limón for shipment abroad. The onerous loans overburdened the treasury as the government paid outrageous interest rates to unscrupulous foreign money lenders. Further, the government bestowed on Chief Engineer Minor Keith 800,000 acres, land that fronted on the railroad and later became the center of the plantations of the United Fruit Company. Even so, the railroad remained in foreign hands. British investors also controlled the ports, mines, electric lighting, major public works, and foreign commerce as well as the principal domestic marketplaces. In short, Costa Rica surrendered all its economic independence and mortgaged its future before 1890 to obtain some of the physical aspects of modernization.

Most of the other Latin American governments also contracted heavy debts to pay for their railroads. Those debts often led to foreign complications and always to some sacrifice of economic independence. One brazen example of foreign intervention triggered by railroad funding occurred in Venezuela. In 1903, German gunboats appeared off the coast to force the government to pay 1.4 million pounds sterling for loans associated with railroad building.

The telegraph furthered the communications revolution in Latin America. Both Chile and Brazil began service over short lines in 1852. In Brazil, the first line connected the imperial palace at São Cristóvão, on the outskirts of the capital, to the military headquarters in the capital. The outbreak of the Paraguayan war caused a flurry of activity to string lines southward toward the battlefields. In a record time of six months a telegraph line joined Rio de Janeiro to the southernmost province of the empire. In the opposite direction, the lines reached Belém, at the mouth of the Amazon, in 1886, and thereafter penetrated the interior. Argentina began to string telegraph wires in the 1860s, and by 1875, sixty stations were transmitting messages.

While on the one hand the telegraph contributed to national unity, on the other it helped to bring nations closer together. In 1866, a cable connected Buenos Aires and Montevideo; and the following year the United States opened cable communication with Cuba. The transandine telegraph united Buenos Aires and Santiago in 1872. Brazil inaugurated telegraphic contact with Montevideo in 1879 and with Buenos Aires in 1883. From the United States, the Central and South American Cable Company, formed in 1879, began stretching its cables southward into Middle America and then beyond. By 1882, its line reached as far south as Lima, and in 1890, it extended to Santiago where it connected with the Transandine Telegraph Company. Transatlantic cables put Latin America in instantaneous communication with Europe. Pedro II dictated the first message to be cabled from Brazil to Europe in 1874. Significantly, then, Rio de Janeiro was linked to Europe by cable long before it could communicate by telegraph with other parts of its own empire.

The number of international steamship lines serving Latin America increased rapidly during the last half of the century. The principal ports of the Austro-Hungarian Empire, Italy, Spain, France, Great Britain, Germany, and the United States were in direct and regular contact with those of Latin America. Sailings became increasingly frequent; ships carried more cargo; service improved. The major ports underwent renovation with the addition of new and larger warehouses, faster loading and unloading machinery, larger and sturdier wharfs, and the dredging of deeper channels.

Clearly not all of Latin America shared fully in the progress. One astonished visitor to the highlands of Ecuador and to Quito in 1885 gasped, "The country does not know the meaning of the words progress and prosperity." At that time, the only communication between Quito, the capital high in the Andes, and Guayaquil, the Pacific port, was still by mule path, a route impassable during six months of the year because of the rainy season. Under optimum conditions, it was possible to make the journey in eight or nine days over the same route in use for centuries. As a port, Guayaquil was in contact with the world and showed signs of modernization long before the isolated capital did. The public streetcar, gas lighting, and other amenities reached Guayaquil years before they could be seen in the capital. Not until the end of the first decade of the twentieth century did a railroad link Guayaquil with Quito. The 227-mile railroad climb from the port to the capital took two days. The slower growth of Ecuador was not unique; it characterized many of the nations that lagged behind the leadership of Argentina, Brazil, Chile, and Mexico.

The concern with improved transportation and communication symbolized the dedication to progress. To a large extent, material advances measured modernization. How many miles of railroads, how much horsepower generated by steam engines, how many tons handled per hour in the ports, how many miles of telegraph wires? The higher the number given in response to these questions, the greater was the progress that the nation could credit to itself. In their general satisfaction with these material advances, the elites seemed oblivious of another aspect of modernization: that the very steamships, railroads, and ports tied them and their nations ever more tightly to a handful of industrialized nations in Western Europe and North America, which bought their raw products and provided manufactured goods in return. They failed to see the significance of the fact that many of the railroads did not link the principal cities of their nations but rather ran from the plantations or mines directly to the ports, subordinating the goal of national unification to the demands of the industrial nations for agricultural products and minerals. As the amount of loans increased to pay for the new material progress, the governments had to budget ever greater sums to pay interest rates. As foreign investment rose, the outflow of profit remittances multiplied. Increasingly the voices of foreign investors and bankers spoke with greater authority in making economic decisions for the host countries. Local economic options diminished. In short, modernization as it took shape in nineteenth-century Latin America adversely affected the quality of life of the majority and contributed to deepening dependency.

INSTITUTIONAL CONFORMITY—THE SALVADORAN EXAMPLE

More regional diversity existed in Latin America during the period when the colonies obtained their independence than there would be at the end of the century. The reasons for the rapid homogenization during the nineteenth century are not difficult to find. Many of the elites in all the newly independent governments had embraced or would embrace the ideas that sprang from the European Enlightenment and later from Positivism. They developed a collective desire to create in the New World a replica of Europe north of the Pyrenees. To emulate the progress the elites believed characteristic of their model nations, they needed capital. This they obtained through loans, investments, and trade, all three of which linked them ever more closely to North Atlantic capitalism. Marvelous advances in communication and transportation facilitated the growing conformity forged by common goals favoring "progress" and trade patterns focusing on the North Atlantic capitalist nations. As one major consequence, the institutional patterns of Latin America showed greater uniformity as the new nations neared the first century of their independence than they had after more than three centuries of Iberian domination. To achieve this conformity, areas and nations that once had been marginal to Iberian interest, and thus more superficially incorporated into European commercial patterns, had to change dramatically. A predominantly export-oriented economy linked to international capitalism became the dynamo propelling this profound, rapid change. In certain cases, radical transformation—almost revolutionary in some instances—challenged the concepts of "changelessness" and "continuity" often applied to the entire area.

El Salvador provides a striking example of the transformation of a once-neglected outpost of the Spanish empire as it rushed to achieve institutional conformity with the rest of Latin America. Further, El Salvador's experience with progress or modernization, accompanied by the increasing impoverishment of the majority of its inhabitants, illustrates how a Latin American nation could modernize without developing.

Spanish institutions had imperfectly penetrated El Salvador. Throughout the colonial period that small area retained closer ties to its Indian past than to any of the bustling centers of colonial Spanish America. Yet, within the short span of three decades, roughly between 1860 and 1890, El Salvador acquired the economic, political, and social institutions characterizing the rest of Latin America. These included a dynamic and modernizing export sector based on monoagriculture; the economic predominance of the large estate producing for foreign trade; a subservient, impoverished, landless rural labor force; the concentration of economic and political power in the hands of the principal planters, who exercised it from a single dominant city, the capital (which, if it fell short of duplicating its urban model, Paris, nonetheless contained districts reflecting the architectural influence of nineteenth-century Europe); and a political rapprochment between an increasingly professional military and the elites. In a number of fundamental aspects, El Salvador became nearly indistinguishable from the rest of Latin America.

In the late 1860s, new socio-economic patterns began to take shape. Greater political stability and closer contact with the North Atlantic nations, principally the United States, France, and Great Britain, partially explain the emergence of the new patterns. Most importantly, the elites found a new crop, coffee, that the country could grow and profitably sell abroad. More than anything else, concentration on the growth and export of that single crop altered old institutions. Before the end of the century, the new coffee estates became the base of economic production, political power, and social organization. Coffee planters and processors emerged as the new elite.

Instrumental in initiating the challenge to the old system, President Gerardo Barrios (1858–63) directed El Salvador's first steps toward modernization and change. Characterizing the nation as "backward," "destitute," and "misgoverned," Barrios determined to introduce progress. Both a military commander and the owner of a medium-sized estate, the president represented the middle sectors in life style, outlook, and aspirations. He advocated the doctrines of both Liberalism and Positivism. He favored individual liberties, opposed dictatorial rule, and sought to end the "feudalism" dominating the countryside. He succeeded in accelerating a radical rural shift toward capitalism. However, in a pattern not unfamiliar in nineteenth-century Latin America, liberty during the Barrios years—as thereafter—smiled exclusively on the elites. Authoritarian rule remained the reality for the rest of the people, despite rhetoric to the contrary. In 1860, the first program Barrios announced for his government included five goals: the promotion of agriculture, industry, and commerce; the introduction into El Salvador of the progress that distinguished other nations; the encouragement of immigration; a reform of the educational system in accordance with the latest European ideas; and the construction of roads and ports to facilitate international communication and transportation.

Understanding the importance of coffee on the world market and the suitability of El Salvador's rich volcanic soil to grow it, Barrios and his successors promoted this crop. The complex process of coffee production engendered a series of crises in traditional institutions that had adequately served a society whose economy relied on the relatively leisurely cultivation of indigo, the primary export, and food crops. Coffee production differed significantly from that of indigo, for the indigo plant required little care or investment. Within a year, the farmer could harvest it. Coffee could be grown under a variety of conditions on lands ranging from a few acres to vast estates. Small coffee planters seemed to flourish in some parts of Latin America—Colombia, for example—but in El Salvador, the growing and especially the processing of coffee took place on medium-sized and large estates. The care, conservation, and fertilizing of the land, and the preparation of the beans—including drying, processing, and sacking—required considerable capital as well as a large, permanent work force that could be augmented during the harvest season. Because they had to wait three to five years for the first harvest, coffee planters required considerably more capital, more patience, and more skill than the producers of indigo. These requirements severely limited the number of coffee growers, particularly the number of processors. Handsome profits, however, repaid the few who met the requirements.

The lure of a lucrative market prompted those planters who could bear the financial burden to expand their estates, which grew at the expense of communal landholdings and small landowners. A shift in landowning patterns fundamentally altered the life style of the majority. Governments encouraged this change, facilitating the concentration of land into fewer and fewer hands. Thus, in the decades between 1860 and 1890, the landholding patterns came to resemble the commercial capitalistic models characteristic of plantation economies elsewhere in Latin America. The first step was to label the Indian communal lands "backward" and "antiprogressive." They were accused of delaying or even preventing modernization. President Barrios initiated the legal attack on the *ejidos*, landholding communities, and the *tierras comunales,* municipally owned and worked lands. The campaign climaxed during the presidency of Rafael Zaldívar (1876–85). In 1881, he abolished the *tierras comunales*. With far-reaching consequences, the decree denounced ancient practices: "The existence of lands under the ownership of *comunidades* impedes agricultural development, obstructs the circulation of wealth, and weakens family bonds and the independence of the individual. Their existence is contrary to the economic and social principles that the Republic has accepted." One year later, a law dissolved the *ejidos* as "an obstacle to our agricultural development and contrary to our economic principles." In both cases, the lands were divided among community members. Such actions disoriented the Indian and folk populations, which little understood private land ownership because they had traditionally identified the community and the land as one. The land existed for the commonweal of the group, and the community cared for the land in an almost religious fashion. Cooperation rather than competition characterized the economic behavior of these populations.

Once the communal lands were distributed into small plots, the coffee planters set about acquiring the land. Experience proved that it was easier to befuddle and buy out the new, small landowner than the well-entrenched and tradition-oriented community. The emerging rural class system, increasingly characterized by a small group of wealthy coffee planters and processors on the one hand and a large body of ill-paid laborers on the other, contrasted sharply with the more egalitarian structures of rural El Salvador prior to 1860.

Export patterns altered radically during the same decades. From the colonial period into the early 1880s, El Salvador had enjoyed varied agrarian production and export: corn, indigo, tobacco, sugar, cacao, coffee, cotton, and tropical fruits. The midcentury invention of synthetic dyes doomed the most important of those exports, indigo. Coffee more than made up for its demise. By 1879, coffee accounted for 48.5 percent of the total value of exports. During the decade of the 1880s, El Salvador became virtually a monoagricultural exporting nation, its economic prosperity largely dependent on the purchase of coffee by three or four nations, which, in turn, supplied investments, technology, and manufactured goods in quantities commensurate with the profits from coffee sales.

The domination of the national economy by coffee obviously affected the rural folk, the overwhelming majority of the population. Dispossessed of their lands, they now depended on the coffee plantations for work. The government passed vagrancy laws in 1881 that required the populace to work under threats of fines, arrests, and punishments. The Agrarian Law of 1907 further regulated the rural working class, while it authorized the organization of a rural constabulary to provide the physical protection the landowners demanded. Agricultural judges—working with a system reminiscent of the Spanish *repartimiento*—made certain that workers were available when and where the planters needed them. The new rural police enforced the judges' decisions, intimidated the workers, protected the plant-ers, and guaranteed the rural order the planters believed essential to their prosperity. The landowners already had identified national well-being closely with their own.

By the end of the century, coffee had transformed El Salvador. The landowning structures, the land-use patterns, and the relationship of the workers to the land were radically different. Whereas in 1860 there had existed a reasonable balance among the large estates, small landholdings, and ejidos, by 1890 large estates dominated. The accumulation of capital in few hands strengthened the coffee estates, improved coffee processing, and further facilitated coffee exportation.

While coffee insured economic prosperity and political stability for the elites, it failed to benefit the majority. The very changes that facilitated the concentration of land also precipitated the disintegration of the social and economic life style of the overwhelming majority of Salvadorans. The changes squeezed off the land those who grew food for their own consump-tion and sold their surpluses in local markets. The dispossessed were forced to depend on seasonal plantation jobs. Some began to trickle into the towns and capital, propelled by rural poverty to search for urban jobs that they were unprepared for or that did not exist. The extent of the new social and economic disequilibrium was not immediately appreciated, for impressive economic growth masked for a time the weakness of the increasingly nar-row, inflexible, and dependent economy.

Meditating on those changes, Alberto Masferrer, a nationalist political writer of the early twentieth century, classified the landowning system as well as the relations between the landlords and rural workers as "feudal": "The lord in this case is the landowner, he who gives and takes, he who permits the worker to reside on his lands or expels whoever does not obey or please him." "Feudalism," as frequently happened, was an emotional charge emphasizing the rural disequilibrium in which the few exploited the many. In reality, capitalism had emerged in El Salvador. Masferrer assessed its impact in this way:

> There are no longer crises; instead, there are chronic illnesses and endemic hunger. . . . El Salvador no longer has wild fruits and vegetables that once everyone could harvest, nor even cultivated fruits that once were inexpen-sive. . . . Today there are the coffee estates and they grow only coffee. . . . Where there is now a voracious estate that consumes hundreds and hundreds of acres, before there were two hundred small farmers whose plots produced corn, rice, beans, fruits, and vegetables. Now the highlands support only coffee estates and the lowlands cattle ranches. The cornfields are disappear-ing. And where will the corn come from? The coffee planter is not going to grow it because his profits are greater growing coffee. If he harvests enough coffee and it sells for a good price, he can import corn and it will cost him less than if he sacrifices coffee trees in order to grow it. . . . Who will grow corn and where? . . . Any nation that cannot assure the production and regulate

the price of the most vital crop, the daily food of the people, has no right to regard itself as sovereign. . . . Such has become the case of our nation.

Masferrer condemned the progress charted by the elites because it had failed to benefit a majority of the Salvadorans. His judgment questions Salvadoran modernization and economic growth since neither addressed the needs of the majority. In key aspects, the Salvadoran experience typifies that of the other Latin American regions—Honduras, Nicaragua, Paraguay, Uruguay, northern Mexico, southern Argentina, and the Amazon—that once had been marginal to Iberian trading patterns but before the end of the nineteenth century were drawn into the export trade and the orbit of North Atlantic capitalism. These basic and common experiences imposed a degree of conformity on all of Latin America in its rush to modernize.

MODERNIZATION AND THE SOCIAL MILIEU

Industrialization grew from the intensifying effort to modernize, and both trends accompanied the accelerating growth of the cities in size and number. For purposes of definition, most of the Latin American nations classify as urban those localities that have some type of local government and a population of at least 1,000 to 2,000 inhabitants. The three trends of modernization, industrialization, and urbanization, among the dominant characteristics of much of Latin America by the last quarter of the nineteenth century, were inextricably intertwined, each acting as a catalyst on the others. Together they challenged some of the traditional values and patterns of the past and often modified them, if they did not change them.

The cities played ever more important roles in each nation. The government and administrative apparatus, commerce, and industry were located in the cities. Increasingly they served as hubs of complex transportation and communications networks. Further, they provided important recreational, cultural, and educational services. Rapid urban growth resulted from the arrival of greater numbers of foreign immigrants, a constantly increasing population (Latin America counted 60 million inhabitants in 1900), and an attraction the city exerted over many rural dwellers. Promises of better jobs and a more pleasant life lured thousands each year from the countryside to the city, a road that became increasingly more heavily trodden. On the other hand, even where that promise was lacking, the grinding poverty and modernization of the countryside pushed many desperate folk into urban areas.

But cities failed to play the role they might have in encouraging national development. The urban facade of modernization deceived. Dependency shaped the cities just as it molded other aspects of life. The high concentration of land in a few hands dictated the function of cities just as it molded other aspects of life. As combined agrarian-industrial units, the large estates did not require the intermediary services that support small trading, servicing, and processing towns. The export-oriented economy encouraged the prosperity of a few ports, a transportation system focusing on them, the expenditure of export wealth to beautify the capital city, and the concentration of absentee landlords in the capital to be near the center of power. The capital and the ports (in the case of Argentina, for example, the capital is also the principal port) absorbed the wealth of the export economy. The large estates, the overreliance on an export economy, and the resultant dependency help to explain why only one or two major "modern" cities dominated each Latin American nation and why urban modernity remained little more than a facade.

A correlation between class status and participation in the modernization process existed. Broadly speaking, in the upper levels of society people could more readily accept modern values. They were the ones most in contact with the world and knew what was going on. They more readily imitated the advances and changes that most struck their fancy. Indeed, they had the time and resources that permitted them the luxury of experimentation.

Individuals who subscribed to the process of modernization were willing and able to experiment, to change, to alter their environment to suit their needs. On the other hand, many of those immersed in poverty and tradition simply could not afford to experiment for fear that failure would bring the ultimate disaster. In short, institutional structures rather than personal choice kept most Latin Americans locked into a marginal existence without much possibility of experimentation with change. Although the conditions hostile to experimentation and change also existed in the cities, they permeated the countryside. As basic as agriculture was to the prosperity of the new nations, by midcentury few changes had been made in timeless production methods. The son used what his father had used, just as the father had copied his own father. An agricultural report on northern Brazil in the early 1860s characterized the local agrarian practices as "primitive" if compared to those observed on the farms of Western Europe and the United States. The hoe was the single farm implement, and the workers faithfully followed past procedures.

Urban culture with its capitalist-consumer imprint imposed a particular mentality on many city dwellers, which in turn shaped an outlook differing from that of most of the rural inhabitants. In an urban environment, traditional relationships tended to bend under necessity or examples of newer ones. In very general terms, the more intimate living conditions of the city and the greater familiarity of the city dwellers with foreign cultures exposed them to different ideas and alternative values. Many read newspapers and participated in public events. They were aware of changes the world was undergoing; they knew of the opportunities open to the trained and talented and were willing to strive for those opportunities. Consequently they laid plans for the future, and exerting every effort to realize those plans, they worked to shape their own destiny. The educational opportunities, varied careers, and job possibilities afforded by the city encouraged them to aspire toward upward mobility.

The statistics on Latin America's urban boom are impressive. Argentina's urban population doubled between 1869 and 1914, so that in the latter year the urban sector represented 53 percent of the population. In 1869, Buenos Aires had a population of a quarter of a million, a figure that increased eightfold by 1914 to encompass a quarter of the national population. Brazil witnessed similar urban growth. Between 1890 and 1914, the government created approximately 500 new municipalities. During the three decades after 1890, the population of the major cities jumped: Recife and Rio de Janeiro doubled in size, Niterói and Pôrto Alegre tripled, and São Paulo increased eightfold. São Paulo grew faster than any other major Brazilian city—in fact it was one of the fastest-growing cities in the world. It increased in population at a rate above 25 percent every five years after 1895. In 1910, the distinguished British diplomat and author James Bryce described São Paulo, a city then approaching half a million, as "the briskest and most progressive place in all Brazil. . . . The alert faces, and the air of stir and movement, as well as handsome public buildings, rising on all hands, with a large, well-planted public garden in the middle of the city, give the impression of energy and progress."

Chile well represented the urban surge in Latin America. In 1875, approximately 27 percent of the population could be classified as urban dwellers, but a quarter of a century later the figure reached 43 percent. Santiago's population shot up from 160,000 in 1880 to 400,000 in 1910, while the population of the second city and principal seaport, Valparaíso, more than doubled to 200,000 during the same period. Foreign visitors always had praise for the modernity of Chile's two major cities. Frank Vincent, who called at Valparaíso in 1885, rhapsodized:

> I was struck by the very civilized look of the famous Chilean seaport. . . . In the dining-room of the hotel the electric light was used, as well as in very many of the stores. In the streets is a "Belgian" pavement, and the sidewalks are smoothly and neatly flagged. The architecture of some of the buildings is very fine, and there are several rich and elegant churches. The principal streets are threaded by tramways. The trams, or cars, are of two stories as in Paris and other European cities. But a Valparaíso conductor is not paralleled in any other city anywhere—for it is a woman.

Visitors to Chile usually commented on those female streetcar conductors. However, the Chilean women of the lower class held a variety of other jobs in the cities by the end of the nineteenth century. In addition to running the streetcars, they did most of the streetcleaning and sold meats, vegetables, and fruits in the markets and on street corners. A well-known figure in Chilean society at the time was Isadora Cousiño, one of the wealthiest persons in Latin America, if not in the world. She administered her vast estates (said to number in the millions of acres), mines, and factories, with a business acumen few could equal and lived amid a splendor that would have been the envy of European monarchs.

By the beginning of the twentieth century, nearly all the capitals and many of the largest cities boasted of electricity, telephones, streetcar service, covered sewers, paved streets, ornamental parks, and new buildings reflecting French architectural influence.

Nurtured in an increasingly prosperous urban environment, intellectual activity flourished. Some of Latin America's most prestigious newspapers were founded: *El Mercurio* in Chile and the *Jornal do Commércio* in Brazil, both in 1827; *El Comercio* in Peru in 1839; and *La Prensa* in 1869 and *La Nación* in 1870 in Buenos Aires. Starting with the University of Chile in 1843, the major universities of Latin America began to publish reviews, journals, annuals, and books, an activity that further stimulated intellectual development. Romanticism, with its individuality, emotional intensity, and glorification of nature, held sway in literary circles for much of the nineteenth century. José Mármol of Argentina, Jorge Isaacs of Colombia, and José de Alencar of Brazil were masters of the romantic novel. Excesses in romanticism prompted literary experiments by 1880 in modernism and realism, already in vogue in Europe. The brilliant Nicaraguan poet Rubén Darío helped to introduce modernism into Latin America, and by the end of the century he dominated the field of poetry. Critics considered him one of the most original and influential poetic voices of his time. Under the sway of realism, the urban writers depicted and denounced the injustices they observed in their society. Clorinda Matto de Turner wrote the first significant novel, *Aves sin Nido* (Birds Without a Nest, 1889), protesting the abysmal conditions under which the Peruvian Indians lived. She saw the Indians as victims of iniquitous institutions, not least of which in her opinion was the Church. With two notable exceptions, Latin American culture aped European trends, particularly those set in Paris. The exceptions were Ricardo Palma, whose original "*tradiciones peruanas*," delightful historical anecdotes of Peru, recreated with wit and imagination his country's past; and the Gaucho poets, foremost of whom was the Argentine José Hernández, creator of *Martín Fierro*, a true American epic, picturing life among Argentina's rugged cowboys.

Education continued to be a privilege of the elite. Overwhelming numbers of the masses remained illiterate. What few schools there were could be found concentrated in the larger cities. In Brazil, the illiteracy rate never dropped below 85 percent in the nineteenth century. In the 1880s, with a population exceeding 13 million, the number enrolled in primary schools totaled less than a quarter of a million. Three Argentine presidents, Bartolomé Mitre, Domingo Faustino Sarmiento, and Nicolás Avellaneda, dedicated much of their energy and the nation's budget to improving education. As a result, literacy in Argentina rose from 22 percent in 1869 to 65 percent in 1914, an enviable record throughout most of Latin America. In Uruguay, during the 1870s, José Pedro Varela preached that education should be free, obligatory, coeducational, and secularly controlled. Under his direction, the Uruguayan educational system expanded rapidly and the illiteracy rate dropped proportionately. Chile, too, extended its schools to ever larger numbers of children. During his long administration (1873–85), President Justo Rufino Barrios of Guatemala devoted as much as 10 percent of the national budget to education. Still, at the end of his regime, Guatemala had only 934 schools enrolling 42,549 pupils, out of a population of approximately 1.25 million. In truth, despite the efforts of a number of farsighted statesmen, the illiteracy rate remained high throughout Latin America during the last half of the nineteenth century, varying from 40 to 90 percent. It was always much higher in the countryside than in the city. A marked contrast existed between the well-educated few and the ignorant many. The unschooled masses silently witnessed the events that surrounded and affected them but in which they could play only the most limited role. The children of the elite, however, seldom set foot in a public school. Their parents hired tutors or sent them to private schools for a typically classical education. Such segregation further removed the future leaders from national realities.

The rising national income, gross national product, and level of technology changed the standard of living of the masses little, if at all. Their condition remained constant throughout the nineteenth century. On the other hand, the landowners grew richer, while the middle sectors shared in the prosperity. Amorphous and small throughout much of the nineteenth century, the middle sectors began to take a more definite shape and increase in numbers during the last half and certainly the last quarter of the nineteenth century. Members of the liberal professions, schoolteachers and professors, bureaucrats, military officers, businessmen, merchants, and those involved in the nascent industrialization composed the ranks of that group. The common denominator of the middle sectors rested on the fact that they were neither admitted to the ranks of the traditional elite nor associated with the lower and poorer ranks of society. The observant James Bryce noted during his tour of South America at the end of the first decade of the twentieth century, "In the cities there exists, between the wealthy and the workingmen, a considerable body of professional men, shopkeepers, and clerks, who are rather less of a defined middle class than they might be in European countries." They possessed a strong urge to improve their lot and tended to imitate, as far as it was possible, the elite. Still, they were not cohesive enough or sufficiently defined to compose a "class," and for that reason the purposely chosen, more nebulous term "middle sectors" is applied to them. Although the heirs of the creoles and mazombos tended to predominate in the middle sectors, increasing numbers of mulattoes and mestizos entered. Education and military service provided two of the surest paths of upward mobility, but the climb was too steep for any but the exceptional or the favored. Although few in number, the dominant presence of the middle sectors in the capital city of each nation allowed them to wield influence far out of proportion to their size. A high percentage of the intellectuals, authors, teachers, and journalists came from their ranks, and they had a powerful voice in expressing what passed for public opinion in the late nineteenth century.

Only an educated guess permits some approximation of the size of the middle sectors. At the end of the nineteenth century it is estimated that Mexico had an urban middle group numbering roughly three-quarters of a million, while another quarter of a million constituted a rural middle group. In contrast, there was an urban proletariat of over one-third of a million and a huge peon class of eight million working on the haciendas. In Mexico, Chile, Brazil, Argentina, and Uruguay, the middle sectors may have included as many as 10 percent of the population by the turn of the century. In many of the other countries, it fell far short of that.

The swelling tide of foreign immigration contributed to the growth of the middle sectors. Many of the new arrivals were from the lower class, but still a high percentage represented Europe's middle class, and besides there was a high incidence of upward mobility among the immigrants in the lands of their adoption. Argentina has been one of the largest recipients of immigrants in modern times. Between independence and 1914, approximately three million arrived, a majority of them Italians and Spaniards. In 1914, 30 percent of Argentines were foreign-born. These immigrants provided 60 percent of the urban proletariat and held 46 percent of the jobs associated with the middle sectors. Half of the population of Buenos Aires in 1914 was foreign-born. Alberto Gerchunoff, a Russian who arrived in Argentina in 1895, left a moving account of the problems and satisfactions of assimilation in his *The Jewish Gauchos of the Pampas* (1910). About 100,000 Europeans migrated to Chile before World War I. They constituted at that time only 4 percent of the population. Yet the foreign-born owned 32 percent of Chile's commercial establishments and 49 percent of the industries. Brazil welcomed large numbers of Europeans, particularly Italians, Portuguese, and Spaniards. Between 1891 and 1900, approximately 112,500 immigrants arrived annually. The trend continued and reached record yearly averages just before World War I. From 1911 through 1913, half a million immigrants entered. However, the proportion of immigrants to the total population in Brazil was never more than 6.4 percent, a figure reached in 1900. Nonetheless, because of their concentration in the south and southeast, and particularly because of their importance in the cities of these two regions, they exerted an influence far greater than their numbers might indicate. The traditional elite soon grew wary of the immigrants and blamed them for many of the ills the burgeoning urban centers were beginning to experience.

Immigrants disembark in Buenos Aires, Argentina, 1907

The new ideas, methods, and skills introduced by the immigrants helped to accelerate modernization.

CONTINUITY AND CHANGE

During the last half of the nineteenth century, new forces appeared that challenged the social, economic, and political institutions deeply rooted in the colonial past. Urbanization, industrialization, and modernization formed a trinity menacing to tradition. Once introduced, these mutually supporting forces could not be arrested. The center of political, economic, and social life, once located on the plantations and haciendas, shifted gradually but irreversibly to the cities.

In the cities the middle sectors grew in size and influence. The white descendents of the creoles and mazombos no longer dominated that group unchallenged. In many of the Latin American nations the mestizos and/or mulattoes formed the largest part of the population. Mexico, Guatemala, Ecuador, Peru, Bolivia, and Paraguay, for example, had large mestizo populations, while the Dominican Republic, Venezuela, and Brazil had large mulatto populations. Representatives of the mestizos and mulattoes entered the middle sectors in large numbers during the last decades of the nineteenth century and claimed their right to play a political and economic role in their nation's destiny. In some cases, the traditional social elites accommodated their ambitions; in others their frustrations mounted as they were excluded from positions of control, prestige, or wealth.

By the beginning of the twentieth century, some of the Latin American states—certainly Argentina, Brazil, Chile, and Mexico—conveyed at least the outward appearance of having adopted the patterns and modes of the most progressive European states and of the United States. Their constitutions embodied the noblest principles of Western political thought. Their governmental apparatus followed the most progressive models of the day. Political stability replaced chaos. Expanding transportation and communication infrastructures permitted the governments to control a larger area of their nations than they ever had before. New industries existed. An ever larger banking network facilitated and encouraged commerce. Society was more diversified than at any previous time. In the capitals and the largest cities, the architecture of the new buildings duplicated the latest styles of Paris—in how many Latin American cities do the local citizens proudly point to the opera house and claim it to be a replica of the Paris Opera? To the extent that some of the Latin American states formally resembled the leading nations of the Western world, which they consciously accepted as their models of modernity, it is possible to conclude that those nations qualified as modern. However, many would argue that such modernity was only a veneer. It added a cosmetic touch to tenacious institutions while failing to effect the changes implied by the concept. Modernization in Latin America lacked real substance.

The superficiality of modernization guaranteed the continued domination of the past. The rural aristocracy still enjoyed power; their estates remained huge and generally inefficient; their control over their workers was complete. The latifundia actually grew rather than diminished in size during the nineteenth century, at the expense of the Indian communities and their traditional landholdings, the properties confiscated from the Church, and the public domain. One visitor to Chile in the early twentieth century noted:

> The owner of the land, however, has much more authority over his tenant than obtains in the United States. He is usually the local magistrate, and does not hesitate to adjudicate cases in which he is personally interested. He also runs a store to supply his tenants with necessary articles, and as credit is easily obtained, the tenant is seldom free from debt.

With twenty-five years of residence and travel in South America, Albert Hale observed of Brazil in 1906, "There exist traces of a feudal system, in that sharp line which divided the upper class, the aristocracy, from the lower class, the laborers. . . . The monarchy was so recently destroyed that in their [the laborer's] minds an aristocracy of blood still prevails, but this aristocracy is really one of land, of money." In 1910, James Bryce vividly described the large planter in Brazil as living "in a sort of semi-feudal patriarchal way" in his "little principality." He compared the situation to that in England a century earlier, when country squires controlled local affairs and selected the members of Parliament.

By early 1888, the nefarious institution of slavery had been abolished. Still, former slaves and their descendants occupied one of the lowest rungs of the social and economic ladder. The doors to education, opportunity, and mobility remained tightly closed to them except in the rarest instances. The Indians fared no better. Debt servitude of one or another variety characterized part of the labor market. Clorinda Matto de Turner recorded in her novel *Aves sin Nido* how debt servitude worked in one shocking case. To borrow 10 pesos, the Indian had to agree to repay 120 at a specific date. Unable to repay, he saw his daughter seized by the lender and sold into servitude to make good the debt. It would have been foolish to have expected the law to intervene to restrict such abuses since the making, enforcing, and judging of the laws rested in the hands of the landowners and their sympathizers.

The wealthiest and most powerful class in Latin America in general was white or near white in complexion. Heirs of the creoles and mazombos, they enjoyed age-old economic advantages, to which, after independence, they added political power. The group that surrounded Porfirio Díaz spoke of themselves, symbolically enough, as the "New Creoles."

Neofeudalism comfortably allied itself with the invigorated capitalism of nineteenth-century Latin America. Positivism even provided a handy ideological umbrella for the two. Like so much of the economic and political thought in Latin America then and since, it recognized no incompatibility in the imposition of capitalist industrialization on a neofeudal, rural base. With its emphasis on order and hierarchy, Positivism assured the elites their venerable privileges, relative prosperity, and selective progress and held out promise of the same to the restless middle sectors. Subsumed was the inferiority of the masses who stood very little chance of "progressing" in a society in which all the institutions repressed them.

Dependency accelerated rather than diminished after independence. Latin America depended for its prosperity on the sale of a few natural, raw products to the industrialized nations. Further, it depended on foreign loans, investments, inventions, technology, technicians, merchant ships, middlemen, and ideology. The very accoutrements of its modernization tightened its dependency. Latin America was able to grow under such conditions, but it hardly developed. Even the growth rates tended to be more modest than historians once concluded.

Social inequality, neofeudalism, paternalistic rule, privilege, and dependency clearly were incompatible with the new trends started during the last half of the century. The Chilean intellectual Miguel Cruchago Montt pointed out in his *Estudio sobre la organización económica y la hacienda pública de Chile* (Study of Chile's Economic Organization and Public Finances), published in 1878, that the colonial past dominated the present and frustrated development. The past could no longer exist unchallenged once Latin Americans began to think in terms of national development.

At the opening of the twentieth century, the Colombian Rafael Uribe stated that the basic economic question concerned the quality of life of the "people": "Are they able to satisfy their basic needs?" The reality was they could not. A majority of the Latin Americans were no better off at the dawn of twentieth century than they had been a century earlier. In fact, a persuasive argument can be made that they were worse off. The negative response to Uribe's question foretold conflict.

THE POPULAR CHALLENGE

The Latin American nations marched toward progress to a tune played by the elites, but not without discordant chords sounded by large numbers of the humble classes. For the majority of the Latin Americans, progress was proving to mean increased concentration of lands in the hands of ever fewer owners; falling per capita food production with corollary rising food imports; greater impoverishment; less to eat; more vulnerability to the whims of an impersonal international market; uneven growth; increased unemployment and underemployment; social, economic, and political marginalization; and greater power in the hands of the privileged few. Ironically, the more the folk cultures were forced to integrate into world commerce, the fewer the material benefits the folk reaped. But poverty through progress must be understood in more than the material terms of declining wages, purchasing power or nutritional levels. A tragic spiritual and cultural impoverishment debased the majority, who were forced by circumstances to abandon previously satisfactory ways of life and to accept alien ones that provided them little or no psychic benefits.

The impoverished majority both bore the burden of the inequitable institutional structure and paid for the modernization enjoyed by the privileged. The deprivation, repression, and deculturalization of the majority by the minority created tensions that frequently gave rise to violence. The poor protested their increasing misfortunes as modernization increased. For their own part, the privileged were determined to modernize and to maintain the order required to do so. They freely used whatever force was necessary to accomplish both. Consequently, the imposition of progress stirred social disorder.

Indian rebellions flared up from Mexico to Chile. The Indians refused to surrender their remaining lands quietly as the large estates intensified their encroachment. The arrival of the railroads, which accelerated those encroachments, spawned greater violence. Doubtless the major Indian rebellion in terms of length, carnage, and significance in the Americas of the nineteenth century was the Caste War of Yucatan between the Mayas and the peninsula's whites and mestizos.

In the years after Mexico declared its independence, the sugar and henequen plantations had expanded to threaten the corn cultures of the Mayas by incorporating their lands into the latifundia and by impressing the Indians into service as debt peons. The Indians fought for their land and freedom. They defended their world. On the other side, the Yucatan elite professed that they fought for "the holy cause of order, humanity, and civilization." Much of the bloodiest fighting occurred during the period from 1847 to 1855, but the war lingered on until the early twentieth century. During those decades the Mayas of eastern and southern Yucatan governed themselves.

Free of white domination, the Mayan rebels took the name of Cruzob, turned their backs on the white world, and developed their own culture, a synthesis of their Mayan inheritance and Spanish influences. Four hundred years of conquest had erased the intellectual and artistic heritage from the Mayan mind, but the Cruzob retained their knowledge of agriculture and village and family organization from the pre-Columbian past. Unique to the Cruzob was the development of their own religion, based largely on their interpretation of Christianity. Unlike other syncretic regions of Latin America, it developed without dependence on the sporadic participation of Roman Catholic priests (to perform baptisms, marriages, or an occasional mass) and free from the critical eye of the white master. Incorporating the Indian folkways, it strengthened the Cruzob and provided a spiritual base for independence other Indians lacked. What was notable about the Cruzob was the emergence of a viable Indian alternative to Europeanization. Although infused with Spanish contributions, it bore a strong resemblance to the pre-Columbian Mayan society. Reviving their Indian culture by repudiating "foreign" domination and substituting their own values for "foreign" ones, the Cruzob revitalized their society. They became masters of their own land again.

Powerful forces at work in the closing decades of the nineteenth century overwhelmed the Cruzob. The poor soil of Yucatan, exhausted under corn cultivation, no longer yielded sufficient food. Disease reduced the Indian ranks faster than battle did. At the same time, Mexico, increasingly stable under Porfirio Díaz, showed less tolerance for the Cruzob and more determination to subdue them in order to exploit Yucatan. A treaty between Mexico and Great Britain closed British Honduras to the Cruzob, thus cutting off their single source of modern weapons and ammunition. Finally, the expanding wagon trails and railroads from northern Yucatan, which accompanied the spread of the prosperous henequen plantations, penetrated the Cruzob territory. A growing market for forest woods even sent the whites into the seemingly impenetrable forest redoubts of the Cruzob. Consequently a declining Cruzob population and relentless Mexican pressures brought to an end the Mayan independence of half a century. The long and tenacious resistance testified to the Indian preference, a rejection of the modernization preferred by the elites.

The Indians were not the only rebels. In Brazil, where slavery lingered after midcentury, the blacks vigorously protested their servitude. Sober members of the elites regarded the slave as "a volcano that constantly threatens society, a mine ready to explode," as one nineteenth-century intellectual phrased it in his study of Brazilian slavery. Foreign visitors also sensed the tensions created by slave society. Prince Adalbert of Prussia visited one large, well-run plantation, which he praised as a model. After noting the seemingly friendly relations between master and slaves, he revealed, "The loaded guns and pistols hanging up in his [the master's] bedroom, however, showed that he had not entire confidence in them [the slaves] and indeed, he had more than once been obliged to face them with his loaded guns." The decade of the 1880s, just prior to emancipation, witnessed mounting slave resistance. The slaves fled the plantations, killed the masters, and burned fields and buildings. One fiery black abolitionist leader, Luís Gonzaga de Pinto Gama, declared, "Every slave who kills his master, no matter what the circumstances might be, kills in self-defense." He also preached the "right of insurrection." Free blacks throughout the Americas protested their poverty and the institutions that they felt perpetuated their problems. For example, Panama City seethed with racial tensions during the decades from 1850 to 1880. The black urban masses resented their depressed conditions and used violence—robberies, fires, rioting—as a means of protest. Many referred to the situation as a "race war," exacerbated by an economic reality in which the poor were black and the rich, white.

Peasant rebellions abounded, signifying still other challenges to the elitist institutions and commitment to modernization. More often than not, the ideology behind those rebellions was vague and contradictory. Somehow, the rebels hoped to save their lands, improve their standards of living, and share in the exercise of power. Two popular revolts, one in Brazil, another in Argentina, illustrate the motives, the violence, and the repression.

The Quebra-Quilo Revolt, from late 1874 to early 1875, ranked high in significance because the peasants of Brazil's interior Northeast succeeded in checking the government's new modernization drive (underway by 1871 but ineffectual by 1875). The causes of that revolt were not unique: new taxes and the threat peasants felt from the large landowners absorbing their farms, complicated by the imposition of the metric system with the requirement of fees for official alteration and authentication of weights. A journalist covering the revolt called it "the direct consequence of the suffering and deprivation . . . of the working classes of the interior"; while a peasant participant claimed, "The fruit of the soil belongs to the people and tax ought not be paid on it." As riots multiplied in the marketplaces, the municipal and provincial authorities feared the "forces of Barbarism" were poised to sweep across the Northeast. The peasants were unusually successful. They ignored the new taxes, destroyed the new weights and measures, and burned official records and archives (thus protecting their informal title to the land by reducing to ashes the legal documentation). The peasants in most cases had taken physical possession and worked the land over the generations without title. They faced possible eviction by anyone who could show the proper paper authenticating legal ownership. By destroying the records, the peasants removed evidence—the local notorial registers of land, for example—from use in judicial proceedings, thereby putting themselves on equal legal footing with the local landed elite. Momentarily, then, the sporadic riots that constituted the revolt achieved the peasants' goals, while temporarily frustrating the penetration of the elites into their region.

In Argentina, revolts shook the province of Santa Fé in 1893. Small farmers there protested a tax on wheat to pay for the government's innovations, including railroads, that seemed to favor the large landowners. Furthermore, they resented the fact that immigrants received land and preferential treatment denied the locals. In the meantime, social disorder rose dramatically in the Argentine province of Tucumán between 1876 and 1895. During those two decades the number of arrests, ones involving mostly illiterate workers, jumped from under 2,000 per year to over 17,000, while the total population only doubled during the same period.

Popular protest also assumed forms other than rebellion. Banditry and millenarian movements flourished in the nineteenth century, although serious studies of them are still rare. Thanks to the conceptual framework offered by E. J. Hobsbawm, it is possible with many cautions to consider banditry as a form of social protest and millenarianism as a type of popular revolution.

Religious in content, advocating a radical change in the world, millenarianism profoundly and totally rejects the present while expressing a passionate hope for a happier future. Those faithful to such ideas believe the world will come to a sudden, apocalyptic end but are vague about how this will happen and about the details of the new society that will replace the old. Although political revolutionaries also advocate a new society, they diverge from millenarianism because revolutionaries plan for and express ideas about how society will be remade. Millenarianists, on the other hand, expect the change to take place through divine intervention according to God's will and plan. Their duty is to prepare themselves for the new world. Obviously people hoping for a new and better life are expressing a form of dissatisfaction with the life they currently lead. Although they do not want confrontation, events may frequently force violence.

Brazil witnessed a remarkable array of millenarian movements. Doubtless the best known took place in the dry, impoverished backlands of the state of Bahia where the mystic Antônio the Counselor gathered the faithful between 1893 and 1897. Thousands flocked to his settlement at Canudos to listen to the Counselor preach. They stayed to establish a flourishing agrarian community. He alienated the government by advising his adherents not to pay taxes. Furthermore, his patriarchal ideas smacked of monarchism to the recently established republican government in Rio de Janeiro. The Church authorities denounced him, resenting his influence over the masses. The local landlords disliked him because he siphoned off the rural workers and stalmated the expansion of their fazendas. Those powerful enemies decided to arrest Antônio and scatter the settlers at Canudos. However, they failed to consider the strength and determination of his followers. It took four military campaigns, all the modern armaments the Brazilian army could muster, and countless lives to suppress the millenarian movement. The final campaign directed by the minister of war himself devastated the settlement at Canudos house by house. The people refused to surrender. The epic struggle inspired one of the masterpieces of Latin American literature, *Rebellion in the Backlands* by Euclydes da Cunha (1902).

Messianic movements flourished among the Andean Indians after the conquest. They yearned for a return to an order, basically the traditional Incan destroyed the Spanish conquest, that would benefit them rather than the outsider. Exemplary of such movements in the nineteenth century was one that occurred among the Bolivian Indians of Curuyaqui in 1891—92. An individual called Tumpa and known as "the supreme being" appeared in the community announcing his mission "to liberate them from the whites." "My kingdom is not of this world," he advised his adherents. Under his prophetic new system Tumpa promised that the whites would work for the Indians. His followers took up arms as urged by the messianic leader; the whites fled to the cities, and the army arrived to brutally crush the uprising. The carnage disproved at least two of Tumpa's prophecies: first, that only water would issue forth from the soldier's guns, and second, that anyone who did die for the cause would return to life in three days.

Northwestern Mexico was the scene of the miracle cures of Teresa Urrea, referred to by hundreds of thousands of devotees as Teresita or the Saint of Cabora. In 1889, after a severe psychological shock, she lapsed into a comatose state. Considered dead, she regained life just prior to her burial. She reported having spoken to the Blessed Virgin, who conferred on her the power to cure. By 1891, pilgrims flooded Cabora seeking her help. Teresita's compassion for the poor earned her the devotion of the masses and the suspicion of the Díaz government. The Yaqui and Mayo Indians confided in her and unburdened their sufferings before her. Believing she enjoyed influence with God, they pressed her for help and advice. In 1890, the Tarahumara Indian mountain village of Tomochic adopted Teresita as their saint, placing a statue of her in their church. The village began to modify its Roman Catholicism to a more indigenous religion focused on the Saint of Cabora. The next year Tomochic rebelled against the government and requested Teresita to interpret God's will to them. The government reacted immediately and harshly, but it still took several armed expeditions to quell the rebellion. The village was destroyed, and not a man or boy over thirteen years of age survived the slaughter. In mid-May of 1892, a group of approximately two hundred Mayo Indians attacked the town of Navojoa shouting, "Viva la Santa de Cabora!" Considering her a dangerous agitator of the masses, the Díaz government exiled Teresa Urrea to the United States. Teresita, herself opposed to violence, had served more as a figurehead, a catalyst, a remarkable charismatic personality, whose compassion gave unity of expression to the miserable masses of northwestern Mexico.

Banditry attracted the desperate, those who had lost out in the system whether they were the poor or members of the impoverished gentry. Whatever else banditry might have signified, it was as much a means of protesting injustice or righting wrongs as it was of equalizing wealth or taking political revenge. Although unsympathetic to banditry, the Brazilian jurist of the mid-nineteenth century, Tavares Bastos, realized that the bandits often were victims of the state who, no longer confiding in its laws, made their own justice.

Bandits roamed the Brazilian interior in the nineteenth century, particularly the impoverished Northeast, where many won the admiration of the poor and the respect of the wealthy, who not infrequently coopted them and utilized their services. Some scholarship correlates the rise of banditry in the late nineteenth century with the breakdown of the patriarchal order in the countryside. Brazilian popular poetry abounds with tales of the bandit hero. A well-known one, sung at the beginning of the twentieth century, related the history of Antônio Silvino, who became a bandit in 1896 to avenge an injustice: his father was slain by a police official who went unpunished by the government. Others relate the adventures of Josuíno Brilhante, also seemingly forced into banditry to avenge injustices against his family. He assaulted the rich and distributed their goods and money among the poor, boasting that he never robbed for himself.

Banditry characterized much of Spanish America as well. Mexican banditry flourished, and interestingly enough, regions that produced bandits, such as Chalco-Río Frío, eastern Morelos, and northwestern Puebla, spawned agrarian revolutionaries before the century ended, providing further evidence of the social dimension banditry could assume on occasion. Peru offers numerous examples of peasant bandits. In his study of them, Enrique López Albujar described banditry as "a protest, a rebellion, a deviation, or a simple means of subsistence." He concluded that nineteenth-century Peruvian banditry produced an array of folk heroes because those bandits corrected injustices, robbed to help the poor, and protested social and economic inequities. For their part, Chilean officials tended to lump together Indians and bandits of the rugged Andes as "criminals." They also routinely complained that local populations supported the bandits, thus facilitating their antiestablishment activities.

The motives and activities of the bandits varied widely, but at least in part they could be explained as protests against the wrongs of society, as they viewed it. Because of their strength and because they often opposed the elites and official institutions, they received the support, indeed the admiration, of large numbers of the humble classes, who often hid them, lied to the authorities to protect them, guided them through strange terrain, and fed them. To the poor, the bandits were caudillos who by default helped them to sustain their folk cultures and the deflect modernization.

The folk by no means rejected change simply to preserve the past unaltered. Rather, they wished to mediate change over a longer period of time, and hopefully in their favor. The elites showed little patience with that desire. They dealt severely with any protest and thus further raised the level of violence. In the last analysis they triumphed. After all, they controlled the police, militia, and military. Furthermore, the popular protests tended to be local and uncoordinated (with the exceptions of the folk caudillos discussed in an earlier section). Thus, despite the frequency of such protests, the elites imposed their will and thus their brand of progress. The triumph of that progress set the course for twentieth-century history in Latin America. It bequeathed a legacy of mass poverty and continued conflict.

6

New Actors
on an
Old Stage

United States troops marching into Havana, 1898

As Latin America approached its independence centennial, two trends, one of external origin and the other internal, emerged with greater clarity. The first was the emergence of the United States as a major world power, preoccupied with its security in the Western Hemisphere and possessing a strong drive to invest in and trade with Latin America. The other was the emergence of better-defined middle sectors within Latin America. The growing middle sectors were looking for their own sources of inspiration, their own example. The industrializing and progressing United States attracted their attention. They visited New York before Paris; they learned English rather than French. Above all else, they admired the new technology associated with the United States. They saw in industrialization their key to advancement, and no country industrialized more rapidly and more thoroughly than the United States. They may have feared the expansion of their mentor and ridiculed its materialism, but nonetheless they were drawn toward it, and the life style of the Latin American middle sectors increasingly reflected that of the United States. Together the United States and the Latin American middle sectors, evolving rapidly into a well-defined middle class, helped to shape Latin American history during the twentieth century. What were their motivations and goals? How would they influence the flow of history?

THE PRESENCE OF THE UNITED STATES

Foreign influence—and none more so than Great Britain's—shaped much of Latin America's development in the nineteenth century. The primary challenge to British interests came from the United States, which was determined to spread across the North American continent and to dominate the Caribbean. By the early twentieth century, the United States had succeeded in doing both and was well on its way to replacing Britain's century-long domination of Latin America. U.S. attitudes and policies toward Latin America were shaped by concerns for security and desires for trade. Obviously the United States and Latin America shared the same geography, the Western Hemisphere, thus being—in a certain romantic sense—neighbors, even though much of the United States was closer to Europe than it was to most of South America.

After the bold proclamation of President Monroe in 1823, officials in Washington chose to ignore the doctrine for several decades. The British reoccupied the Falkland Islands despite vigorous Argentine protests, the French intervened in Mexico and the Plata area, and the French and British blockaded Buenos Aires, all without the United States reminding these European interlopers of the content or intention of Monroe's statement. Only when the British and French maneuvered to thwart the union of Texas with the United States did President John Tyler invoke the principles of the doctrine in 1842 to warn the Europeans to keep out of hemispheric affairs. Indeed, as later used, the doctrine provided a handy shield for North American expansion, well underway by the mid-1840s. As President James Polk gazed westward toward California, he notified the Europeans that his country opposed any transfer of territory in the New World from one European state to another or from a nation of the Western Hemisphere to a European nation. However, by his interpretation the Monroe Doctrine did not prohibit territorial changes among the nations of this hemisphere. Such an interpretation complemented the annexation by the United States of Texas in 1845 and of Arizona, New Mexico, and California later in the decade. Expansionist sentiment rose to a fever pitch as the Stars and Stripes fluttered across the continent toward the Pacific Ocean. An editorial in the influential *De Bow's Commercial Review* in 1848 expressed the ebullient mood of a confident nation:

> The North Americans will spread out far beyond their present bounds. They will encroach again and again upon their neighbors. New territories will be planted, declare their independence, and be annexed. We have New Mexico and California! We will have Old Mexico and Cuba!

Such rhetoric aroused cheers in the United States. Reacting quite differently, the Latin Americans watched with apprehension the division of Mexico and debated how best to stem the expansion of the menacing "Colossus of the North." Their old fears of European intervention faded as the shadow of the United States lengthened.

Great Britain served as the major check on United States expansion southward into Middle America and the Caribbean during the mid-nineteenth century. British interests in the area were considerable, United States interests were growing, and the diplomatic maneuverings between the two to protect and extend those interests intensified. The best the United States could arrange at the time was an agreement in 1850, the Clayton-Bulwer Treaty, in which both nations promised not to occupy, fortify, colonize, or otherwise exercise domination over Central America. The treaty temporarily checked the territorial expansion of both nations into troubled and tempting republics that otherwise stood helpless before the two aggressive Anglo-Saxon powers. At about the same time the attention of the United States focused inward once again as a divided nation girded itself for internal strife.

While civil war rent the United States, several European nations pursued their own adventures in the New World. Spain reannexed the Dominican Republic and fought Peru and Chile. France intervened in Mexico. Only after it became apparent that the North was winning the Civil War and was determined to oppose European adventures in this hemisphere did Spain depart from the Dominican Republic and return the Chincha

Islands to Peru. When Napoleon III hesitated to withdraw French forces from Mexico, the government in Washington dispatched a large army to the Mexican border to help the French emperor make up his mind. Once these European threats to Latin America had ended, the United States seemed content to ignore the region—at least for the moment—while the nation concentrated its energies on reconstruction, railroad building, and industrialization.

Rapid industrial growth eventually prompted United States business people and leaders to search for new markets, and none seemed more promising than Latin America, long the domain of European salespeople. One of the most remarkable secretaries of state, James G. Blaine, understanding the need for friendship and cooperation among the nations of the hemisphere, sought to stimulate more intimate commercial relations as a logical means to solidify the inter-American community. The United States had long appreciated the strategic importance of Latin America but had been slow to develop its trade relations with the huge area. During the last half of the nineteenth century, North American commerce with and investments in Latin America rose gradually. In the vigorous industrial age that had begun in the United States, Secretary of State Blaine envisioned a fraternal hemispheric trade in which the United States supplied the manufactured goods and Latin America the raw products. With such an idea in mind, he presided over the first Inter-American Conference, held in Washington in 1889–90. Although cordiality characterized the sessions, it became increasingly obvious that the Latin Americans were less interested in placing orders for the new industrial products than they were in containing the expansion of an ambitious neighbor by obtaining a promise of respect for the sovereignty of their nations. The times augured ill for such a promise. In fact, at that very moment, a rising tide of sentiment favoring expansion once again swept the United States.

Others in the United States realized as Blaine did that Latin America contained great wealth and potential, but unlike the secretary of state they showed less subtlety in coveting it. In the eyes of many, the Latin Americans appeared too slow in fulfilling the destiny nature had charted for the area. Doubtless some "Protestant virtues and Yankee know-how" were needed to turn potential into reality—or at least so thought a growing number of citizens of the prospering United States, well satisfied that they had discovered the secrets of success. The Reverend Josiah Strong summed up much of the opinion of his fellow countrymen in his influential book *Our Country,* published in 1885, when he asked, "Having developed peculiarly aggressive traits calculated to impress its institutions upon mankind, [the United States] will spread itself over the earth. If I read not amiss, this powerful race will move down Central and South America, out upon the islands of the sea, over upon Africa and beyond. And can anyone doubt that the result of this competition of races will be the 'survival of the fittest'?" Imbued with the Spencerian and Darwinian philosophy popular at the time, the good Reverend spoke with the enthusiasm, confidence, and arrogance of his generation. Other powerful voices soon echoed his views. Senator Henry Cabot Lodge spoke of "our rightful supremacy in the Western Hemisphere." Naval officer, historian, and strategist Alfred T. Mahan lobbied for a bigger and better navy. Senator Albert J. Beveridge put his faith in a still more potent force: "God has marked the American people as His chosen Nation to finally lead to the regeneration of the world. . . . We are trustees of the world's progress, guardians of its righteous peace." Secretary of State Richard Olney announced to the world in 1895 that the United States was supreme in the Western Hemisphere where its will would be done.

Thus, by the end of the nineteenth century, government and business leaders alike spoke approvingly of expanding world markets and of a global foreign policy. Their talk soon led to action: American overseas expansion into the Pacific and the Caribbean. Significantly that expansion began after the conquest of the western frontier, after several decades of impressive industrial growth, and during the economic difficulties of the 1890s. The United States challenged Spain in 1898 and easily wrested from its remaining empire the Philippine Islands, Cuba, and Puerto Rico. The quick victory marked the debut of the United States as a world power embarked upon a new international course of extracontinental expansion, which one influential journalist of the day characterized admiringly as "the imperialism of liberty." Washington annexed Puerto Rico and made Cuba a protectorate, a state of dependency that officially lasted thirty-five years.

The six-week war against a once mighty Spain heightened the confidence, not to mention the feeling of superiority, of the United States. National rhetoric reflected that attitude. In his study of the relations between the United States and Latin America published in 1908, George W. Crichfield spoke pompously of the duty to impose "civilization" on the Latin Americans: "The United States is in honor bound to maintain law and order in South America, and we may just as well take complete control of several of the countries, and establish decent governments while we are about it." More than half the nations, he huffed, had "sinned away their day of grace. They are semibarbarous centers of rapine. . . . They are a reproach to the civilization of the twentieth century." Diplomacy dictated that such ideas be expressed more subtly, but there can be no doubt that the same sentiments governed Washington's twentieth-century behavior in Latin America in the twin pursuits of trade and security.

Under the influence of "Dollar Diplomacy," foreign policy pronouncements, nonetheless, could be surprisingly frank. As more and more U.S. capital entered Latin America, the U.S. government encouraged the trend and stated its determination to protect it. President William Howard Taft (1908–12) left no doubt of where his government stood on those matters.

Doubtless influenced by his experiences as the first civil governor (1901–04) of the U.S.–controlled Philippine Islands and provisional governor of Cuba (1906), he announced his foreign policy would "include active intervention to secure our merchandise and our capitalists opportunity for profitable investment." Indeed, the United States already had involved itself physically in the region that most strategically concerned it, the Caribbean and circum-Caribbean.

In the period between 1898 and 1934, the United States intervened militarily in Cuba, Mexico, Guatemala, Honduras, Nicaragua, Panama, Colombia, Haiti, and the Dominican Republic. In some nations, such as Honduras, Panama, and Cuba, the interventions occurred repeatedly. In others, like Haiti, the Dominican Republic, and Nicaragua, they lasted for years, even decades. In Haiti, the marines landed in 1915 and did not depart until 1934. Tolerating no opposition, the marines fought continuously during their interventions against outraged local patriots. For example, in Haiti, Charlemagne Peralte organized a guerrilla army in 1917 to fight the U.S. Marines. Betrayed, he died in an ambush two years later. The newspapers in the United States invariably branded those armed opponents as "bandits." Of course viewpoints conflicted. Those termed bandits by the U.S. Army were labeled "freedom fighters" or "guerrillas" by others who were bearing the brunt or feeling the humiliation of the intervention.

While its interventions in Nicaragua dated back to 1849, the United States never occupied that country in the nineteenth century. Annoyed with President José Santos Zelaya (1893–1909), a fiery nationalist who talked of enlisting Japanese, British, and/or German help to build a canal across Nicaragua, the United States dispatched a fleet in 1909 to overthrow him. Thus began a prolonged occupation, 1909 to 1933 (with one break in 1925–26). Denouncing the seemingly endless occupation by the Yankees who "murder us in our own land," Augusto César Sandino launched a rebellion on July 16, 1927: "I am accepting the invitation to combat." For five and a half years, Sandino led the fight to expel the foreign occupiers. For that challenge, the international press vilified him as a bloodthirsty bandit. His skill in harassing the marines, avoiding capture, and embarrassing the United States won the support of large numbers of Nicaraguans and the admiration of many Latin Americans. On repeated occasions, Sandino advocated changes for a "free Nicaragua": a popular, independent government, the revision of all treaties that limited Nicaragua's sovereignty, and the recovery of the nation's riches and resources for the benefit of all. He favored land reform: "I believe the state owns the land. . . . I favor a system of cooperatives to work the land." Nationalism was the force propelling and shaping his struggle and the revolution it promised. To an occupied people, he was a patriot, a man who nourished their self-respect.

The treacherous assassination of General Sandino opened a new chapter in Nicaraguan history that is still being written. After the U.S. Marines

Augusto César Sandino, 1934

withdrew in January of 1933, Sandino agreed to a cease fire and signed with President Juan Bautista Sacasa a protocol of peace. The guerrilla chief swore loyalty to the president, while repeatedly warning him to beware of the new Guardia Nacional (National Guard), created, equipped, and trained by the U.S. Marines. He particularly suspected the ambitions of the Guard's commander, Anastasio Somoza. In the spring, Sandino issued a "Manifesto" declaring his moral support of President Sacasa and his intention to remain in the Segovia mountains where he would "organize agricultural cooperatives in these beautiful regions that for centuries have been ignored by the statesmen." In February 1934, Sandino returned to Managua for more talks with the government. On that occasion, General Somoza and officers of the Guardia Nacional planned the assassination of Sandino, who was seized after leaving a dinner with Sacasa and executed. Somoza waited until 1936 to depose Sacasa and to establish a dynastic rule that lasted until 1979. But the ghost of Augusto César Sandino did not rest. Most Nicaraguans—and many Latin Americans—accorded him a position of honor as a folk hero. From his grave he would defeat the Somozas.

The rationale for U.S. interventions varied. In the cases of the Dominican Republic and Haiti, the marines landed ostensibly to forestall threatened European intervention to collect debts; in Nicaragua, the country's alleged chaotic finances partially explained the United States presence, but probably more significant was the rumor that the Nicaraguan government might sell exclusive canal rights through its territory to either Japan or Great Britain. Threats, real or imagined, against U.S. citizens or property occasioned other U.S. interventions. Nor were they limited to small republics; both Colombia and Mexico felt the weight of the "Colossus of the North." (The U.S. intervention in Mexico during the second decade of the twentieth century will be discussed in Chapter 7.)

Near the turn of the century opinion in the United States favoring the construction of an interoceanic canal was growing, spurred by military and commercial considerations. The first step toward the realization of a canal was to abrogate the old Clayton-Bulwer Treaty. Under international pressure, London agreed in the Hay-Pauncefote Treaty in 1901 to permit the United States to build, operate, and fortify a canal across the isthmus. Washington then proceeded to negotiate with Colombia for rights across Panama, but the Senate in Bogotá balked at the terms suggested. At that point, the Panamanians seceded from Colombia and declared their independence on November 3, 1903. The Panamanians found their new sovereignty heavily compromised by the treaty signed fifteen days later by U.S. Secretary of State John Hay and the Frenchman Philippe Bunau-Varilla, an international adventurer who purported to represent Panama's interests. He pocketed $40 million from the United States for which no public accounting was ever given, received the Legion of Honor from the French government, and never returned to Panama. The treaty he signed in Panama's name granted the United States "in perpetuity" control of a ten-mile strip across the Isthmus with power and jurisdiction "as if it were sovereign." It was negotiated without consulting the Panamanians during those chaotic days when they were fighting physically for their independence. Work on the canal began in 1904 and terminated a decade later. Controversy over the canal and the treaty that made it possible has raged between the United States and Panama ever since.

The trespassing of the North American giant on Latin American sovereignty evoked protest and aroused distrust. Many Latin American intellectuals of the period spoke out to denounce "the Yankee imperialism." Physically unable to prevent the interventions, Latin American governments sought recourse in international law. They labored long and determinedly to persuade Washington to renounce by treaty recourse to intervention.

Meanwhile, the United States eclipsed Great Britain as the dominant foreign economic influence. Investments from the United States rose rapidly. By 1897, U.S. capital in Latin America totaled $320 million, chiefly in Mexico, Cuba, and Central America. Railroads ranked as the most important investment, followed by mining and then agriculture. In the next decade and a half investments jumped fivefold with Chile and Peru joining the Middle American nations as the chief recipients of attention. By 1929,

U.S. citizens had invested $3.5 billion, or 40 percent of all overseas investments, in Latin America.

Trade between the United States and Latin America increased with equal rapidity. The United States supplanted Europe in economic importance in Middle America. By 1914 the United States was purchasing 75 percent of Mexico's exports and supplying 50 percent of its neighbor's imports. By 1919 the United States consumed two-thirds of Central America's exports, while furnishing that area with three-quarters of its imports. Domination of the South American markets was less complete but nonetheless very important and growing. New steamship lines and telegraph cables tightened the links between the United States and Latin America.

The North Americans, who had forged particularly strong economic links with Brazil, were the principal customers of Brazil's three-major exports: coffee, rubber, and cocoa. Since 1865, the United States had taken the single largest share of Brazil's coffee, after 1870 buying more than half its coffee beans sold abroad. The result was that by 1912 the United States bought 36 percent of Brazil's exports, while the second most important market, Great Britain, purchased only 15 percent. Indicating the increasing importance of trade with Brazil, the National City Bank of New York in 1915 established the first two U.S. bank branches there. In the same year, an American Chamber of Commerce opened in Rio de Janeiro. Those growing commercial relations strengthened a diplomatic understanding and cooperation between Brazil and the United States. In 1904, the Brazilian Foreign Office classified Washington as the "number one" diplomatic post and the following year raised its legation to the rank of embassy in the North American capital, the first South American nation to do so. The United States immediately reciprocated. The United States enjoyed a friendship with the South American giant unique in the annals of hemispheric diplomacy, a counterpoint to tensions prevailing in other regions created by U.S. concerns for security and Latin American fears of aggression.

THE MIDDLE SECTORS IN POLITICS

The rhythm of Latin America's population growth quickened. Increasing at a rate of 1.3 percent per year in the last half of the nineteenth century, the population doubled between 1850 and 1900, from 30.5 to 61 million—exceeding by two-thirds the rate of growth during the previous century. Latin America's population was growing at a much faster rate than Europe's. The rate accelerated slightly in the period from 1900 to 1930, averaging 1.7 percent per year, so that population totaled 104 million by 1930. The most rapid increase was in the southern temperate zone of South America, especially in Uruguay and Argentina.

As the population increased so did it diversify. By the end of the nineteenth century, the middle sectors, whose previous emergence was noted in the last chapter, reached sufficient numbers and had enough direction to exert an influence then and increasingly thereafter on the course of events in some nations, most particularly in Argentina, Brazil, Chile, Mexico, Uruguay, and Costa Rica. Only later were they large and articulate enough to wield a similar influence in other countries. Commerce, business, and industry contributed heavily to the widening ranks of the middle sectors, and foreign immigrants continued to compose a disproportionately large percentage of their numbers. Certain characteristics of the middle sectors increasingly became evident. The majority of those so classified lived in the cities and boasted of an above-average education. Their income level placed them between the wealthy few and the impoverished many. Although the heterogeneous middle sector never unified, on occasion a majority of them might agree on certain goals, such as improved or expanded education, further industrialization, or more rapid modernization, and on certain methods to achieve them, such as the formation of political parties or the exaltation of nationalism. They consented to the use of the government to foment change, and with minimal dissension welcomed the government's participation in—even direction of—the economy. Still, political preferences within their ranks varied from far right to far left.

While, on the one hand, the middle sectors expressed strong nationalistic sentiments, on the other, they, like the elites, looked abroad for models. Further displaying a degree of contradiction, while tending to regard the United States as their model, they did not hesitate to criticize the more aggressive tendencies of their powerful neighbor. Their nationalism prompted frequent outcries against "Yankee imperialism." Yet the middle sectors regarded the United States as the example of a New World nation that had "succeeded," an example of the "progress" preached but not always practiced in aristocratic Europe. True, the United States embraced impressive examples of wealth and poverty, but it seemed that large numbers, even a majority, lived somewhere between those extremes so characteristic of Latin American society. The aggressive strength of their counterparts in the United States inspired the Latin American middle sector. They attributed part of the apparent success of the United States to industrialization and education. In prescribing industrialization as a panacea for their national ills, they hoped to emulate the Yankee model. The high North American literacy rate seemed to provide the proper preparation for an industrial society, and the middle sectors appreciated the mobility education afforded the citizens of that technological nation. The American educator Horace Mann became a revered figure to many Latin American leaders, and they eagerly imported not only his doctrines but also the Yankee books and schoolteachers to go with them. Domingo F. Sarmiento, for one, met Mann, imbibed his ideas, and as president of Argentina (1868–74) hired New England teachers to direct the new normal schools he established. President Justo Rufino Barrios in Guatemala (1873–85) encouraged the North American missionaries to set up Protestant schools. Finally, the comfortable life style of the U.S. middle class with its increasing arsenal of consumer goods impressed the Latin American candidates for middle-class status.

The middle sectors favored reform over revolution. They sought entrance into the national institutions, not necessarily destruction of them. In fact, they demonstrated a preference for economic improvement and less concern with altering political structures. Although the elites at first had distrusted the middle sectors, they eventually understood their potential as allies and not only incorporated them into their privileged institutions but also in due course let them administer them—a trust that the middle sector did not betray.

As urbanization and industrialization expanded, a larger, more cohesive, and militant proletariat appeared. Slowly becoming aware of their common problems and goals, these workers unionized despite relentless government opposition. The first unions appeared after 1850, evolving from mutual aid societies. They tended to be small, ephemeral, and local organizations. The typographers, stevedores, railroad employees, artisans, miners, and textile workers were the first to organize, and most of the early union activity concentrated in Buenos Aires, Montevideo, Havana, Santiago-Valparaíso, and Mexico City as well as in the mining regions of northern Chile and central Mexico. By 1914, about half a dozen nations boasted well-organized unions, and at least some attempt had been made in the rest to institute them. At any rate, the foundation for future expansion was laid.

In the following two decades, the local unions expanded into national organizations, recruiting ever larger numbers from all urban sectors as well as from some of the rural proletariat. The economic dislocations caused by World War I and the financial collapse of 1929 induced labor unrest, mounting militancy, and strikes. A working-class consciousness took shape as labor thought in terms of changing the national institutions to suit its own needs.

In their periods of formation and expansion, the unions could and did cooperate with other urban elements, specifically the middle sectors. Both sought change, however modest, and realized they had to challenge the traditional elites to get it. The privileged oligarchy resented and opposed that alliance. Once the middle sectors achieved their more limited goals and began to participate in the national institutions, they broke their alliance and aligned with the elite.

In Brazil, the middle sectors were strong enough to help overthrow the monarchy in 1889 and for a time, in conjunction with the military, to rule the nation. The composition of Brazilian society had altered considerably in the nineteenth century. At the time of independence the new empire counted barely 4 million inhabitants of whom probably half were slaves of African birth or descent. Sixty-five years later there were 14 million Brazilians, roughly 600,000 of whom were slaves. At the other end of the social scale stood 300,000 plantation owners and their families. Most of the population fell somewhere between the two extremes. True, most of them were impoverished, illiterate rural folk who unknowingly contributed to the status quo. But there was an important, growing body of urban dwellers, many of whom qualified for the ranks of the middle sectors. The gulf between the countryside with its many vestiges of the colonial past and the city with its increasingly progressive outlook widened during the last decades of the nineteenth century. The urban dwellers were less favorably disposed to two basic institutions inherited from the past, slavery and monarchy, than was the rural population. They saw these institutions as buttresses of the position of the elite and uncomplementary to their own best interests. Indeed, they viewed the two institutions as the means by which the traditional rural elite retained most of what was colonial in Brazilian society and in the economy while still rejecting, in the stricter legal sense, colonial status. The military, hostile to slavery, ignored by the emperor, and restless, shared the view of the urban middle sectors to whom the officers were closely related both by family ties and philosophy. Together, they brought an end to both slavery and monarchy.

Not surprisingly the new republican government established by the military in 1889 reflected the goals and aspirations of Brazil's middle sector. The new chief of state, Deodoro da Fonseca, was the son of an army officer of modest means, and his cabinet consisted of two other military officers, an engineer, and four lawyers. They were sons of the city with university degrees, a contrast to the aristocratic scions who had formed previous governments. During its early years, the republic was identified with both the military and the urban middle groups much more than the monarchy had ever been. As one of their goals, they hoped to transform the nation through industrialization. The government raised the tariff on items that competed with national goods and lowered the duty on primary goods used in national manufacturing. To augment the number of technicians, four new engineering schools were opened in the 1890s. A high income from coffee exports, generous credit from the banks, and the government's issue of larger amounts of currency animated economic activity to a fever pitch. Speculation became the order of the day. Bogus companies abounded, but unfortunately for Brazil the speculation resulted in little real industrial progress. In 1893 a political crisis complicated the economic distress. The navy revolted and the southern state of Rio Grande do Sul rose in rebellion; together they threatened the existence of the republic.

The powerful coffee planters with their wealth and control of the state governments of São Paulo, Minas Gerais, and Rio de Janeiro held the balance of power between the government and the rebels. They promised aid to the government in return for a guarantee of an open presidential election in 1894. Both kept their sides of the bargain, and in the elections the coffee interests pushed their candidate into the presidential palace. The political victory of the coffee interests reflected the predominant role coffee had come to play in the Brazilian economy. Cheap suitable land, high profits, large numbers of immigrant workers, and a rising world demand made coffee a popular and lucrative crop. By the end of the nineteenth century it composed half of the nation's exports.

The alliance of the coffee planters and the federal government in 1894 superseded all previous political arrangements. Thereafter, the political dominance of the coffee interests characterized the First Republic (1889–1930). The new oligarchy, principally from São Paulo but secondarily from Minas Gerais and Rio de Janeiro, ruled Brazil for its own benefit for thirty-six years. The coffee interests arranged the elections of presidents friendly to their needs and dictated at will the policies of the governments. Sound finances, political stability, and decentralization were the goals pursued by the coffee presidents.

The urban middle groups, whose unreliable ally, the military, was torn by disunion and bickering, lost the power they had exercised for so brief and unsettled a period. These middle groups increasingly resented the economic and political monopoly the large planters wielded in the republic. They decried the many favors the government lavished on the planters. Occasionally they supported a presidential candidate, such as Ruy Barbosa in 1910, who understood their aims and objectives. For the elections of 1922, the urban groups and the military united in an unsuccessful effort to wrest the presidency from the coffee elite. They failed. Thereafter, violent protest erupted in Brazil.

In July of 1922, shortly after the coffee interests had once again imposed their presidential preference on the nation, a handful of junior officers revolted in Rio de Janeiro in a poorly planned effort to overthrow the moribund republic. It signaled the beginning of an eight-year period of unrest, which climaxed in 1930 with the fall of the republic. The discontented elements centered in the cities.

By 1926, the movement of the junior military officers, known in Portuguese as *tenentes* (meaning lieutenants), had acquired a somewhat more identifiable philosophy, even though it never became precise. The tenentes maintained a mystical faith that somehow the military could alter the habits of the country and provide the impetus to propel it into the modern age. Their primary concern was not democracy but reform. For the remainder of the discussion, reform denotes a gradual change or modification of established economic, political, or social structures. The tenentes wanted to retire the entrenched politicians and modernize the nation. Then, and only then, they would consent to return the nation to constitutional rule. They hoped to expand the base of the government and to eradicate regionalism. They favored a very strong, centralized government. Revealing "social democratic" tendencies, the tenentes proposed government recognition of trade unions and cooperatives, a minimum wage, maximum working hours, child-labor legislation, agrarian reform, nationalization of natural resources, and expanded educational facilities. Obviously much of the program favored the urban middle groups. However, those groups failed to understand that the various military rebellions and movements in the 1920s could have been turned to their advantage. Indicative of the weakness of the middle groups was their inability to coordinate their desires for modernization with the similar desires of the young officers. Still, by the end of the decade of the 1920s, the middle groups had some accomplishments to their credit: they had helped to abolish slavery, to bring down the monarchy, to encourage education, to promote industrialization, and to stoke the fires of nationalism, but they did not achieve the influence their counterparts did in some of the Spanish-speaking nations.

At the same time the middle sectors were maturing and tasting their first political power in gigantic Brazil, the small nation of Costa Rica felt the initial influences of its own middle group. Always remote from the activities of the Spanish empire, and even isolated from the political turmoil of the rest of Central America, Costa Rica contained little wealth and engaged in minimal foreign trade until the last quarter of the nineteenth century. Consequently no privileged wealthy class to speak of had existed. Poverty created a kind of equality in a nation that contained only slightly more than a quarter of a million inhabitants at the close of the century. The nation's disastrous experience with financing a railroad further constrained the acquisition of wealth. Costa Rica probably had a higher percentage of small and middle-range farmers than any other Latin American country at the end of the century. A society without the sharp edges of economic extremes offered good conditions for the growth of a middle class. The period from 1882 to 1917 boasted a remarkable record of constitutional government in which four-year presidential terms were honored and peacefully exchanged. Politicians and parties supported platforms substantively middle class in their goals. In the last half of the 1880s, Minister of Education Mauro Fernández laid the foundation for a system of free and compulsory public education that eventually would produce Latin America's most literate population. Likewise, the government began to pay greater attention to public health. The widespread medical and health care the government provided its citizens made them the healthiest of Central America. The relatively equitable patterns of land ownership, the positive emphasis on education, and the comparatively widespread participation of the citizenry in politics marked Costa Rica as an essentially middle-class nation.

In Argentina, elements representative of the urban middle groups founded the Unión Cívica Radical in 1892. That party campaigned for free elections; obviously under the rigged elections perpetuated by the oligarchy it had scant hope of reaching office. An enlightened president, Roque Saenz Peña, promulgated laws in 1912 to guarantee the secret ballot for all males, a reform that paved the way of the middle sectors to power. In the next presidential election, 1916, the candidate for the Radicals, Hipólito Irigoyen, won.

The Radicals had worked hard for their victory, but once in office they revealed a lack of commitment and a confusion of objectives. Irigoyen showed an interest in and sympathy with the poor, unusual for an Argentine president. To reward his working-class supporters, he saw that some mild social-welfare legislation was enacted. He encouraged unionization, but, on the other hand, he was not reluctant to brutally suppress strikes in Buenos Aires in 1919 when he felt the workers had become too violent. Characteristic of the middle sectors everywhere in Latin America, the Radicals gave encouragement to education and made a great fetish of democracy. Irigoyen recognized the inequity of land distribution and hoped to rectify it by making land available on the frontier; he thereby sidestepped the issue of the predominance of the latifundia in the most fertile and populous area of the nation. He also established a national petroleum agency to develop that vital natural resource. By preventing foreign exploitation of oil and thereby opting for greater national economic independence, his action became a model for nationalists both in Argentina and in other Latin American nations.

In retrospect, the achievements of the Radicals over a period of a decade and a half were disappointingly few. As it turned out, once in office, the middle sectors manifested a conservatism not too far removed from

The inauguration of President Hipólito Irigoyen, Buenos Aires, 1916

that of the displaced oligarchy. Enjoying their taste of power, they muted their cries for reform. During the years the Radicals enjoyed power, they made no structural or institutional changes in Argentine society or economy. In the crisis of 1930, which was precipitated by the international economic depression, the Radicals proved incapable of reacting. The army swept them from power and returned the government to the traditional oligarchy, although thereafter the military remained as the arbiter of the nation's political destiny.

In Chile, the middle sectors allied with the working classes in 1918 to form the Liberal Alliance, an electoral force dominant enough to win control of the Chamber of Deputies that year. The Alliance, under the banner of the popular Arturo Alessandri, went on to win the presidency in a closely contested election in 1920. Alessandri had promised many socioeconomic reforms, but once in office he found his efforts to fulfill those promises frustrated by the conservatives in congress hostile to his program. The conservatives, from their stronghold in the Senate, clearly represented the traditional values of the oligarchy as they fought off the efforts of the urban middle and working groups to implement change. A congressional election in 1924 favored Alessandri by giving him a working majority. The new congress promptly enacted his broad social-welfare program. It recognized labor unions and assured their independence. Alas, congress voted itself a handsome pay raise at an economically inopportune moment when paychecks to the military had been delayed. Contrary to its previous constitutional behavior, the army rebelled and sent Alessandri packing in September of 1924. A liberal countercoup in 1925 brought him back from exile. He served six more months in office during which time he was able to push a new constitution through congress, a document that replaced the ninety-two-year-old constitution written by Portales. It ended Chile's experiment with parliamentarianism and returned to the president the full measure of power he had lost in 1891. It also contained advanced labor and social-welfare provisions and authorized the state to intervene in social and economic matters. The middle sectors have remained a dominant force in Chilean politics ever since the Alessandri presidency.

In Uruguay, the Latin American middle sector won their greatest victory in the early twentieth century. Uruguay changed dramatically under the government of the middle sectors, providing one of the best such examples of peaceful change in Latin America. Independent Uruguay emerged in 1828 as a result of the stalemate between Argentina and Brazil, which had continued the centuries-old Luso-Spanish rivalry over the left bank of the Río de la Plata. Uruguayans divided into two political camps, the conservatives (Blancos) and the liberals (Colorados). From independence until 1872 they fought each other almost incessantly for power. When the liberals got power in 1872, they managed to hang on to it, despite challenges from the conservatives and the military, until 1959. During the

Paraguayan army officers, 1915. Throughout Latin America, the military kept a sharp eye on the middle class during its initiation into the exercise of political power.

last decades of the nineteenth century, relative peace settled over the small republic, by then in the process of an economic metamorphosis. Prosperity helped to pacify the nation. Exports of wool, mutton, hides, and beef rose. New methods of stock breeding, fencing, the refrigerated ship, and railroad construction (the mileage jumped five times from 200 to 1,000 miles between 1875 and 1895) modernized the economy.

During the same period, Uruguay constructed the foundation of its enviable educational system. New teacher-training institutes and public schools multiplied. Uruguay was on its way to becoming South America's most literate nation. Expanded and improved education was among the foremost concerns of the middle sectors, and the attention given to education in Uruguay reflected their increasing influence.

The outstanding political representative of the middle sectors at that time, not only in Uruguay but in all of Latin America, was José Batlle. He first exerted influence as the articulate editor of a prominent newspaper in Montevideo that spoke for the interests of the middle sectors and, by providing them with a voice, helped to organize that always amorphous group. By the end of the nineteenth century, he led the Colorado Party. He served twice as president (1903–7, 1911–15), but his influence over the government lasted until his death in 1929. During those decades, he sought to expand education, restrict foreign control, enact a broad welfare program, and unify the republic. He succeeded brilliantly in each instance, and through his force and foresight he transformed Uruguay into a model bourgeois nation.

At the turn of the century, the conservatives controlled some of the departments (local territorial units) to the extent that they were virtually free of the control of the central government. Batlle extended the power of his government over them by assuring the conservatives proportional representation in the central government. He managed to balance the budget, repay foreign creditors, and strengthen the national currency. National banks grew in confidence and were able to lend to Uruguayans so that they no longer had to look abroad for much of their capital. To protect national industry, congress raised the tariffs. The government began to enter business, taking over light, power, insurance, and many other formerly private enterprises and continued to do so on an ever-increasing scale. The government entered the meat-packing business to offer competition to the foreign companies that had long been engaged in the industry, so vital to a nation dependent on stock raising. The enactment of advanced social-welfare legislation guaranteed workers their right to unionize, minimum wage, an eight-hour day, pensions, accident insurance, and paid holidays. Batlle felt the government should play a positive role in improving the living conditions of the less-favored citizens. On one occasion he announced, "There is great injustice in the enormous gap between the rich and the poor. The gap must be narrowed—and it is the duty of the state to attempt that task." These reforms, like others taking place in Latin America at the time (with the exception of Mexico), affected only the urban areas and never extended into the countryside. Strong as Batlle was, he never directly challenged the landowners or the rural socioeconomic structures. In fact, he saw no reason to, as he stated in 1910: "There is no pressing agrarian problem requiring the attention of the government. The division of the landed estates will take place in response to natural forces operating in our rural industries." It was a point of view shared by the middle-sector leaders of the period. Thus they permitted the continuation of the oldest and most fundamental land and labor institutions. Obviously such a neglect restricted national reforms and circumscribed the limits of change. The neglect of rural reforms reflected the middle sectors' fear of the power of the landowners, their preoccupation with the city, their own intermarriage and connections with the landowning families, and a desire to acquire estates of their own.

The climax of the Batlle reforms came in the new constitution, written in 1917 but promulgated in 1919. It provided a model of the type of government the middle sectors of the period wanted, one, of course, that guaranteed them power. It authorized direct elections, reduced the powers of the president and created a National Council of Administration to share the presidential powers (with the hope of eliminating any future threat of dictatorship), established a bicameral legislature elected by means of a proportional representative system, reduced the military to a minor institution, separated the Church and state, and provided a comprehensive program of social welfare. In creating the first welfare state in the Western Hemisphere, the middle sectors acknowledged their political debt to the working classes and rewarded them for their support.

Uruguay prospered in the years after World War I thanks to a lively demand abroad for products from the nation's fertile pampas. The good times were auspicious for the new reforms. Batlle died in 1929, just before the Great Depression challenged his democratic welfare state. In the first three decades of the twentieth century, Batlle demonstrated to the Latin Americans how a nation once immersed in chaos, tyranny, illiteracy, social inequality, and foreign exploitation could change peacefully. Compact in size, with a small and homogeneous population, with rich land and no adverse geography, Uruguay enjoyed advantages of which few other nations could boast. These advantages doubtless smoothed the path to reform. Still, Uruguay provided an example of a nation that could peacefully alter its course. In the three decades during which Batlle exerted his greatest influence, he accomplished much of what many progressive Latin Americans of the period desired. His constitution provided the blueprint for Uruguay's development in the twentieth century. The middle sectors throughout Latin America venerated it.

The middle sectors, complaining loudly of their precarious economic position, felt confident that education, industrialization, and nationalism charted a course to enhance their positions. In theory, some of them advocated a wide variety of reforms, but in practice they proved to be essentially conservative, fearful that too much reform might harm rather than benefit them.

7

The Past Repudiated

José Clemente Orozco, "The Revolutionary Struggle"

By the opening of the twentieth century, some Latin Americans began to express a desire for genuine reforms, change, and development. Differing from their nineteenth-century predecessors, the new reformers sought to alter basic institutions. Understanding that the cosmetic touches applied by the liberals had changed little or nothing, they made more radical demands: a redistribution of the land, more effective curbs on the wealth and power of the Church, a limitation on the control that foreigners exerted over the national economies, and a wide range of social benefits and political innovations. The new elements in Latin American society—larger urban middle sectors, immigrants, new business people and industrialists, and labor unions—brought stronger pressure to bear on the established elites and the governments they dominated to break with the past, to eradicate vestiges of the colonial era still widespread. The ambitious new groups struggling in an increasingly complex Latin American society opposed the rigid institutions that impeded their rise. They required a more fluid society. If the old institutions and elites proved unwilling to accommodate their ambitions, they, then, were determined to use force to transform the traditional society. At the same time, repressed groups—peasants, rural and urban workers—articulated more forcefully their needs and demands. Large groups sought national development rather than simply the unsatisfactory growth of the past. Meanwhile, under skillful direction, nationalism emerged as a potent catalyst for change and development. Understanding why many advocated institutional changes and how opposing forces frustrated their aspirations challenges our historical insight and imagination. How do nations change? What changes? Can fundamental societal changes occur rapidly, if at all?

MEXICO'S VIOLENT RESPONSE TO THE PAST

In Mexico, intellectuals, representatives of the middle class, the urban working class, the rural proletariat, and peasants united to alter violently many of the nation's oldest institutions. In doing so they precipitated Latin America's most profound revolution of the first half of the twentieth century, one of the world's major social upheavals. In certain aspects the Mexican Revolution (as a landmark in Latin American history, this Revolution merits capitalization) continued the movement initiated and directed by Hidalgo and Morelos from 1810 to 1815. Many considered it at least until about 1950, the prototype for nationalistic revolutionary change in twentieth-century Latin America. For the remainder of this discussion of the twentieth century, revolution means sudden, forceful, and violent overturn of a previously relatively stable society and the substitution of other institutions for those discredited. Change by revolution thus denotes the destruction of old social, political, and economic patterns in favor of newer ones. Use of this definition divides genuine "revolutions" from the innumerable palace coups, military takeovers, civil wars, and the wars of independence, which were nothing more than shifts in the holding of power within the same or similar groups unaccompanied by fundamental economic, social, or political changes.

Mexico in 1910 clung tenaciously to its neocolonial structures and institutions. Porfirio Díaz and the "New Creoles" had ruled for thirty-four years without popular mandate for the benefit of a privileged native elite and foreign investors. The economy still depended upon foreign whims and direction. The masses were brutally suppressed. The real wages of the working class declined throughout that long period. Land, a principal source of wealth, remained in the hands of a few. Ninety-five percent of the rural population owned none. Not even 10 percent of the Indian communities held land. Fewer than 1,000 families owned most of Mexico. In fact, fewer than 200 families owned one-quarter of the land, while foreigners had another quarter. Private estates reached princely proportions. The De la Garza hacienda in the state of Coahuila totaled 11,115,000 acres; the Huller estate in Baja, California, sprawled over 13,325,650 acres. Productivity was low; absentee landlords were common. The fact that a majority of the Mexicans lived in the country and worked in agriculture made the inequity of the land distribution all the more unjust. The desire of the repressed rural population to cultivate its own land was welling into an irrepressible force.

An economy reminiscent of colonial mercantilism and with vestiges of feudalism prevented the growth of democracy. It condemned liberal reform to failure. It also goaded the growing mestizo urban classes to express dissatisfaction with the inequitable institutions inherited from the past. The mestizos had grown rapidly in number over the centuries. By the end of the nineteenth century they surpassed the Indians in number and totally overshadowed the tiny "creole" class. It was obvious from their size, skill, and ambitions that the mestizos held the key to Mexico's future. The mestizo working and middle sectors of the cities voiced discontent with their inferior and static position in Porfirian Mexico. The inflexibility of Mexico's neocolonial institutions retarded their mobility and inhibited their progress. In common with the peasantry, they advocated change in order to improve their conditions.

A political event, rather than vague aspirations for change, set in motion the forces culminating in the Revolution. The Mexicans tired of the long Díaz dictatorship and the electoral farces that perpetuated the aging *jefe* in office. In the elections scheduled for 1910, Francisco I. Madero, a liberal landowner from the North, announced his intention to run against Díaz. To the surprise of no one, Díaz declared his victory at the polls and took office for the eighth time. Madero, by then, had seen the popular response his political opposition to the old dictator had aroused. In November of 1910, he crossed the frontier from the United States into Mexico with the intention of overthrowing the government. His Plan of San Luis Potosí announced the simple motivation of his movement: the forced resignation of Díaz and electoral reforms. Repeatedly his followers voiced the slogan "Effective suffrage and no reelection," a clue to the exclusively political, urban, and middle-sector origin of the Revolution. Díaz resigned in May of 1911, and fled to a European exile. (He died in Paris in 1915.)

Madero took office quite unprepared for the task he faced. His political platform contained some vague planks on political reform and almost nothing solid on social or economic change. He represented the traditional liberalism of the nineteenth century, which at last many realized had not benefited Mexico. At any rate, it did not harmonize with the newer demands being made. Madero's importance derived first from his significance as a symbol of the revolt against the Porfirian past and second from the political freedom he permitted for open discussion in which the needs and aspirations of the nation were thoroughly ventilated.

While Madero demonstrated his incompetence, the demand for agrarian reform mounted, encouraged by Emiliano Zapata in his Plan of Ayala in 1911. Crying "Land and Liberty," he and his determined rural followers demanded land, and in many cases they seized haciendas for themselves. A new force had been unleashed and it represented what distinguished the Mexican Revolution from previous movements in Latin America: the stirring of the masses. It became clear that a social revolution had begun.

To enact change or to redirect the course of the Revolution required power and many were the leaders vying for it. In February 1913, General Victoriano Huerta, a representative of the *porfiristas*, overthrew the ineffectual Madero and then permitted his assassination. Uniting to oppose the reactionary general, Venustiano Carranza, Alvaro Obregón, Plutarco Elías Calles, Francisco Villa, and Emiliano Zapata, all of whom played fundamental roles in the Revolution, marched against Huerta's armies. After Huerta fell in March of 1914, the victors began to struggle among themselves for supremacy. To broaden his support, Carranza appealed to those who regarded the Revolution as a social movement. By mid-1915, he and his allies emerged to direct the Revolution, but Zapata in the South and Villa in the North continued to challenge him until 1919 and 1920, respectively. In May of 1920, Carranza, attempting to rig the presidential elections, was deposed, then assassinated. The moderates made one final effort to gain control of the Revolution in 1924 but failed.

In all the political changes and chaos of the preceeding years, one major political fact stood out: the era in which the "creole" had commanded was over. The mestizos dominated Mexican politics after 1914, and they were determined to recreate Mexico in their own image. The emerging leadership of the Revolution was overwhelmingly mestizo: Zapata, Villa, Obregón, Calles, Cádenas, et al. Impoverished, sons of peasants, virtually illiterate in their childhood, looking more to their Indian than to their

Spanish past, unknown, and unheralded, they rose to positions of prominence during the Revolution. The Revolution made them and propelled them to the forefront.

During the early years of the Revolution, as the winds of change blew with gale force across Mexico, the absence of a plan, a philosophy, intellectual leadership, or a directing party became painfully obvious. The Revolution assumed its general characteristics slowly. In time, it became apparent that many of the institutions closely identified with the Spanish past—foremost of which, and most fundamental, was the land-tenure system—would be destroyed or altered beyond recognition. To solve national problems, the Mexicans looked deeply into themselves for an answer. As a result, the Revolution became increasingly native and conversely more antiforeign.

The Revolution swept all before it. The destruction was as total as the chaos. It cost more than a million lives. It ruined much of the agrarian, ranching, and mining economy. No major bank or newspaper that predated the Revolution survived. Exceptions to the economic dislocation were the henequen and oil industries, whose output rose. By 1921, Mexico ranked third among the world's oil producers, furnishing one-quarter of the world's total. From the disorder and destruction that lasted throughout most of the period of 1910 to 1920, a new Mexico arose.

The constitution promulgated in 1917 contained the blueprint for the future, the first general statement of the aims of the Revolution. Carranza called a constituent assembly, expecting it to approve a document similar to the liberal constitution of 1857, but it quickly became apparent that he exercised little control over the proceedings. Ideological differences split the delegates. The radicals, supported by Obregón, gained control and imposed their views. The constitution that emerged after two months of bitter debate at Querétaro contained many of the traditional enlightened ideas characteristic of the former constitution. In the customary Latin American fashion, the constitution conferred strong authority on the president. However, it went on to alter significantly some fundamental and traditional concepts, to eliminate some hoary institutions, and to point the way to new solutions for old problems.

The new constitution exalted the state and society above the individual and conferred on the government the authority to reshape society. The key articles dealt with land, labor, and religion. Article 27 laid the basis for land reform and for restrictions on foreign economic control. It declared government ownership of mineral and water resources, subordinated private property to public welfare, gave the government the right to expropriate land, annulled all alienations of ejidos since 1857, and recognized communal ownership of land. Article 123 protected the Mexican workers from exploitation by authorizing the passage of a labor code to set minimum salaries and maximum hours, provide accident insurance, pensions, and social benefits, and guarantee the right to unionize and to strike. Since foreign investment in Mexican industrialization was heavy, this article potentially could be used as one means of bridling the operations of the foreign capitalist. Finally, Article 130 placed restrictions on the Church and clergy: churches were denied juridical personalities, they could not own property, states could limit the number of clerics by law, no foreigner could be a minister or priest, nor could foreigners vote, hold office, or criticize the government, and the Church could not participate in primary education.

Carranza dutifully promulgated the constitution, but he showed little intention of carrying out most of its provisions, many of which were not put into effect for years. For example, fourteen years passed before the enactment of a labor code to give meaning to Article 123. Nonetheless, the constitution stands as the single most important event in the history of the Revolution, marking off Mexico's neocolonial past from the modernized nation that was rising from the holocaust of revolution. It provided the point of departure for the creation of a new national state based on local experience. The history of Mexico since its promulgation has been the story of the struggle to carry out the provisions of the document and thereby to put into effect the social, economic, and political changes it envisaged.

With the inauguration of Obregón in 1920, the first efforts were made to implement the socioeconomic changes authorized by the Constitution. After years of slogans, the land-reform program got underway. Obregón distributed 3 million acres to the peasants. To combat illiteracy, the president appointed the energetic José Vasconcelos as Minister of Education. Accelerated school construction and teacher-training programs received an impetus from him. With the encouragement of the Revolution, educational opportunities continued to expand, and illiteracy, from a high of 80 percent in the early 1920s, slowly declined. Vasconcelos was a fiery cultural nationalist, in the vanguard of a movement enveloping Latin America. Negating the pessimistic racism of the past, a form of European cultural imperialism the confused Latin American intellectuals had accepted in the nineteenth century, he preached the triumph of the new mestizo "race," *la Raza Cósmica* (the Cosmic Race). He made available space and funds to encourage Diego Rivera, José Orozco, and other artists to paint monumental murals glorifying Mexico's Indian past. With his encouragement, Carlos Chávez composed music in a Mexican idiom. Desirous of an authentically Mexican culture, Vasconcelos declared the nation's spiritual and cultural independence of Europe: "Tired, disgusted of all this copied civilization . . . we interpret the vision of Cuauhtémoc as an anticipation of the . . . birth of the Latin American soul. . . . We wish to cease being [Europe's] spiritual colonies." Mexico's intellectuals rallied to the cry. A new sense of nationality and pride—brilliantly evident in art, architecture, music, dance, and literature—engulfed Mexico.

Calles, who became president in 1924, carried forward the trends

Mexico

begun during his predecessor's administration, but he soon found himself embroiled with the Roman Catholic Church. The Constitution horrified the Catholic hierarchy, who saw in several of its articles the power to debilitate the Church. The Church-state issue exploded in 1926 when Archbishop José Mora y del Rio publicly announced, "The Episcopate, the Clergy, and all Catholics disavow and combat Articles 3, 5, 27, and 130 of the present Constitution." The government reacted by enforcing those articles much more rigidly than ever before. In response, the Church went on strike. The priests refused to perform their functions, although the government kept the churches open for the faithful. Conservative Catholics revolted against the government, and blood flowed anew in Mexico. Not until the late 1930s did the Church and state show more tolerance toward each other, and since then relations have gradually improved.

The bullet of a religious fanatic felled Obregón before he could return to the presidency to which he was reelected in 1928. Calles continued to dominate politics, and in 1929 he founded the National Revolutionary Party (PNR) to help fill the political vacuum. The PNR assumed responsibility for selecting and electing presidents as well as insuring that the transfer of power took place—and took place peacefully. It thus helped to solve a problem that had nagged Mexico, indeed most of Latin America, since the declarations of independence. In 1938, the party reorganized as the "official party" under the name of Mexican Revolutionary Party (PRM) and broadened its base of support. In 1946, the party once again changed its name, this time to Party of Revolutionary Institutions (PRI). With each change the party strengthened itself so that it, an institution, not individuals, came to dominate Mexican politics. It gave Mexico a remarkable political stability, a sharp contrast to the nation's own past and unusual in Latin America.

As stability increased, the role of the military diminished. The Constitution assigned the military the conventional tasks of maintaining order and defending the nation from outside attack, and the officers accepted their more restricted position. After 1929, the budget provided increasingly less funds for them. In that year, one-third of federal expenditures went to the military; by 1950, the figure had dropped to one-fourteenth; by 1964, to one-thirtieth.

Basic to the Revolution was land reform. If carried out successfully, it threatened to destroy the hacienda, perhaps the most debilitating and influential institution from the past, and substitute for it communal and small private holdings. Obregón modestly initiated the redistribution of the land, and his successors continued the policy. The titles the president handed out conferred on the small farmers a new dignity, a vital step in changing them from exploited workers into responsible citizens. The reform put into use formerly idle or inefficiently cultivated lands. It also strengthened the powers and prestige of the government, which could grant land or withhold it for political considerations. Lázaro Cárdenas, president from 1934 to 1940 (the presidential term had previously been extended from four to six years), accelerated the redistribution of land by handing out titles to 45 million acres, a staggering amount when one considers that between 1910 and 1945 the grand total of land redistributed was 76 million acres. By 1984, the government had distributed 253 million acres to 2.3 million small farmers. Despite that trend, 4 million landless rural workers clamored for land that year. In absolute numbers, Mexico had more landless people in 1984 than during Zapata's time.

After 1940, following a period of decline, agricultural productivity began to rise. It increased 46 percent during the following two decades, far above the world's average increase of 12 percent and contrary to the general decline in Latin America's agricultural output. One prominent Mexican economist, Edmundo Flores, affirms that the rapid industrialization of his nation has been achieved only because of the reformed agrarian structures that made possible political stability, high rates of capital formation, and increased agricultural production and productivity.

In many respects, the six-year term of Cárdenas marked the apogee of the Revolution. Cárdenas based his energetic use of the presidency on the support of the peasants and the urban laborers, who in turn benefited the most from his reaffirmation of revolutionary principles. He was the first Latin American president in the twentieth century to shift the power base to the popular masses. He also well understood the potential force of economic nationalism. Cárdenas boldly declared Mexico's economic independence by nationalizing the railroads in 1937 and the oil companies in 1938. The foreign oil companies, accustomed to a privileged status in Mexico, had refused to accept a decision of the Mexican Supreme Court ruling as legal the pay raise requested by the workers. In response to the companies' defiance of the court, Cárdenas expropriated the oil firms and thus became a national hero. All Mexicans, of every level and background, enthusiastically supported the government. Even the Church nodded its approval, the first gesture of cooperation between the two in several decades. What was more, Mexico proved to itself, to the former oil monopolies, and to the world that it could produce its own oil, and contrary to predictions it proceeded to do so more efficiently than the foreigners had done. Oil production climbed. By 1950, it doubled the output reached during the low point of 1932; by 1963 it doubled again. By the early 1970s, vast new deposits were discovered. Meanwhile, engineers exploited rich offshore reserves. The bulk of Mexican oil no longer flowed to Western Europe and the United States to buttress their industrialization. The Mexicans refined and used it at home as an intricate part of national industrialization, which was then moving forward at an accelerating pace. Using their own oil for national development, the Mexicans challenged and changed old economic patterns, which were all too reminiscent of the mercantilism of the past. In addition, the state began to remove from foreign control the production of electrical power and to direct that vital industry itself. Mexico was in the process of redeeming itself, of limiting foreign control over its land and its industry.

The major governments of Western Europe and the United States endorsed none of these changes. The endangered investments of their citizens prompted them to complain bitterly to the Mexican government about the new laws, to apply pressure to thwart them, to threaten reprisals, and to speak of intervention. Also, the Roman Catholic Church maintained strong pressures on other governments to force the Mexican officials to accommodate themselves to the interests of the Church. No nation intervened in Mexican affairs more vigorously than the United States, whose officials, with the exception of Ambassador Dwight W. Morrow and President Franklin D. Roosevelt, lacked even the haziest notion of the significance of the Mexican Revolution. Ambassador Henry Lane Wilson unabashedly supported General Huerta, although the brutal assassination of Madero shocked President Woodrow Wilson into refusing to recognize the Porfirian general. The U.S. Navy blockaded the Gulf coast in 1914, then shelled and occupied the port of Vera Cruz. After Villa raided Columbus,

New Mexico, and killed seventeen Americans, President Wilson ordered General John Pershing and an army into northern Mexico in a quixotic search of nearly a year for the evasive Villa. The Constitution of 1917 caused further concern in Washington over U.S. investments in Mexico as talk of confiscation circulated. The United States did not want Article 27 to be applied retroactively. Because of the violent death of Carranza, the Department of State refused to recognize Obregón when he became president in 1920. It used the issue of recognition as a lever to pry from the Mexicans an agreement to pay compensation for any land expropriated. Relations between the two neighbors improved in 1927 when Dwight W. Morrow arrived as ambassador to Mexico. Astute and able, he understood the significance of the Mexican Revolution and attempted to deal fairly with the Mexicans in their drive for rapid change. Later, President Roosevelt possessed a similar perceptiveness and withstood heavy pressures from the Roman Catholic Church and the oil companies for intervention. Mexico's agreement to compensate the oil companies and the improvement of Church-state relations within Mexico in the late 1930s lifted at least part of the pressures on him, and improved relations between Mexico and the United States were the result.

Cárdenas was the last strong man to dominate Mexico. After 1940, Mexican presidents derived their power from the office they held, not from their own personal strength, prestige, or following. In short, the institution possessed greater strength than the individual, a new development in Mexico and Latin America. At the same time, public opinion grew in influence to the point where it exerted considerable pressure on the government. The Revolution created a novel social flexibility, and as one consequence the middle sectors grew both in size and importance.

Impressive as the material results of the Revolution were, the psychological changes in the Mexicans surpassed them. The hacienda system was not uprooted nor the oil expropriated just for economic benefits. Those measures were taken to give the Mexican people greater control over their own destiny and to enhance the dignity of the workers and to include them in the national life. The Mexican historian, Daniel Cosío Villegas, judged, "The present dignity which the Indian has achieved was worth the blood and destruction of the Revolution." What the Revolution meant to the people can be seen in the powerful murals of Diego Rivera, the daring architecture of the National University, the rhythmic movement of the Ballet Folklórico, or heard in the vibrant music of Carlos Chávez. Together they reveal the soul of a proud Mexico emancipated by a ferocious but necessary revolution.

It became increasingly apparent after 1940 that the Revolution had entered a conservative phase. Institutions took on a greater rigidity. Indeed, the Revolution itself had become institutionalized. A new privileged elite emerged to absorb most of the national income, with the sharp division between wealth and poverty all too evident. Foreign capital reentered to play a dominant role, and growth began to outstrip development.

The increasingly conservative course of Mexico disturbed many Mexicans and not least of all the intellectuals. Carlos Fuentes' exciting novel *La Muerte de Artemio Cruz* (The Death of Artemio Cruz, 1962) offers one explanation of what was happening in Mexico and to the Revolution. Cruz, the novel's central figure, fought in the Revolution but later became a business tycoon. He illegally acquired large estates despite the land reform and allied himself with foreign capital to exploit his native land. Both actions obviously betrayed the Revolution. The novel shows him cynically turning the Revolution to his own advantage. The change from revolutionary fighter to businessman that Cruz underwent in the novel represented the emergence of a new privileged class capable of exploiting change for its own selfish advantage. The persistent and perplexing question "Is the Mexican Revolution dead?" receives a resounding "Yes" from Fuentes. Daniel Cosío Villegas is just as emphatic. He explains the failure of the Revolution in historical terms:

> The drive and the energy of the Revolution were consumed much more in destroying the past than in constructing the future. As a result, the past certainly disappeared, but the new present came into being and began to develop haphazardly, so that, for lack of another image to imitate, it finally ended by becoming equal to the destroyed past. From this standpoint the reaction won a complete victory over the Revolution, since it has succeeded in taking the country back to the exact point where it was when the Revolution broke out. I mean "the exact point" where Mexico was before the Revolution in the sense of the general mental outlook prevailing now in the country, but not in the sense that the country itself is like the Mexico of 1910.

Cosío Villegas and Fuentes have ample reason to be pessimistic. Mexico in the 1980s lived through one of its major crises, a contrast to the great hopes of the previous decade when new petroleum discoveries quickened plans for development. By 1974, Mexico produced 2.75 million barrels of oil per day, half of which was exported. The government plunged into a spending spree only to experience falling world prices for its oil and other exports. Meanwhile, a rural exodus brought peasants into the already overcrowded cities in pursuit of new industrial jobs for which, as they soon discovered, they were unqualified. While unemployed in the cities, they no longer contributed to agriculture. Production of food staples, corn and beans, fell or remained constant at the same time as the population was growing at 2.5 percent annually. By 1980, Mexico imported one-sixth of its rice and nearly one-quarter of its corn and wheat. Between 1976 and 1981, the value of food imports jumped sevenfold. The government during the 1980s spent billions of dollars it could not afford to buy food abroad, while at home unemployed and landless farmers could have produced the food on lands that stood idle.

In the crisis of overextended industrialization, extravagant government spending and food imports, the government borrowed imprudently at high interest rates. Mexico's foreign debt jumped from $14.5 billion in 1975 to $85 billion in early 1984, surpassing $110 billion by 1989. A monetary crisis choked Mexico by 1982. President López Portillo declared a temporary moratorium on debt payments and nationalized all the country's banks. However, in 1983, President Miguel de la Madrid, following the recommendations of officials of the International Monetary Fund, cut government spending in half, eliminating subsidies for some basic foods. While inflation continued in the 75 to 100 percent range, the president held wage increases between 15 and 25 percent. From 1981 to 1987, consumer prices increased 13.8 times. Unemployment and underemployment rose to approximately 45 percent; the austerity program created no jobs, even though Mexico needed 700,000 new jobs a year to absorb the new entrants into the work force. In the 1980s, Mexico experienced neither development nor growth. While President de la Madrid's austerity measures might have rehabilitated Mexico's international credit rating, they further impoverished the average Mexican. And the average Mexican reacted in the presidential elections of July 1988. The PRI candidate collected barely 50 percent of the votes from the heavy turnout at the polls. The Mexican political commentator Adrian Lajous observed, "The [one-party] system is dead, but it doesn't know it yet." Thus, after sixty years of PRI domination, Mexico stood on the threshold of political change.

Clearly the Revolution did not change all the institutions, and its failure to make a total transformation permitted the resurgence of old neofeudal and capitalist practices that apparently have thwarted many of the original revolutionary goals of those who wanted to alter Mexican society. The weaknesses of the Revolution obviously are great, but nonetheless it will stand as a major landmark in Latin American history: the first effort of the twentieth century to divide the past from the present and future. It made significant social, economic, and political transformations. It indicated a path for Mexico to follow, but the question now is whether that path can lead to real change and development and, if it can, why the Mexicans deviated from it.

NATIONALISM AS A FORCE FOR CHANGE

Nationalism, perhaps more than any other single force, impels change in twentieth-century Latin America. Difficult to define precisely, nationalism in this text means a group consciousness that attributes great value to the nation-state, to which total loyalty is pledged. Members of the group agree to maintain the unity, independence, and sovereignty of the nation-state as well as to pursue certain broad and mutually acceptable goals. Two of these goals in the twentieth century have been modernization and economic independence. The nationalists have been in the vanguard of those encouraging the development of Latin America, and thus they have served as eager agents propelling change. Nationalism can trigger a powerful emotional response. Much of the nationalistic sentiment intertwines with feeling, loyalty, and group spirit.

Nationalism is not a novelty introduced by the twentieth century. It can trace its roots far back into the Latin American past. It evolved slowly over the centuries, at different times assuming different characteristics. During the colonial period, particularly during the eighteenth century, the local elite developed a literature praising their surroundings and extolling the beauty and purity of the New World. The intensifying conflict between the creoles and the mazombos on the one hand and the reinóis and peninsulares on the other sharpened the "nativism" of those born in the New World, consequently deepening their alienation from the Iberians. Through such a psychological process, the nation in the historical sense preceded the nation in the political sense. Indeed, Latin American historians affirm that the spiritual and emotional maturity of their countries predates political independence. Two Peruvians, Víctor Andrés Belaúnde and Jorge Basadre, speak of "colonial nationalism" and "*conciencia de sí*," a self-consciousness, evident in Peru in the eighteenth century—if not before. Daniel Cosío Villegas concludes that Iberian colonial oppression encouraged a "nationalist sentiment and ardor" foreshadowing Latin American independence. Such native pride and growing self-consciousness had its inevitable triumph in the proclamations of independence. Transformed from nativists into nationalists, the elite created and defended their new nations.

The declarations and wars of independence gave a much sharper focus to nationalism. The rhetoric, symbols (flags, anthems, heroes), and battles infused enthusiasm and determination into many ranks of the Americans, particularly into the elite, the intellectuals, and the urban dwellers. Wars, boundary disputes, and foreign threats helped to maintain or intensify that political nationalism throughout the nineteenth century. Juan Manuel de Rosas ably manipulated the Argentine distrust of foreigners to weld diverse and distrusting regions into a national union. In Brazil, the throne of the emperor provided a convenient focal point that rallied the loyalty of all regions and classes of the enormous, sprawling, and disconnected empire. During the course of the nineteenth century, internal trends buttressed the sporadic demonstrations of defensive nationalism. The fast rate of racial mixing obscured ethnic origins to create a homogeneous mestizo citizenry distinctive to the New World, and some of the racial combinations were unique to specific countries. As the nations became more conscious of their peculiar personalities, they developed a stronger sense of national identity. Railroads, telegraph lines, and steamships further unified each nation. Together they successfully combated the major threat to national unity: regionalism.

As the twentieth century opened, a wave of cultural nationalism swept the hemisphere. The intellectuals, long slavish imitators of European styles, turned their backs on their former mentors to seek the indigenous roots of national culture. They probed national psychology, questioned national motives, and reexamined the past. Scholars such as José Enrique Rodó in Uruguay, João Capistrano de Abreu and Euclydes da Cunha in Brazil, Ricardo Rojas in Argentina, José Vasconcelos in Mexico, and José Carlos Mariátegui in Peru offered novel introspective theories to explain national development (or the lack of it) that relegated the usual emphasis on Europe to a secondary plane. In reinterpreting the past, historians paid greater attention to the influence of the interior, the hinterlands, and the frontier. Nowhere was that trend more evident than in Brazil. In a brilliant essay presented in 1889, Capistrano de Abreu was the first to point out the influence of the interior on the formation of Brazil. According to him, the interior was the true Brazil; the more heavily populated coast was just an extension of Europe. Only when the coastal inhabitants turned their backs to the sea and penetrated the interior did they shed their European ways and become Brazilianized. Da Cunha confirmed that thesis in *Rebellion in the Backlands* (1902). From his perceptive study of the interior, he concluded that on the frontier, in the hinterland, he beheld the real Brazil and the true Brazilian. He spoke of the backwoodsmen as "the very core of our nationality, the bedrock of our race," and of their society as "the vigorous core of our national life." Rojas came to similar conclusions about the Argentina interior. Essays, poems, and novels on the gaucho, now perfectly romanticized as the frontier "type," were the vogue in the Platine region.

As the battle lines hardened between nationalism and foreign influences, Ricardo Rojas cried for the salvation of Argentine youth "from the foreign clergy, from foreign gold, and from foreign books." At the same time in Brazil, Ronald de Carvalho, one of the major exponents of the new cultural nationalism, exhorted his followers, "Let us forget the marble of the Acropolis and the towers of the Gothic cathedrals. We are the sons of the hills and the forests. Stop thinking of Europe. Think of America!" A Latin American renaissance in art, literature, music, and dance resulted from these proddings. It originated in Mexico, then appeared in Brazil, and spread thereafter—sometimes with less effect—to the rest of the republics.

Architecture, too, bore the impress of nationalism. The architects turned their attention away from Europe to contemplate the environment in which they built. Slowly, they suggested a new architectural idiom, notable for its integration with the arts (murals, sculptures, tiles) and nature

The Ministry of Education and Health
(1937–43), Rio de Janeiro, Brazil.
Both Lúcio Costa and Oscar
Niemeyer contributed to the design
and planning of this major landmark in
Brazilian architecture.

(gardens and decorative plantings). In some regions, bold splashes of color enhanced the buildings. In Brazil, Lúcio Costa led a vigorous movement to adapt architecture to the tropical environment. One of the first and finest examples of the distinctively Brazilian architecture was the Ministry of Education and Health (1937–43) in Rio de Janeiro, a project that combined the genius of Costa, Oscar Niemeyer, and others. In Venezuela, Carlos Raúl Villanueva led a movement to create distinguished modern architecture. Certainly one of his masterpieces was the Aula Magna (1954) of the University of Caracas, an impressive example of the combination of many arts—murals, stained glass, sculpture, painting, and architecture—into a unified whole. The National University of Mexico, constructed in the early 1950s, stands as a major tribute to the new Mexican architecture. Mexico produced one of the major architects of the twentieth century, Luis Barragán. His design for the Jardines de Pedregal on the edge of Mexico City blended stark buildings influenced by the monumental structures of the Indian past with lava formations in a masterful combination of nature and architecture. In 1980, the world of architecture awarded him his profession's most prestigious prize, the Pritzker Architectural Prize. Oscar Niemeyer received the same prize in 1988. As in many other fields, Latin American architecture began to make significant international contributions only when it incorporated local inspiration and perspectives. That uniqueness won admiration; the distinctive Latin American contribution aroused the very international approval the Latin Americans had sought for so long.

The invention of the motion picture camera coincided with a rising tide of nationalism in Latin America, and the Latin Americans at once seized on film as an appropriate means to encourage the nationalism. It offered an obvious advantage in those countries where a majority of the citizenry was illiterate.

The fledgling Mexican film industry actively promoted fictional documentaries to glorify the past. As part of the centennial celebrations in 1910, Felipe de Jesús Haro produced *El Grito de Dolores* (*The Cry of Dolores*), a patriotic hymn to Miguel Hidalgo, the hero of Mexican independence. The appearance of *Cuahtémoc* in 1918 reflected the revived interest in Mexico's Indian past, so notable in music, literature, dance, and art as well. At about the same time the Ministry of War expressed an interest in filmic interpretations of the Revolution and financed such films as *Juan Soldado* (*John Soldier*), *El Precio de la Gloria* (*The Price of Glory*), and *Honor Militar* (*Military Honor*). The Revolution provided filmmakers with a seemingly endless inspiration.

Lacking the intense nationalistic impetus that the Revolution gave Mexicans, the early Brazilian filmmakers paid only partial attention to historical themes. In 1911, Salvatore Lazzaro made the first film version of

The Aula Magna of the University of Caracas, Venezuela (1954). The architect was Carlos Raúl Villanueva; the sculptor, Antoine Pevsner; the muralist, Matteo Manaure.

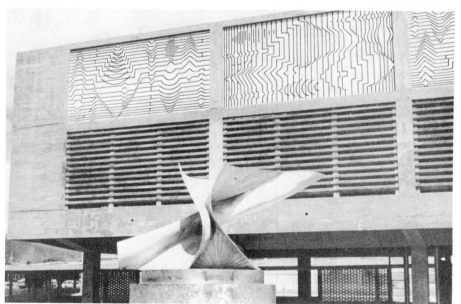

O Guarany (The Guaraní Indian)—four other versions were produced during the following decade!—that quintessence of Brazilian nationalism. In its romantic plot, an Indian chief and the daughter of a Portuguese noble fall in love, the symbolic intertwining of the New World and the Old to create Brazil. First as a novel, then as an opera, and, after 1911, as a movie, *O Guarany* appealed mightily to the national spirit. In fact, the overture to the opera (always played along with the film) is considered on a par with the national anthem as a major hymn to Brazilian patriotism.

Beginning in 1915, filmmakers paid greater attention to historical themes. Doubtless the approach of Brazil's first centenary celebration of independence encouraged the new film industry to turn to historical epics. In 1918, Brazilians could watch *Tiradentes*, episodes from the life of a martyr to independence, and *O Grito do Ipiranga (The Cry of Ipiranga)*, an account of events surrounding the declaration of independence. As in Mexico, the Ministry of War favored such enterprises with its cooperation and encouragement.

The Argentines shared a fascination with historical films with other Latin American filmmakers of the early twentieth century. Likewise, part of the impetus to explore the past through film came from the elaborate preparations underway to commemorate the first centenary of Argentine independence in 1910. In fact, the first story-film made in Argentina concerned the independence period; called *El Fusilamiento de Dorrego (The Execution of Dorrego before the Firing Squad)*, it was filmed in 1908 by Mario Gallo. In 1910, the public viewed an entire series of patriotic films based on history.

In their concern with national identity and reality, early Argentine films, like those of Mexico and Brazil, dealt with the Indians, the prime symbol of the uniqueness of America and of nationality. Starkly contrasting with the romanticism of the Mexican and Brazilian treatment of the subject, one of the early Argentine masterpieces of the screen depicted the Indian with a realism unusual for the time. The remarkable *El Ultimo Malón (The Last Indian Uprising)* filmed in 1917 by Alcides Greca, focused on an uprising of the Mocovi Indians in Santa Fé in April 1904. The first part was purely documentary, showing the conditions of the Mocovi in 1917 and commenting on their poverty and exploitation by the local landowners. The second part recreated, using the Indians themselves, the actual uprising. The film identified the Indians with the land as the worthy progenitors of Argentine nationality.

Also, as might be expected, the filmmakers focused on the gaucho, a mixture both culturally and ethnically of the Indian and European, who offered an obvious symbol for national identity. The gaucho already had left his stamp on Argentine literature and art. José Hernández published his epic *Martín Fierro* in 1872 and 1879; the highly successful gaucho novel, *Juan Moreira,* by Eduardo Gutiérrez appeared in 1879–80. The novel was dramatized to much acclaim in 1886. By then a group of Argentine artists, among whom Prilidiano Pueyrredón and Juan Carlos Morel would be outstanding representatives, had painted vivid scenes of gaucho life. Therefore, it seemed only natural for the new medium, the film, to take up that highly national theme, and the filmmakers did, producing in 1915 one of the great hits of the Argentine screen, *La Nobelza Gaucha* (*Gaucho Nobility*). Many of the explanatory titles for this silent film came directly from *Martín Fierro*. The plot concerned a beautiful country girl, sweetheart of a hardworking gaucho, who was kidnapped by a city villain and of course eventually rescued by the brave gaucho so they could live happily ever after in the simplicity and wholesomeness of the countryside. A simple plot, indeed a melodramatic one, it gave another perspective to an intensified search for national identity, at least part of which became increasingly associated with the broad pampas and its distinctive gaucho inhabitants. *La Nobleza Gaucha* also contained social commentary in its implied denunciation of the precarious situation of the gaucho in a society that still exhibited neofeudal characteristics. Within a few years, the theme of the gaucho emerged in yet another form: music. Felipe Boero's *El Matrero,* which premiered in 1929, projected a romanticized vision of the gaucho, in some respects akin to the tragic *Martín Fierro,* and has been sanctified as the national opera.

Argentina's first professional film director, José Augustín Ferreyra (1889–1943), one of the most prominent of the nation's twentieth-century blacks, freely drew inspiration from the growing exaltation of the gaucho and made four early popular films on the gaucho theme. However, in the final analysis, he was a devoted son of Buenos Aires, a city he knew intimately and always loved. His best films, in fact, testify to that devotion. He used his camera to explore and dissect the city, and he found beauty in the most commonplace incidents and localities. Almost invariably his films showed the life styles of the ordinary people, and many of them were shot in the suburbs, rather than using the more sophisticated locales in the center of the capital. These films provide a subtle study of changing Buenos Aires, 1915–40, a city multiplying in size and illustrative of the dominant role cities were assuming in the twentieth century, not only in Argentina but throughout Latin America. The film *Calles de Buenos Aires* (*Streets of Buenos Aires*, 1933) typified the director's style, concerns, and themes. The simple plot focused on the lives of two young ladies of humble origin— many of his films depicted and moralized on the contemporary roles of women. One sought to escape her poverty and fell victim to the easy promises of a seducer and the ruin that followed. In contrast, the other, steadfastly maintaining her honesty and faith in the face of adversity, found true love and fulfillment in the arms of an impoverished singer.

Like so many of his plots, that of *Calles de Buenos Aires* recalled tango lyrics. Indeed, it should. Ferreyra loved tangos; he composed lyrics for them. Many of his films included the singing of that distinctive music of

Buenos Aires. In one of his earliest films, *El Tango de la Muerta* (*The Tango of Death*, 1917), he made clear his association of the tango with the film. To the female lead in this film, the tango simultaneously symbolized her condemnation to misery and her final liberation. More often than not, Ferreyra's films were visual recreations of the sentiments pervading the tango. Appearing first in Buenos Aires in the 1880s, the tango offered a partial insight into the spirit and feelings of all Argentines. Ferreyra succeeded in combining the city (particularly the poorer districts), the common people, and the tango into films that both depicted a broad segment of the nation and expressed popular sentiments. No other Argentine filmmaker has succeeded so brilliantly in making that combination.

Film reached huge audiences, proved to be the most effective medium to address the populace at large, and often discussed national themes. Still, its importance should not be exaggerated, since most of the screens in Latin America showed foreign movies that had nothing to do with local realities. In fact, they contained antinational messages and served more as social soporifics than stimulants.

Strong political undercurrents swirled within the waters of cultural nationalism. The arts were not separate from politics; those participating in one often took part in the other, though it was truer of intellectuals than of politicians. The nationalists initiated a search for new indigenous solutions to old political problems. The Cuban José Martí set the tone in his plea:

> In order to govern well, one must pay attention to reality. The wise leader in America is not he who knows how the German or the Frenchman is governed, but he who knows of what elements his own country is composed and how he can guide them as a unity—by means of methods and institutions native to his own country—toward that desirable condition in which each man knows himself and exerts himself. . . . The government must be born of the country. The spirit of the government must be that of the country. The form of the government must adjust itself to the inherent structure of the country. Government is nothing more than the balance of the natural elements of the country.

The Mexican Constitution of 1917 was the first example of a constitutional document reflecting indigenous experiences and needs rather than merely copying the political ideologies of Western Europe and the United States.

The collapse of the international economy in 1929 and 1930 and the prolonged derpression that followed caused attention to shift to yet another form of nationalism: economic or developmental. The difficult years emphasized once again to the Latin Americans the dependency and vulnerability of their economies. Their monocultural export economies collapsed. Cuba's economy broke down: foreign trade in the early 1930s was 10 percent of the 1929 figure. Uruguay's exports dropped 80 percent in the early 1930s. Brazil's exports plummeted from $445.9 million in 1929 to $180.6 million in 1932. In short, by 1932, Latin America exported 65 percent less than it had in 1929, proving once again that foreign trade contributed mightily to the cyclical fluctuations of the Latin American economy. The nationalists demanded that steps be taken to increase the viability of the national economies and conversely to reduce their dependency on the gyrations of the international market caused by the buying whims of a few highly industrialized nations. Plans were made to increase economic diversification and to promote industrialization. Industrialization appealed to both common sense and pride. For one thing, it promised to diversify the economy; for another, it kept foreign exchange from being spent to import what could be manufactured at home. At the same time, an acute shortage of foreign currencies meant that either the nations manufactured their own goods or they did without.

The economic crisis motivated the governments to play an increasingly active role in the national economies. They introduced long-range economic planning, exerted new controls, and offered incentives. Devalued currency, import controls, and higher tariffs stimulated national industry, and all these measures received the support of the nationalists. Still, few understood the hazards of imposing the invigorated industrialization on the neofeudalistic rural institutions that were, after all, the base for the entire economy. It would take considerable time to reveal some of the unrealistic planning behind Latin America's industrialization.

The wider participation of the governments in the economies and the mounting demands for faster development shifted the leadership of the nationalist movement from the intellectuals, who had long enjoyed a near monopoly in directing it, to the governments themselves, which began to understand the potential power of the movement. At the same time the base of support of nationalism expanded to include, on occasion, the masses, or more specifically the urban working classes. They were told and they believed, rightly or wrongly, that the foreign investor exploited them, extracting huge profits from Latin America while paying minimal wages. In other words, the foreigner perpetuated the local poverty. It was a simple argument with great emotional appeal.

Nationalism remained an amorphous sentiment, but passions could be brought to a boil over certain issues and none was more inflammable than oil. It symbolized economic nationalism—it was representative of the longing many Latin Americans felt to control their own natural resources. Nationalists argued that the discovery and exploitation of their own petroleum was not only economically desirable but also the guarantee of real national independence and, in the case of several of the larger countries, of world-power status. "Whoever hands over petroleum to foreigners threatens our own independence," one Latin American nationalist leader warned. No acts in recent memory received more popular acclaim than the nationalization of foreign oil industries in Bolivia in 1937 and in Mexico in 1938. On the other hand, the alienation of a nation's petroleum through concessions to foreign companies has contributed to the fall of several recent Latin American governments, as President Arturo Frondizi (1958–62) learned in Argentina and President Fernando Belaúnde Terry (1963–68) learned in Peru.

When the oil question is handled adroitly, it can become a strong prop buttressing a nationalist government. President Getúlio Vargas of Brazil (1930–45, 1951–54) ably used the oil issue to his advantage. Sensing the growing importance of oil, emotionally and economically, he created the National Petroleum Council in the 1930s to coordinate and intensify the search for oil. In 1939, the first successful well was drilled, and it brought forth oil from Brazil's soil. The excited nationalists at once called for the creation of a national oil industry. In a bid for wider popular support, Vargas urged the creation of a state oil monopoly to oversee exploration and to promote the development of petroleum resources. Its creation in 1953 followed a passionate national campaign and marked a major victory for the nationalists. They had triumphed over those who argued that it would be more economical for experienced foreign companies to drill for oil and pay Brazil a royalty on whatever was pumped out. The nationalists denounced that argument. After all, the issue was an emotional, not an economic, one. They wanted Brazil to retain control over one of its most precious and important resources. Their arguments convinced the masses that a national oil industry represented sovereignty, power, independence, and well-being. The masses responded with enthusiastic support, a demonstration of the power economic nationalism can muster.

In the decades after World War II, economic nationalism assumed four distinct characteristics. First, the political left took over much of the leadership, imposing their ideas and their vocabulary. As one result, contemporary nationalism relies heavily on the Marxist lexicon, a fact that exposes the movement to constant denunciations that the communists dominate or direct it. The accusation is not only false but it vastly oversimplifies the complexity of nationalism and hinders efforts to better understand it.

Second, the nationalists have increased the criticism of foreign economic penetration. They accuse the foreign investors and companies of perpetuating Latin America's underdevelopment by keeping the population poor, ignorant, feeble, and imbued with a feeling of inferiority. They harken to the warning of José Martí: "A people economically enslaved but politically free will end by losing all freedom, but a people economically free can go on to win its political independence." As a cruel irony, the figures seem to demonstrate that foreign investment aids the investor and debilitates the host nation, at least in Latin America. Former foreign minister Gabriel Valdes of Chile noted:

We can assert that Latin America is contributing to finance the development of the United States and other affluent nations. Private investments have meant, and mean today for Latin America, that the amounts that leave our continent are many times higher than those that are invested in it. Our potential capital is diminishing, while the profits of invested capital grow and multiply at an enormous rate, not in our countries but abroad.

In a speech before the United Nations General Assembly on September 26, 1960, Fidel Castro explained some of the causes of the Cuban Revolution, one of which concerned the exploitation by foreign capitalists. He illustrated in concrete terms the general charge made by Valdes:

Public utilities, electricity and telephone companies were owned by United States monopolies. A large part of the banking and import business, the oil refineries, the greater part of the sugar production, the best land, and the chief industries of all types of Cuba belonged to United States companies. In the last ten years, the balance of payments between Cuba and the United States has been in the latter's favor to the extent of $1,000 million, and that does not take into account the millions and hundreds of millions of dollars removed from the public treasury by corrupt and tyrannical rulers and deposited in United States or European banks—one thousand million dollars in ten years! The poor and underdeveloped country of the Caribbean, with 600,000 unemployed, contributing to the economic development of the most highly industrialized country in the world!

Figures released by the United Nations Economic Commission for Latin America fully corroborate the charges. During the years 1960–66, the flow of private investment into Latin America reached $2.8 billion, while the repatriation of profits and income amounted to $8.3 billion. A net loss of $785 million per year in Latin America's balance of payments resulted. According to the figures released by the U.S. Department of Commerce for 1970, U.S. investments in Latin America earned $1.3 billion, while the capital outflow from the United States to that area totaled only $302 million. One need not be an economist to see a four-to-one return on the investment dollar. The U.N. Economic Commission reported in 1988 that fully $147 billion flowed from Latin America to "developed countries" between 1982 and 1988 as a "net transfer of resources." All statistics confirm the charge that the rich, developed nations profit handsomely at the expense of impoverished, underdeveloped Latin American nations.

Third, the nationalists have mounted their most vitriolic attack against the United States. The reason is obvious: the United States is the largest single investor in Latin America. In 1972, the United States had invested over $14 billion in Latin America, nearly three-quarters of which was concentrated in minerals, petroleum, and manufacturing industries. The presence of U.S. business is overwhelming, not just in the small Caribbean republics but also in the major nations: fifteen of the twenty-five largest companies in Argentina are owned by North American companies and six of the thirty largest companies in Brazil are U.S. firms. Consequently, any campaign against foreign capital automatically assumes anti-Yankee tones. Then, too, the U.S. government and the major U.S. investors have become closely identified with the Latin American oligarchy and, in the eyes of the nationalists, with the preservation of the status quo. Action occasionally replaces accusation. The Peruvian government in 1968 seized the International Petroleum Company, a Jersey Standard subsidiary, and in 1969 expropriated W. R. Grace's rich sugar estates. In late 1969, the Bolivian government nationalized Gulf Oil's subsidiary. In mid-1971, Chile nationalized the copper industry, taking over the huge operations of Anaconda, Kennecott, and Cerro. On January 1, 1976, the Venezuelan government took over ownership of the foreign oil companies that for decades had pumped, refined, and sold that country's lucrative resource.

Finally, the nationalists pay ever greater attention to economic development in a desperate attempt to modernize their countries. Developmental nationalism continues to call for government control of natural resources, limitations of foreign capital, accelerated industrialization, and trade with all nations regardless of their political or economic ideologies. The developmental nationalists show a greater impatience with the ideologies of the past and more interest in experimenting with new ones. The Secretary-General of the Organization of American States, Galo Plaza, concluded in the late 1960s, "One of the most powerful forces in Latin America today, and one of the least understood outside the region, is the upsurge of economic nationalism." His remarks retain their validity.

In the twentieth century, the thrust of nationalism has altered dramatically. While once the nationalists were absorbed in tracing the historic roots of their country and in glorifying the potential wealth and natural beauty of their land, now they are concerned with the future. As the twenty-first century nears, nationalists challenge institutions and behavior still rooted in an ever more distant colonial past. They find in nationalism the motor to propel change. That change will take many forms, but it will have one goal: national development.

CHANGING RACIAL ATTITUDES

The nationalists in the twentieth century came to appreciate a long-neglected fact: the rich and varied racial heritage of Latin America accounted for the region's uniqueness and vitality. Unfortunately, although the Indian, African, and European contributed jointly to the formation of Latin American civilization, the three groups by no means enjoyed equality. The European and his New World descendants occupied the highest level of society, with the mestizos, mulattoes, Indians, and blacks relegated to lower rungs of the social ladder. Without the benevolent protection of the Iberian monarchs, the position of the Indians and blacks, if anything, deteriorated in the nineteenth century. Some intellectuals contributed to their misery as well as to national psychosis. In their eagerness to mouth European ideas, they circulated the specious racist doctrines so in vogue among Europeans in that century.

The wealth of biological thought in the nineteenth century, the popularity of Darwinism and Spencerianism, and the complex ethnic composition of Latin America aroused a lively interest in race and racial theories. Latin America's cultural mentor, France, offered a poisonous array of pseudoscientific books attesting to the superiority of the Northern European. Widely read by the end of the century was the social psychologist Gustave Le Bon, who methodically classified all humankind into superior and inferior races with the Europeans indisputably at the top. Among other things, he asserted that miscegenation produced an offspring inferior to either parent. Another champion of the Aryan, the anthropologist Georges Vacher de Lapouge, minced no words in his chief work, *L'Aryen, son Role Social,* to support the theory of racial significance in cultural development. In line with his thesis, he characterized Brazil as "an enormous Negro state on its way back to barbarism." Bombarded by such influence and inheritors of a sociopolitical system in which the European and his offspring ruled while the Indian, the African, and their offspring obeyed, most Latin Americans equated whiteness with beauty, intelligence, and ability. Conversely, the darker the people the less likelihood there was that they could possess those desired characteristics. Intellectuals such as Francisco Bulnes in Mexico, Carlos Octavio Bunge and José Ingenieros in Argentina, Alcides Argüeda in Bolivia, and Manuel Bonfim in Brazil blamed miscegenation for the backwardness and anarchy of Latin America. In doing so, they condemned their peoples to a feeling of inferiority.

The rising tide of nationalism caused some Latin Americans to question these dreary racial concepts. To accept the European doctrines, they finally realized, would condemn Latin America perpetually to a secondary position. The nationalists concluded that the doctrines were simply another means devised by the Europeans to humiliate and subjugate Latin America. In due course, the Latin Americans rejected the foreign racist doctrines, and in so doing they took a major step toward freeing themselves from European cultural domination.

In the early twentieth century, the Latin Americans began to take a new interest in the Indians, who had been cheated, robbed, overworked, suppressed, and massacred throughout the nineteenth century. Disturbed by the rapid decline of the Indian population as well as by the terrible tales of brutal exploitation of the natives by the rubber barons of the Amazon, the Brazilian government created the Indian Protection Service in 1910 to defend them and to incorporate their diminishing numbers into the national family. The *Apista* movement appeared in Peru by the end of the second decade of the twentieth century and spread thereafter to other countries. Advocating an Indian renaissance, it strove to uplift the Indian and glorified America's indigenous past. In 1919, President Augusto Leguía of Peru declared the Indian community once again to be a legal corporation. Accelerating change after taking power in 1968, the reformist military government recognized Quechua in 1975 as an official language of Peru along with Spanish. The Indians benefited handsomely from the Mexican Revolution. Under the banner of Emiliano Zapata, they fought for the restitution of their lands. Eventually the Revolution did return some lands to them, as well as offer them an education and a place in the new Mexican society. Lázaro Cárdenas, more than any other Mexican president, served the Indians; in order to institutionalize his concern, he created the Department of Indian Affairs in 1936. Unjust biases against America's Indian past were finally uprooted, and Indian themes became respectable for art, literature, music, and dance. Latin Americans at last pointed with justifiable pride to their Indian past. Still, the lot of the Indian in the national societies remains far from satisfactory. In some regions the Indians are disappearing rapidly. Such is the case in Brazil, where, by the late 1980s, probably fewer than 100,000 Indians survived. The government has been moving them onto a huge Amazonian reservation, the Xingú National Park, as a means of saving them, but the cultural and physical shock of the move amounts almost to genocide. Their plight arouses considerable international sympathy.

At the same time attitudes toward the black also underwent change. As the first step, it was necessary to end black slavery. The Spanish-speaking republics abolished it between 1821 and 1854. The institution lingered on in Spain's Caribbean islands and in Brazil. Tremendous international pressures bore down on Spain and Brazil to free their slaves. After midcentury internal pressures welled up. Spain feared that to manumit (liberate) the slaves would drive the insular landowners to declare their independence. Cautiously the Spanish government abolished slavery in Puerto Rico in 1873, freeing approximately 31,000 blacks. The process in Cuba was slower. The Moret Law, passed in 1870 but only published in Cuba in 1872, liberated children born of slaves after September 18, 1868, although subjecting the freeborn black to a system of tutelage until eighteen years of age. In 1880, the government ended slavery but with the proviso that former slaves had to continue to work for eight years for their former masters. Finally, in 1886, the crown abolished the tutelage system, freeing all blacks from compulsory labor.

The abolition movement in Brazil was even more protracted. No one in authority seriously advocated an immediate end to slavery. The economy could not absorb the shock of so radical a move. The abolitionists therefore favored a gradual emancipation, to take place over a lengthy period of time. The emperor, too, counseled the gradual approach in order to avoid disturbing the economy and committed his prestige to such a course. The conservative government headed by the Visconde do Rio-Branco enacted the Law of the Free Womb in 1871, which declared all children born to slave mothers to be free. At the time there were approximately 1.5 million slaves and a free population of 8.6 million. The law slowly doomed slavery in Brazil. Africa as a source of slaves had been closed since 1850; after 1871, the only other source, the womb, could bring forth no more slaves. However, patience with the slow results of the Rio-Branco Law wore thin. Before the end of the 1870s, the slavery question once again confronted the public. The concern for the welfare of the remaining slaves called forth some forceful spokesmen and prompted the formation of some active abolitionist societies.

Several highly articulate blacks contributed to the leadership of the abolitionist campaign: José Carlos do Patrocínio, a persuasive journalist, wrote ceaselessly for the cause and became a symbol of the campaign; André Rebouças, one of the empire's most prominent engineers, organized abolitionist clubs and spoke and wrote profusely in support of abolition; and Luís Gonzaga de Pinto Gama spent his youth as a slave and later became a distinguished lawyer who specialized in defending slaves in court. He claimed credit for freeing 500 slaves through the courts. A fiery advocate of immediate abolition, he declared, "Every slave who kills his master, no matter what the circumstances may be, kills in self-defense." He also preached "the right of insurrection." Given to poetry, he began one of his better-known verses, "My loves are beautiful, the color of night."

The slavery issue forced itself to the forefront of politics as one group after another favored the abolitionist cause until only the slave owners themselves were left as apologists of a discredited institution. Finally, on May 13, 1888, to cries of approval from those in attendance, the parliament passed the Golden Law liberating the remaining three-quarters of a million slaves. When Princess-Regent Isabel put her signature to the law, slavery finally disappeared from the Western Hemisphere. If the slaves expected the Golden Law to transport them to a promised land, they became disillusioned quickly enough. Life continued to be hard for them, as they lamented in this popular verse:

> Everything in this world changes,
> Only the life of the Negro remains the same:
> He works to die of hunger,
> The 13 of May fooled him.

The battle for their freedom had ended, but they faced a second struggle, psychological emancipation from the feeling of racial inferiority derived from long centuries of slavery. The assumption of racial inferiority was by

Firemen in Havana, Cuba, circa 1885. This photograph illustrates a racial reality common to Latin America, particularly at that period: the officers (extreme right and left of the photo) are white, while the firemen are black or mulatto.

no means limited exclusively to the blacks. Whites, too, had to overcome ingrained prejudices to reevaluate the ability of the blacks and their role in the Americas.

During the early twentieth century, interest in the blacks' new struggle as well as in their contributions to the New World grew. The new interest was most evident in those areas where the populations of African descent were largest, the Caribbean and Brazil. In Cuba, the prolific intellectual Fernando Ortiz began publishing his studies of the black as early as 1906. Together with the black Nicolás Guillen, the originator of the *negrismo* school of poetry, he founded the Society for Afro-Cuban Studies in 1926 and thereafter devoted himself with increasing fervor to the study of the Negro. The intellectual search for black identity did not preclude violence generated by frustration and injustice. In Cuba in 1912, the black leader Evaristo Estenoz, disillusioned by the failure of the island's independence to institute equality of all peoples, organized the Independent Party of Color to support the blacks' rights. Regarding the new party as subversive, the government sent troops to disband it, and a race war erupted that claimed the lives of 3,000 blacks and engendered lasting hostilities.

Meanwhile the concept of "Negritude" swept the Caribbean. In Haiti in the 1920s, Jean Price-Mars took up his pen to urge fellow blacks to accept their African heritage and to use it as a cultural resource. Aimé Césaire, an outstanding intellectual from Martinique whose contributions include the widely read *Return to My Native Land,* defined Negritude as follows:

> I have always thought that the black was searching for identity. And it has seemed to me that if what we want is to establish this identity, then we must have a concrete consciousness of what we are—that is, of the first fact of our lives: that we are black; that we were black and have a history, a history that contains certain cultural elements of great value; and that the Negroes are not . . . born yesterday, because there have been beautiful and important black civilizations. . . . Therefore we affirmed that we were Negroes and that we were proud of it, and that we thought that Africa was not some sort of blank page in the history of humanity; in sum, we asserted that our Negro heritage was worthy of respect, and that this heritage was not relegated to the past, that its values were values that could still make an important contribution to the world.

Generations of Caribbean intellectuals have pursued the goals of Negritude.

At the same time, the Brazilians looked with clearer vision on their African past. A contemporary of the racist Bonfim, Afonso Celso, refused to accept his colleague's negative predictions about Brazil's innate inferiority. In his blatantly nationalistic *Porque Me Ufano do Meu Pais (Why I Am Proud of My Country)*, Celso proudly affirmed, "Today it is a generally accepted truth that three elements contributed to the formation of the Brazilian people: the American Indian, the African Negro, and the Portuguese. . . . Any one of those elements, or any combination of them, possesses qualities of which we should be proud." His book contained a chapter praising the heroic resistance of the blacks to slavery. The pioneer of anthropological studies of the black in Brazil, Dr. Raimundo Nina Rodrigues, worked in Bahia from 1890 to 1905. Although not free of the prejudices of his day, he felt a great sympathy toward the blacks and manifested a lively interest in their condition. He studied the African cultures in order to identify their survivals in Brazil, and in that manner was able to indicate more correctly than previously the contributions of various African civilizations to the formation of Brazil. For example, he disproved the long-accepted idea that the Bantu predominated among Brazilian blacks by pointing out the strong cultural presence of the Sudanese groups, particularly the Yoruba, in Bahia. A few years later, another scholar, Manuel Raimundo Querino, emerged in Bahia to write about the blacks, their religions, and their contribution to Brazilian history. Querino is of special interest and significance because he was Brazil's first black historian, and he has provided a unique and extremely valuable perspective on Brazilian history. His major historical essay, "The Black Colonist as a Contributor to Brazilian Civilization," first reached print in 1918. It was fitting that the intellectuals of Bahia—an area where the African always predominated—first discovered the Brazilian blacks and began to emphasize the heroic role they had played in Brazil's development.

Writers also turned their attention to the same subject. Several novelists of the late nineteenth century, Aluísio Azevedo in his *O Cortiço* (The Tenement), and Adolfo Caminha in his *O Bom Crioulo* (*The Good Negro*), described at length the black as a member of the urban proletariat. In some of his best novels, Afonso Henriques Lima Barreto raised his voice to protest the discrimination against the black that manifested itself in Rio de Janeiro, described it in some of its ugliest aspects, and called for justice. Menotti del Picchia characterized the Brazilian as a mulatto in his lengthy poem "Juca Mulatto"; it was the first time in Brazilian poetry that a mulatto appeared as the hero. The more enlightened attitudes toward the races removed embarrassments that earlier had inhibited or confused the intellectuals. Thus freed, they became increasingly proud of the nation's racial amalgamation, which they began to view as an achievement, not a disgrace.

Gilberto Freyre helped to break the last chains binding the intellectuals to their racial uncertainties when he published *Casa Grande e Senzala* (*The Masters and the Slaves*) in 1933. The national and international acclaim that greeted his study freed the intellectuals from any remaining cultural complexes. Freyre's cogent discussion of the creation of a unique, multiracial civilization in Brazil opened vast new areas for research and study. In 1934 the first Afro-Brazilian Congress met in Recife, and three years later a second one convened in Salvador. The papers read during those sessions and the discussions that followed emphasized the revised opinion about the blacks and their newly assigned place within the Brazilian family.

The more realistic appraisal of the African presence improved the black's position in Brazilian society, but it would be wrong to conclude, as is so often done, that Brazil knows no racial prejudice. The facts prove otherwise. Newspapers regularly ran help-wanted advertisements seeking whites only. Until well after the mid-twentieth century, both the diplomatic corps and the naval officer corps remained lily-white. After World War II, it was necessary to promulgate a law to punish overt discrimination. Black cultural and political leaders, such as Abdias do Nascimento and Alberto Guerrero Ramos, have spoken out to denounce subtle but insidious aspects of local racism. In all fairness, though, it must be pointed out that Brazil probably has less racial tension and less racial prejudice than any other multiracial society, past or present. The races mix freely in public places. Interracial marriage is reasonably common. A more formidable barrier than race may well be class. Class membership depends on a wide variety of factors and their combination: income, family history and/or connections, education, social behavior, tastes in housing, food, and dress, as well as appearance, personality, and talent. As it happens, the upper class traditionally has been and still remains mainly white, the lower class principally colored. The significant point, though, is that colored people can and do form a part, albeit a small part, of the upper class, just as whites are by no means uncommon in the lower classes. Upward mobility exists and education promotes it. With effort, skill, and determination (plus a little luck) class barriers can be hurdled, but it is not easy.

There have always been movements afoot among the black community to improve the conditions of its members. Often these movements have stressed the value of education as the principal means of raising the social and economic position of the black, but on occasion the trend was to encourage a back-to-Africa migration, a movement noticeable during the last half of the nineteenth century. Rarely sounded is a note of militancy equal to that heard in the United States or in the Caribbean, although by the decade of the 1980s, evidence of such militancy was visible. Some young blacks showed more of an interest in Brazil's African past than the immediately preceding generation had.

Racial attitudes in the hemisphere have changed considerably during the twentieth century. The myth of racial inferiority or superiority has been destroyed. As one result the Indian and the black occupy a more favored position today than they did at the opening of the century. Everywhere important steps have been taken to eradicate racial prejudice. However, although much has been accomplished, much still remains to be done.

NEW NATIONS IN THE CARIBBEAN

The Caribbean region boasts an overwhelmingly black population, although in Trinidad, Guyana, and Surinam there are large numbers of Asians, particularly from India. Black militancy has become increasingly

TABLE 7-1   The Caribbean Nations

NATIONS	AREA (SQ. MILES)	POPULATION	YEAR OF INDEPENDENCE
Antigua	171	82,000	1981
Bahamas	5,386	245,000	1973
Barbados	161	254,000	1966
Belize	8,866	176,000	1981
Cuba	44,401	10,500,000	1898
Dominica	290	88,000	1978
Dominican Republic	18,919	7,000,000	1821
Grenada	133	100,000	1974
Guyana	83,000	850,000	1966
Haiti	10,808	7,500,000	1804
Jamaica	4,247	2,400,000	1962
St. Lucia	238	143,000	1979
St. Vincent	150	116,000	1979
Surinam	62,934	415,000	1975
Trinidad and Tobago	1,930	1,200,000	1962

characteristic of the Caribbean, and there has been an interaction between such militancy there and in the United States, as the biographies of Marcus Garvey and Stokely Carmichael, among others, demonstrate.

The areas still under European tutelage in the twentieth century protested vigorously, particularly from the 1930s onward, social and economic injustices with their attendant racial prejudice. In many cases these areas sought their independence. In 1962, after an unsuccessful attempt to federate, Jamaica and Trinidad and Tobago separated to become independent states. Barbados asserted its sovereignty in 1966, the same year Guyana, after many difficulties, achieved its independence. The Bahamas became independent in 1973 and in 1974 so did Grenada. Belize, formerly British Honduras, gained its independence in 1981. Although its most important city remains Belize, the port, the country has a newly constructed capital, Belmopan. Similar to the arrangement in some other former colonies, Belize recognizes the English monarch as the official head of state, while a prime minister actually runs the government. The new nation requires the protection of Great Britain since neighboring Guatemala claims it as an historic part of its territory.

With the exceptions of Haiti, the Dominican Republic, and Surinam, the nations of the Caribbean enjoy a high rating (80 or above) on the Physical Quality of Life Index, a measurement devised by the Overseas Development Council (Washington, D.C.), and based on literacy, longevity, and infant mortality. Nations offering ready access to medical care and education rank high on this index. The people of the Caribbean generally have better Physical Quality of Life rankings than the inhabitants of the other parts of Latin America. Regardless of that important advantage, they suffer the same economic problems as those found throughout most of Latin America. Poverty predominates. Unemployment and underemployment are high. The agrarian structure is fragile, overly dependent on a few exports, principally sugar. The region imports food. Its major export seems to be people. Since 1945, approximately 5 million Caribbeans have entered the United States; millions more have migrated to Central and South America, Canada, and Europe. Because of the small size and population of most Caribbean nations, there are few resources, low savings, and limited markets to encourage industrialization.

Independence has solved few of the region's problems. That failure is easily explained: The plantation export economies historically have dominated the Caribbean; they still predominate and do not permit development. In Jamaica, 1 percent of the farms occupy 56 percent of the total acreage, and unemployment among the impoverished and poorly educated masses can reach on occasion as high as 50 percent. An unbalanced distribution of wealth menaces social tranquility. Approximately 50 percent of the economy is controlled by only 1 percent of the population, and that small segment is not black but Chinese, Lebanese, American, Canadian, and

British. In Jamaica, as throughout the Caribbean, foreign companies continue to dominate primary industries. In short, relatively few of the Caribbean blacks have managed to reap much benefit from independence.

Disappointments arising from economic frustrations encouraged the growth of the Black Power movement, which reached its height in the Caribbean just as black leaders were replacing whites. The years 1968–70 witnessed Black Power demonstrations across the breadth of the Caribbean from the Bahamas to Trinidad. The Black Power advocates called for radical solutions to the area's lingering problems of poverty, illiteracy, unemployment, underemployment, and exploitation, demanding a new order based on nationalism and populism. They extolled as their principal goal local, black control of the economy, thus moving beyond nominal political independence to economic independence. That economic power still rests in the hands of nonblacks has become a source of deepening resentment in the area. In the Bahamas, for example, the blacks, fully 80 percent of the population, may control the government, but the white minority runs the economy, which is fueled by income from tourism and tax havens. For complex reasons, the new governments, despite the nationalist rhetoric, tolerate their economic dependency. What happened in Guyana in 1971 was the exception rather than the rule. In that year, to the applause of the nationalists, Prime Minister Forbes Burnham nationalized the big Canadian-owned Alcan bauxite operation, a move closely watched by leaders throughout the Caribbean. Psychological rather than economic benefits resulted. In 1982 Burnham acknowledged the bankruptcy of Guyana. It could pay neither for imports nor its debt installments. The government blamed the crisis on the acute foreign exchange shortage, low productivity in key sectors of the economy (especially in bauxite), mismanagement of state enterprises, corruption, waste, and poor marketing practices. Guyana's crisis, however, reflected the problems of all dependent nations: imported goods, chiefly oil, rose in price, while exports, all natural products, declined in price.

Perplexing economic problems do not characterize only the new nations of the Caribbean. Haiti, independent since 1804, still has not resolved its major problems, and the situation looks more desperate than ever. Long dictatorships, first of "Papa Doc" Francois Duvalier (1957–71) and then of his son "Baby Doc" Jean-Claude Duvalier (1971–86), submerged Haiti in a sea of corruption and brutality devoid of any trace of economic development. The popular overthrow of the family dictatorship in 1986 led to political instability, while the poverty index continued its downward slide. The United Nations has singled out Haiti as the only Latin American nation among the twenty-five "least developed" nations of the world. Of its 6.5 million inhabitants, approximately 90 percent are illiterate. Half of the children die before reaching their fifth birthday. Haiti has the lowest Physical Quality of Life rating in the Western Hemisphere, a sobering 41.

Not all the islands of the Caribbean are independent. Since Columbus's visit to Puerto Rico in 1493, the inhabitants of the island have searched to define their status within larger imperial spheres. After nearly four centuries, during which Puerto Ricans remained voiceless in their own affairs, they won representation in the Spanish parliament in 1876. Just as they gained autonomy to exercise authority over the internal affairs of their island, U.S. troops stormed ashore in one of the campaigns of the Spanish-American War. Falling spoils to the United States, the Puerto Ricans had to start all over again to define their political status.

For decades the political fate of the island remained ambiguous: not a part of the United States, not autonomous, and certainly not independent. Ambiguity bred frustrations that, in turn, stoked the fires of nationalism, passionately fanned in the 1930s by Pedro Albizu Campos, a major figure in the Puerto Rican nationalist movement. Not until 1948 did Puerto Ricans elect their own governor, Luis Muñoz Marín. Four years later, the Commonwealth of Puerto Rico was established, again a political status fraught with ambiguities.

While the Puerto Ricans, like the English Caribbeans, enjoy higher indices of education, health services, and nutrition than their counterparts in Latin America, the island's economy, like those throughout the region, never developed and for many of the same reasons. "Operation Bootstrap" of the 1950s emphasized capital-intensive industrialization. Yet, persistent unemployment, gross inequalities of income, and debt continued. Economist James L. Dietz characterizes the much ballyhooed Operation as "a monument not to economic progress but to the costs and dangers inherent in a development program based upon capital-intensive, foreign owned, vertically integrated, and export-oriented corporate expansion." Such a judgment recalls disappointments with the industrialization experience and capitalist development schemes elsewhere in Latin America. Sharing yet another characteristic with that region, Puerto Ricans no longer produce the food they eat, ringing up monumental deficits to import it. Current frustrations have prompted one scholar of Puerto Rico to wryly conclude that it is a society in which the ruling class does not rule and the working class cannot work. Puerto Rico still awaits the solution of its political status as it pursues elusive economic development.

In its efforts to alter the institutional patterns of the past, Cuba remains the only Caribbean nation in the process of development. Chapter 9 will discuss the unique Cuban experience.

8

Development and Democracy Frustrated

The facade of the National Congress. Buenos Aires, 1973, with graffiti reading "Bourgeoisie Executed—The Workers in Power"

In the decades after 1945, Latin America grew rapidly, and during part of that time the forces favoring democracy seemed to triumph. Aspirations for change and development mounted as greater numbers of the population understood the potential benefits of a more modern or a more rational society. Unfortunately aspirations outpaced change. Too few enjoyed the benefits of what change took place, and too many of the old political, economic, and social structures and patterns lingered. Development was more illusion than reality. As the rate and extent of change and development failed to fulfill expectations, frustrations and tensions mounted. In many nations, the military, also the victim of accelerating frustration, imposed its own political solutions that, more often than not, were a reaffirmation of older patterns. The failure to develop at the speed and to the extent desired created a widespread disillusionment with democracy and capitalism. Disillusionment as well as frustration and desperation sparked violence. Two old questions surfaced again: why has Latin America not developed and how can it? Specters of the past, dependency and underdevelopment, haunt contemporary Latin America.

THE MODERNIZATION OF UNDERDEVELOPMENT

The modernization process accelerated in the twentieth century as some parts of Latin America adopted more recent techniques, methods, and ideas to replace more time-honored ones. Continuing the conflict of the nineteenth century between the folk and the Europeanizing elites, modernism struggled with traditionalism in what was essentially a contest between the static countryside and the more dynamic cities. Certainly the process and effects of modernization revealed themselves more readily in and near the urban areas than elsewhere, even though much that was traditional also flourished in metropolitan environments. Likewise, the effects of modernization continued to be more visible among the elite, middle class, and urban working class than among the peasants and rural proletariat.

Various indicators pointed to a quickening movement of part of Latin America from a traditional to a modern society by mid-twentieth century. In some countries, such as Argentina, Brazil, Chile, Mexico, and Uruguay, the movement was quite noticeable; in others, such as Paraguay, Bolivia, Ecuador, Honduras, and Haiti, it would take a careful observer to discern a significant inclination toward modernization.

The following comments, contrasting traditional with modern societies in mid-twentieth-century Latin America, are of an extremely general nature, applicable to some areas of some countries but questionable with regard to other areas of the same country or to other countries. The discussion suggests some indicators by which a Latin American country's progress toward modernization might be measured. It should be stressed that the models that follow represent one stage of social science conceptualization. Models may be useful as a means to study society, but they are more creations of conjecture than of reality.

Traditional societies are agrarian: they have as high as 80 percent of their work force engaged in agriculture, while modern societies can get by with as few as 10 percent on the farms. At midcentury, Latin America still had about 50 percent of its work force concentrated in agriculture, although that percentage had been steadily declining. Between 1945 and 1955, the percentage of the work force engaged in agriculture dropped from 57.4 percent to 51.6 percent. By 1950, Latin America stood on the threshold of becoming more urban than rural, a reflection of major population shifts in the previous half-century. A high degree of literacy characterizes the modern society, while illiteracy—with the exception of a well-educated elite—plagues the traditional. Approximately 50 percent of Latin America's working age population did not know how to read and write. Further, traditional society divides into a large peasantry and a small elite with sharp distinctions between the two. It is as difficult as it is rare to cross class lines. On the other hand, in the broadly stratified modern society, class distinctions blur, easing social mobility. Urban Latin America enjoyed far greater flexibility in its social structure than the rural area. Nonetheless, in both, there existed a well-defined elite whose ranks were difficult for outsiders to join. Traditional and modern societies revere different values. The traditional accepts the world as it exists, including of course the class and power structures. The traditional individuals adapt to their surroundings. They are person-oriented. Individual relationships matter most to them and consequently they place primary emphasis on their dealings with people. Treatment in an impersonal way by doctors, lawyers, social workers, or governmental bureaucrats alienates them. They suspect anyone who seeks to exert leadership or rise above the group. They refuse to make long-run plans. In contrast, the individuals embracing the benefits of modernization become increasingly object-oriented. Their goals outside their group often take precedence over personal relationships: an education, a profession, a better standard of living, a different style of life. Change and flexibility constitute the keystones of modern societal values. The conflict between activism and fatalism continued in Latin America, but by and large the struggle over values took place in the cities. The peasantry and rural proletariat accepted their lowly status. Latin America had an extremely low level of technology; it seemed content with methods passed down from generation to generation. (Some would argue convincingly that the impoverished have little room to experiment, since failure means disaster, possibly in the form of starvation.) A modern society, in order to maintain and to accelerate its advance, innovates and invents freely, questioning past practices with the intention of improving them and in the process raising the level of technology. Finally, the traditional society has a subsistence economy that

TABLE 8-1 Income Distribution in Chile in 1968. Estimates of Relative Shares of Personal Income and of Total Income-Earning Population

	SHARE OF INCOME-EARNING POPULATION	SHARE OF PERSONAL INCOME	APPROXIMATE PER CAPITA INCOME IN US DOLLARS
Lower Income Groups	71.5	26.0	220
Middle Income Groups	24.1	28.5	710
Higher Income Groups	4.4	45.5	6,200

Source: Stefan de Vylder, *Chile 1970–73. The Political Economy of the Rise and Fall of the Unidad Popular* (Stockholm, Sweden: Civiltryckeriet i Kristianstad, 1974), p. 9. Reproduced with the permission of the publisher.

centers on local markets, although it often furnishes one primary product for the international market. Conversely, in a modern nation a complex commercial network covers the breadth of the land, and its links with the outside world are many.

As a consequence of intensive, efficient economic activity, the per capita income in a modern nation far exceeds that of a more traditionally oriented one. Whereas the average per capita income in the United States at midcentury approximated $3,000, in Latin America it was less than $400, ranging from a high of $800 in Venezuela to a low of $40 in Haiti. As might

A Mexican postcard, circa 1920, was meant to convey the idea of the nation's modernization. It contrasted "yesterday's" stagecoach with "today's" locomotive, a sure sign of progress.

be expected, the income was badly distributed. In Argentina, Brazil, and Mexico, those in the top 10 percent income bracket received 40 percent of the national income, while those in the bottom 40 percent earned only 10 percent. In all of Latin America, 20 percent of the population received 60 percent of the national income. Over 70 percent suffered abject poverty. Income continued to concentrate in the hands of a few during the years following midcentury, as exemplified in the case of Chile. The figures in Table 8-1 provide a clear idea of the deceptiveness of the general per capita income figures. Although most sources list the per capita income in Chile at somewhere near $600 at the end of the 1960s, the breakdown of incomes in Table 8-1 shows that more than two-thirds of the population received a per capita income of only $200 in 1968, while a favored 4.4 percent enjoyed a per capita income of $6,200. A major weakness of studies dwelling on modernization is their acceptance of the values, vocabulary, and goals of the elites. Judgments, thus, become skewed by the experience of the foreign models preferred by the elites. Students of Latin America must continue to exercise great caution not to overrely on such models.

It is evident that despite great advances made in the twentieth century, few of the Latin American societies qualified in their entirety as modern. While the elite and middle classes enjoyed many of the benefits of a modern society, the fact was that conditions for the masses had not improved. A majority of the population remained immersed in the past. Modern society had penetrated but slightly into rural Latin America, a fortress

A magnificent baroque church in Potosí, Bolivia, no longer serves its original purpose. In 1974, it housed a movie theater.

The sign welcomes the visitor to El Agustino, Peru, in 1975. Combining the past with the present, it advertises "Inca Kola," the drink with which the military government replaced Coca Cola. The top of the billboard announces, "In Peru, we work," while the bottom lettering assures Peruvians that Inca Kola is "The national taste!"

The Plaza of the Three Cultures, Mexico City, perfectly illustrates the past and present. In the foreground is an excavated Aztec temple foundation, upon which the Spaniards constructed a church, while in the background stand modern apartment buildings.

of traditionalism, where a majority of the Latin Americans lived. As in the nineteenth century, modernization signified growth and provided a cloak of change to shelter traditional institutions. Modernization seldom meant development. Indeed, so long as the neocolonial and neofeudal institutions remain, it is unrealistic to expect much significant development in Latin America. Modernization's major contribution continued to be growth.

The latifundia, more than any other institution, preserved the past. In 1960, 54 percent of the population lived in the countryside. Although this dropped to 46 percent in 1970, the total rural population rose during that decade from 108 to 133 million. Consequently, change in Latin America, whether by reform or revolution, can be truly effectual only when it reaches the overwhelming number of landless too. Land tenure has been the key to agriculture, indeed the key to the economy since agriculture has remained the economic base for Latin America. During the 1960s, 52 percent of Latin America's total international earnings came from agriculture. These exports have been extremely important because they determine the availability of foreign exchange for capital goods. True, during the twentieth century, the agricultural sector of the economy gradually reduced its contributions to the gross national product, but nonetheless it continued to play the decisive role in the economy.

Despite the fact that agriculture formed the basis for the area's economy, few nations tried to reform the centuries-old agrarian structure—Mexico being the sole exception until the 1950s—or to modernize agriculture. The landowning system in most of Latin America remained flagrantly unjust, based, at least in part, on the accumulation of huge tracts of land often by means of force, deceit, and dubious measures approved by the passage of time and the connivance of bureaucrats. The following testimony of the chief of the Mapuche community of Anacón Grande, Argentina, taken in early 1975, points to a remarkable continuity of methods used to divest Indians of their lands over the course of nearly five centuries:

> I went to the land office with this problem of land and presented it to the commissioners. They said to me, "What land are you occupying? Where is your permission to occupy it? You don't have any document showing title to that land. If you want to occupy that land you have to file a claim for it." That's what they told me. Well, I said that I couldn't file the claim. Why must I claim my own land? If I am to file that claim, I have to go far away. I have to leave the land to exert my rights. And if I do, who will feed my family?
>
> And then they said to me, "So-and-so has made a claim to the land, and if you don't make a counterclaim then you'll have to leave there because you will be trespassing." How can it be that I am a trespasser? We didn't come from the other side of the ocean. Today those who come to claim our land have been here only ten or maybe twenty years, but we have been on this land for at least one hundred years. Our great-grandfathers lived here. How can we be the trespassers? They are the trespassers not us Mapuches who were born on

this land. Like the trees which shade it, we were planted and grew here. We are the true owners of the land.

In no other area of comparable size in the world did there exist a higher concentration of land in the hands of a few than in Latin America. As of 1950, 2 percent of the Argentine estates accounted for 60 percent of the land; in Brazil, 1.6 percent of the fazendas covered 50 percent of the land; in El Salvador, 1 percent of the haciendas included 50 percent of the land; in Paraguay, 11 haciendas controlled 35 percent of the land. The figures were comparable in most of the rest of the countries. And the general tendency in this century has been for the large properties to increase in both number and size. (By the late 1960s, 17 percent of the landowners controlled 90 percent of the land.) On the opposite end of the scale lay another problem: the minifundium, a property so small that often it failed to sustain its owner, much less to contribute to the regional or national economies. That problem, too, was widespread. As of 1950, 42 percent of the farms in Argentina claimed only 1 percent of the land; in Brazil, 22 percent of the rural properties possessed only 0.5 percent of the land; in El Salvador, 80 percent of the farms had fewer than 12 acres each; in Paraguay, 44 percent of the farms had fewer than 12 acres each. Table 8-2 illustrates the plight of the minifundia and the dominance of the latifundia. Looking at the statistics available for the early 1960s, the researcher can conclude that 63 percent or 18 million adult farmers owned no land; another 5.5 million owned insufficient amounts of land; 1.9 million possessed sufficient land; and 100,000 owned too much land for the social and economic good of the area.

Latin Americans traditionally have farmed their land inefficiently. The large estates included much land their owners either did not cultivate or undercultivated. Experts estimated that Latin Americans in the mid-twentieth century farmed only about 10 percent of their agricultural holdings. In Brazil, Venezuela, and Colombia, approximately 80 percent of the farmland was unused or unproductively used for cattle raising at the end of

TABLE 8-2　Land Ownership in Latin America, 1960

SIZE OF FARMS IN HECTARE (1 HECTARE = 2.47 ACRES)	PERCENTAGE OF FARMS	PERCENTAGE OF LAND AREA
0–20	72.6	3.7
20–100	18.0	8.4
100–1,000	7.9	23.0
Over 1,000	1.5	64.9

Source: Richard P. Schaedel, "Land Reform Studies," *Latin American Research Review*, I, no. 1 (Fall 1965), 85. Reproduced with the permission of the publisher.

the 1950s. A 1960 study of Colombia revealed that the largest farmers in control of 70 percent of the agricultural lands, cultivated only 6 percent of it. Farmers of fewer than thirteen acres, on the other hand, cultivated 66 percent of it. Another study illustrating the underuse of farm land showed that only 14 percent of Ecuador's tillable land was cultivated in the early 1960s. The landowners continued to hold their property, not to farm but for purposes of prestige, investment, and speculation. As in the past, control of the land insured control of the work force as well. For those parcels of land under cultivation, the owners seldom took full advantage of the work force available or used any but the most antiquated farming techniques. The slash-and-burn method remained the most popular means of clearing the land. The farmers rarely spread fertilizer or did so sparingly. Consequently, the land eroded, became easily exhausted, and depleted quickly. Productivity, always low, fell. A person of routine and custom, the farmer used the hoe, unmodified for centuries. The plow was rare, the tractor even rarer.

That the Latin Americans were never able to feed themselves well and during the past few decades have been incapable of supplying their own food requirements are a major indictment of Latin America's agrarian structure and farming methods. With 16 percent of the world's cultivatable land and only 6 percent of the world's population, Latin America contains proportionately more hungry people than India, Pakistan, or Bangladesh. For this there are at least three explanations: most of the tillable land lies fallow, the cultivated land is inefficiently exploited, and much of the land is used to raise export crops. More and more the use of land to produce export crops rather than staples creates food scarcity. Nicaragua vividly illustrated that trend. During the 1950s and 1960s, cotton production swept through the nation's corn belt. While Nicaragua increased its exports, food production plummeted. For its part, Brazil throughout the 1970s encouraged the cultivation of soybeans for export, to the neglect of black beans, the major food staple. Between 1964 and 1974, per capita production of export crops in Latin America rose 27 percent, while that of staple crops fell 10 percent. Statistics from throughout Latin America during the last half of the twentieth century confirm the emphasis on export over subsistence agriculture.

Increasingly Latin America must import food. Chile, for example, shifted in the 1940s from being a net agricultural exporter to becoming a net importer. By the mid-1950s, agricultural products accounted for 25 percent of Chile's total imports. In short, that nation was spending about 18 percent of its hard-earned foreign currency on food that Chile could grow itself, a tragedy by no means unique to Chile. By 1965, foodstuffs constituted 20 percent of Latin America's purchases abroad. That percentage rose in the succeeding years. These three examples typify the tragedy in 1989: Mexico imported 25 percent of its food, including nearly half of its staple grains. Having cultivated only 15 percent of its arable land, Belize also bought abroad 25 percent of the food its population consumed. Haiti, once the agricultural jewel in the imperial crown of France, became the hungriest nation in the hemisphere and imported 75 percent of its food.

Even with imports supplementing careless local production, the food available to feed the population properly was insufficient. Starvation was not unknown and malnutrition was common in wide regions of Latin America. In Chile during the period from 1965 to 1969, 7,000 children died of malnutrition each year; more than one-third of the population consumed fewer than 2,000 calories per day; 50 percent of the youth were underfed. In Mexico during the decade from 1965 to 1975, childhood deaths due to malnutrition jumped 10 percent. Food shortages, high cost of staples, malnutrition, and starvation occurred in regions that, agrarian experts agreed, had the potential of not only feeding their populations well but also of becoming net exporters of food.

Agriculture in the twentieth century lost none of the speculative, reflexive nature so characteristic of the mercantilist past. For its prosperity, it continued to rely heavily on a few export commodities, which were always very vulnerable on the international market. Prices depended on the demands of a few industrialized nations. Further, new producers and substitutes appeared to challenge and undersell them, thus increasing Latin America's economic vulnerability. Africa, in particular, emerged as a formidable competitor for international markets. After World War II, the prices of agricultural products gradually declined to the dismay of the Latin Americans (while at the same time the prices of imported capital goods spiraled upward). Still, the latifundia by and large followed their usual practice of offering one crop for sale. On a fair price for coffee alone, for example, depended the well-being of an alarming number of Latin Americans at the end of the 1950s; coffee composed 67 percent of Colombia's exports, 42 percent of El Salvador's, 41 percent of Brazil's, 38 percent of Haiti's, 34 percent of Guatemala's, and 31 percent of Costa Rica's. On the export of sugar, bananas, cacao, wheat, beef, wool, and mutton depended other Latin American economies.

The economic inefficiency of the land structure was one matter, the human misery it perpetuated quite another. Rural society with its hereditary social positions resisted change. The few landlords lived in comfort; the rural masses existed in misery. They earned a pittance in wages—if, indeed, they received wages—and most probably were heavily in debt to their employer. Debt peonage was as common as it had been in the eighteenth and nineteenth centuries. The Brazilian Graciliano Ramos captured the pathos and hopelessness of the rural proletariat in his novel *Barren Lives,* set in the drought-tortured Northeast. The herdsman Fabiano realizes that everything conspires to prevent his escape from poverty:

In the division of stock at the year's end, Fabiano received a fourth of the calves and a third of the kids, but as he grew no feed, but merely sowed a few handfuls of beans and corn on the river flat, living on what he bought at the market, he disposed of the animals, never seeing his brand on a calf or his mark on the ear of a kid.

If he could only put something aside for a few months, he would be able to get his head up. Oh, he had made plans, but that was all foolishness. Ground creepers were never meant to climb. Once the beans had been eaten and the ears of corn gnawed, there was no place to go but to the boss's cash drawer. He would turn over the animals that had fallen to his lot for the lowest of prices, grumbling and protesting in distress, trying to make his meager resources yield as much as possible. Arguing, he would choke and bite his tongue. Dealing with anyone else he would not let himself be so shamelessly robbed, but, as he was afraid of being put off the ranch, he would give in. He would take the cash and listen to the advice that accompanied it. He should give thought to the future, be more careful. . . .

Little by little the boss's brand was put on Fabiano's stock, and when he had nothing left to sell, the backlander went into debt. When time came for the division, he was in the hole, and when accounts were settled he received a mere nothing.

This time, as on other occasions, Fabiano first made a deal regarding the stock, then thought better of the matter, and leaving the transaction only half agreed upon, he went to consult with his wife. Vitória sent the boys to play in the clay pit, sat down in the kitchen, and concentrated . . . adding and subtracting. The next day Fabiano went back to town, but on closing the deal he noted that, as usual, Vitória's figuring differed from that of the boss. He protested, and received the usual explanation: the difference represented interest.

He refused to accept the answer. There must be some mistake. . . . The mistake couldn't be found, and Fabiano lost his temper. Was he to take a beating like that his whole life long, giving up what belonged to him for nothing? Was that right? To work like a slave and never gain his freedom?

The boss became angry. He refused to hear such insolence. He thought it would be a good thing if the herdsman looked for another job.

At this point Fabiano got cold feet and began to back down. All right, all right. There was no need for a fuss. If he had said something wrong, he was sorry. He was ignorant; he had never had any learning. He knew his place; he wasn't the cheeky kind. He was just a half-breed. He wasn't going to get into any arguments with rich people. He wasn't bright, but he knew how to show people proper respect. . . . The boss calmed down and Fabiano backed out of the room, his hat dragging on the brick floor.[1]

The plight of Fabiano seemed typical of millions of other rural inhabitants. For them, housing was primitive, the diet inadequate, health and sanitary conditions abysmal, and education generally nonexistent, and where existent, substandard.

Josué de Castro entitled his study of the depressed agricultural region of northeastern Brazil *Death in the Northeast* and concluded, "The Northeast of Brazil remains a region of crisis where hunger and misery, instead of

[1]Graciliano Ramos, *Barren Lives* (Austin: University of Texas Press, 1969), pp. 93–95. Reprinted with the permission of the publisher.

gradually subsiding, increase in intensity." In that huge region, scarcely 4 percent of the population owned most of the land. Poverty, hunger, social waste, illiteracy, and chronic illness predominated. Life expectancy barely reached 30 years, a child died every 42 seconds, 85 per hour, 2,040 per day. Even in more developed regions like the Central Valley of Chile, the rural laborers (known locally as the *inquilino*) led a marginal existence. Families dwelt in one-room mud huts, with earthen floor and thatched roof, without sanitary facilities, running water, or heating. The *patrón* granted them use of a small plot for a garden, and from it came the meager rations for an always hungry family. The caloric intake barely sustained life; malnutrition predominated; death was expected momentarily. Obviously the rural masses in Latin America existed rather than lived. The human plight staggered the imagination, but it failed to produce sufficient reforms. Only when it became all too apparent that the changeless countryside delayed modernization of the nation did reformers expand their customary urban perspective to contemplate the rural tragedy.

THE CITY AS HOPE

The city represented hope: economic redemption for the poor and development for the nation. However, as it turns out, no city can fulfill those hopes as long as it remains engulfed by the rural institutions of the colonial past.

The city folks demanded more food at a lower price and the haciendas and fazendas proved their inability to comply. As part of the rural population migrated toward the city, farming needed to become increasingly efficient to feed the growing nonagrarian population. Failure to produce more efficiently necessitated the food imports mentioned previously. To function properly, the urban factories demanded efficient, abundant production of raw goods in the countryside, a demand the landlords were ill prepared to meet. At the same time, an industrial economy required expanding markets for the manufactured goods. The industrialists saw their capacity to produce far exceed the ability of their compatriots to purchase. The countryside offered little encouragement to the industrial process since the workers earned little money and often the patrón paid them in kind rather than in currency, a feudal vestige incompatibile with modernization. To further expand industrialization required rural reforms. Hemispheric leaders meeting at Punta del Este, Uruguay, in 1961, finally voiced a concern with agrarian problems. They signed a declaration "to encourage . . . programs of comprehensive agrarian reform leading to the effective transformation, where required, of unjust structures and systems of land tendure. . . ." It proved easier to make that declaration than to carry it out. Nonetheless, if the growing cities were to be viable, the governments and urban populations would have to address festering rural problems.

Until the 1950s, Mexico remained the only nation that had broken the colonial land patterns and structures to experiment with the redistribution of land and with communal landholdings. Mexico made many errors, from which both the Mexicans and other Latin Americans learned. It became apparent that just to divide up the land worked to the disadvantage not only of the national economy but also of the peasants, since it deprived them of some necessary services formerly provided by the patrón. For the rural workers to be transformed into independent farmers required much more than just a piece of land; they needed advice, instruction, seeds, equipment, and credit, the absence of which doomed reform to failure. Nor was it desirable to split the estates into plots too small to be productive. Such a reform would simply substitute the problems of minifundia for those of latifundia. Mexico experimented, and over the decades solved some of its agrarian problems. It became increasingly apparent to both friends and foes of agrarian reform that Mexico's experiment succeeded after 1940. Agricultural production rose. Also, and far more important, the Mexican peasants enjoyed a higher standard of living. They formed a new market for transistor radios, toothpaste, shoes, bicycles, wristwatches, and other products of the burgeoning consumer industries. Mortality rates among them fell. Life expectancy lengthened by as much as 50 percent. In some favored areas, the peasants enjoyed those social services previously reserved for urban dwellers.

Torn by many considerations, reformers proposed a variety of new solutions to the old land problem, not all of them germane. In those nations where land reform was actually taking place, the most common procedure was to divide the land into units considered economically viable and distribute them to the landless. Mexico in many instances delivered individual land grants but in others returned to the communal landholding patterns of its Indian past, the *ejido*. The government of Fidel Castro in Cuba refused to subdivide the land. The estates taken from individuals or companies were operated by the workers as cooperatives under government supervision. The land reform advocated by President Salvador Allende in Chile in 1971 favored the cooperative over individually owned units. Many of the reformers sidestepped the main issue—and thus avoided a direct confrontation with the entrenched landowner class—by proposing the resettlement of the landless in distant unused lands, often the jungles. These cautious reformers failed to face honestly the question of why the unused lands had never been occupied. The reason was simple: they were marginal at best, of no value at worst. The lands either were a long distance from the markets or possessed low fertility of soil or suffered from bad weather or were plagued with an unhealthy climate or any combination of the above. In short, there were execellent reasons why the conquistadores, the Church, the landed aristocrary, or the government had never taken possession of those lands. To use scarce capital in opening up such marginal territory was questionable economics. Rather, it seemed wiser that first efforts and available capital should go toward making the high-potential land already accessible to ready markets produce more than it did. Latin America's rural problem, with few exceptions, has not been so much the need for more land as the necessity to exploit more intensely and productively the land already available.

Many factors delayed the process of land reform. Obviously the large landowners refused to consider any plan, automatically labeling such efforts as communist. Even the progressive middle class found it difficult to move from the splendid-sounding theories of land reform to practice. The rural masses themselves—at least through the 1940s and with the exception of Mexico—remained passive, inarticulate, and disorganized. Not until 1955 were the first Peasant Leagues founded in the Northeast of Brazil. In truth, land reform was far too radical a process for many Latin Americans to embrace. In taking land from one group and bestowing it on another, the reform would give property to a new group, and of course, status, prestige, and dignity would accompany ownership so that the new group would possess the potential for power, the potential to challenge other interest groups and iniquitous institutions. For that reason, those in power, with a few exceptions that will be examined later, have paid lip service on occasion to land reform but generally have shied away from actually enacting and implementing it. Almost every Latin American country today boasts of some grandiose land reform in its law books, but few have bothered to implement it. The Colombian Social Agrarian Reform Law promulgated in 1961, for example, impressed everyone as progressive. Yet, a decade later, it had distributed only 0.25 percent of the total cultivated land to a paltry 0.45 percent of the farmers.

Those who would change society lavished their attention and energy on industrialization, regarded by ever-increasing numbers of people as the key to modernization. The blow the Depression dealt agriculture in the 1930s made industrialization seem all the more desirable, even inevitable. The jolt cleared away much of the former resistance to industrialization. Falling prices and demands for primary products precipitated an acute balance of payments crisis. Latin America possessed scant funds to meet its foreign debts or interest payments abroad or to import the manufactured items to which it had become so accustomed. At that point, economic nationalists argued cogently that industrialization would diversify the economy, prevent scarce foreign exchange from being spent abroad for what could be produced at home, and raise national self-sufficiency. Sympathetic to these arguments and compelled to experiment, many of the governments enacted laws favorable to the encouragement of local industry: higher tariffs, multiple exchange rates, import controls, subsidies, tax privileges, and so on. By reducing foreign competition, the governments made investment in local industry more profitable and, hence, more attractive. Industrial growth during the 1930s was impressive, and it continued thereafter. Statistics indicated that industry grew at a much faster rate than agriculture. In Brazil, in 1950, agriculture accounted for 25 percent of the gross domestic product (GDP) and industry 26 percent. By the early 1980s, the agricultural contribution had fallen to 10 percent, while the industrial had jumped to 37 percent. During the same time span in Mexico, agricultural imput to the GDP slid from 23 to 10 percent, and industrial rose from 30 to 38 percent.

Industrialization throughout Latin America shared a number of characteristics. It tended to concentrate in only a few cities in each of the countries. Most of the manufacturing was done in small plants employing only a few workers. Manufacturing processes depended heavily on hand labor. The level of capitalization remained low and so did output, mainly because of the limited markets. The factories produced principally consumer items: washing machines, blenders, wristwatches, plastic toys, shoes, toothbrushes, and the like. In certain countries—notably Argentina, Brazil, and Mexico—the consumer industries became so well developed that it was no longer necessary to import certain items. On the negative side, limited and well-protected local markets tended to encourage inefficiency in production. Although textiles and foodstuffs constituted the most important segment of the growing volume of manufacturing, a slight shift toward capital goods became noticeable in the largest countries by the late 1930s. As the national industries increasingly bought more local raw products and sold their finished goods in the local markets, it became apparent that the economy depended less on export than it had in the past. In short, the industrializing process was modifying the economic structure of the nation.

At first all manufacturing was done for local markets with few items for sale abroad. That pattern changed after midcentury, particularly for the larger nations. In 1950, only 6 percent of the Latin American exports consisted of manufactured goods, but by 1974, that figure reached 18 percent. Such a diversification of exports at first pleased the Latin Americans, but soon enough the sale of industrial goods abroad indicated some of the old structural weaknesses. Industrialization imposed on antiquated institutions was handicapped, and the prospects of industrialization by itself changing the nations and their ingrained institutions seemed dimmer than they had only a few years earlier. The basic problem remained: since few could afford to buy manufactured goods, the markets were small. To survive, the big industries of the major nations had to export. Industrial dependency—a new form of an old malady—appeared, and nowhere was it more evident than in Brazil by 1980. Particularly in the Caribbean and Central America, plants often did more assembly than manufacturing. They imported component parts, usually from the United States, assembled them with cheap labor, and then exported the finished products. Such assembly plants created a few jobs, but their triple dependency—on foreign capital, foreign parts, and foreign markets—made them weak, perhaps even negative, contributors to national industrialization.

The economic crises of the 1930s compelled the governments to play a more active role in the economy and to become a major decision maker. Adopting the concept of long-range planning, the state increasingly supervised what it thought would be national development but what in reality turned out to be unprecedented growth. The government directed, operated, or owned certain industries where it could not induce or find private capital to do so. Within less than a quarter of a century, the Brazilian government came to dominate the vital fields of oil, electricity, and steel. Steel, considered a key industry for serious industrialization, demonstrated the new attitude of the Latin American governments toward planning of and participation in the economy. President Getúlio Vargas of Brazil, encouraged by the military and the nationalists, ordered plans drawn up in 1940 for a steel mill—Brazil possessed the largest known iron reserves in the world, although the country was deficient in coal. The following year he organized the National Steel Company, which at once initiated work on a steel plant at Volta Redonda, situated between Brazil's principal cities, São Paulo and Rio de Janeiro. The mill began to operate in 1946. By 1955, Volta Redonda was producing 646,000 tons of steel, an annual output doubled by 1963. At the same time, the Mexican government was in the process of expanding national production of steel by increasing the capacity of the mill at Monterrey and building a new plant at Monclova, which became the largest integrated iron and steel producer in Latin America. Argentina and Chile began to operate their own steel mills in the 1940s.

The period following World War II witnessed a surge of industrialization. The trend toward the production of capital goods increased, despite the continuing speculative nature of industrialization. Brazil amply illustrated the growing importance of industry within the economy. Whereas in 1939, the industrial sector provided 17.9 percent of the national income, it furnished 35.3 percent by 1963. Native capitalists continued to prefer quick and high profits over a definite and limited period of time rather than long-term, slow-growing investments, the type needed to really promote the production of capital goods. Partially for that reason, the governments became ever more involved in financing larger and more risky industries. The trend toward government planning of and participation in the economy became characteristic of Argentina after Juan D. Perón assumed the presidency in 1946. His first Quinquennial Plan aimed to accelerate industrialization and to promote greater economic independence. Hence, it fell well within the confines of the economic nationalism engulfing Latin America at the time. A National Economic Council oversaw the economic progress of the nation and a Trade Promotion Institute encouraged exports. The government began to take over banks, railroads, and the telephone and telegraph system. Traditional British influence over the economy

TABLE 8-3   Argentine Progress toward Industrialization

	1946	1954
Number of Industrial Establishments	84,985	148,363
Number of Workers	889,032	1,007,270
Wages and Salaries (in thousands of pesos)	2,462,742	13,713,769
Value of Production (in thousands of pesos)	14,793,358	76,586,271

waned. Table 8-3 indicates Argentina's progress toward industrialization during the Perón years.

All nations of Latin America did not participate equally in the industrial surge. Industrialization concentrated in a few favored geographic areas. At the end of the 1960s, three nations, Argentina, Brazil, and Mexico, accounted for 80 percent of Latin America's industrial production. In fact, more than 30 percent of the total factory production was squeezed into the metropolitan areas of Buenos Aires, Mexico City, and São Paulo. Five other nations, Chile, Colombia, Peru, Uruguay, and Venezuela, produced 17 percent of Latin America's industrial goods, leaving the remaining 3 percent of the manufacturing to the twelve other republics. By 1970, for the first time, the portion of the GDP represented by manufacturing exceeded that accounted for by agriculture and mining, an enduring characteristic for the remainder of the twentieth century.

Following World War II, foreign investment in Latin America rose spectacularly, showing a decided preference for petroleum, manufacturing, mining, and public utilities. United States investment—by far the most predominant—reached $9 billion by the mid-1960s and $35 billion in 1980, about 80 percent of U.S. private investment in the Third World. While the total sum of U.S. investment in Latin America increased impressively, the U.S. share of foreign investment declined, dropping from 38 percent in 1950 to 18 percent in 1980. Foreign capital controlled a disproportionate share of the industries in each nation. For example, the extent of foreign investment in Brazilian industry in 1970 was substantial: approximately 22 percent of the capital of all industrial firms, or 32 percent of medium and large firms. Of the fifty-five largest companies operating in Brazil during the 1960s, thirty-one were foreign-owned. Argentine industry likewise felt the influence of foreign capitalists. Of the ten principal industrial firms operating in Argentina in 1971, eight were owned by foreigners and the remaining two by the government. Foreigners also owned more than half of the private banks in Argentina. In Mexico, too, foreign economic influences remained considerable. Well over $1 billion of U.S. direct investment concentrated in Mexico, and over two-thirds of that was in manufacturing. It has been asserted that in the early 1960s, foreign interests—predominantly those of the United States—controlled 28 percent of the 2,000 largest companies in Mexico. Furthermore, their influence was clearly evident in another 14 percent. Despite, then, impressive industrial growth and diversification in Latin America, the area still relied heavily on foreign interests and capital.

High profits attracted foreign investments. Indeed, investors received more return than they could expect from similar investments in the United States, Canada, or Western Europe. Between 1950 and 1965, U.S. citizens invested $3,800 million in Latin America and earned $11,300 million, a mind-boggling profit of $7,500 million.

Industrialization sowed the seeds of new problems for Latin America. For one thing, it was creating a new type of dependency in which Latin America relied ever more heavily on foreign investment, technology, technicians, and markets. For another, it funneled wealth increasingly into the hands of a few. While technological advances resolved many problems, they also accentuated economic inequality. University of Chicago anthropologist Marshall Sahlins has concluded that "poverty has grown as civilization has advanced." The industrial megalopolis of Buenos Aires offers a thought-provoking example of the economic power of relatively few industrialists. By the early 1970s, 0.2 percent of the industrial proprietors controlled 65 percent of the production and employed 50 percent of the workers. In 1975, the Secretary General of the Economic Commission for Latin America, Enrique Iglesias, confirmed the growing concentration of wealth throughout the region.

The ties between industrialists and large landowners seemed to be closer than most people either realized or cared to admit. It can be misleading to think of separate landowning and industrialist classes because in many instances—although it must be emphasized not in all—the two groups are one and the same or the overlapping of the two may be partial. Thus, one could observe—and this was as true in the larger and more prosperous nations such as Argentina and Brazil as it was in the smaller nations—a growing industrial concentration in the hands of a few alongside a great concentration of land ownership, and very often the same persons played the dual role of landowner and industrialist. Such an interrelationship of interests confused efforts made in favor of reform.

One significant consequence of industrialization has been the growth of a better-defined urban proletariat class conscious of its goals and powers. As the labor movement expanded in the decades between 1914 and 1933, its leadership spoke increasingly in terms of major social changes. The ideological content of the labor programs, the increasingly efficient organization of the unions, and the new power labor wielded worried the elite and later the middle class. One result was that governments yielded to some basic labor demands to limit working hours, set minimum wages, provide vacations, insure sick and maternal leave, and legislate other social-welfare laws. At the same time they moved to dominate, control, and finally coopt the labor movement.

Political parties and politicans have tried and continue to try with varying degrees of success to harness labor to their own goals and ambitions. While they certainly exploited labor for their own political purposes, they also gave labor a greater role in politics than it had exercised before. Although a relatively small percentage of the working class is unionized, perhaps less than 15 percent in the late 1970s, the unions can serve as an effective means of mobilizing and controlling the masses. Their power, real or potential, has become increasingly important. Professor H. O. Spalding Jr., a specialist in labor history, has concluded, "The development of organized labor in Hispanic America can be viewed as a process in which labor has evolved from a group totally outside the system to one controlled by the state and/or elites and political parties. While waging great struggles at times, organized labor has not functioned as an independent or revolutionary force. Despite this fact, under certain conditions, workers have played a progressive role."

In that progressive role, labor helped to form coalitions to challenge the traditional elite and to bend—if not break—some of the old institutions. Uruguay provided an early example. In the first decades of the twentieth century, Batlle encouraged labor organization and favored the workers with some of the most advanced social legislation of the day. Labor, in turn, enthusiastically supported him. Irigoyen in Argentina, Alessandri in Chile, and Carranza in Mexico were also among the first Latin American presidents to court labor and to rely in part on labor for their support. In return, they conferred some benefits on working people. Later, labor played an even more prominent role, particularly during the administrations of Getúlio Vargas (1930–45; 1951–54) in Brazil, Lázaro Cárdenas (1934–40) in Mexico, Rafael Calderón (1940–44) in Costa Rica, and Juan D. Perón (1946–55; 1973–74) in Argentina, all four of whom qualify, at least in part, as populist presidents. Charismatic, those leaders spoke the nationalist vocabulary. Rhetorically convincing, ideologically weak, they offered immediate benefits— better salaries, health services, the nationalization of resources—rather than institutional reforms. With the notable exception of Cárdenas, they focused their attention on the cities.

Vargas clearly understood the importance of the growing proletariat in Brazil. Almost at once after taking power in 1930, he created the Ministry of Labor, which served as the means by which the government dealt with the workers. By careful maneuvering, he used the urban workers to help check the formerly overwhelming power of the traditional elite. The workers pledged their support to him in return for the benefits he granted them. With a highly paternalistic—and some say demagogic—flourish, Vargas conceded to the workers more benefits than they had previously obtained through their own organizations and strikes. A decree ordered the Ministry of Labor to organize the workers into new unions under governmental supervision. By 1944, there were about 800 unions with a membership exceeding half a million. The government prohibited strikes but did establish special courts and codes to protect the workers and to provide redress for their grievances. Under the government's watchful eye, the unions could and did bargain with management. Further, Vargas promulgated a wide variety of social legislation favoring the workers. He decreed retirement and pension plans, a minimum wage, a workweek limited to forty-eight hours, paid annual vacations, maternal benefits and child care, educational opportunities and literacy campaigns, safety and health standards for work, and job security. In short, Vargas offered to labor in less than a decade the advances and benefits that the proletariat of the industrialized nations had agitated for during the previous century. Little wonder, then, that the urban working class (for the benefits did not extend into the rural areas) rallied to support the president. In 1945, Vargas created the Brazilian Labor Party, which frankly and aggressively appealed to the urban worker. Small at its inception, the party grew in size and strength during the following two decades, while the other two major parties declined in strength.

Simultaneously Cárdenas wooed the Mexican urban laborers in order to counteract the growing influence of the conservatives in the government. He won their endorsement for his revolutionary government. To strenghten labor, he advised the workers to organize into one monolithic confederation. To that end, he oversaw the establishment of such an organization that in 1936–37 included most of the nation's unionized labor. At the same time, he restructured the official governmental party so that it rested on four "sections" of support, one of which was labor. Organized labor, thus encouraged and directed by the government, achieved an unprecedented importance in Mexico. Both sides benefited. The standard of living of the workers rose and so did their sense of dignity as active participants in the national government. The government intervened to settle most labor-management disputes in favor of labor. Further, the workers assumed management of the National Railways Company and cooperated in the management of the petroleum industry. With the encouragement of Cárdenas the labor movement reached its highest degree of organization, greatest prestige, and strongest influence. Cárdenas profited from the vigorous and loyal labor organization. Partially as a result of the strength labor lent him, he triumphed over party and political rivals, promulgated the revolutionary reforms he favored, and improved his position in bargaining with foreign economic interests and local industrialists.

Perón, too, based much of his political power on an alliance with labor. Previous Argentine governments had done little to favor the workers despite the industrial surge and the expansion of labor's ranks. Perón perceived the potential of the working class and utilized it after the military coup d'état of 1943 to project himself into power. As secretary of labor in the new government he lavished attention in the form of wage increases and social legislation on the hitherto neglected workers, who responded with enthusiastic endorsement of their patron. During the two years Perón held the labor portfolio, the trade unions nearly quadrupled in size. Perón adroitly manipulated the labor movement so that only leaders and unions beholden to him were officially recognized. When military leaders, suspicious and resentful of the growing power of Perón, imprisoned him in October of 1945, workers from around the country angrily descended on the center of Buenos Aires and paralyzed the capital. The military, devoid of any visible popular support, immediately backed down and freed Perón. With the full backing of labor, he easily won the presidential elections of 1946 with 56 percent of the vote, and his followers dominated the new congress.

During his decade of government, Perón relied heavily on the approval and support of organized labor. Urban workers, many of whom were inadequately integrated into city life, constituted the basis for Perón's highly successful mass movement. He offered the leadership they had awaited. Their goals were more reformist than revolutionary. They sought admission to the nation's institutions rather than destruction and replacement of them.

Eva Duarte de Perón (1919–52) had played a fundamental role in organizing and coordinating the popular support of the working class that first brought her husband to power and then helped to maintain him there. Probably more radical than he, she exhibited a greater sensitivity to the needs and aspirations of the masses. She partially contributed to their well-being through the huge Social Aid Foundation she administered. She devoted much time to strengthening the Peronist Women's Party and was instrumental in achieving the enfranchisement of Argentine women in 1947, when they got not only the vote but also equal rights with men. In the 1951 elections, over 2 million women voted for the first time, and six women senators and twenty-four deputies, all Peronistas, were sent to Congress. "Evita," as the Argentine masses affectionately called her, handled at least in part the relations of the government with the workers. She helped weld the workers into an effective force complementary to the government's goals.

It would be too simplistic to lament the demise of labor's freedom under the Peróns. In truth, it never had enjoyed much liberty—at best it was tolerated—under previous governments, and certainly prior to Perón the unions had gained few victories for their rank and file. They did compromise their liberty but they did so in return for undisputed advantages and for a greater feeling of participation in government than they had ever felt under the elitist leaders who had governed Argentina, with, of course, the possible exception of the middle-class government of Irigoyen. Perón's nationalist rhetoric cheered the workers, who identified more closely with his programs than with those of any previous government. They rallied behind him to taunt the foreign and native capitalists who they believed had exploited them. Perón, like the other populist leaders of the time, exuded a charismatic charm. He never lost the support of the working class. His fall from power in 1955 resulted from certain economic errors he made, a loss of Church approval, the firm and increasingly effective opposition of the traditional oligarchy, and—most important—the withdrawal by the military of its previous support. The middle class and the elite rejoiced in his fall; the event stunned great multitudes of the masses who had given their leader enthusiastic support in return for more benefits and dignity than they received from all the previous governments combined.

The faith of the working classes in the Peronist doctrines did not disappear. His supporters constituted the single largest cohesive political group in Argentina. Despite all the handicaps subsequent governments imposed on them, they continued to make impressive showings at the polls. Finally in 1973, the Peronists succeeded in bringing their leader back to Argentina in one of the great popular triumphs of the century. The army, which had controlled politics since 1955 and proscribed Perón, capitulated before the populist forces. In March 1973, Héctor Cámpora, a front for Perón, won the presidential elections with 49.5 percent of the vote. He took office only to schedule new elections in which Perón himself ran and received 62 percent of the vote. Isabel Martínez de Perón, his third wife, ran and won as vice-president. These electoral victories legitimized the reentry of the masses into Argentine political life.

After eighteen years in exile, Perón entered Buenos Aires hailed by the masses as a savior. Indeed, for the first time since he left, both government and real power were lodged again in one person. His devoted following represented a diverse and difficult political alliance. On the right stood the labor leaders whose loyalty could be traced back to the 1945–55 period. They controlled the huge labor apparatus that provided the fundamental support for Perón. Linked to the past, they occupied a place very close to Perón. The far left consisted of the new generataions, some of whom had never seen their leader before. Radicalized by the frustrations of the two decades, they looked to future reforms to make some basic societal changes. Although his charisma was still evident, Perón clearly had lost some contact with political realities in an agitated Argentina. He had little chance to pacify his homeland. Whatever talents he might once have possessed, they did not measure up to the complex demands of the mid-1970s. He died on July 1, 1974, at age 78. Isabel Martínez de Perón immediately assumed the presidency and thus became the first woman to govern in the Western Hemisphere. The broad divisions within the Peronist movement became increasingly visible. The violent struggles between left and right within the Peronist ranks and a faltering economy plunged Argentina into renewed and continuous crises. *La presidente* exhibited scant ability to govern, and the Peronist cloak could not hide her confusion. In late March of 1976, the military intervened, once again removing a Perón from the presidential palace. The officers, however, brought no formula to solve the complex problems of one of Latin America's richest, best educated, and most urbanized nations.

Obviously such populist governments as the one Perón so well represented found little favor among Latin America's elite, both the traditional elite and those who, thanks to greater social fluidity in the twentieth century, had recently achieved that exalted status. They resented any erosion of their power from below. Increasingly the middle class, as a group, seemed frightened by the prospects of populist government and consequently tended to align with the elite. Certainly the previous arrangements between urban labor and the middle class, noticeable in some instances during the first decades of the twentieth century, disintegrated as the middle class became apprehensive of a threat, real or imagined, to their status and ambitions from labor. By the mid-twentieth century, identifying more with the elite against whom they had once struggled but whose life style they incessantly aped, the middle class when forced to select between the masses and change and the elite and the status quo tended to opt for the latter.

The new power struggles took place in the cities, which were playing an ever more dominant role in the growth of Latin America. In the decades after World War II, the cities in Latin America grew at a faster rate than those in any other part of the world. During the decade 1945–55, the urban populations of seven countries—Brazil, Mexico, Bolivia, Peru, El Salvador, Panama, and the Dominican Republic—increased approximately 55 percent, while those in another four countries—Cuba, Chile, Venezuela, and Uruguay—went up nearly 45 percent. During the 1960s, the rate of urban growth averaged 4.5 percent annually—or three times the rate of urban growth in the United States. During the 1970s, it averaged 3.8 percent annually. The population surge of Colombia's four major cities, indicated in Table 8-4, exemplified the broader trend throughout Latin America.

Uruguay, where more than 80 percent of the population lives in cities, has become the most-urbanized Latin American republic. Three nations, Argentina, Chile, and Uruguay, ranked among the fifteen most-urbanized nations of the world. Much of the urban population concentrates in the

TABLE 8-4   Growth of Colombia's Major Cities, 1951–70 (in thousands)

	1951	1964	1970	1985
Bogotá	720	1,700	2,400	4,208
Medellín	360	770	1,030	2,095
Cali	280	640	870	1,742
Barranquilla	280	500	620	1,137

capitals, which with few exceptions are disproportionately large. Fully one-half of Uruguay's population lives in Montevideo; one-third of all Argentines resided in metropolitan Buenos Aires; one-quarter of the Chileans, Cubans, and Panamanians inhabited their capital cities; in Peru, Venezuela, Paraguay, and Costa Rica, one-fifth of the populations live in the capitals. Reversing historical roles, the countryside had become dependent on the cities. As of 1980, over 60 percent of Latin America's population lived in cities of 20,000 or more inhabitants. Latin America is the most urbanized region of the Third World. In Africa in 1980, only 26 percent of the population was urban; in Asia, 27 percent.

Urban population growth can be attributed in part to the continuing high birthrate. Between 1920 and 1960, Latin America witnessed a phenomenal demographic rise, an average of 2.9 percent per year, which amounted to a 126-percent increase. The figure becomes even more impressive when compared to Europe's population growth of only 23 percent for the same period. City and countryside did not share equally in the growth. Better health-care and medical facilities in the city meant infant mortality rates were lower and life expectancy higher there than in rural areas. Further, fast urban growth could still be explained in terms of the push exerted by grinding rural poverty on the peasant to move into the city to seek a better life, as well as of the pull exercised by the industries, glitter, and promise of the city. Thus, the statistics for Mexico reveal that between 1930 and 1968, the urban population grew at the rate of 4.5 to 5 percent per year, while the rural population increased by only 1.5 percent per year. That pattern seemed representative of much of Latin America. The rural migrant families faced the serious problem of adapting their traditions to the different pace and demands of the city. Despite the challenges and hardships, the nuclear family remained as important in the city as it had in the countryside.

The creation of new cities embodied economic and political hopes. New capitals symbolized new starts, the opening up of marginalized territory, the unleashing of new energies. Six hundred miles inland from coastal Rio de Janeiro, President Juscelino Kubitschk inaugurated Brasilia, the new Brazilian capital, in 1960. Thirty years later, its population of nearly 2 million lived amidst the finest architecture of the century, the portal to the economic exploitation of the country's vast far west. In 1970, the British built a new capital, Belmopan, for Belize. The Argentine Congress approved in 1987 the plan of President Raul Alfonsín to move the capital from cosmopolitan Buenos Aries to Viedma, hundreds of miles south, a gateway to the underpopulated Patagonia region.

On the Orinoco River, where hydroelectric potential, iron ore, and bauxite could be found in abundance, the Venezuelan government built a new city, Ciudad Guyana, in 1961. It sought to take economic advantage of the natural resources. Despite monumental difficulties, Ciudad Guyana grew into an impressive industrial city of nearly half a million inhabitants in 1989. Its steel mills and aluminum smelters helped the nation through a severe economic crisis when oil income had slipped from $19 billion in 1981 to $7.7 billion in 1986. The city's industrial exports earned over $1 billion in 1986. In 1989, it produced more than half of Venezuela's electricity.

As the cities grew in size so did the ranks of the middle class and proletariat. Though always a minority within the total population, these two groups were highly articulate. Their concentration near the seat of government afforded them power disproportionate to their numbers, and they did not hestitate to wield it to push their goals aggressively. At some times and in some countries, these two urban classes had the strength to put into the presidency those who favored their ambitions. Little wonder then that political power focused ever more sharply on the cities.

The middle class exerted a strong influence in the reshaping of the cities to fit its image of the good consumer society. Like their prototypes, these cities catered to the demands of the automotive age. Thus, increasing numbers of public works were freeways, viaducts, bridges, tunnels, and subterranean underpasses. In fact, these facilities for the automobiles of the middle class became the symbols of "progress," "modernization," and even "development" to such an extent that opposition to them was equated with subversion. They drained the modest public treasuries of funds needed for public services, and of course they frustrated sincere efforts at urban planning. Quito provides a thought-provoking example for the mid-1970s. The discovery of deposits of oil in the Amazonian lowlands turned the solemn Ecuadorian capital into a boomtown. Those profiting from the new riches congregated in the northern sector of the city, which for the first time boasted all-night liquor stores and drive-in hamburger palaces amid a nightmare of traffic problems. The rural migrants attracted by the building boom and construction jobs clustered on the steep slopes of the mountains overlooking Quito in hovels without light, water, or sewerage. Meanwhile, the government received a $8.9 million loan from the Wells Fargo Bank to be used to solve the city's traffic problems by constructing some spectacular new bypasses and fly-over junctions in the northern sector of the capital.

For some, taking advantage of the more broadly stratified urban society with the blurred distinctions between classes, the city facilitated social and economic mobility and thus fulfilled its promise of hope. However, for the illiterate, inexperienced, and technically untrained, the city offered little more than misery. Unsuitable for employment in a modern city, they had difficulty finding jobs. Unemployment rates were high. In 1970, Lima had 16 percent of its working-age, male population unemployed; the figure for Barranquilla, Colombia, was 19 percent. These figures do not take into account underemployment, which prevails throughout the area. Many of those who were fortunate enough to find jobs soon discovered that the jobs paid so little that it was a struggle to keep families housed and fed. Many became the scavengers of society. An urban family of average income spent 50 percent of its earnings on food, 10 percent on clothing, and 10 percent on transportation, leaving little to be divided among housing, education, medicine, and other necessities. The average urban worker in Costa Rica earned $2.25 a day in 1973, but just to eat the balanced diet advised by nutrition experts the worker would have to spend $3.45 a day. A study published in Guayaquil, Ecuador, in 1975 showed that a family needed to spend more than the legal minimum wage of 1,250 *sucres* a month on food alone. Little wonder then that slums developed and squatter hovels sprang up in all major Latin American cities. The squatter settlements were conglomerations of one-room shanties, where Latin America's most precious resource, its people, wasted away with bloated bellies, underdeveloped bodies, dysentery, fever, and myriad diseases. In 1970, more than one-third of Latin America's urban population lived in submarginal housing. On the average, 40 percent of the inhabitants of the capital cities lived in "spontaneous settlements," a euphemism for squatters' shacks. Caracas offered a sobering example: of its 2 million inhabitants, 800,000 lived in *ranchos* (shanties). In Brazil in 1975, more than half the urban residences had no running water and more than three-quarters no sewers. Statistics from Chile for the decade of the 1960s revealed the growing shortage of urban housing. In that decade, the average number of individuals per existing housing unit rose from 6.8 to 7.0.

The tens of millions of Latin Americans who lived in such misery drew little satisfaction from the industries, boutiques, high-rise apartment buildings, and skyscrapers that bespoke modernization. For them, the hopes held out by the cities had not materialized. The trends of history in twentieth-century Latin America indicate that the potential of the cities cannot be realized without a reformation of the countryside.

THE EXPANDING ROLE OF WOMEN

From the earliest colonial times, relations between men and women in Latin America have been shaped by *machismo*, an attitude mixing the code of chivalry with distorted views that relegate women to subservience. Both the legal systems and Roman Catholicism have reinforced the lowly status of women. Part of the history of women concerns their efforts to raise their social, economic, and political status to correspond to the role they play in society.

Women played a major, albeit unsung role in Latin America. For centuries women of the lower classes worked side by side with men in the field, tended shop, bartered in the markets, and handled the minor duties of commerce. They bore primary responsibility for raising children. The more privileged households offered their women greater opportunity for

This 1875 photograph by Eadweard Muybridge focuses on five major domestic tasks of Guatemalan Indian women: transporting water, grinding corn meal, spinning cotton, combing cotton, and weaving.

education and a fuller social life. Still, they dedicated much of their time to directing the management of the home and caring for the children. Until after 1850, the home and convent remained the principal domains of upper-class women, but within those confines they expressed a restlessness and a resourcefulness that indicated a desire to expand their roles.

The accounts from the past century paint varied pictures of those females, ones that still permit different interpretations. The earlier conclusion that upper-class women lived secluded lives was probably overdrawn, somewhat caricatured. Certainly Maria Graham's ample descriptions of the women she knew during the early 1820s in Brazil revealed them to be educated, French-speaking, lively conversationalists, and much in evidence in well-appointed drawing rooms. In the pages of her diary, Frances Calderón de la Barca frequently mentioned the presence and participation of upper-class Mexican women at social events of the early 1840s. Generally she regarded them as charming, elegantly dressed, and well educated. She lauded the family life of the Mexican elite as exemplary. In the account of his travels in Colombia in the 1850s, Isaac F. Holton penned an intriguing portrait of one "middle-class woman" of the provinces, or, to use his words, "an intermediate link between the aristocracy and the peasantry." An attrac-

Margarita López, a Bolivian schoolteacher, circa 1890. By the end of the nineteenth century, women taught in elementary schools throughout Latin America.

A Costa Rican public health worker, circa 1910. Women increasingly took up careers in public health in the early twentieth century.

During the Mexican Revolution, women fought alongside men. Their participation in Latin America's struggles can be traced well into the colonial period, and they exercised major roles in the wars of independence.

tive eighteen year old, Isabel Gamba alternated her clothing between peasant dress and the styles of the well to do. Without an opportunity for formal education, she had managed to educate herself and enjoyed reading French novels in translation. Sir Horace Rumbold, an English resident of Buenos Aires in 1880–81, observed that each succeeding generation of nineteenth-century Argentine women received a better education. At parties, dances, and dinners, the younger women entered fully into the conversation, exhibiting wit, intelligence, and humor, a contrast to the older women present. Sir Horace concluded, "The women of the higher classes here certainly strike one at once as decidely superior to the men."

The female search for equal rights in the nineteenth century began with the desire for improved education and increased respect and proceeded with a quest for the enhancement of their legal position. Finally,

Receiving lower wages than men, women were widely employed in the factories as Latin America industrialized in the twentieth century. These women manufactured helmets in Santiago, Chile, circa 1929.

A female basketball team, Nicaragua, 1927

women sought new careers outside the home, beginning in the cities where the traditional patriarchal families had to adapt to urban pressures. By midcentury, Brazilian women could administer their own property. The Commercial Code of 1850 permitted women to marry without disturbing their commercial rights. In 1852, Brazil's first female editor, Joana Paula Manso de Noronha, called for "social betterment and moral emancipation of women."

Determined women scaled barriers to enter professional life. At the mid-nineteenth century, Nina Luisa traveled from Tegucigalpa to Havana to study photography; and upon her return to Honduras, she established that nation's first photographic studio. The Austrian traveler Carl Scherzer met her and recalled, "I had the pleasant task of congratulating a clever and very gracious lady on the success of her artistic efforts. A lady artist, I may observe, is a most uncommon phenomenon to meet with in Central America." Nina Luisa persevered and succeeded in her career.

Teaching was the first profession conquered by Latin American women. By the end of the century, it was common to find them in charge of the classroom. By then, they also worked in offices, and women of the lower classes worked in factories.

Chile pioneered in offering professional education to women. A special governmental decree in 1877 permitted women to receive professional degrees, and in 1886 Eloísa Díaz became the first woman in all of Latin America to receive a medical degree. In 1892, Matilde Throup graduated from the law school in Santiago and became the first female lawyer in Latin America. The Brazilian government opened professional schools to women in 1879.

Throughout Latin America women predominated in the marketplaces. This indoor market scene in Port-au-Prince, Haiti, circa 1930, shows only women buying and selling.

Brazilian women actively participated in the abolitionist movement during the 1880s. Before that decade ended, a few advocated the extension of Brazil's limited suffrage to include females. In the opening decades of the twentieth century, women organized to demand equality. Pioneer feminist fighters, such as Camelia Horne de Burnmeister and Julieta Lanteri of Argentina and Paulina Luisi of Uruguay, proclaimed the case of equality for women. A distinguished physician, Dr. Luisi campaigned during the second decade of the twentieth century for social reforms, including political suffrage. In 1916, Dr. Lanteri, one of Argentina's first female physicians, wrote, "A hope begins to shine on the dark horizon; the awareness of her own value begins to awaken in woman." In 1922, Chilean women established the Feminine Civic Party (*Partido Cívico Femenino*) to obtain universal suffrage. Brazilian feminists were active too. In 1923, Bertha Lutz founded the Brazilian Federation for Feminine Progress (*Federação Bra-*

Eva Perón, shown here addressing a rally in Buenos Aires in 1951, exercised significant influence in Argentina, 1945–52, and remains after her death one of the most revered and controversial public figures.

Female participation in Cuban life was broadened after 1959 by women's inclusion in the militia. These women marched in Havana in 1961.

sileira pelo Progresso Feminino), one of the largest women's organizations in Latin America.

As women's determination for political equality soared, Anesia Pinheiro Machado literally took to the air. A Brazilian pioneer of aviation, she held the oldest valid pilot's license for a woman in the world. She began flying in 1922 at age twenty and flew for more than half a century.

Women contributed to the fine arts. The distinguished Peruvian novelist, Clorinda Matto de Turner (1852–1909) has already been discussed as the author of the first Indianist novel, *Birds Without a Nest* (1889). Also editor of *El Perú Ilustrado,* she presided over literary gatherings in Lima. Two other outstanding novelists of the nineteenth century were Gertrudis Gómez de Avellaneda (1814–73), a Cuban, and Juana Manuela Gorriti (1818–92), an Argentine. Gorriti led a singular life. She married the president of Bolivia, Manuel Belzu, already discussed in this text as a folk caudillo, but in a most unusual step for an aristocratic woman of the nineteenth century, she left her husband, moving to Lima where, along with Clorinda Matto de Turner, she helped to direct Peruvian intellectual life. Today little is known about women's participation in nineteenth-century music. But, in 1883, Teresa Tanco presented her light opera *Similia Similus* in Bogota, where it was applauded by the flower of Colombian society, including President Rafael Núñez.

The revolutionary government of Nicaragua appointed Vilma
Núñez de Escorcia (left) and María Lourdes Bolanos de
Rodríguez as two of the five members of the Supreme Court.

In 1914 a young schoolteacher won first prize in a Chilean poetry
contest. So humbly dressed was she at the contest that she refused to stand
up before the audience to read her poems. Her name was Gabriela Mistral.
In 1945, she received the Nobel Prize in literature for her poetry, the first
Latin American so honored. Fittingly, "The Teacher's Prayer" remains one
of her well-remembered poems:

> Let me be more maternal than a mother; able to love and defend
> with all of a mother's fervor the child that is not flesh of my flesh.
> Grant that I may be successful in molding one of my pupils into
> a perfect poem, and let me leave within her my deepest-felt melody
> that she may sing for you when my lips shall sing no more.
>
> * * *
>
> Make me strong even in my weakness as a woman, and particularly as a poor
> woman. Make me scorn all power that is not pure, and all duress that is not
> your flaming will upon my life.
>
> * * *
>
> Let me make my brick schoolhouse into a spiritual temple. Let the radiance of
> my enthusiasm envelop the poor courtyard and the bare classroom. Let my
> heart be a stronger column and my goodwill purer gold than the columns and
> gold of rich schools.[2]

Doris Dana has translated for the English-reading public some of the Chilean's most memorial verses, *Selected Poems of Gabriela Mistral.*

All these achievements came at the cost of much energy and frustra-

---

[2]Reprinted by permission of Joan Daves. Copyright © 1961, 1964, 1970, 1971 by Doris
Dana.

tion because, although society was changing, it still resisted the desire for equality women sought and merited. Two magnificent Brazilian documents have been translated into English and bear testimony to the ambitions and feelings of two remarkable women. *The Diary of "Helen Morley,"* a true diary, views the world of a small town in the interior at the end of the nineteenth century through the eyes of a sensitive young woman. The novelist Rachel de Queiroz brilliantly portrayed in her autobiographical novel *The Three Marias* the frustrations she felt in the state of Ceará as she was growing up in the 1920s. She wanted a career of her own; she longed to direct her own life. A small, provincial city did not readily concede her the liberty she sought. The novel remains a masterly statement on the status and role of a woman in Brazilian society.

Rights for women came slowly in the twentieth century. Many years were to pass before women received the right to vote. Ecuador in 1929 made voting obligatory fo men and voluntary for women. The women of Brazil in 1932, Venezuela and Argentina in 1947, Chile in 1949, Mexico in 1953, and Colombia in 1954 were enfranchised. By the mid-1950s, with a few exceptions such as Paraguay and Nicaragua, women in most of Latin America voted. They soon entered public office in greater numbers. In 1956, for example, Argentina had seven female senators and twenty-four female deputies; Chile two deputies; Costa Rica three deputies; and Cuba one senator; while, for comparison, the United States Congress had one female senator and sixteen female representatives. In 1970 a woman judge sat on the Argentine Supreme Court, and in 1975 Dr. Maria Josefa Saavedra became the first woman appointed to the Bolivian Supreme Court. When Alfonso López took his oath of office as president of Colombia in 1974, he appointed a woman as minister of labor and six women as state governors. The Feminist Party of Uruguay nominated Celica Guerrero de Chiappa, a professor of education, as its candidate for the presidency in the 1971 elections. Maria Eugenia Rojas de Moreno Díaz ran in Colombia in 1974 as the presidential candidate of the National Popular Alliance (Alianza Nacional Popular) and received 10 percent of the vote. Isabel Perón's Argentine presidency has been noted already, but she no longer bears the distinction of being the only female Latin American president.

In November of 1979, in the midst of a constitutional crisis set off by a military coup, Bolivia's congress elected Lidia Gueiler Tejada, leader of its lower house, as president. Long a supporter of women's rights and the author of essays on the subject, she once wrote and pushed through Congress a bill creating a ministry to provide social benefits, principally for women and children. In her inaugural address in the tense capital of La Paz, she declared, "My fighting spirit, my willingness to assume responsibilities will allow me to contribute to democracy in Bolivia." Seldom had a new Latin American president faced more challenges. By the mid-1960s, women had gained the vote throughout Latin America. Only the constitution of Paraguay prohibits a female president.

Women also made significant—if perhaps less spectacular—political contributions on the regional and municipal levels. By the end of the 1960s it was not uncommon to find female mayors. An interesting if somewhat unusual example of the participation of women in local government was the town of Miguel Pereira in the state of Rio de Janeiro, Brazil. It boasted a population of 22,000 in 1972, when it elected a mayor named Aristolina Queirós de Almeida, who had been a schoolteacher most of her life. Other women occupied the posts of municipal accountant, director of education, director of social assistance, municipal judge, state prosecutor, municipal registrar, director of the post office, director of the electric power company, state doctor in charge of rural health, and chief of federal social security. In 1985, Fortaleza, a city of 1.7 million in northeastern Brazil, elected Maria Luisa Fontenelle as mayor. A social worker, sociologist, and socialist, she pared the bloated city payroll, restored the municipal hospital to full service, tripled the fleet of public buses, paved scores of streets, and stimulated popular participation in city government. While at the end of the 1980s Brazil boasts of many female mayors, Senhora Fontenelle holds the distinction of being the one administering the largest city.

In agriculture, the potential base of Latin American well-being, women historically have played a primary role. The role increased in the twentieth century, due in part to the rising male migration to the cities. Never a male-dominated institution, the small farm required the cooperation of the entire family. In 1988, 11 million small family farms produced 41 percent of the food consumed in Latin America and 32 percent of the agrarian exports. One of the worst forms of discrimination against women lingers in the countryside: unequal access to land ownership. Land reform apparently has done little to rectify this iniquitous situation for women, Mexico and Cuba excepted.

Clearly the role of women was broadening, although they still encountered ingrained prejudices. They still had to win equality in their work. They received neither equal pay nor proportional managerial positions. In 1970 in Argentina, although 1.6 million women held jobs, only 1 out of every 100 had a supervisory or executive position. In 1973 in Colombia, approximately 19 percent of the labor force was female, but female factory workers almost always earned less than their male counterparts. Colombian women professionals received only about one-fifth the salary of male lawyers, architects, and engineers. Within most of the cities, women often manage and run the great marketplaces that sell food, clothing, and other consumer goods to the vast majority of the population. These hardworking and savvy merchants, reflecting the Indian and African heritages of Latin America, bear the responsibility for the daily economic well-being of the cities.

Complex causes explain the changing role of Latin American women in the past 100 years. Certainly the potent forces of urbanization, industrialization, and modernization—coupled with foreign models and influences—

and the determination, example, and leadership of Latin American women go a long way to provide an explanation. One major benefit of their more active participation in Latin American political life has been to strengthen the potential for democracy.

A FLIRTATION WITH DEMOCRACY

The rhetoric to which the United States marched into World War II wafted throughout the rest of the hemisphere. The Latin Americans in general supported the effort of the United States in the struggle against the Axis powers. At a special conference in Rio de Janeiro in January of 1942, the representatives of the various republics voted to recommend that their governments break diplomatic relations with the Axis nations. All complied, although Chile delayed any action until January of 1943 and Argentina until March of 1945. Brazil dispatched troops to fight in the Italian campaign and Mexico sent an air squadron to the Pacific. The war brought Latin America and the United States into even closer contact than previously. Because trade with Europe was difficult if not impossible during the war years, the economies of North and South America meshed more intimately than ever before.

The Allies' march to victory in Europe in 1944 marked democracy's triumph over dictatorship, and the consequences shook Latin America. Questioning why they should support the struggle for democracy in Europe and yet suffer the constraints of dictatorship at home, many Latin Americans rallied to democratize their own political structures. A group of prominent middle-class Brazilians opposed to the continuation of the populist Vargas dictatorship mused publicly, "If we fight against fascism at the side of the United Nations so that liberty and democracy may be restored to all people, certainly we are not asking too much in demanding for ourselves such rights and guarantees."

In the surge toward democratic goals, the ideals of the nineteenth-century liberals revived. Lofty rhetoric extolling reform and development disguised mundane programs that permitted cosmetic changes and growth. The times favored the democratic concepts professed by the middle class. Governments out of step with them toppled. In 1944, Fulgencio Batista fell in Cuba, Hernández Martínez abandoned office in El Salvador, and Jorge Ubico fled Guatemala; in 1945, four strongmen, Alfonso López Pusmarejo of Colombia, Manuel Prado of Peru, Isaías Medina of Venezuela, and Getúlio Vargas of Brazil, were forced from office. A wave of freedom of speech, press, and assembly engulfed much of Latin America and bathed the middle class with satisfaction. New political parties emerged to represent broader segments of the population. Democracy, always a fragile plant anywhere, seemed ready to blossom throughout Latin America.

Certainly nowhere for the previous century and a half had more homage been paid to the virtues and trappings of democracy than in Latin America. The democratic facade often existed but the substance was missing. In most cases the idealists or the cynics had trusted in imported democratic constitutions with scant consideration of local realities. In exasperation, the Peruvian intellectual César Vallejo had noted,

> How is it possible that the few owners of our country are able to maintain in our Republic a regime of castes with its consequent social, political, and economic injustices? They are able to do so because of the democratic farce they perpetuate. . . . The republican process has been nothing but an uninterrupted and chaotic series of contradictory make-shifts and accommodations to make the system viable.

His short, sharp criticism of republicanism contains a powerful indictment of Latin America's institutions, an indication of why underdevelopment prevailed, and an historical interpretation of national history. It calls into question the meaninglessness of democracy in Latin America: form without substance.

Putting aside the exotic aspects of transplanted institutions, a functional democracy would have been difficult in a society that had still not integrated all its members. Even among those included in the mainstream of national life, few could vote. In the presidential elections of Brazil prior to 1930, never more than 3 percent of the population cast a ballot. Prior to World War II few women and few illiterates voted. Power struggles among the elite took little account of the desires of the masses. Democratic experience and tradition were limited. The patterns of authoritarian rule and change of government by coup d'état, once set, were difficult to alter. Nonetheless, for about two decades after World War II, there seemed to be a genuine movement toward the democratization of Latin America. During those years, the middle class perceived that its interests would be best served by the democratic process as they defined and manipulated it. Brazil provided an interesting case study, which in its broadest interpretation typifies the fate of the democratization process in much of contemporary Latin America.

The Brazilian military quietly removed Vargas from office in 1945 and guaranteed free elections. Three major, national political parties formed, representing left, center, and right in the most conventional liberal-democratic definitions of these political positions. A constituent assembly prepared a new constitution, promulgated in 1946, which provided all the safeguards for a democratic republic. Although the military did intervene in politics in 1954, 1955, and 1961, the officers retired at once, leaving the government in the hands of civilians, and the democratic process continued. The elections of 1945, 1950, 1955, and 1960 were totally free. Different parties won the presidency and there was a peaceful democratic transfer of power. All regarded the elections as generally honest. An elaborate system of electoral courts removed the control of the elections from those in power and guaranteed the voters complete freedom at the polls and an accurate tabulation of the votes cast. The electorate steadily increased in size. Illiterates were still excluded from the voting rolls, disenfranchising at least half the population over 18 years of age. Nonetheless, the percentage of the population registered to vote increased from 16 percent in 1945 to 25 percent in 1962. The number of voters climbed rather steadily during that period at approximately 20 percent every four years. Two new groups, the urban proletariat and the industrial middle class, took important positions in the political spectrum. The vocal urban groups created a lively public opinion, which the governments increasingly heeded. Further, the judicial system as it evolved under the Constitution of 1946 provided another bulwark for nascent Brazilian democracy. Elaborate constitutional safeguards promoted a judicial independence unique in Latin America. The Federal Supreme Court had jurisdiction to rule on the constitutionality of all legislation, federal, state, or local. Although the bench never exercised the power of its counterpart in the United States, it did inhibit, check, and reverse arbitrary actions of the executive and legislature. All indications were that Brazil's experiment with democracy was succeeding.

Throughout Latin America, the democratization process, in general terms, followed a similar pattern. Two crucial tests for democracy were whether the elections were free and whether the president left office at the end of his constitutionally prescribed term. Although the presidents continued to wield considerable power, they were limited to a definite period of office, a maximum of six years, and seldom permitted to run for immediate reelection. In a surprising number of cases the constitutional mechanism functioned more effectively than it had in the past. Peaceful and honest elections were held and the results acknowledged by all candidates. In many cases, presidents quietly turned over their sashes of office after serving their legal terms of office. The political process accommodated itself nicely to the interests of the middle class without threatening the traditional elite.

Public opinion as a political force strengthened during the experiments with democracy. Governments consulted and heeded it more than they had in the past. More often than not, large numbers of the working class, middle class, intellectuals, and students advocated and defended democracy. Representatives of these groups formed new political parties whose platforms called for many needed reforms. Two such parties that attracted considerable attention were the Christian Democratic Party of Chile and the Democratic Action Party of Venezuela. Both offered hope for change and reform through the democratic process.

The Christian Democratic Party in Chile, as elsewhere in Latin America, advocated an ideology based on the humanistic writings of the French philosopher Jacques Maritain. Stressing Christian values, the party sought to modernize society and improve the conditions of each citizen. It emphasized reform. Running on the Christian Democratic platform, Eduardo Frei swept into the Chilean presidency in 1964. Advocating democratic and evolutionary change, Frei warned, "Democracy will not be saved by those who, praising it as it now exists, petrify its abuses." His government, meeting with strong opposition in congress, moved by necessity slowly, apparently too slowly. Instead of resettling 100,000 families on land of their own, which was his goal, Frei managed to bestow farms on only 11,200. He also failed to reach his other goals. The party compromised its reform program to such an extent that it became virtually meaningless. The Christian Democrats by the end of the Frei administration looked more like a party favoring status quo rather than change.

The Democratic Action Party of Venezuela, under the forceful leadership of Rómulo Betancourt, was democratic in conviction and mildly leftist in action. It advocated land reform and declared the government's right to expropriate oil properties, both of which, if carried out, promised considerable change for Venezuela. In the elections of 1958, Betancourt won the presidency. Two years later, he promulgated the Agrarian Reform Law. Exempting productive farms up to 370 acres, it expropriated large estates after indemnifying the owners and distributed them among the landless with the goal of making Venezuela self-sufficient in foodstuffs. The reform promised more than it delivered. The Democratic Action Party held the presidency through 1968, first under Betancourt and then under Raúl Leoni. In the elections of late 1968, the Christian Democrats triumphed.

The Roman Catholic Church, at some times and in some places, raised an influential voice in favor of democracy and reform. While the Church's tolerance of the status quo and thus tradition and iniquity had long been its hallmark, a new, young, and socially conscious clergy began to question the reasons for the poverty of the masses and the social injustices that perpetuated it. They received assistance from the highest level of the Roman Catholic Church during the 1960s. The Vatican's Council II (1962–65) expressed concern for a more democratic Church and for greater social and economic justice. Pope Paul VI visited Bogotá in 1968 where he identified with Latin America's poor and tried to stir the social conscience of the elite. Thus encouraged, a small but dedicated part of the clergy spoke out convincingly for change. Some abandoned the neighborhoods of the wealthy and middle class to enter the slums, where they set up schools and clinics. A new "theology of liberation" eclipsed traditional dogma in those areas. It held that the poor must understand the causes of their poverty as well as the Church's desire to support them in their quest for justice. It possessed a tremendous potential as a catalyst for change.

From the pulpit sounded appeals for reform. In 1962 and again in

1963, the National Conference of Brazilian Bishops recommended basic land reforms. Bishops in Colombia, Chile, Peru, Bolivia, and Ecuador also advocated land reforms, as did the Latin American Bishops Conference. That the Church might do more than just talk was indicated in Ecuador in 1971. There the hierarchy announced its decision to turn over to 2,000 landless families about 250,000 acres of the Church's arable land as a demonstration of support for land reform. The discussions among the concerned clergy inevitably led to diagnoses of the hemisphere's economic problems and thence to broad suggestions for their solution. Archbishop Aloisio Lorscheider, president of the Brazilian Conference of Bishops, observed, "We also believe that the economic system does not take sufficient account of the need for respect and development of the human being, but emphasizes money and profits instead." In these ways, the Church—or at least a vocal and concerned segment of it—seemed to acquire a persuasive voice favoring change and to encourage a sorely needed grass-roots democracy.

Together the forces favoring democratization wielded considerable strength. They needed to since they faced innumerable obstacles, not least of which were unemployment, underemployment, hunger, undernourishment, illiteracy, lethargy, and a legacy of institutions that in no way favored democracy. Democracy faced serious challenges in fragmented societies. The activities of certain groups, totalitarian political parties, ambitious politicians, and the military further retarded and then reversed the democratization process. However, the major weakness of Latin American democracy was that it served only the elite and middle class—who by midcentury recognized that they had mutual, not conflicting, interests—and did not embrace the majority of the populations. The privileged groups continued to import their democratic ideology and used it for their own rather than their nation's benefit, confusing as always their welfare with that of the nation at large. They therefore instituted no serious programs to abolish poverty, illiteracy, hunger, and unemployment; instead, they squandered the national resources on armaments, superhighways, color television, luxury cars, and a cornucopia of inconsequential consumer items. After the last echoes of their rhetoric disappeared, it became all too apparent that the democratic parties could not effect reform. Their constant compromise and procrastination insured a long life for the old neofeudal and neocapitalistic institutions inherited from the past and still very much a characteristic of Latin America as it entered the last half of the twentieth century. At best, democracy, at least in its Latin American manifestation, safeguarded the status quo.

The democratic experiments that characterized Latin America after World War II reached their apogee in 1959. In that year only four military governments held sway in Latin America, a record low. However, throughout the 1960s, democratic government was challenged and the previous trend reversed as much of Latin America returned to military rule. In the brief span between 1962 and 1964, eight countries fell victim to military takeovers. With rare exceptions, the military governments were more conservative than their predecessors, a reaction to attempts by popular groups to actually enact whatever limited reforms a democracy might permit.

Once again it is instructive to look at Brazil as an illustration of how that reversal occurred. Just as the action of the Brazilian military in 1945 had opened the way for the experiment with democracy, so it was the military in 1964 that terminated the experiment. The constitutional ascendancy of Vice-President João Goulart to the presidency in 1961 seemed to signal the triumph of public opinion and the democratization process in Brazil. After a momentary intervention, the military were forced by public opinion to step aside and turn the presidency over to the constitutional authority. Following the populist ideology initiated by his mentor, Vargas, President Goulart promised broad reforms. He loosened Brazil's ties with the United States in a bid for leadership in the Third World. Dedicated to a highly nationalistic program, he persuaded congress to enact a law limiting profit remittances abroad by foreign companies and encouraged the building of hydroelectric dams in order to challenge foreign control over Brazil's electrical power. He spoke of reforming the land structure. Labor unrest, strikes, and inflation disturbed the middle class, which felt its security and well-being were threatened. At that point the middle class allied with the traditional elite in complaint over Goulart's policies. Then, the president made a grave tactical error by appealing to the enlisted men of the armed forces for their support over the heads of their officers. The move alienated the officers, who decided to remove the president. The military, cheered on by the elite and the middle class, marched against Goulart and unseated him on April 1, 1964. The generals who controlled Brazil reduced congress and the courts to pliant tools, ruled by decree, purged all their political adversaries, abolished elections, substituted two sterile "approved" political parties for those that had developed in the 1945–64 period, established censorship of all the media, and filled the jails with political prisoners. Brazil's experiment with democracy ended, replaced by an old-fashioned, brutal military dictatorship that enjoyed the support of a large part of the upper and middle classes.

The alliance of the military with the frightened middle class and elite emerged as a major obstacle to the continued experiment with democracy and to any meaningful reform. The military is an extension of the privileged classes. The officers too enjoy remarkable privileges in their impoverished societies. They receive excellent salaries and fast promotions, enjoy good housing and free medical care, divert themselves in handsome clubs, and in general partake of a wide variety of benefits. Most of them come from the lower and middle classes, and probably a majority have urban backgrounds. The military provides a splendid means of social mobility. On frequent occasions it has been the avenue from obscurity to the presidency.

Although proportionately the size of armed forces in Latin America is small, the military is expensive. It absorbs, on the average, 25 percent of the national budgets, a hefty figure when one realizes that it fights no foreign war.

By tradition, the military considers itself the guardian of nationality. Whenever the senior officers agree that the well-being of the nation is threatened, they intervene in politics to eradicate the threat and to control the government for as long as they feel it necessary. The military interventions can be frequent. One authority on military behavior in Latin America estimated that between 1930 and 1965 the officers staged forty-four coups d'état. Generally the officers see the political left as more dangerous to the nation and intervene most often when radical reforms are imminent. Thus, they tend to favor the status quo over change. On the other hand, the military is capable of advocating reform and enforcing change. The Brazilian military in the period 1930–53 enthusiastically supported the establishment of a national state-owned petroleum company. The officers who took control of Peru in 1968 voiced reformist, even revolutionary, rhetoric, and they imposed a sweeping land reform on the nation.

By 1970, the military governed most of Latin America. They held sway in Argentina, Brazil, Bolivia, Paraguay, Peru, Panama, Honduras, Guatemala, and El Salvador. The democratic experiment continued in Costa Rica, Uruguay, Chile, Mexico (countries with a relatively long democratic experience), Colombia, and Venezuela. Under siege, Latin American democracy received very little support from the major democracy in the hemisphere. In outlining U.S. policy for the 1970s, President Richard Nixon stated with regard to Latin America, "The United States has a long political interest in maintaining cooperation with our neighbors regardless of their domestic viewpoints. We deal with governments as they are." (With the convenient exception of Cuba, of course.) The policy was in reality just a continuation of the doctrine followed during the Johnson administration, when the State Department declared in early 1964 that it would not distinguish between dictatorship and democracy.

The inevitable conclusion emerges that democracy has not been a great success in Latin America during the past century and a half. Perhaps democracy's difficulty has been its preoccupation with political formalities and formulas. With that emphasis, the democrats and the democracies they encourage and manage have failed to provide solutions for most of Latin America's major economic and social problems. The democrats have seemed content to apply a veneer of political democracy over institutions unsuitable to a democratic society. They have failed to create social and economic institutions compatible with a political democracy. Overconcern with form and lack of sufficient concern with reform have made most of Latin America's democracies, even when they are functioning at their best, sterile.

9
The Revolutionary Option

Armed to defend the revolution, a Nicaraguan peasant in Jalapa, near the Honduran frontier, 1983

Much of the change produced by democratization, populism, nationalism, urbanization, industrialization, and modernization proved to be superficial: it affected only a small part of the life of the nations or touched only a minority of the populations. Often the capital cities took on a veneer of change that did not extend to the rest of the country. In most nations and for major segments of the populations, reforms came too slowly and too ineffectively, if, indeed, they came at all. On five occasions thus far in the twentieth century, Latin Americans despairing of evolutionary change and reform opted for revolution as a quicker and surer path to change. The Mexican experience has been related; it remains to look at the more recent experiences of Guatemala, Bolivia, Cuba, and Nicaragua.

In his *The Natural History of Revolution,* Lyford P. Edwards outlines the steps through which revolutions pass and charts their behavior. Widespread social restiveness and the belief that legitimate aspirations and ideals are repressed sound the overture to revolution. Advanced symptoms include the alienation of the intellectuals, the growing psychological strength of the repressed, the loss of faith of the governing class in themselves, and the appearance of the "social myth," a combination of the ideas of the intellectuals and the desires of the discontented. One event, demonstrating both the strength of the repressed and the incompetence of the governing class, sparks the revolution. Once underway, the revolution moves through four phases: (1) the triumph of the moderates, the enactment of reforms, the emigration of conservatives, and their appeal to a foreign power for help; (2) the triumph of the radicals over the moderates; (3) the imposition of revolutionary change; and (4) a return to normality once the radicals impose their program and no longer fear either foreign invasion or internal uprising. In short, the revolution has been accepted. The radicals become tolerant once they win toleration for themselves and the revolution.

In reviewing the causes and consequences of the Latin American revolutions, it may be useful to keep Edwards's social science model in mind. What do these revolutions want to achieve, why, and how do they go about it? Why has the metropolis vigorously opposed them?

GUATEMALA

Guatemala, in many respects a microcosm of the problems besetting Latin America in the 1940s, had a population of 3 million of whom three-quarters were Indian (many did not speak Spanish) and the rest were mestizo. The illiteracy rate topped 75 percent and surpassed 90 percent in some areas. The per capita income was meager, life expectancy low, and nutrition substandard. The few who owned most of the land farmed it inefficiently and allowed much of it to lie fallow. The Indians labored on the large estates under abysmal conditions, characterized by at least one

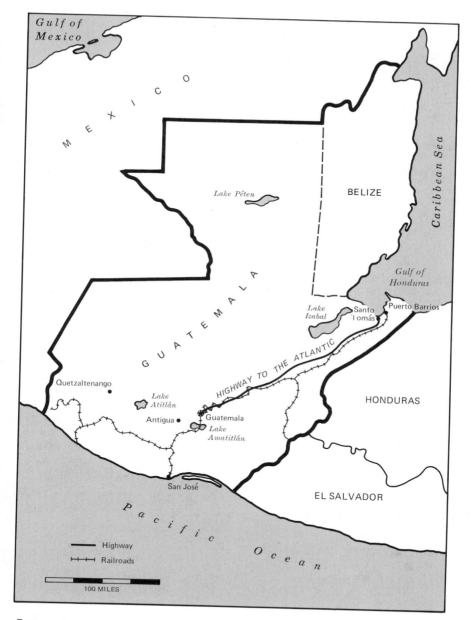

Guatemala

economist, Elizabeth E. Hoyt, as less humane than those on a feudal estate of the Middle Ages. Guatemala exported a few agricultural products, principally bananas and coffee, and remained at the mercy of an international market over which it had no influence, much less control. The taxes rested lightly on the wealthy—property and income taxes provided less than 10 percent of the tax revenue—but heavily on the masses, since most governmental revenue came from taxes on consumer goods.

A desire to change some of the institutions and patterns that perpetuated the national misery pervaded the small, heterogeneous middle groups within Guatemala City. Intellectuals, the lower ranks of the civil service, students, labor, and young army officers were the principal groups which rose up to throw General Jorge Ubico out of office in 1944 and to terminate the harsh rule he had exercised over the country for thirteen years. The new, provisional government encouraged the formation of political parties and guaranteed an honest election. Indeed, Guatemala witnessed one of the first free elections in its history when, in December of 1944, the voters selected by a six-to-one majority a forty-two-year-old professor, Juan José Arévalo, the candidate of the National Renovation Party (*Renovación Nacional*, or RN). He looked past the foreign interests and traditional oligarchy that had buttressed the Ubico regime to a new power coalition of peasants and workers, particularly the latter. In promising the nation a change, he categorized his government as one of "spiritual socialism." A new constitution, promulgated in 1945, regulated Guatemala's experiment with democracy and change. It owed much of its inspiration to the Mexican document of 1917. Like its model, it authorized a land reform and many new rights for labor.

Dependent upon the support of labor, Arévalo lavished attention on the workers. He abolished the discredited forced-labor system used by Ubico, created a Social Security Institute, and promulgated an advanced Labor Code. On the books at any rate, the Guatemalan workers enjoyed many of the social benefits of their contemporaries elsewhere in the world. With the encouragement of Arévalo, labor rapidly unionized, and the president consistently supported the unions in their struggles with the management of the United Fruit Company, the largest foreign company and the most powerful business in Guatemala. Arévalo skillfully used these disputes to stir nationalistic sentiments among Guatemalans, who were quite willing to endorse the charges of foreign exploitation hurled against the American-owned company. The preponderant presence of the foreign concern provided a convenient focal point for nationalist ire, which the leadership of the RN knew how to use for political purpose. The Industrial Development Law of 1947 sought to encourage industrialization. Although it permitted foreigners to participate, it forbade any special privileges for them. In short, they were put on an equal footing with nationals. Education, too, occupied much of the attention of the government, which launched an intensive literacy campaign. During his five years in office, Arévalo headed a government that can be characterized as leftist, progressive, non-Communist and highly nationalistic. The *Area Handbook for Guatemala,* published by the U.S. Army in 1970, referred to Avévalo as a "reformist." Certainly within the terms used after 1961 in the Alliance for Progress, it was a moderate government. Yet, within the context of the Guatemalan historical experience, it constituted the initial phase of a real revolution.

A mysterious and brutal assassination eliminated Francisco Arana, the most popular candidate to succeed Arévalo in the presidency, and opened the door to power for Colonel Jacobo Arbenz. Leading the RN Party, he received 65 percent of the vote in an election all observers agreed was fair and honest. When Arévalo handed him the sash of office in 1951, Guatemalans witnessed one of the rare instances in their history of a peaceful and legal transfer of presidential power. Arbenz entered the presidency with one major nationalist goal: to convert Guatemala from a dependent nation with a semicolonial economy to an economically and thus politically independent nation. His goal harmonized perfectly with that of nationalists then and thereafter throughout Latin America.

As his first step, he sought to transform Guatemala's inefficient, semi-feudal economy into a modern, efficient one. To do so required a far-reaching land reform. That step brought him into direct conflict with the powerful landowning oligarchy and the United Fruit Company. Arbenz had a firm legal base for the reform he intended. The Constitution of 1945 declared large estates to be illegal and conferred on the government the power to expropriate and redistribute land. The Agrarian Reform Law of 1952 declared that uncultivated land on estates over 220 acres where less than two-thirds of the estate was under cultivation was subject to expropriation and redistribution. The law provided compensation for expropriated estates. It affected only uncultivated land. The landowning elite immediately and vociferously charged that the reform was communistic. In their eyes, the Arbenz government had become a puppet of Moscow.

In Washington, the State Department watched apprehensively but said nothing until in 1953 the Guatemalan government seized 233,973 acres of unused land claimed by the United Fruit Company, a figure later raised to 413,573 acres. As it had maintained consistently throughout, the Guatemalan government said it intended to put all uncultivated land into use and would make no exceptions, either for nationals or for foreigners. The United Fruit Company argued that it needed reserve lands for future use and in case of the destruction of any of its present plantations by a banana disease. United Fruit had operated in Guatemala for many decades. It received its first concession from the Guatemalan government in 1906, and banana production climbed steadily thereafter. In 1947, Guatemala was the second largest producer of bananas in the world. During that time the economic power of the company multiplied. Not only was it the largest single agricultural enterprise in the country but it also owned and controlled the principal railroad and the facilities in the major port, Puerto Barrios. The company had brought many benefits. Its workers enjoyed better housing and medical care than the average Guatemalan laborer. It paid its workers twice the wages of the coffee workers, but then the banana worker produced two or three times the wealth of his counterpart on the coffee plantation. Regardless of any benefits the company might have provided, it was extremely unpopular among the nationalists and vulnerable because it was foreign and exercised too powerful an influence over an economy being challenged as semifeudal and exploitative. As a matter of record, the company paid the Guatemalan government in duties and taxes about 10 percent of its annual profits, a sum regarded by indignant nationalists as far too low.

The State Department rushed to support the claims of the United Fruit Company against the Guatemalan government on the basis that the compensation offered was insufficient. Yet, the sum offered equaled the value of the lands declared by the company for tax purposes. At that point, the State Department began to charge that the Guatemalan government was infiltrated with, if not controlled by, Communists. Some critics of U.S. foreign policy wondered at the motivations of the U.S. government. They pointed out the close connections between CIA Director Allen Dulles and Secretary of State John Foster Dulles and the United Fruit Company, a relationship that might have suggested some conflict of interests. The law office of John Foster Dulles had written the drafts of the United Fruit Company's 1930 and 1936 agreements with the Guatemalan government. Allen Dulles had served as president of the United Fruit Company. For that matter, the family of John Moors Cabot, then assistant secretary of state for inter-American affairs, owned stock in the banana company. Further, Henry Cabot Lodge, senator from Massachusetts, the home base of the United Fruit Company, already had denounced Arévalo on the Senate floor as "communistically inclined," and he remained unbendingly hostile toward Guatemala. As the verbal attacks of the State Department on Guatemala mounted, it became difficult, indeed, nearly impossible, to distinguish its charges from those of the United Fruit Company, and both of them sounded remarkably similar to the statements of the native oligarchy. All three manifested a preoccupation with the Communist "menace," but none of them seemed concerned with the abysmal misery on which communism might well feed in Guatemala and other underdeveloped nations in the hemisphere.

Despite the mounting pressure, Arbenz pushed ahead with his program to decrease Guatemala's dependency. He announced the government's intention to build a highway from Guatemala City to the Atlantic coast and thereby end the transportation monopoloy of the International Railways of Central America, owned and operated by the United Fruit Company. Further, he decided to construct a national hydroelectric plant.

Until that time, foreigners produced Guatemala's electrical power, and the rates charged were among the highest in Latin America.

Cultural nationalism also flourished. Following patterns evinced elsewhere in the Americas, the Guatemalan intellectuals turned their attention to the nation's rich Indian past for inspiration. Certainly the monumental novel of Miguel Angel Asturias, *Hombres de Maíz* (Men of Maize), published in 1949, ranked as the major Indianist statement—the Indians' view of Guatemalan history—and as a cultural landmark for Guatemala and Latin America. Other writers, painters, and musicians contributed to the reevaluation of the Indian roots of modern Guatemala. Nationalist and leftist rhetoric adorned the plans and pronouncements of Arbenz and his political supporters. By 1953, anti-Yankee sentiments proved very popular in governmental circles as well. The Guatemalans were enjoying a freedom of speech, assembly, and press to a degree that they rarely had in the century before 1944. Opposition parties thrived.

Local and foreign Communists signified their approval and identified with the Guatemalan goals, but the sentiment for change, nationalist pride, and distrust of the United States were too genuine and too popular to bear out the claim that the Guatemalan people blindly followed Communist leadership. The social legislation of the Arévalo-Arbenz period was not nearly so radical as that enacted in the United States during President Franklin Roosevelt's New Deal or in England under the Labor governments. Nonetheless, critics of President Arbenz, principally from the native oligarchy, the United Fruit Company, and the U.S. State Department, intensified their accusations that his government had succumbed to Communist pressures.

The Agrarian Reform Law figured as a major argument in the charge of communism. However, time has more than exonerated that misquoted law. Thomas F. Carrol of the United Nations' Food and Agricultural Organization stated some years later, "Decree 900, the agrarian reform, which had its roots in the Constitution of 1945, is a remarkably mild and a fairly sound piece of legislation." Even the State Department—in 1961—had to own up to the fact that the law was mild, and what had been labeled "communistic" in 1954 became one of the models approved by the Alliance for Progress in 1961.

By late 1953, the Arbenz government feared intervention from the United States. Pressures and retaliations from the United States had plunged the Guatemalan economy into a tailspin. The State Department embargoed arms sales to Guatamala. Arbenz repeatedly requested arms since he felt his more conservative neighbors, Honduras and El Salvador, were encouraging exiles to prepare an attack on his country. Unable to equip the army with matériel from the United States, the president turned to a source only too eager to comply with the request. On May 17, 1954, a shipment of arms arrived from Poland. To the State Department, its arrival served as final proof that Guatemala had fallen under Communist control. The U.S. Air Force at once ferried military supplies to Tegucigalpa in order to equip a small army under the command of a Guatemalan army exile, Colonel Carlos Castillo Armas. On June 18, 1954, Armas and approximately 150 men crossed the border into Guatemala. They penetrated about twenty-five miles and engaged in no significant action. They did not need to. The Arbenz government fell because the army refused to act and the workers were not armed. A series of air attacks on the unarmed capital terrorized the population and broke the morale of the people. The attacks caused more psychological than physical damage. The planes were furnished by the CIA and flown by U.S. pilots, as former President Dwight D. Eisenhower revealed in a publicly recorded interview. U.S. Ambassador John Peurifoy handled the changing of the government and with the enthusiastic endorsement of Washington installed Castillo Armas in the presidency. In a radio address on June 30, 1954, John Foster Dulles informed the American people of the changes in the Guatemalan government, which prompted him to declare, "The events of recent months and days add a new and glorious chapter to the already great tradition of the American States." One cannot be sure if the statement was a master stroke of cynicism or satire.

The CIA intervention in Guatemala was the first of many that would occur in the succeeding decades throughout Latin America. It introduced a cast of unsavory characters who would emerge repeatedly and disastrously in both international and U.S. politics. Perhaps the most notorious of them was E. Howard Hunt. He participated in the planning and execution of the bombardment of Guatemala City, the invasion of Guatemala, and the substitution of Castillo Armas for Arbenz; later he took an active role in the preparation for the invasion of Cuba in 1961 at the Bay of Pigs; a decade later he served on the White House staff of President Richard M. Nixon as a special consultant. He supervised the Watergate break-in. His case—and it was by no means an isolated example—linked international and national political immorality. As Hunt complained to the Senate Watergate Committee on September 25, 1973, "I cannot escape feeling that the country I have served for my entire life and which directed me to carry out the Watergate entry is punishing me for doing the very things it taught me to do." The sad situation of E. Howard Hunt revealed in a broader context that an intelligence mechanism constructed to subvert foreign governments could easily be directed to subvert national government. The great tragedies of U.S. political life, 1972–74, had part of their origins in the CIA intervention in Guatemala in 1954, exactly as the Iran-Contra scandals, 1986–87, had origins in the CIA interventions in Nicaragua during the 1980s.

A year after the United States placed Colonel Carlos Castillo Armas in power, Vice-President Richard Nixon wrote, "President Castillo Armas' objective, 'to do more for the people in two years than the Communists were able to do in ten years,' is important. This is the first instance in history where a Communist goverment has been replaced by a free one. The whole world is watching to see which does the better job."

In a yes-or-no plebiscite echoing the Ubico practice of the 1931–44 period, Castillo Armas confirmed himself in power. Deriving his major support from the local elites, the United Fruit Company, and the U.S. State Department, he ruled for three years without ever offering to hold elections, free or otherwise. Nonetheless, he took the precaution of abolishing all political parties that did not please him and disenfranchising all illiterates, thus canceling the voting rights of more than half the adult population. The police jailed, tortured, exiled, and/or executed all political opponents, excusing their crimes with the accusation that the victims were Communists. Castillo Armas eradicated whatever traces of communism could be found but in the process also eliminated democracy and reform.

Guatemala after 1954 offered the first Latin American example of the reversal of a land reform. Castillo Armas returned to the United Fruit Company the lands his predecessor had nationalized. What is more, he signed a new contract that facilitated the company's exploitation of Guatemala until 1981, limiting its taxes to a maximum of 30 percent of the profits. (That figure contrasted with the 69 percent oil companies had to pay Venezuela.) Approximately 1.5 million acres, which under the 1952 Agrarian Reform Law had been confiscated as idle and distributed to 100,000 landless rural families, reverted back to the original owners. The newly created peasant class suffered severely. A report published in 1965 by the Inter-American Agricultural Development Committee noted the tragic fate of one such small farmer dispossessed by Castillo Armas:

> Under Decree 900 he was granted a small piece of land and the credits to work it. Filled with enthusiasm, he used his own savings (over $90) to cultivate the land. Some time later he was arrested for the crime of being an "agrarian reformer," and had to take refuge in the mountains. Now the Banco Agrario is demanding payment of the loan plus nine years of interest, and since he cannot pay he is being persecuted.

Much of the land returned to the original owners lies fallow. One consequence is that for Guatemala to feed its population it must spend its hard-earned foreign reserves to import the food that the country is perfectly capable of growing.

One of the presidential guards assassinated Castillo Armas in mid-1957. Since that time political repression has continued amid considerable instability and repeated military interference. The CIA found it necessary to intervene again in November 1960, when a coup led by young, nationalistic officers deposed President Miguel Ydígoras Fuentes because he had allowed the United States to train Cuban exiles on Guatemalan soil for the invasion of Cuba. To return Ydígoras Fuentes to power, U.S. planes piloted by U.S. Air Force personnel bombed and strafed the headquarters of the young officers in Guatemala City, forcing them to surrender. Further, the U.S. military participated directly and indirectly with the Guatemalan army to suppress the guerrilla attacks that originated in the countryside throughout most of the 1960s. Bombings, assassinations, kidnappings, and terrorism shattered the urban tranquility during the same period. In the decade ending in 1971, the undeclared civil war between the right and the left claimed between 8,000 and 10,000 victims, a figure reaching 100,000 by 1986.

The frustrations of those Guatemalans desiring change intensified. The statistics of the early 1970s clearly substantiated the need for change. The average per capita income was $160, although 73 percent of the population earned $83 a year. Guatemala was one of three Latin American countries where the least taxes were paid by the wealthy. The tax on landed property amounted to 0.6 percent. Average life expectancy was only forty-five years. Although Guatemala's infant mortality rate ranked among the highest in the world, Guatemala was one of seven Latin American countries commended by the U.S. State Department for having "joined with the United States in aid to South Vietnam by sending medicines." The quality of life for the majority continues to erode. By 1987, Guatemala suffered the most skewed land distribution system in Latin America: 54 percent of all farmers owned but 4.1 percent of the land; more than 420,000 peasant families were landless. The weighty catalog of social ills provides convincing evidence that the governments since 1954 have done nothing to benefit the majority of the Guatemalan people. The whole world watched and, after three and a half decades, has had ample opportunity to judge, as President Nixon once challenged them to, whether Guatemalans received more benefits during the Arévalo-Arbenz decade or during the decades of military dictatorship. The young Guatemalan poet Otto Rene Castillo evaluated the present and indicated the future in these words:

> You have a gun
> And I am hungry
>
> You have a gun
> Because
> I am hungry
>
> You have a gun
> Therefore
> I am hungry
>
> You can have a gun
> You can have a thousand bullets and even another thousand
> You can waste them all on my poor body
> You can kill me one, two, three, two thousand, seven thousand times

But in the long run
I will always be better armed than you
If you have a gun
And I
Only hunger.

Reflecting on the brutality and arrogance of decades of military rule in Guatemala, the *Los Angeles Times* (July 5, 1984) termed the CIA intervention in 1954 and its dismal aftermath "one of the most shortsighted 'successes' in the history of U.S.–Latin American relations."

BOLIVIA

At the same time as Guatemala struggled with revolutionary change, Bolivia, too, chose to experiment with some radical solutions to old problems. Although Bolivia is ten times larger than Guatemala (Bolivia includes 424,163 square miles), they had in the early 1950s almost the same population. The similarity did not end there. Approximately three-fourths of the Bolivians were Indians, most of whom did not speak Spanish; the rest of the populations was mestizo. Illiteracy, undernourishment, sickness, low per capita income, and short life expectancy characterized the population. Starvation was one of the major causes of death. The majority of the population were landless Indians. In the cities, particularly in the capital, La Paz, dwelt the middle groups and industrial workers, two small groups. Bolivia's political record had been particularly chaotic: during the first century and a quarter of independence something like 125 presidents had sat in the governmental palace. During that period, the economic and social structures continued practically unchanged since the colonial era. Like Guatemala, Bolivia depended on one major export, but unlike the Central American republic, Bolivia's export was a mineral, tin, rather than an agricultural product.

Bolivia's defeat at the hands of smaller and more impoverished Paraguay in the Chaco War, 1932–35, the major Latin American conflict of the twentieth century, jolted Bolivia from its colonial lethargy. Both nations claimed the Chaco, Bolivia as part of the colonial territory from which it was formed and Paraguay by right of possession. They bickered over it for a century, but when these hinterlands promised to produce oil, the arguments heated up into armed clashes. In the three-year war that followed, the Paraguayans soundly routed their larger foe. The defeat stunned Bolivia, which in its history had surrendered territory to all its neighbors. The humiliation of losing land to its smallest and weakest neighbor sobered the nation and caused anguished soul-searching. The disillusioned middle groups, young army officers, students, and intellectuals turned to socialism and Marxist ideology in hope of discovering some solution to national

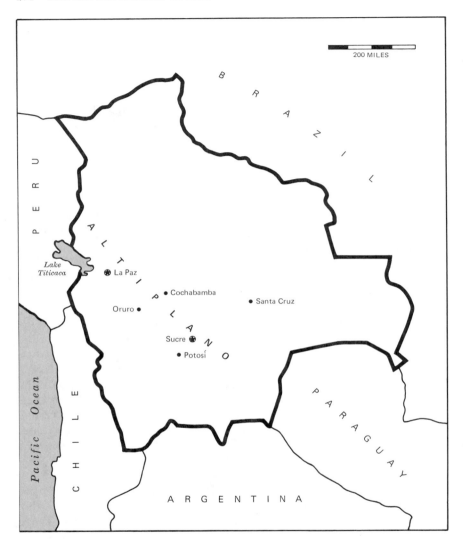

Bolivia

problems. They laid the blame for the war on international oil companies, claiming that two rival companies pushed Bolivia and Paraguay into war with the hope of obtaining favorable exploitative agreements from the victor. To show its ire, Bolivia nationalized the property of the Standard Oil Company of Bolivia on March 13, 1937, an action antedating Cárdenas's expropriation by a year. The government claimed and proved that Standard Oil had defrauded the state by illegally exporting oil. Colonel David

Toro, the president who signed the expropriation order, expressed the sentiments of many frustrated Bolivians when he announced that the defeat in the Chaco necessitated fundamental changes in society. He proclaimed the obvious: Bolivia lacked social justice. The Chaco disgrace demanded that the people and their government correct past errors in order to build strong, new equitable institutions. Bolivian politics took many a turn before these sentiments could be acted upon. Those proposing change found it easier to expropriate a foreign company than to alter national institutions. When Toro attempted to impose a higher tax on the "tin barons" of Bolivia, he found himself bounced from the presidency.

Urban intellectuals under the leadership of Víctor Paz Estenssoro organized the National Revolutionary Movement (*Movimiento Nacional Revolucionario,* or MNR) in 1941. Its two primary goals were to nationalize the tin mines and to combat international imperialism. The decade of the 1940s was unusually chaotic, even for Bolivia. During those ten years, eight coups d'état disturbed the nation and seven different presidents held office. In one four-year period, there were eighteen ministers of labor; in another eight-month period, there were eight ministers of finance. The elite on the wildly whirling political carousel seemed oblivious to the restless discontent welling up in the rural and urban workers.

In the presidential election of 1951, as was customary, the government controlled the electoral machinery and the suffrage remained restricted to literate males, about 7 percent of the population. Despite these handicaps, an opposition party, the MNR, won a resounding victory. The government evinced no intention of letting the winner, Paz Estenssoro, take office, and the army seconded that decision. A bloody struggle erupted in April of 1952 in which the MNR seized power by force and placed Paz Estenssoro, the winner at the polls, in office. The revolution represented a broad-based alliance of the progressive elements of the middle class, intellectuals and students, organized labor, and the rural landless. The urban and rural workers' militias provided the backbone of armed strength and emerged as a key power group.

President Paz Estenssoro moved at once to implement the first goal of the MNR: to nationalize the tin mines, the primary source of Bolivia's wealth. Three Bolivian families owned the mines: Patiño, Hochschild, and Aramayo. Patiño controlled most of the mining. His annual income exceeded that of the national government during any year. In fact, the annual allowance of one of his sons was greater than the government's budget for education. They took most of the profits from mining out of Bolivia in order to live opulently in Europe. Clearly, the mining companies exercised greater power than the government, and no previous government had dared undertake any project or make any major decision without the approval of the Patiños, Hochschilds, and Aramayos. Because nearly the entire population opposed the arrogant power of the three families, the expropriation decree proved to be very popular. The government took over the mines in October 1952 without giving any remuneration to the owners. Unfortunately, the price of tin on the world market fell at about the same time, a vivid demonstration of the vulnerability of an economy dependent on one export. To guarantee the support of the well-organized and armed miner's unions, the government raised wages and benefits, moves that further threatened the fragile national economy. Not until 1966 did the mines report a profit for the first time since 1952.

Rural agitation forced the government to turn its attention to land reform, a demand the MNR had been unprepared to meet. If "feudalistic" could be a proper adjective to describe rural life in Latin America, it was nowhere more applicable than in Bolivia, where the huge rural estates had changed little, if at all, since the sixteenth century. A United Nations report of 1951 observed, "The land tenure system almost completely blocked the development of a progressive agriculture." Six percent of the farm owners controlled 92 percent of the land, most of which was fallow and the rest of which was inefficiently worked. At the same time Bolivia imported more than one-fifth of its food necessities.

The MNR confronted one of the major peasant rebellions of the twentieth century. After the close of the Chaco War, restive Indians demanded land only to meet impenetrable bureaucracy, unfulfilled political promises, or harsh repression. The revolution carried out by the urban MNR triggered an Indian uprising in the countryside. The Indians seized the land; the landlords fled to the city. Civil war between the urban "whites" and the rural Indians threatened. President Paz Estenssoro responded to the reality. He formalized the reform undertaken by the Indians in a decree-law of August 2, 1953. Although the MNR had plans for an eventual rural reform, it would not have been as complete as that carried out by the Indians themselves. The Indian triumph was a reform designed to end the extreme concentration of land ownership and put the land into the hands of the rural workers. Article 30 of the new law abolished latifundia, but Article 35 exempted from expropriation large farms on which the owner had made substantial capital investments, used modern farming methods, and personally worked the land. The former owners receive virtually no compensation. The government handed out land titles to almost 60,000 heads of family by 1960.

As one immediate result of the reform, the index of agricultural production fell. The period of adjustment with its general confusion, as the Mexican case also proved, is not always beneficial for the economy in the short run. Students of agrarian reform point out that the peasants tend to sell less of their product because they are able for the first time to eat better. Cold statistics also ignore the immeasurable psychological results and benefits for the nation. Land ownership turns the rural proletariat into responsible citizens; it bestows dignity reflected in the peasants' new pride in self and country. It redistributes power. Fortunately, in Bolivia, the agricultural production index began to rise slowly in the late 1950s and by the mid-1960s had equaled and even surpassed the prereform levels.

The MNR at once turned upon the army, the political arbiter since independence. The senior officers had employed force in an effort to prevent the MNR from legally taking office in 1952. Paz Estenssoro distributed arms to the workers and peasants, whose militias gave the government the force it needed to impose its will. Then the government reduced the military to near oblivion, where it remained throughout most of the 1950s. In 1957, expenditures for the military dropped to a mere 6.7 percent of the national budget but rose steadily thereafter when the government began to rebuild the military as a counterweight to the powerful and radical militias. By the early 1960s, the military had regained most of its former strength.

After serving his four-year term, Paz Estenssoro turned over the presidency to another MNR stalwart, Hernán Siles, who won the elections of 1956. A term out of office permitted Paz Estenssoro to run again for the presidency in 1960, and the voters enthusiastically endorsed his new bid for office. The free elections and peaceful transfers of power from one president to the next, each of whom served his full legal term, were phenomena novel to Bolivian political life. Unfortunately when election time came around again in 1964, President Paz Estenssoro made the error of tampering with the constitution to permit himself to be reelected, a genuinely unpopular maneuver. The army stepped in, a reversion to its prerevolutionary role, and took the reins of power.

Revolutionary activity declined, then disappeared. Generals monopolized political power. Cocaine traffic and corruption pervaded the barracks and the halls of government. Between 1978 and 1982, political and economic chaos reached bewildering proportions. An editorial in the *Los Angeles Times* (August 20, 1980) commented, "Diplomatic sources . . . say that corruption and greed are the overriding motivations of the new order in Bolivia. In essence, the generals are really grabbing control of the profitable drug traffic. The secret-police chief himself is said to be a major trafficker in cocaine." The Department of State terminated the U.S. anti-narcotics program in Bolivia, suggested that key personnel in the military governments were "engaged in drug trafficking," an involvement that seemed to reach into the cabinet itself. By 1987, Bolivia's cocaine industry was the largest in the world and the nation's primary export. Most of the Bolivian cocaine found its way to the streets of the United States.

When Paz Estenssoro returned yet again to the presidency in 1985, age—he was seventy-eight—had turned the revolutionary into a reactionary. He set out to dismantle whatever remained of the revolution he had forged three decades earlier. For the poorest nation of South America, he imposed a brutal austerity program, economic medicine drawn from the pharmacopeia of the free-market economic model. In 1986, Bolivia paid

$621 million on its foreign debt, while exports earned only $544 million. Such economic medicine promises to kill the patient.

Bolivian political and economic patterns after 1964 contrast sadly with the positive efforts made toward development in the 1950s. The authentic revolution that the MNR initiated in 1952 was coopted by the moderates in the late 1950s, terminated by the military coup d'état in 1964, and reversed by the military governments of the 1970s. Bolivia's revolution and most of its proud achievements have passed into history.

The varying reaction of the United States to the Bolivian and Guatemalan revolutions seems at first blush paradoxical. While opposing the course of events in Guatemala and contributing to the overthrow of the Arbenz government, Washington lavished funds, technical aid, and support on the MNR governments of Bolivia. When Paz Estenssoro reached power by revolution in 1952, the State Department cautiously waited three months before extending recognition. President Eisenhower sent his brother Milton on a mission to Bolivia in 1953, a visit that proved to be the turning point in the relations between Washington and the MNR. Showing an unusual flexibility during the John Foster Dulles years, the State Department made the distinction that although the Bolivian revolution might be Marxist, it was not Communist, a distinction that, alas, the State Department rarely has been able to repeat. In short, to Washington officialdom, Paz Estenssoro seemed to offer the only viable alternative to communism in Bolivia, and on that basis, the U.S. government granted aid on a generous scale. During one year, the United States provided up to one-third of the national budget of Bolivia.

The financial and technical aid to Bolivia was channeled by the U.S. government in such a way as to support the moderate, middle-class leaders of the revolution, Paz Estenssoro and Siles, against the radical, workingclass factions. Thus, aid, skillfully directed, helped to shape the course of the Bolivian Revolution and, in the opinion of many scholars, to set its limits. One U.S. official, George Jackson Eder, whom the Bolivian government was required to accept in 1956–57 as the director of its stabilization program, reminisced in his book *Inflation and Development in Latin America* (1968) that he helped to break the power of the radical labor unions over the government. He stated that his stabilization program "meant the repudiation, at least tacitly, of virtually everything that the Revolutionary Government had done over the previous four years." Much subtler then the bombardment and invasion of Guatemala, the cooption of the moderate forces in Bolivia proved just as effective in overturning revolutionary change.

Perhaps two reasons can partially explain the option of the United States for subtler diplomacy with Bolivia. First, Guatemala had the temerity to expropriate property belonging to North American investors, while Bolivia, until seizing the property of the Gulf Oil Company in 1968, confiscated mainly the property of nationals. (North American investments in Bolivian tin and land had been minimal.) Second, because of its geographical location,

Guatemala fell within the sphere of immediate U.S. interest and concern. The proximity of the United States limited Guatemala's choices and facilitated intervention. Bolivia is farther removed from the United States, and its isolation complicates direct intervention.

CUBA

In 1959, Cuba became the fourth Latin American nation in the twentieth century to choose revolution as the means of changing inflexible patterns inherited from the past. The Cuban situation differed considerably from that of Guatemala and Bolivia. By Latin American standards, Cubans enjoyed a high literacy rate and a very high per capita income. It was an urbanized nation with a large middle class. Nonetheless, Cuba suffered from a number of serious problems. Proximity to the United States—the famous ninety miles—meant that Washington dominated Cuba. Economically, even politically, Cuba depended on the United States, and Washington showed a preference for governments in Havana that complemented international trade rather than instituted reforms at home. Cuba depended on a one-crop export, sugar, for its prosperity, and, as the Depression amply proved, the Cuban economy was as vulnerable as that of Bolivia. Corruption flourished in Havana, often on a spectacular scale. The nation's wealth concentrated in the lively capital and failed to trickle down to the impoverished provinces. Finally, years of dictatorship—Fulgencio Batista had controlled the government firmly but efficiently from 1933 to 1944, but his second exercise of power, 1952–59, proved to be more brutal and less efficient—aroused a genuine and deep yearning among the Cubans for change.

Cuba

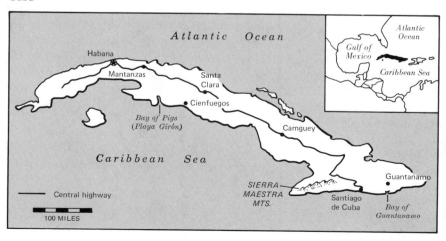

Fidel Castro, a brash young representative of middle-class students and intellectuals, audaciously challenged the powerful Batista dictatorship, first in his quixotic 1953 attack on an army barracks and then after his "invasion" of 1956 as a very effective guerrilla fighter in the Sierra Maestra Mountains. Castro visualized a reformed Cuba. He said his struggle was to end the latifundia, limit foreign ownership, establish cooperatives, nationalize public services, enact social legislation, spread education, and industrialize the nation. These programs appealed to broad segments of the Cuban population and stirred the island's nationalism. They echoed the basis upon which Grau San Martín founded his middle-class party in 1935: "nationalism, socialism, anti-imperialism." In fact, a surprising amount of the change Castro advocated for Cuba rested on a strong historical precedent.

José Matrí, the island's most revered national figure, died in 1895 struggling for Cuba's independence. His voluminous writings constitute a formidable legacy that inspired succeeding generations with patriotism and national identity. One of his observations was particularly pertinent not only for Cuba but also for all of Latin America: "Political liberty is possible only when it is accompanied by economic independence." A kind of quasi-political independence came in 1898 as a result of U.S. intervention in the Cuban-Spanish conflict. The United States fastened the Platt Amendment on Cuba, converting the new republic into a protectorate. The key clause of the amendment read, "Cuba consents that the United States may exercise the right to intervene for the protection of Cuban independence, the maintenance of a government adequate for the protection of life, property, and individual liberty." Such political domination, however, was secondary to the economic control U.S. interests soon exerted over the monocultural sugar production. The Cubans resented Washington's hegemony and succeeding generations of patriots challenged it, repudiating their compatriots who profited by cooperating with it.

Twice Cuban patriots nearly succeeded in altering their country's relationship with Washington. After the popular overthrow of the repressive regime of Geraldo Machado in 1933, a radical government took power with the promise of change. Subtle and effective U.S. diplomacy undercut the radicals and pushed the moderates into the political arena. In return for marginalizing the radical reformers, Cuba received a sugar preference in the U.S. market and the United States abrogated the Platt Amendment. Cuba, however, lost the opportunity to make some fundamental institutional changes. In 1940, the nationalists wrote and promulgated a new constitution, one of the most important to emerge from Latin America because it indicated the reforms progressive Latin Americans desired to institute in their societies. The Constitution of 1940 banned latifundia, discouraged foreign ownership of the land, permitted the expropriation of property "for reason of public utility or social interest," authorized the state to provide full employment, claimed the subsoil for the nation, empowered

Fidel Castro addressing a rally, Havana, Cuba, 1964

the government to "direct the course of the national economy for the benefit of the people," and conferred on the state control of the sugar industry. The succeeding middle-class governments turned their backs on the new constitution and governed as though it never existed. In the writings of Martí, in the rhetoric of the forces that overthrew Machado, and in the Constitution of 1940, Fidel Castro found much of the inspiration for the changes he proposed.

What startled both Cubans and the rest of the world was that Castro, after the collapse of Batista on January 1, 1959, carried out his promises. Unlike his predecessors, he mixed action with talk. As a symbol of reform, Castro rode into power on a wave of unprecedented popularity, not only in Cuba but throughout Latin America. He seemed to represent purity over corruption, change over status quo. He captured the imagination of the masses with his panache, his intensity, and his concern with their plight. His nationalism and antiimperialism immediately brought him into open conflict with the United States. When he felt that the government and businesses of the United States were trying to impede Cuba's revolution, he confiscated approximately $1 billion in North American property and investments. Washington broke diplomatic and consular relations with Cuba on January 3, 1961.

Realizing that his small nation of only 7 million inhabitants handicapped with a vulnerable sugar economy could not defy its colossal neighbor alone, Castro turned to the one nation—the Soviet Union—capable of and willing to stand up to the United States and provide Cuba with protection, technical aid, loans, military hardware, and markets. Moscow was only too delighted to find an ally in the Western Hemisphere. Castro's daring defiance of the United States won for him and the Cuban Revolution admirers among many Latin Americans who found in his charges that "Yankee imperialism" perpetuated the status quo in Latin America enough truth to make them applaud his frankness and boldness.

It became abundantly clear after he assumed power that Castro intended to alter Cuba radically. He announced:

> The only thing that can resolve the problems of hunger and misery in the underdeveloped countries is revolution—revolutions that really change social structures, that wipe out social bonds, that put an end to unnecessary costs and expenditures, the squandering of resources; revolutions which allow people to devote themselves to planned and peaceful work.

He regarded education as one key to the new future. Teacher-training institutes sprang up; in a decade the number of teachers tripled; the number of schools quintupled; young, eager volunteers fanned out into the remotest corners of the island to teach reading and writing. Within a few years illiteracy virtually disappeared. By 1971, nearly one-quarter of the country's 8 million inhabitants were in school. Education was free from nursery school through the university. Reading became a national pastime. In 1958, Cuba published 100 different titles and a total of 900,000 books. In 1973, it published 800 titles and a total of 28 million books. Cuba has the highest per capita book production in Latin America. Hospitals were built in remote cities and doctors became available in the countryside for the first time. All medical services were free. By 1965, Cuba spent $19.15 per person per year for medical care, a figure that contrasted sharply with the $1.98 Mexico spent or the $.63 Ecuador spent. As a consequence the health of the nation improved dramatically and life expenctancy lengthened (See Table 9-1). Public housing received attention from the government, and the living conditions of the masses were better than ever before. No family needed to pay more than 10 percent of its income for rent.

The government encouraged the arts, and painting, literature, and music flourished. The National Ballet of Cuba emerged as one of the principal dance companies of the world, which it frequently toured to critical and popular acclaim. Alicia Alonso and her young partner Jorge Esquivel dazzled their New York audience in 1975, received a twenty-minute tumultuous ovation, and inspired rave critical notices in all the press. The Ballet Nacional de Cuba again toured the United States in the summer of 1979 to universal acclaim. It was probably in film, however, that the Cuban Revolution reached its maximum cultural achievement.

TABLE 9-1   Cuban Health Record, A Comparison between 1958 and 1983

	1958	1983
Population	6.5	10 million
Life Expectancy	58 years	73.5 years
Infant Mortality	70 per 1000 live births	17.3 per 1,000 live births
Percentage of Hospital Births	20	98.9
Physicians	6,250	16,936
Dentists	250	3,986
Nurses	394	31,855
Medical Technicians	478	29,109
Hospitals	96	256
Polyclinics for Outpatient care	0	397
First Aid Stations	0	225
Dental Clinics	0	142
Blood Banks	1	21
Homes for the Elderly	20	75
Homes for the Handicapped	2	18
Medical Schools	1	17
Dental Schools	1	4

The first law of the revolutionary government in the field of culture created the Cuban Film Institute (*Instituto Cubano del Arte e Industria Cinematográficos*) in March 1959. It has produced documentaries, newsreels, and feature-length films in addition to publishing the most serious Latin American journal on the film, *Cine Cubano*. Much of the Cuban filmmakers' attention focused on reinterpreting their country's past. In his alternatingly lyric and realistic *Lucia*, Humberto Solas studied the woman's role in three Cuban struggles that have shaped the history of modern Cuba: the war for independence in 1895, the fight to overthrow the Machado regime in 1933, and the literacy campaign of the 1960s. In another effective look at the past, Manuel Octavio Gómez recreated in his *La Primera Carga al Machete* (The First Machete Charge) events from the guerrilla warfare against Spain in 1895; in the film he used the technique of the on-the-spot cameraman to simulate newsreel reporting. Besides *Lucia* the film most accessible to audiences in the United States is *Memorias de Subdesarrollo* (Memories of Underdevelopment), a witty and penetrating analysis of attitudes of the former bourgeoisie toward the revolution. New York, San Francisco, and Los Angeles organized Cuban film retrospectives, and Cuban films became regular features of film festivals. Cuban films have been projected throughout the world, have won a disproportionate number of international awards, and have earned enthusiastic reviews from a wide variety of critics. Between 1959 and 1985, the Cuban Film Institute made 2,000 feature, documentary, and newsreel films. In 1988, Fidel Castro established a film school for the Third World outside of Havana.

The revolution has lavished attention on athletics. Cubans boast of their prowess on the playing field and enjoy enviable world records in boxing and baseball. Cuba dominates, and has for several decades, world amateur baseball. The Cuban National Team has won ten World Series of Amateur Baseball and four gold medals for baseball at the Pan American games.

During his first months in office, Fidel Castro focused his attention on agriculture. The agrarian problems challenged the imagination. Sugar companies owned 70 to 75 percent of the arable land. Three percent of the sugar producers controlled more than 50 percent of the production. At the same time, while most of the arable land stood uncultivated, 70,000 Cubans had no jobs and the country imported fully 50 percent of the food its people ate. In June of 1959, the Castro government issued the Agrarian Reform Law. As it turned out, the confiscated estates, for which no indemnity was paid, were not divided and turned over to the rural proletariat but were worked by them as cooperatives under the management of the omnipotent National Institute of Agrarian Reform. In the early 1970s, approximately 34 percent of Cuba's tillable soil still remained in private hands, divided into family-sized farms of no more than 165 acres each. The Cuban economy still depends heavily on the production, preparation, and sale of sugar, although the markets for that product have been more widely diversified. Effort to lessen the dependency on sugar have prompted the increased planting and production of rice, coffee, cotton, tobacco, pineapples, bananas, and citrus fruit. Cattle raising has become a more efficient and widespread industry. The initial surge toward industrialization has been slowed and put on a more rational base. The government succeeded in ending the unemployment and underemployment that always plagued the Cuban workers. In the 1950s, one out of every four of the employable work force had no jobs either for the entire year or a major part of it. Since 1959, a serious labor shortage has existed. Women entered the work force in large numbers and enjoyed equality with men. In the late 1960s, Professor Robin Blackburn of the London School of Economics concluded about the Cuban economy, "Though many of Cuba's economic problems cannot be resolved in isolation from those which afflict the developing world as a whole, her new economic system has at least already shown itself to be much more dynamic, and more egalitarian, than that which it replaced."

The traditional power of the old oligarchy, military, and Church vanished; the state, that is, the popular dictatorship of Fidel Castro, filled the vacuum. Eschewing the sterile forms of the democratic farce that had previously characterized Cuban government, Castro claimed his government to be one of the people. To prove his confidence in popular support, he distributed arms to the peasants and workers to defend their new government—

TABLE 9-2   Selected Standard of Living Indicators for Cuba

INDICATOR	PERCENTAGES		
	1953	1970	1981
Children between Ages 6–12 Years Enrolled in School	56.4	88.0	97.3
Population with at Least a Sixth Grade Education	20.1	31.6	61.0
Homes with Indoor Sanitary Facilities	74.9	82.0	91.0
Homes with Electricity	56.4	70.7	82.9
With Radio Sets	49.0	61.0	82.0
With TV Sets	6.0	17.0	58.0
With Refrigerators	16.0	24.0	51.0
With Sewing Machines	—	40.0	50.0
With Washing Machines	—	—	28.0

and they did. He frequently convoked the people to mass meetings where he sought—and received—their approval. It is all too easy for the sophisticated to scoff at those hectic mass rallies, but to the peasants and workers, neglected or exploited in the past, they provided a participation in the governing process they previously had not known. It brought them closer to the source of power than they had even been. In short, most of them were able to identify with the aims and methods of the Castro government. Most of the elite and middle class abhorred the changes that divested them of influence, prestige, and property. They fled Cuba in large numbers to escape the popular socialism that was rapidly changing the Cuba from which they had benefited so much.

In the United States the Cuban exiles received a warm official welcome. Washington used their testimony in an effort to discredit Fidel Castro and the new socialist experiments in Cuba. Successive U.S. governments employed the CIA to finance and influence myriad Cuban exile organizations in support of U.S. policies toward the Castro government. The machinations of the CIA included commando raids on the island, false news reports, assassinations, the overthrow of Latin American governments that refused to break relations with Cuba (the government of President J. M. Velasco Ibarra of Ecuador in 1961, for example), and the cynical manipulation of the patriotic sentiments of many sincere Cuban exiles. Perhaps the most notorious plot of the CIA was the planning, preparation, and execution of the invasion of Cuba in 1961. One of the agents involved in the madcap scheme was E. Howard Hunt, whose book on the invasion, *Give Us This Day* (1973), inadvertently exposed the real character of the invasion and the type of government it intended to establish in Havana. It revealed a greater concern with property than progress: "This time I told [Justo] Carrillo American money was not being spent for hoped-for good will, but on the certainty that the post-Castro government would honor the constitution and restore confiscated property to its rightful owners, Cuban or foreign" (p. 84). An admiration for Batista proved hard to suppress: "True, Batista had been a corrupt dictator, but under him and his predecessors the Cuban standard of living was far above the Latin American average, while every passing day demonstrated how precipitously Castro communism was lowering it" (p. 217). The CIA really had contempt for the Cuban exiles and used them only when it suited its convenience: "Cuban plans, in any case, were not the ones that would be used on I-Day, but plans that were being developed by the CIA and the Pentagon through the Joint Chiefs of Staff. Cuban military planning, therefore, was a harmless exercise and might prove tangentially useful if they became known to Castro's agents and served as deception material—disinformation. To paraphrase a homily: this was too important to be left to Cuban generals" (pp. 61–62).[1] Guided by the most faulty intelligence mixed with wishful thinking, the badly trained Cuban exiles landed at the Bay of Pigs on April 17, 1961 to meet instant disaster. Rather than a popular uprising that would embrace them and cast out Castro, they encountered a well-trained and determined Cuban army and militia that inflicted immediate defeat despite support from U.S. planes flown by U.S. pilots. The Cubans hailed it as their greatest victory, and Castro emerged stronger and more revered than ever.

The U.S. blockade of Cuba was no more successful than the CIA—Cuban exile invasion, although it certainly inflicted considerably more hardship on the island. In fact, despite all the efforts of the United States to effect the contrary, the quality of life in Cuba for the average Cuban improved and did so to such an extent that even former critics had to acknowledge it. By the early 1970s the testimony of the overall success of the Cuban experiment became irrefutable and much of it emanated from surprising sources. Mr. Pat M. Holt, chief of staff of the Senate Foreign Relations Committee, made a brief visit to Cuba and then wrote *A Staff Report Prepared for the use of the Committee on Foreign Relations, United States Senate* in which he concluded that the Cubans were on the verge of making their system work. All Cubans enjoyed the necessities of life and indeed as a group had an impressive standard of living. On August 7, 1974, *The Times of the Americas,* a conservative newpaper published in Washington by Cuban exiles, concluded a nine-part essay on Cuba written by John P. Hoover, who had served in the U.S. Embassy in Havana for eight years and was U.S. Consul General there from 1954 to 1956. He published his essay after returning from a visit to Cuba. It spoke favorably of the changes he observed in Cuba and concluded that a new Cuban had emerged. The November 1974 issue of *The Progressive* carried another essay by Hoover in which

---

[1]Copyright © 1973 by Howard Hunt. From *Give Us This Day* (New Rochelle, N.Y.: Arlington House). All rights reserved. By permission.

he affirmed, "My observations lead me to agree with them that the Castro government is giving more material and social good for a higher proportion of the people than any other regime in the island's history." The *Los Angeles Times* carried an article by Frank Mankiewiez on September 22, 1974, that concluded:

> I traveled throughout Cuba for nearly four weeks in July, and during that time did not see one shoeless child or one child with the classic signs of malnutrition. Cuba now has the lowest infant mortality rate of all Latin American nations, illiteracy is practically nonexistent, and by a shrewd concentration of resources in the countryside—where the great majority of development has taken place—Castro has avoided the terrible problem of almost every developing country, namely the flight of hundreds of thousands to the capital city. As a result, Havana is the only Latin capital I have seen which does not have the typical ring of shantytown misery surrounding it. . . . What it does have is a government free of corruption, with the support of the people who live there, whose economy appears to be stable and indeed is growing without our assistance.

Indeed, the *Los Angeles Times* had concluded in an editorial as early as July 11, 1972, that Washington's policy toward Cuba needed revision since it no longer served the national interest.

During those years of revised assessments of Cuba, its economy boomed. Growth statistics hovered between 9 and 10 percent. Both agrarian and industrial production expanded impressively. High international sugar prices explain part of the economic prosperity. In a mood of experiment in 1975, the government adopted the "Economic Management System" but did not start to implement it until three years later. The system called for greater decentralization and democratization of the economy as well as offered incentives to workers. Meanwhile, in 1976, Cuba adopted a new constitution, approved by popular referendum, the first of the Revolution, and interestingly enough about 40 percent of it came from the Constitution of 1940. Among other things, the new constitution called for popular elections of municipal councils, which, in turn, would elect provincial and national assemblies. Consequently popular participation in local government increased. Those innovations marked a significant step toward the political institutionalization of the Revolution. Castro released thousands of "political" prisoners, and at the same time opened Cuba for exiled Cubans to visit. A trend toward better relations between Cuba and the United States climaxed in September of 1977, when both nations opened "interest sections" in each others' capitals, a subtle means of initiating direct relations without according formal diplomatic recognition.

During those years of fulfillment of the Revolution, shifting international winds began to lash Cuba. The island's increasing involvement in Africa and falling international sugar prices precipitated new crises in the last years of the decade. The United States bitterly denounced the Cuban military presence in Africa, particularly in Angola and Ethiopia. Nature dealt Cuban agricultre some cruel blows: hurricanes, floods, sugar rust, and tobacco mold. Falling sugar prices rocked the economy. These reverses seemed to tighten Havana's dependence on aid from Moscow. They also slowed down the growth rate. The heady rates of the decade's first half fell to 4.5 percent by 1979 and 2.9 percent by 1980. Such reverses occurred at the same time that previous baby booms provided educated young recruits for the labor market. Demands for scarce consumer items and housing continued unabated, while failure to fulfill all those demands generated frustration. The crises of the last years of the 1970s forced the Revolution to "tighten its belt." As it did, the Revolution alienated that part of the labor force in a precarious or marginal position, people who had sacrificed all they were able to for the Revolution and who could accept no more discipline in the name of socialism. They wanted out. Castro opened the doors (the safety value?) in mid-1980, and over 100,000 Cubans migrated to the United States. Although the overwhelming majority of the immigrants successfully integrated into American life, a small minority did not. Included in the refugee groups were criminals and others whom Cuban authorities labeled "socially undesirable." Their abuse of American hospitality further embittered feelings in the United States toward Cuba.

Cuba was proving that the road to socialism was long and hard. Because such is the case, socialists who intend to succeed seem to require a heavy dose of discipline and hard work from the population. Some changes, even under revolution and socialism, come slowly. After more than a quarter-century of revolution, sugar still dominated as the principal crop and export. Cuba is, after all, a relatively poor island with no coal, and no hydroelectric resources. It possesses few minerals. Its soil consistently produces good sugar, however, which is a major resource but a crop often as inconsistent in quality as the international prices paid for it. Although no one would deny its preponderant importance as an export, observers tend to ignore that its contribution to the total Cuban GNP has slipped from 25 to 17 percent, a healthy but overly slow trend. Cuba, inconvenienced by the U.S. blockade, needs Soviet aid and relies on it. Critics with some justification stress the island's continued monoculture and dependency.

Despite persistent problems, the economy made a welcomed rebound in 1981, when the economic growth rate skyrocketed to 15.6 percent. The growth rate averaged 7.5 percent annually for the period 1980–85, contrasting sharply with the negative growth rate registered in many parts of Latin America during those years of economic crises. Furthermore, external debt to the West declined from $3.2 billion (1980) to $2.8 billion (1983), while it continued to climb throughout Latin America.

On January 1, 1984, Cubans celebrated the twenty-fifth anniversary of the revolution. Those festivities sparked renewed assessments of its successes and failures. *The Economist* (January 14, 1984) gave it surprisingly high marks, concluding

> A quarter of a century of socialism has brought Cuba an average annual growth rate of 4.7%, one of the highest in Latin America. By third-world standards, Cubans live well. They are well clothed, and enjoy free education and health care. . . . For Cuba's poor majority, life has improved, though it remains austere. An increasing variety of goods is available in Cuba's free markets. With a maximum rent set at 10% of income, Cubans have money to spend. . . . Mr. Castro remains popular and Cuban nationalism—which has always focused on anti-Americanism—is ferocious.

Although by no means uncritical, the *Los Angeles Times* nonetheless acknowledged the revolution's real achievement: It had eradicated illiteracy, hunger, destitution, and unemployment. It had diminished racial and sexual discrimination. Conformity, limits on freedom of expression, and the economy's overdependence on sugar and Soviet aid headed the list of criticisms. Certainly the life styles of the former elite and middle class had been reduced, but, at the other end of the spectrum, those of the once impoverished had been improved. Concluded one essay in the *Los Angeles Times* (April 29, 1984):

> There is no question that living conditions for those who constituted the poorest segments of Cuban society before 1959—and their children—have improved enormously as a result of the revolution. In the rural areas, for example, there is year-round employment, decent housing that never before existed and access to first-rate health services and high-quality education—accompanied by indoctrination.

An outdoor cafe in Havana, Cuba, 1978

In addition to studying, these high school students in the model Lenin School also manufacture clothing in Havana, 1978.

As most critics realize, the majority of Cubans enjoy more benefits and a higher quality of life today than the majority ever did in the past. To put the revolution in the perspective of the living conditions of the majority of Latin Americans, it has provided an abundance that tens of millions of Mexicans, Brazilians, Bolivians, Guatemalans, Ecuadorans, Paraguayans, Chileans, and other Latin Americans would hardly believe and certainly do not experience in their own countries.

The debates over the merits and demerits of the revolution seldom convey a perception of the significance of the Cuban revolution within the entire Latin American experience. What would, or could, it mean to the impoverished multitudes, to that majority who have stood for so many generations at the base of the social, economic, and political pyramid? An exceptionally sensitive evaluation came from the pen of Joe Nicholson, Jr., when he compared his impressions of Cuba and Mexico in 1973:

> I looked out at the palm trees and orchards to get a last glimpse as we taxied down the runway of the José Martí Airport. We passed yards of cranes, trucks, and buses. A small banner, the airport's only sign, said "Yankees Out of Vietnam." The plane turned toward Mexico City and the orchards became increasingly difficult to see.
>
> A skyline dominated by massive billboards along the airport runway greeted us in Mexico: "Beefeater Gin for Perfect Martini," "Pepsi," "Enjoy Coca-Cola," "Nescafe Symbol of Friendship," "Holiday Inn Host To The World." The Americanization of Latin America seemed glaring after de-Americanized Cuba.
>
> Mexico was building a new Colonel Sanders Kentucky Fried Chicken emporium, the Colonel's "finger lickin' good" slogan translated to read, "It will make your fingers good to lick." I passed up the Colonel's chicken and asked for a taco from a street vendor whose cart was parked on the Paseo De La

Reforma. He had only hot dogs. The store window diplays along the Paseo offered Maxwell House instant coffee; Hershey bars; Aunt Jemima hotcakes; V-8 vegetable juice; Del Monte canned tropical fruit; Gordon's distilled dry gin; Ballantine's finest Scotch whiskey; Toastmaster air conditioners; Hoover vacuum cleaners; Aqua Velva; and Max Factor lipstick. At the movie theater Jacqueline Susann's *The Love Machine* was playing, and the kiosk in front of the theater displayed Spanish versions of *Reader's Digest* and a selection of comic books, including Woody the Woodpecker (translated as the Crazy Bird), Tarzan of the Apes, Mickey Mouse, Donald Duck, Batman, and Dennis the Menace.

That evening I walked down Genova Street where the American businessmen from the Sheraton and Hilton hotels spend their evenings dancing and drinking at the nightclubs. Outside Los Incognitos, one of the clubs, an Indian woman sat on the sidewalk clutching two shivering children and a half-dozen bouquets of roses. She wore her black hair in a bun, and she kept pulling her torn blanket around the girl, who was coughing. Inside, the revelers could be heard clapping and thumping on the tables in time with the mariachi bands. Every few minutes the door would open on several halfdrunk patrons. A doorman in red cap and yellow shoulder tassels would escort the reveler down the marble steps and signal for a taxi. Each time, the Indian woman would get to her feet and edge into the canopy's floodlights, holding the rose boquets. Most of the patrone simply looked past her. Once she got into the path of a departing couple. The man pushed his date ahead of him and stepped around the stooped Indian, giving her one of these kindly, phony smiles with the sides of his mouth pulled up, as if to tell her he took her supplications as just a good joke between old friends.

The poor are undoubtedly worse off in some other Latin American countries. I've seen thirteen-year-old prostitutes in Guatemala and children in Ecuador and Nicaragua with stomachs distended from malnutrition. But I couldn't help thinking how life would be for that Indian woman in Cuba. She wouldn't be assured of all the civil liberties of a Jeffersonian democracy. Nonetheless, she would be spared some of her problems. She would be entitled to a decent job. Her children would be enrolled in day-care centers or schools. They wouldn't be wearing rags, and they wouldn't have to worry about getting enough to eat. And if their mother went to a nightclub, she would go to revel, not to sit outside on the sidewalk.[2]

Since the Cuban experiment remains unfinished, any judgment of it would be premature. Within Cuban history it seems to be the continuation of the movement begun in 1895 and thwarted in 1933 but codified in the Constitution of 1940. Within the larger confines of the development of Latin America, one might make the preliminary assessment that this Revolution is one more attempt by Latin Americans to challenge and change the institutions of the past in an effort to accelerate modernization, to unchain themselves from a colonial heritage of dependency and propel themselves into the twentieth century. Certainly it is the most radical experiment with change to date. For the first time in the Western Hemisphere, a revolution

[2]Joe Nicholson, Jr., *Inside Cuba* (New York: Sheed and Ward), 1974). Originally published in *Harper's Magazine*, April 1973. Reprinted by permission of the author.

has been put through in the name of socialism. Scarcely any of the prerevolutionary institutions remain and much of the prerevolutionary privileged class is gone and without ready access to power. Cuba thus provides an example of socialist solutions to the old problems that beset Latin America.

NICARAGUA

The dominant reality of twentieth-century Nicaraguan history has been the lack of opportunity the Nicaraguan people have had to govern themselves. The United States intervened in 1909 to overthrow President José Santos Zelaya and occupied the country, with some brief interruptions, until early 1933, a period characterized by the disintegration of both the state and the economy. During its final years of occupation, the United States created the Guardia Nacional and appointed as its commander Anastasio Somoza. The maintenance of order and stability were the primary duties of the Guardia, and it had received the training, financing, and equipment to fulfill them. The Somoza dynasty, the father and two sons, ruled from the mid-1930s until 1979. One wry political scientist termed the Somoza rule as "government by kleptocracy." The family robbed everyting it could put its hands on. By 1979, the Somozas owned 20 percent of the arable land (the best lands with good soil and ready access to roads, railroads, and ports); the national airline; the national maritime fleet; and a lion's share of the nation's businesses and industries. The Somoza hand never left the national coffers; the once economically modest family built up accounts in foreign banks that in time ranked it among the world's wealthiest. The Somozas were loyal only to the Guardia, a small coterie of relatives and members of the old elite, who supported the regime, and the United States. Nicaragua's voting record in both the Organization of the American States and the United Nations, for example, conformed 100 percent with that of the United States. During the long Somoza decades, the Nicaraguan people exercised neither political power nor influence, and the Guardia dealt swiftly and brutally with anyone courageous or foolish enough to try. The voice of the Nicaraguans remained muted from 1909 to 1979.

An opposition group emerged in 1961 to challenge the Somozas. Its youthful leadership drew inspiration from the struggle of Augusto César Sandino against the U.S. Marines. His example and ideas guided them in the creation of the Sandinista Front for National Liberation (*Frente Sandinista de Liberación Nacional*, F.S.L.N.). The Sandinista program advocated entrusting political and economic power to the people; agrarian reform; national unity; emancipation of women; the establishment of social justice; and an independent foreign policy. The struggle of the Sandinistas against the well-armed and trained Guardia Nacional proved to be long and bloody. Determination sustained them; the greed, corruption, and brutality of the Somozas were their effective allies. By the late 1970s, even the small but potent middle class and members of the tiny elite joined the opposition to the third dynastic dictator, Anastasio Somoza, Jr., whose military arsenal could no longer repel popular wrath. The Guardia, and thus the government, collapsed in mid-July 1979, and the victorious rebels led by the FSLN entered Managua triumphantly on July 19.

The challenge of reconstruction surpassed even the task of overthrowing the Somozas. The victors inherited an economy in shambles. Somoza had bombed the cities and industries. War damages amounted to approximately $2 billion; 40,000 were dead (1.5 percent of the population); 100,000 wounded, 40,000 children orphaned; 200,000 families without homes. The national treasury was empty; the foreign debt exceeded $1.6 billion. Add to these woes the reality of a debased population and an underdeveloped country; 52 percent of the population was illiterate; life expectancy was slightly more than 53 years; infant mortality was 123 per 1,000 live births; malnourishment plagued 75 percent of the children.

During the early months after the victory, a wide variety of political groups supported and participated in the revolution. However, as the realization dawned on some of the representatives of the middle and upper classes that the revolution had been made by the peasants and workers and was to benefit them, they withdrew their cooperation and became critical, some even hostile. Such behavior followed the classic model of revolutions. United to overthrow a common enemy, a heterogeneous group brings about the final victory. Later, the temporary alliance disintegrates as some realize that their own interests will not be served by revolutionary change. As a last resort, the disaffected try to stop the revolution by force, more often than not allying themselves with some sympathetic foreign power in order to enhance their strength. Events in Nicaragua followed that predictable pattern.

The Roman Catholic Church split in its support of the revolution. The Nicaraguan Church had taken a stand against Somoza and, finally, in favor of armed resistance to him. Thus, the religious hierarchy gave its blessings to the revolution, an extremely unusual position for the Church in Latin America. Many priests participated in the revolution, and a few still hold high office, including cabinet posts, in the Sandinista government. Liberation theology played an active role in the overthrow of the Somoza dynasty and contributes to Sandinista ideology. The revolution, according to those theologians, embraces three Christian-related principles: satisfaction of basic needs through a new economic development model; broad popular participation; and the emergence of a new consciousness, a new dimension of human awareness and justice. As the hierarchy of the Church became uncomfortable with the revolutionary process, perhaps fearful of losing some of its own power and authority (in particular to the so-called "popular Church" based on liberation theology), the archbishop and bish-

After the revolution, Nicaragua's two medical schools vastly increased enrollments. More than half the students are female. This second-year class is studying microbiology in the Faculty of Medicine, the National University, Managua, 1984.

ops sought to distance themselves from it. Yet, many priests and religious through the Christian base communities and the popular Church maintain close ties with the revolution. A papal visit to Managua in 1983 widened rather than bridged the growing split in the Church.

The government embarked on an ambitious program to improve the quality of life of the majority. A literacy campaign in 1980 reduced illiteracy from 52 to 12 percent. Following up that campaign, the government doubled the number of schools in four years, quintupled the number of public libraries, and made education free from preschool through graduate studies. In 1988, more than a million Nicaraguans (40 percent of the population) were studying. Attention focused on expanded health care. Nicaragua eliminated measles, diphtheria, and polio, diseases that once took a heavy toll among children. Clinics and hospitals sprang up in the countryside and in small towns. The number of health centers multiplied from twenty-six to ninety-nine. Infant mortality fell 50 percent. Despite the shortage of medicine, medical equipment, and physicians, health-care delivery was so impressive that the World Health Organization cited Nicaragua in 1983 as a model nation. A proper diet further explains the improving health of Nicaraguans. Caloric intake has risen because more basic foods are now available to larger numbers of people.

One of the three founders of the FSLN, Carlos Fonseca, had vowed, "In Nicaragua, no peasant will be without land, nor land without people to work it." A far-reaching agrarian reform law based on Sandino's hopes, Fonseca's promise, and global experiences with rural restructuring was promulgated in 1981. It provides land for anyone who wants it and will work it. As the largest nation in Central America, Nicaragua (54,864 square miles) has more than enough land for its relatively small population (3.2 million). The principal goal of the reform is to put the land into use so that Nicaragua can both feed itself and export crops for needed foreign exchange. For six years, the government distributed only land that once belonged to the Somozas or their closest allies, abandoned lands, and unused lands. On January 11, 1986, after successfully distributing nearly 5 million acres of land to 83,000 families, the government made significant changes in the Agrarian Reform Law, permitting the expropriation of any unused land without compensation and, indeed, of any land needed for the goal of assuring anyone who wants to farm access to land. For the first time the government began to distribute lands already in production in areas where rural workers demanded land. At the same time, the government continued to guarantee the right to private property, and as of 1987, the majority of the land remained in private hands.

In redistributing the land, preference is given to those willing to organize themselves into cooperatives. The government prefers cooperatives because it is easier to provide them with services: clinics, schools, child-care centers, credit, machinery, etc. Also, they are considered to be more efficient producers. Nonetheless, individual land titles are also given. While the land is free, it cannot be sold or alienated, in order to prevent future

The revolutionary goverment quintupled the number of public libraries in Nicaragua between 1980 and 1984. This photo depicts the public library of Bluefields, 1983.

Grade school children line up outside a medical clinic in a workingclass suburb of Managua for their biannual health checkup, 1984. Fully 50 percent of Nicaragua's population is under 16 years of age. They are the primary beneficiaries of the revolution.

land concentration. While land titles can be inherited, the land cannot be divided among heirs, in order to avert the problems of minifundia.

Within this revolution, Nicaraguans looked into themselves to rediscover their own roots and were busy expressing them in music, dance, a resurgence of folk arts, painting, and poetry. Nicaragua is a land of poets, and the Popular Poetry Workshops sprung up in barracks, factories, cooperatives, and neighborhoods.

Nationalism, socialism, and Christianity converge in Nicaragua to of-

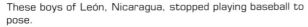

These boys of León, Nicaragua, stopped playing baseball to pose.

fer on a modest scale one model of change for the Third World. The model has attracted international attention because it addresses the major concerns of most of the world's population. It challenges dependency, pursues economic development, embraces human dignity, and seeks social justice. After all, the access to land, the availability of health care, and the education that the revolution provides the Nicaraguan people are the very benefits that most of the people of the Third World crave.

Thus, in the final half of the twentieth century, Nicaragua enacted the drama of the Third World. One Nicaraguan revolutionary, Bayardo Arce, captured that reality when he asked:

> Isn't the true threat of what is happening in Nicaragua and Central America that the small, poor, underdeveloped countries are offering a new term of reference to all of the Third World? How are the new social changes made that are needed by two-thirds of humanity so as to reach a minimum level of life and survival, while at the same time retrieving the dignity, respect, and self-determination that as independent nations our peoples are demanding now at the end of the twentieth century? These questions are not rhetorical. They attempt to raise a whole problematic: what we have called a challenge for the peoples of Europe, for the international community and its institutions, and very particularly for the North American people.

In the eyes of the majority of the planet's population comprising the Third World, Nicaragua represents the dynamic of change.

In the eyes of Washington, however, it represents the dynamic of challenge. The revolution, the rhetoric of the Sandinista government, and a nonaligned foreign policy annoy Washington. The U.S. government expressed deep suspicions of the socialist inclinations of the Sandinistas, fearful that Managua might become a focal point for the "destabilization" of the rest of Central America, too friendly with Havana and Moscow, a security threat to the Panama Canal and to the United States itself.

Washington allied itself with the remnants of the discredited National Guard, the dispossessed elite, and members of the frightened middle class to terminate the revolution and drive the Sandinistas from power. That profound changes alienated many Nicaraguans at all social levels was not an uncommon trend in any revolutionary history. That challenge angered the metropolis was no less uncommon.

The CIA financed, trained, and armed counterrevolutionaries. They invaded Nicaragua as early as November 1979, from Honduras and later from Costa Rica. The war, intensified after 1984, brought destruction and death to Nicaragua. In 1984, the CIA mined the harbors of Nicaragua in violation of international law, drawing the outrage and condemnation of the international community. In 1985, President Ronald Reagan, an implacable foe of the revolution, imposed a trade embargo on Nicaragua. With an annual budget of less than $2 billion dollars, Managua tried to meet the goals of the revolution while fighting a war against the surrogates of the most powerful nation in the world. The war plunged Nicaragua into multiple crises. It deflected funds and people from development projects, although it also has strengthened the unity, determination, and resolve of the Nicaraguan people.

On July 19, 1989, the Nicaraguans celebrated the tenth anniversary of the triumph of their revolution. They have made, taking into consideration their limited resources, the hostility of the United States, and the disastrous contra war, impressive strides toward development. The quality of life for the workers and peasants has improved; the new social statistics for Nicaragua stand in marked contrast to the dismally declining ones for Guatemala, El Salvador, Honduras, and even, sadly enough, Costa Rica. Nicaraguans clearly manifest a new pride in themselves and profess great hopes for the future. Undeniably, the opposition from the United States has greatly complicated the efforts of the Nicaraguans to carry out the goals of their revolution.

Five nations—Mexico, Guatemala, Bolivia, Cuba, and Nicaragua—underwent violent revolutions in the twentieth century and tried extreme solutions for nagging national problems. Similarities characterize the five revolutions (although notable differences also distinguish each from the others). All five of the revolutions had in common a desire to modify or eradicate hoary institutions considered incompatible with the drive for modernization. All recognized the importance of land reform in the restructuring of society and set about to radically change the ownership patterns. All were manifestations of intense nationalism. All involved the participation of the masses. All accelerated efforts to educate the masses. All favored one or another form of socialism. All hoped to increase their economic viability and the independence of their nations. All favored greater industrialization. All removed from power—at least temporarily—representatives of the old oligarchy. Revolution was the most extreme effort of the Latin Americans to bring about change.

The fates of the five revolutions varied. The Mexican Revolution seemed to be succeeding until it grew rigid and conservative after 1940. The Guatemalan Revolution was first halted and then reversed. The Bolivian Revolution accomplished much in its first years, grew increasingly timid after 1956, and expired with the military coup d'état in 1964. The Cuban and Nicaraguan revolutions continue.

The United States reacted unsympathetically to four of the five revolutions. It took nearly three decades for Washington to reconcile itself to the new turn of events in Mexico. Washington steadfastly opposed the Guatemalan and Cuban revolutions. In alliance with Guatemalan dissidents, the CIA succeeded in ending the Guatemalan experiment, and in cooperation with Cuban exiles, the CIA—perhaps with its Central American success in mind—later tried (at least once) to remove Castro and blunt the Cuban

Revolution. Thus far, its efforts have failed. The United States armed, trained, and financed the Nicaraguan counterrevolutionaries; mined the Nicaraguan harbors; and brought economic pressure to bear on Nicaragua. The impoverished Nicaraguans withstood but only at great expense to their aspiration for development. Only the Bolivian Revolution received support from the United States, and that aid went to the moderate wing that eventually came to dominate and then to blunt the revolutionary process. Such a record doubtless reflects a nervous metropolis fearful of any change in or challenge from its client states.

10

The Enigma Remains

A political rally in support of President Salvador Allende, 1973, Santiago, Chile

From the vantage point of the present, we survey the Latin American past and contemplate its future. There is much to admire; the blending of races and cultures to create unique civilizations; the beauty of the lands; the talents of the peoples; intellectual achievements such as the brilliant twentieth-century literature of Jorge Amado, Gabriela Mistral, Carlos Fuentes, Gabriel García Márquez, Pablo Neruda, and Jorge Luis Borges; the enviable ability to settle international disputes peacefully; among other things. In our effort to better understand Latin America, major questions confront us: Why has growth predominated and development been minimal? Why does dependency tend to deepen rather than recede? How can the quality of life for the majority be improved? What is the best role for the United States to play in Latin America, and how does a knowledge of the past help us prepare for it? In considering these difficult questions, it might be useful to recall a pertinent historical judgment made by Will and Ariel Durant, authors of the widely acclaimed, multivolume historical survey, *The Story of Civilization*. They capped their long and productive careers with a slender tome based upon their joint observations of the past. Entitled *The Lessons of History*, it observed, "When the group or a civilization declines, it is through no mystic limitations of a corporate life, but through the failure of its political or intellectual leaders to meet the challenges of change." Surely, a major aspect of Latin America's future will be an intensification of such challenges of change.

THE FRAGILITY OF DEMOCRATIC REFORM

Democracy in Latin America has proven to be very fragile and ineffectual. Democratic government (or for that matter the authoritarian governments of the past) has demonstrated scant capacity to develop Latin America, to alter the traditional patterns of the past, or to propel Latin America into the future. One of the most striking characteristics from the early 1960s onward was a growing disillusionment with democracy. By 1975, three-fourths of the Latin American governments were frank dictatorships. Right and left and many with political preferences between the two extremes have despaired of seeing their nation's problems solved through the democratic process. Brazil's military rulers since 1964 have regularly blamed democracy for the nation's ills. In 1970, Minister of Education Jarbas Passarinho asked, "How can we speak of democracy when four out of five of our people are practically outside the economy?" Indeed, who can read Josué de Castro's moving *Death in the Northeast* and conclude that democracy has ever worked in Brazil? The author affirmed that democracy has served to preserve "abstract principles and existing systems of advantages"; it has not provided "the basic domestic reforms," most needed of which would be land reform. Another group in another region of Latin America, the Guatemalan guerrillas, espoused a political position favoring extreme socialist revolution and refused to participate in any democratic process of elections or compromises with the government. The failure of democracy to solve Guatemala's pressing problems has embittered the youth. Guerrilla movements sprang up throughout Latin America in the 1960s, angrily demanding the reforms that democracy has never enacted. Colombia, a nation with a reasonably good democratic record in the past forty years, has been the scene of guerrilla warfare for the same period of time. In 1930–31, armed groups appeared in the mountains demanding an agrarian reform. The most popular guerrilla leader in modern Colombia, a priest named Camilo Torres, advocated in 1965 an extremely radical program: the nationalization of all natural resources, the expropriation without indemnification of all large estates, higher wages for the workers, and a popular government. Those demands typified the programs of most of the guerrilla groups.

Probably one of the most surprising converts from democracy in recent times was Juan Bosch, long a favorite of the liberal democrats. He ranked as one of the leading intellectuals fighting the brutal regime of General Rafael Trujillo—who terrorized the Dominican Republic for thirty-one years—and advocating democratic government for the progress and well-being of his country. In 1962, following the assassination of Trujillo, Bosch ran for the presidency and won, becoming the first democratically elected president to take office in his country in over three decades. The Kennedy administration welcomed the new government as "Democracy in the Caribbean." Seven months after Bosch's inauguration, the old-line Trujillo military overthrew him, revealing a not uncommon and quite convenient confusion in the minds of the oligarchy of "democracy" and "communism." At the time the United States took no action. However, three years later, when civilian and military supporters tried force to return Bosch to power, President Lyndon Johnson, labeling as "communism" what his predecessor had termed "Democracy in the Caribbean," dispatched 23,000 troops to that unhappy country. The intervention facilitated the rise to power of Joaquín Balaguer, longtime aide and confidant of the discredited Trujillo. The maneuvers showed Bosch "the real face of the United States," to use his own words.

Returning to his homeland in 1969, after four years in exile, Bosch was no longer the democrat he had always been. Apparently bitter experience and deeper reflection had brought him to new conclusions. He stated,

Representative democracy cannot work in a country such as the Dominican Republic. It has served to maintain the privileges of a minority of property and wealth, and it has not provided the stability, personal safety, health care, and education that the majority want.

Representative democracy has been a failure in Latin America for more than 150 years. It cannot guarantee true equality for all men, since it is a fundamentally unjust sociopolitical system which is organized and sustained by the principle that there are men who have a right to exploit and that there are others whose duty it is to allow themselves to be exploited.

In the place of the democracy he once had supported so enthusiastically, he advocates a "dictatorship with popular support," one with a socialist orientation. He sees a popular dictatorship as the only way to destroy some formidable institutions that he believes have prohibited Latin America's development. His popular dictatorship would reform the landowning structure by breaking up large, idle estates, draft and implement a master plan for development through diversification of the economy and industrialization, and nationalize all large companies whether foreign or domestic. He foresees support for such a popular dictatorship from the impoverished masses, the bourgeoisie, which has more to gain from such a government than from association with the traditional oligarchy, the part of the hierarchy of the Roman Catholic Church increasingly concerned with the plight of the poor, and those military officers who desire to see their nation reformed and strengthened. His conversion from supporting a reform-oriented democracy to advocating radical change by means of a populist dictatorship indicates a trend among large numbers of Latin Americans disturbed by the dilatory nature of their democracies and eager for economic development and independence, agrarian reform, state ownership of natural resources, popular government, and a greater valuation of the individual.

For many decades, students of Latin American affairs pointed to the middle class as the major hope for growth of Latin American democracy. They further reasoned that a vigorous democracy would bring about the changes so desperately needed in the Latin American societies. Time has more than proved them wrong. The middle class has more commitment to its economic well-being than to democratic theory and practice and is downright fearful of any change. So long as the middle classes controlled the democratic machinery and operated it for their own benefit they proved to be staunch democrats. However, once larger numbers of the population began to participate in the democratic process and came to dominate it, the middle classes did not hesitate to abandon it. Threats of real reform caused the Brazilian middle class to urge the military to intervene in 1964 to jettison the democratic experiment and institute a dictatorship favorable to the bourgeoisie. The Brazilian experience illustrated a wider trend in Latin America, by no means limited to the 1960s.

The bitterest blows to the promises some hoped to find in democracy came in Uruguay and Chile. Uruguay long had been judged the Latin American bastion of reform and democracy, a kind of middle-class paradise, thanks largely to the changes brought about by José Batlle. Commendable as his reforms were, they did not touch the essence of the economy: land monopoly and overdependence on the export sector. When events after the mid-1950s shook and crumbled the foundations of the economy, the edifice of democracy came crashing down. Between 1955 and 1970, the GNP declined 16 percent, while inflation rose 9,000 percent. Uruguay witnessed the worst inflation and the poorest economic performance in Latin America. The cost of living reached a peak that wages could not hope to equal. The complex causation of this disaster had its roots in the countryside. The land provided Uruguay's wealth, but it was used inefficiently. Uruguayan prosperity depended on wool and beef exports, but Uruguayan producers made a poor international showing: a sheep in Uruguay provided 2.9 kilos of wool as compared to 4.5 for one in New Zealand; it took 27 Uruguayan cattle to provide one ton of beef, whereas in the Netherlands it took only 13. As the population of Uruguay increased in the twentieth century, agricultural production declined proportionately. The weakening agrarian sector undermined industrialization.

The classes suffering most responded. They formed the Movement for National Liberation, more popularly known as the Tupamaros, in the early 1960s. By 1968 it was a national force with a program advocating land reform, socialization of the industry, and expropriation of foreign-owned banks, businesses, and industries. In the 1971 presidential elections, the Tupamaro candidate lost by 10,000 votes in an election in which over 1.5 million voted. The new government relied heavily on the military to maintain order in an increasingly restive nation. As the economy continued to deteriorate, the Tupamaros raised their demands; the level of violence escalated; the frightened middle class swung more to favor order and the status quo over reform; the government proved its ineffectiveness; and the military played a more important role in its determination to maintain order at any price. Finally, in 1973, the military overthrew the government. They intervened at the request of the wealthy and middle classes. The generals then imposed one of the most brutal dictatorships in Latin America. To raise one's voice in criticism of their behavior was to risk being charged with an "attack on the moral strength of the Armed Forces." In 1979, fully 1 percent of all Uruguayans were political prisoners. Uruguay jailed the highest number of political prisoners per capita in the entire world. Further, another half million of the four million inhabitants were in exile. Uruguay, for half a century the model of democracy and reform in Latin America, had been reduced to a shameless dictatorship devoid of any freedom, reform, or hope.

At the same time, events in another "model deocracy," Chile, followed an all to familiar course. There, too, the middle class demonstrated an equal distaste for democracy in late 1973. A combination of increased participation of the lower classes in politics, the declining economic position of the poor, and disillusion with the failure of President Eduardo Frei to bring about reforms during his 1964–70 administration brought Salvador Allende to the presidency in the hotly contested elections of 1970. The aim of the Popular Unity (*Unidad Popular*) government headed by Allende was to transform Chile from a capitalist and dependent society into a socialist and independent one and to do so gradually within the democratic and constitutional framework of the nation.

From the start, Washington vehemently opposed Allende. So did the transnational corporations, such as IT&T, with operations in Chile. As early as September 1970, President Richard Nixon commanded the CIA to rid Chile of Allende. The CIA headquarters cabled its station chief in Santiago on October 16, 1970, "It is firm and continuing policy that Allende be overthrown by a coup. . . . We are to continue to generate maximum pressure toward this end utilizing every appropriate resource." The U.S. efforts, first to thwart the election of Allende, then to prevent his inauguration, and finally to destabilize and overthrow his government, are a study in the intimate relationship of multinational corporations, the State Department, and the CIA working together with the common goal of intervening in the political affairs of a Latin American nation.

Once in office, President Allende, with the overwhelming support of Congress, nationalized the foreign-owned copper industry, which produced three-quarters of the value of all Chile's exports. He accelerated agrarian reform, distributing during his first year in office more land than the Frei government had in six years. The government bought control of most of the nation's banks. Allende paid most attention to improving the living conditions of the poor. Salaries rose and real buying power increased. Unemployment dropped sharply. The government rechanneled distribution to favor the underprivileged. These changes took place within a democratic framework; all liberties were respected.

The shifting balance of power frightened the middle class, which was unaccustomed to sharing the nation's political decision making or its limited resources with the poor. Allying with the traditional elite, the middle class refused any cooperation with the Allende government and initiated a series of crippling strikes, the most disabling of which was that of the truck owners, who were covertly financed by CIA money. The *New York Times* reported on October 21, 1972, that the confrontation between the government and its opponents "has begun to take on the character of a class struggle," a conclusion confirmed by the language of both sides. In the meantime, the international banks and the U.S. government had cut loans and aid to the Allende government to a trickle, thus adding to the economic stress created by middle-class strikes. Similar to the events in Brazil in 1964 and in Uruguay earlier in 1973, the middle class persuaded the military to intervene. On September 11, 1973, air force planes bombed the presidential palace, where President Allende died while defending his government. The military fastened on Chile one of the bloodiest dictatorships ever to emerge in Latin America. It murdered, tortured, and imprisoned hundreds of thousands of Chileans, abolished all liberties, canceled the constitution, and terminated all democratic experiments. It then returned to the original owners many of the lands expropriated and distributed by Allende to the landless as well as 800 businesses and industries that the government had nationalized. Indeed, the military even permitted one of the major expropriated copper companies, Anaconda, to return to mine copper again. Above all, the military dictatorship determined to punish the working class. It extended the workweek from forty-four to forty-eight hours without extra pay, canceled wage raises promised by Allende, abolished the unions, and ended the distribution of products to the poorest districts at lower prices. Unemployment soared. Prices rose at rates unknown even in the most inflation-prone Latin American countries, and the purchasing power of the working class plummeted.

Democracy, freedom, and reform in Latin America suffered a staggering blow in Chile on September 11, 1973. Events there, coupled with those in Uruguay and Brazil, indicated that the middle class has no commitment to either democracy or change. The arguments for democracy in Latin America now seem more hopelessly idealistic than ever, as does the case for reform. They simply have no historical support. The Chilean tragedy substantiates the case put forth by Juan Bosch that only a popular dictatorship will be able to bring about any real change to benefit the majority of the Latin Americans. No evidence exists that democratic governments can bring about the basic reforms that Latin America so desperately needs. Sadly, democracy has become a guise to preserve the status quo.

MILITARY MODELS FOR CHANGE

The revolutionaries have had their opportunities to effect change; the reformers, theirs. With the exceptions of Cuba and Nicaragua, all have failed to institute development, to solve the major national problems. The military also has taken its turn to solve the problems besetting modern Latin America. It, too, has paid homage—some, more cynical perhaps, might say lip service—to the concept of development. Since the wars for independence, the Latin American military has played a significant role in shaping the destiny of each nation. An extremely expensive institution, the military has absorbed large portions of national budgets that could have been more fruitfully invested in development. Further, the officers have made far-reaching economic decisions for their nations, which over time have determined the extent of growth and/or development or the lack thereof. The best-organized and best-disciplined civil institution, the armed forces have repeatedly broadened their traditional role from defender of the nation and guarantor of public order to alternate governments in power and more often than not to the exercise of political power itself. Certainly they represent and advance their own corporate interests, but they do not act alone or in a vacuum. They have been a part—significant because of their physical strength—of larger, more intricate political maneuvering.

On balance, rightly or wrongly, the military has not enjoyed a savory reputation in the twentieth century, perhaps because examples of its misbehavior linger longer in the public mind than its acts of benevolence. Some military officers on occasion committed acts that at least superficially seem antinational: The Ecuadoran air force in cooperation with the CIA overthrew the constitutional government in 1961 in order to replace its semi-independent foreign policy with one more complementary to the goals of the United States. The Brazilian generals in the period after 1964 sold national companies to foreigners and opened the doors to greater foreign investment and hence deepened dependency. Military officers have been exposed as corruptible and venal: Colonel Oswaldo López Arellano, while president of Honduras (he had overthrown the democratically elected, liberal government), accepted a $1.25 million bribe from United Brands (formerly the United Fruit Company) to reduce the export tax on bananas by fifty cents a forty-pound box in 1974, thereby saving United Brands $7.5 million. The military bombardment of the presidential palace in Santiago, Chile, in 1973, and the consequent death of the constitutionally elected president, Salvador Allende, repelled the civilized mind just as did the repeated accounts of torture applied to political prisoners by the military in Chile, Brazil, and Uruguay. Increasingly the military has become associated with contraband trade and particularly with drug trafficking. The higher-ranking officers of the military of Paraguay, Bolivia, Panama, Honduras, and Haiti seem most tainted with these charges.

By and large, the military have been associated with the maintenance of the status quo, and they have served as the armed agents of the middle and upper classes. Several excellent films reveal and depict them in that role. The brilliant Argentine film *La Patagonia Rebelde* (Rebellious Patagonia, 1974) showed the army allied with the large landlords in 1920 to brutally suppress a strike of farm laborers who barely eked out a living. An equally gripping historical film from Bolivia, *El Coraje del Pueblo* (Courage of the People, 1971), detailed the massacre of miners by soldiers that took place in a remote area of Bolivia in 1967. Powerful novels of the 1980s, of which Manlio Argueta's *One Day of Life* and Victor Montejo's *Testimony: Death of a Guatemalan Village*, are masterpieces, detail the brutal treatment of the rural poor by the military.

Rare have been the military interventions into political life to precipitate change. Yet, they have occurred. Both Juan D. Perón and Jacobo Arbenz, contemporaries in power in the mid-twentieth century, were army colonels. They drew support from popular sectors of society and to varying degrees benefited them. The years 1968–74 framed a curious period in which military leaders in such diverse nations as Peru, Panama, Bolivia,

Ecuador, and Honduras manifested broad social concerns. They called for increased national autonomy, the diversification of international trading partners and sources of credit, a more independent foreign policy, and land reforms. Some nationalized foreign businesses.

In the 1960s two distinct military governments took power in South America, one in Brazil and the other in Peru. They offered contrasting philosphies for change and became, at least for a time, military models closely scrutinized by other Latin Americans.

When the Brazilian middle class and elite summoned the soldiers from their barracks in 1964, the soldiers responded with alacrity and sent the democratic and constitutional president, João Goulart, into exile on April 1. The five generals who then ruled successively followed the same policies, thus making it possible to speak of those years (1964–85) as a continuum. They highly concentrated all power, while at the same time

Brazil

depoliticizing the people and repressing every form of freedom and liberty. Economically they concentrated on controlling inflation and accelerating the growth rate. A brutal dictatorship, their political model offered little of novelty, except perhaps its efficiency. However, the phenomenal economic growth of Brazil during the years 1969–74, which witnessed annual growth rates averaging about 10 percent, attracted considerable admiration and much envy throughout the rest of Latin America. For that reason, Brazil seemed to offer a worthy model to many.

The military officers strengthened the capitalistic institutions that had become traditional over the centuries. They made no effort to alter the iniquitous rural land structure. As a matter of fact, after 1964 the large estates tended to grow both in size and inefficiency. Foreign investment basking under the sun of official approval rose and not surprisingly dependency deepened. To consider Brazil during those years as a model for "development," as many did, revealed a semantic confusion. Brazil recorded a remarkable growth, a quantitative increase, without a realization of the nation's vast potential for improvement in the lot of the majority of its inhabitants. Further, economic growth concentrated in the consumer industries demanded by the privileged classes centered on a small geographical area, the Southeast, which contained less than one-fifth of the national territory, although about one-third of the population. But there the middle and upper classes concentrated. Absorbing most of the investments, the more dynamic Southeast exerted a kind of "internal colonialism" over the rest of the nation.

Like so many Latin Americans, the Brazilian generals believed in the panacea of industrialization as the solution to most national problems, even though planners had become increasingly skeptical of the "magic solutions" attributed to it, particularly that variety of industrialization based on consumer items. And Brazilian industrialization focused largely on the production of consumer goods. Scant evidence exists to suggest that the drive toward industrialization remedied any of the traditional economic disparities. In fact, the United Nations' Economic Commission for Latin America concluded in 1970 that the region's industrialization "led to an accentuation of the initial disparities and, as a result, of the discordances in the economy as a whole." The rapid Brazilian industrialization proceeded without a commensurate increase in the purchasing power of the population. It thus led to a new form of dependency: the necessity of exporting the manufactured goods in order to operate the factories and to maintain prosperity. While the accelerating industrialization process marked a shift from the traditional agro-extractive primary production, it by no means was either an index of real internal development or an index of reduced dependency. Meanwhile, neglect of the inefficient agricultural system meant that food prices were disproportionately high, forcing potential customers to spend more of their income on food rather than buy manufactured items. The

Brazilian situation offered a thoughtful study of the problems in imposing industrialization on antiquated agrarian structures.

The economic record of the military governments has been one of a rising GNP. Pursuit of an ever higher GNP is never a search for social objectives but a blind chase of numbers that can be expanded to infinity without much social value resulting. Brazil, in fact, provides the perfect example of an upwardly spiraling GNP without much development or resultant social benefits. To complicate matters for the military, the economic growth rate faltered by 1975 and began a sharp decline.

The generals and their apologists have spoken glowingly of an economic "miracle," but the sober might ask what is miraculous about the rich getting richer. As the *Los Angeles Times* pointed out in an editorial on July 21, 1974, "Despite Brazil's impressive growth rate, the gap between the rich and the poor is wider than ever." Grim statistics support that conclusion. Of the total gain in Brazilian income during the 1964–74 period, the richest 10 percent of the population absorbed 75 percent, while the poorest 50 percent got less than 10 percent. Compounding that iniquity was a regressive tax system that put the heaviest burden on the working class.

A political record of brutality, repression, and violence accompanied the economic growth. No ray of freedom or liberty brightened Brazil between 1964 and 1978. Only those who extol the economic "miracle" or praise order have been able to express themselves without fear of reprisal. International labor and legal organizations as well as the Roman Catholic Church repeatedly condemned the practice of torturing political prisoners in the Brazilian prisons. The military government inaugurated by the coup of 1964, which U.S. Ambassador to Brazil Lincoln Gordon lauded as "the single most decisive victory for freedom in the mid-twentieth century," remained wed to terror, torture, and imprisonment for well over a decade following the overthrow of President Goulart.

In examining the years of strictest military control, 1964–1978, one fails to find much real development in either industrialization or agriculture, although, of course, the evidence of growth was overwhelming. While industrialization grew rapidly under the military, it embodied many weaknesses: a concentration on goods for the wealthy and middle class; a dependency on foreign investment, technology, and markets; a denationalization of Brazilian-owned industry; a low rate of labor absorption since it was capital intensive; ecological threats and pollution; and regressive income distribution. The accelerating industrialization process marked a shift from the traditional agro-extractive primary production, but it by no means served as an index of real internal development or of reduced dependency.

The military governments neglected agriculture. That sector of the economy grew at rates averaging 2.5 percent a year, somewhat less than the population growth, which fluctuated between 2.5 and 3 percent. Land concentration continued to characterize rural Brazil. In fact, the concentration of land ownership was one of the highest in the world. In 1988, less than 5 percent of the landowners controlled more than 66 percent of the cultivable land. More and more people depended on fewer and fewer farm workers to feed them, and there was a serious question of whether or not that declining number had the wherewithal or efficiency to fulfill its responsibility. Although Brazil ranked as the world's fifth largest exporter of agricultural products in 1978, nearly 60 percent of the population suffered from an insufficient diet. In 1980, Brazil had to import more than $1.8 billion worth of food. Statistics from the Brazilian government itself in 1984 estimated that 64 percent of the population was undernourished.

The problems intensified. Inflation continued to plague Brazil. By 1984, inflation exceeded an annual rate of 230 percent. Ironically that rate surpassed the figures of the Goulart years, and, after all, the "uncontrollable" inflation of those years had provided the military with a primary motive for intervention in politics, the destruction of democracy, and the establishment of a dictatorship. The rising cost of imported oil dealt the economy a staggering blow. Mounting fuel costs drove Brazil ever deeper into debt. In 1988, the government owed international banks nearly $120 billion. President João Figueiredo reminded the nation in mid-1983, "The moment is critical, the economy is very sick. I ask each Brazilian to understand the importance and the necessity of his sacrifice." He then proceeded to cut back salaries to 80 percent of the cost-of-living index. To close an unfavorable balance of trade as well as to meet the interest payments, the government encouraged the increase of exports. One means to achieve that goal was to intensify the exploitation of the Amazon.

The acceleration of road building in the Amazon and the more intensive use of the land for agriculture and lumbering were upsetting the delicate ecology of that vast region. Roberto Burle Marx, Brazil's most internationally repsected landscape architect, warned, "Immense areas are being destroyed for pasturage and colonization schemes. These areas are being transformed into deserts because there is no precise knowledge of what to plant and what is best for the soil." At the current pace of deforestation, the Amazon rain forest, as we have known it, will disappear before the end of the century.

During the government of President Ernesto Geisel (1974–79), opposition to the military in power mounted. The Roman Catholic Church, through the leadership of people like Archbishop Helder Câmara and Cardinal Paulo Evaristo Arns, raised its voice against social injustice and demanded economic opportunities for the masses and freedom for all. Labor showed a renewed independence. In May of 1978, a strike in São Paulo involving some 50,000 workers was the first in a decade. Those workers sought higher wages, and the government responded with adjustments. The students, too, became vocal again, in 1977 they organized a number of important demonstrations. More surprising, the business community began to voice criticism. In November of that year, some 2,000 businesspeople gathered in Rio de Janeiro and called for democratic liberties, and in July of 1978 a document signed by eight wealthy industrialists advocated a more just socioeconomic system. Finally, within the ranks of the military, reform sentiment was growing, and it became increasingly difficult for the governing generals to disguise the cracks in the facade of unity they wanted to project.

Unlike his military predecessors, Geisel did not consult his colleagues in selecting a consensus candidate to replace himself in the presidency. Arbitrarily he picked General João Baptista Figueiredo, a relatively unknown figure who formerly had directed the National Intelligence Service. Assuming a six-year term presidency on March 15, 1979, President Figueiredo expressed his hope to preside over the political transition from dictatorship to democracy. He announced, "I intend to turn this country into a democracy. . . . I hold out my hand in conciliation." Action followed. Within four months he proposed an amnesty for all those who since 1964 had been accused of political crimes, had had their political rights suspended, and had been punished by arbitrary justice. In 1982, elections for state governors were held for the first time since 1965. In 1985, the government enfranchised illitarates (perhaps as many as 40 percent of the adult population) and conducted elections for the mayors of the state capitals. An electoral college selected a civilian president. Political freedoms triumphed, but "The New Republic" sailed on the stormiest of economic seas. Whether the return to a liberal democratic framework would be accompanied by any basic reforms of Brazil's inquitous institutions remained speculative, not to say dubious. No sign appeared that economic growth might promote development.

Across the continent in Peru, the military provided quite a different model, one singular in the behavior patterns of the Latin American military. The Peruvian armed forces always had buttressed the elite and contributed to the maintenance of the status quo. That country of 496,225 square miles and 18 million inhabitants offered the sharpest social contrasts. A tiny, affluent European-oriented elite ruled a vast, impoverished Indian population whose condition had deteriorated almost constantly since Pizarro conquered the Incan Empire. Feudalism—usually an overworked and much-abused word in descriptions of Latin America—perfectly characterized the relationships between the landlords and laborers in the countryside, where 1 percent of the landowners controlled 80 percent of the usable land. Indeed, one family, the Gildemeisters, owned 1.1 million acres. The military officers had become increasingly sensitive to the social, economic, and political disparities in their homeland during the early 1960s, when they found themselves called upon more frequently to protect the landed gentry from miserable rural Indians who wanted land to farm. The huge, unused tracts of the small, propertied class invited invasions from the landless Indians, and the army was expected to repel the invaders. Their social conscience disturbed, the officers, under the leadership of General Juan Velasco Alvarado, intervened in October 1968 to depose President Fernando Belaúnde Terry, a well-meaning democrat who was unable to fulfill the lofty promises he had made in the presidential campaign five years earlier.

To the astonishment of all, the military set out to change some of Peru's most traditional institutions through what the leading officers termed "a non-capitalistic, non-Communistic revolution." As the first priority, they transformed the land structure. On June 24, 1969, General Velasco issued a sweeping agrarian reform law to expropriate all holdings in excess of 375 acres. By 1978, nearly all large estates had been expropriated, a reform affecting nearly 50 percent of the land. At the same time, the government invested millions in the rural infrastructure to facilitate the changes. Large, efficient estates—such as the coastal sugar plantations, 65 percent of which were owned by U.S. companies—were not broken up but were run by the workers as cooperatives. There was not enough land for the large number of landless Indians, so the government initiated large-scale irrigation projects to bring barren lands under the plough and began to open the Amazonian hinterlands to cultivation. In contrast to the experience elsewhere in Latin America, the expropriation and reform went forward without a decline in production. To the contrary, a modest increase (it averaged 1.6 percent annually between 1969 and 1974) was registered.

Taking an active role in other aspects of the economy as well, the state controlled electric utilities and telecommunications and asserted direction over financial institutions. The military nationalized U.S. petroleum, copper, and sugar companies, although it cooperated with foreign oil companies in the drilling, extracting, and marketing of Peru's petroleum. Peru's hope to become a major oil exporter did not materialize. An apparent overestimation of reserves and an overoptimism of export potential caused the government to invest princely sums in pipelines and equipment, an investment that paid no dividends but rather drove the nation to the brink of bankruptcy. Private enterprise continued in commerce and industry. However, industries had to share their profits with workers and to gradually award them stocks until they controlled 50 percent of the ownership. Thus, industry was to be a joint worker-management enterprise.

The military emphasized Peru's Indian past and present. Some of the land returned to the old Indian communities; Tupac, Amaru, the leader of an Indian rebellion against Spanish rule in 1780–81, was selected as a national symbol and his portrait widely displayed; and in 1975, Quechua, the principal Indian language, took its place alongside Spanish as the national language, thus making Peru officially bilingual. The schools have been giving a new attention to Peru's rich Indian heritage.

Those changes occurred in an atmosphere of relative freedom. There were no reports of torture or executions. Political opposition existed and manifested disapproval of many actions taken by the government. However, the government disbanded the former principal political parties and held no elections until 1980.

In early September 1975, a bloodless coup within the military removed General Velasco from office. The radical phase of military government ended. The government of Velasco counted four major achievements to its credit: land reform, a reduction of the power of the traditional oligarchy, nationalization of major resources, and an expanded economic role of the state. Its chief weakness seems to have been that although it used radical reform rhetoric, it did not seek, nor did it receive, popular support. Neither did it completely restructure the nation. After 1975, under a moderate government, the reforms withered. Lack of government commitment condemned them to failure.

If anything, Peru's problems multiplied in the last years of the 1970s. The foreign debt reached a staggering $16 billion by 1988. Technically Peru was bankrupt. The gap between the richest and the poorest remained as wide as before, possibly even wider.

Unable to solve Peru's problems, the military resolved to retire from politics, leaving government to the civilians. In the presidential elections of early 1980, Fernando Belaúnde Terry, the very man the military had ejected from the presidency in 1968, won handsomely. In July, he returned to office to face challenges more monumental than those he had confronted in the 1960s.

After twelve years of military dictatorship, the Peruvians held out great hopes for the democratic government of President Belaúnde. He failed to realize those hopes. Declining prices for exports, a crippling debt with skyrocketing interest rates, and a poor agrarian performance lashed the economy. The 1980s witnessed a serious decline in the Peruvians' standard of living. Much to their dismay, the Peruvians discovered that free elections and a nominal democracy brought neither desired changes nor improved conditions. In the midst of the frustration, a once obscure guerrilla movement, Sendero Luminoso (Shining Path) gained new adherents and increased its activity. By the end of the 1980s, Sendero Luminoso was the most active guerrilla movement in South America and the most radical.

On the surface, the Peruvian and Brazilian military experiences contrast. The Brazilian military model strengthened the institutions inherited from the past and in doing so accentuated social, economic, and political iniquities. It fostered rapid growth with minimal development. The Peruvian model, on the other hand, attacked some of the fundamental institutions of the past, principally the land structures. Yet, on balance, both approaches strengthened an inherited capitalism, albeit in diverse ways. In both models a select few made decisions and imposed them through military force on the entire population. Both failed to generate broad support from the masses. The inescapable conclusion is that neither the Brazilian

nor the Peruvian military, despite different approaches, instituted development. On the one hand, they did not benefit the majority, while, on the
other, they eventually evoked complaints from the middle class and elites.
The models offered by those two military governments for change proved
to be less than satisfactory.

Economic failure characterized military governments throughout the
hemisphere, and everywhere they brutally suppressed freedom as they
reinforced outmoded and unjust institutions. Chile provides the most recent example of the military's political repression and economic failure.
The military government that replaced the democratic Allende government in 1973 subscribed to monetarist economic policies. Popularized by
the conservative economists of the University of Chicago, monetarism advocates minimizing governmental control over the economy, extensive budget
cuts, reduction of tariffs, and incentives for foreign investments. The Chilean government sought to end its direct participation in the economy. It
virtually dismantled social security and pension plans. Between 1977 and
1980, it balanced the budget, reduced inflation, and witnessed substantial
economic growth. In 1982, Milton Friedman, Chicago's theoretician of
monetarism, wrote, "Chile is an economic miracle."

Economic growth, however, depended largely on a substantial inflow
of foreign credit spent to finance acquisitions rather than for productive
investments, that is to import luxury items rather than to construct industries capable of manufacturing basic needs. It also depended on high prices
for copper, which alone accounted for 95 percent of export earnings. But
after 1975, the world price of copper plummeted from $1.70 per pound to
$.52 in 1982.

To many the miracle was a myth. A rising foreign debt accompanied
by falling export earnings revealed the fragility of Chile's economic growth.
In 1982, the gross national product fell 14 percent; in 1983, it dropped
another 3 percent. (Chile holds a record for the steepest drop in GNP in
Latin America.) By the mid-1980s, the economy lay in ruins. A foreign
debt, by 1988 in excess of $20 billion, gave Chile the dubious distinction of
having one of the highest per-capita debts in the world. Servicing that debt
consumed fully 80 percent of the nation's export earnings. Bankruptcies
multiplied. Unemployment soared. The *Los Angeles Times* (February 22,
1983) reported, "Businesses are going bankrupt at a record pace, the banking industry has all but collapsed, and the country is dangerously near
default on its foreign debt." The poor and the middle class felt the brunt of
the economic deterioration. Chile's Cardinal Raul Silva Enríquez observed,
"I could be wrong, but never in my life have I seen such a disastrous
economic situation." One Chilean wryly observed, "The free-market policies of the Chicago Boys destroyed more private enterprises in the past year
than the most radical sectors of Allende's coalition dreamed of nationalizing in three years; they have turned more middle-class people into proletari-

ans or unemployed than any Marxist textbook ever described." British economist Philip O'Brien labeled the Chilean economy in 1984 as a "spectacular example of private greed masquerading as a model of economic development." Although the economic experiments under the Chilean military bore the fancy name of "monetarist," they were in reality a return to older types of policies that had amply proven their inability to encourage development. Monetarist experiments further impoverished Chile.

In Argentina, the military government not only contributed to the further destruction of the economy but compounded the nation's problems by engaging in a disastrous foreign war. In April 1982, Argentina invaded the Falkland Islands, long claimed by the Argentines but held and populated by the British. The Argentine military proved as ineffective on the battlefield as it was in government. No match for the British forces, the Argentines surrendered in June. Humiliated, the military stepped down from political power and permitted democratic elections in late 1983.

The question arises whether military governments have brought any benefits to the Latin Americans or whether they serve only as barriers to change. While the elites might prosper under military rule and the preservation of outmoded institutions, the majority has not. Also, on balance, the military governments have brought few or no advantages to the middle class. Generally they have proven themselves to be inefficient, ineffective, and unimaginative governors. Every military regime has been as corrupt and venal as the civilian governments. They have been brutal in their repression of dissent. Liberties and freedoms have not fared well at their hands. They have drained the economies of scarce funds to buy military hardware. Surprisingly, they tend to be more internationalist than nationalist in their outlook. In each case, the military has inhibited or halted the drive for change. The record clearly proves that military governments have no solutions for Latin America's problems. In fact, they are a part of the problem.

DEBT AND HUNGER

By the end of the 1980s, Latin America's foreign debt exceeded a staggering $400 billion, several times the region's annual income. Most of that debt was pegged to floating interest rates that followed the U.S. prime rate. Consequently an increase of 1.5 percent in the U.S. prime interest rate in mid-1984 added about $4.5 billion to the debt. Also in 1984, Latin America's combined income from exports totaled $95 billion; interest payments amounted to $40 billion, 42 percent of the income. (These figures included only interest payments, not repayment of principal.) The proportion was even higher in Argentina, Brazil, Chile, and Mexico.

The debt morass reflected Latin America's dependency, the carelessness of governments that borrowed for questionable projects or simply misspent the money on military hardware and consumer luxuries, and the irresponsibility of international bankers who often press loans on governments, always confident that sovereign states will not default. While the first half of the 1970s witnessed fair international prices for Latin America's exports, and consequently economic growth in the region, it also signaled the rise of petroleum prices and hence the costs of imports. In the euphoria of economic growth, Latin American governments borrowed ever larger sums. In the 1970s, inflation drove down the real cost of borrowing, a powerful incentive to borrow strong money and repay it later with weak money. The bankers, flush with petrodollars, were eager to loan. Until the mid-1970s, the economic situation clearly was one of boom—but the bust followed close behind. In the last half of the seventies, prices for Latin America's primary exports dropped drastically. The governments still required loans to import petroleum and ever more costly capital goods and to finance themselves until the crisis, hoped by all to be short-lived, ended. Latin Americans continued to borrow even while their income diminished. The situation for the borrower became critical in the 1980s when low inflation and high interest rates characterized the U.S. economy. By then, the governments found it necessary to borrow just to pay the interest on prior loans. Latin America was caught in a disastrous debt cycle from which its falling income offered no exit.

The International Monetary Fund (IMF) certifies the creditworthiness of nations. States in international financial trouble find it difficult to borrow from any bank without IMF approval. To obtain that approval, they must follow the economic prescriptions of the IMF, which emphasize austerity. They are extremely conservative and include the abolition of subsidies—many Latin American governments subsidize the price of gasoline, electricity, and basic foods—the freezing of wages, and an end to public works projects. Obviously they weigh heaviest on the poor majority. The IMF inevitably recommends greater exportation and highly reduced imports. In 1984, in order to borrow internationally, the government of the Dominican Republic imposed on the nation those conditions demanded by the IMF, which included the reduction or elimination of subsidies on basic food items. The Dominican people rioted for three days, and sixty died before the army restored order. The government was able to borrow to pay interest on its debts, but the cost to the standard of living of the majority was devastating. In general, the IMF policies inhibit economic development, foment political instability, and undermine already fragile democracies. For these reasons, they make all the Latin American governments nervous. They also reinforce Latin America's dependency by emphasizing the export sector of the economy over internal development and by subordinating the debtor nations to the creditor. In effect, the Latin American nations, large and small, have mortgaged themselves to the lender nations.

The quest to repay mounting debts further emphasizes the export sector of the economy. More and more lands are converted from subsistence crops that feed local populations to export crops that earn the hard currencies to meet interest payments. In Brazil, for example, the production of soybeans and oranges for exports utilizes lands once used to grow black beans, rice, manioc root, and corn, all staples of the national diet.

The search for scarce dollars has prompted some Latin Americans to engage in or to tolerate illegal but profitable drug exports. In particular, they have found cocaine and marijuana to be highly profitable new exports. At least four nations, Colombia, Bolivia, Paraguay, and Jamaica, count drugs among their top three exports. In Colombia, for example, cocaine ranks as the second most important export, after coffee. In mid-1984, when the government made an energetic effort to crack down on narcotics, the Colombian peso dropped 30 percent in value.

For their part, the international bankers fear debt default. In 1984, both Ecuador and Bolivia unilaterally suspended their debt payments. In 1985, President Alan García of Peru announced that his country would limit debt payments to 10 percent of export earnings. That same year trade union leaders from twenty-six Latin American and Caribbean countries meeting in Havana declared the debt to be "the most glaring manifestation of present-day imperialism" and advocated no further repayment. In 1987, Brazil temporarily halted debt payments. Argentina, too showed signs of being unable to meet the economic and political costs of repayment. It had fallen behind in its interest payments. A major Latin American debt default could send shock waves through the U.S. banking community and probably precipitate a financial crisis in this country. Charles Maechling, Jr., an international lawyer, cautioned, "Today, Latin America is in the grip of a financial crisis whose potential for damaging the economy of the United States reduces the threat of subversion to insignificance."

Ironically and tragically, Latin America has become a net exporter of hard currencies, a situation greatly exacerbated by the debt crisis. Between 1982 and 1986, the net transfer from Latin America to the capitalist nations surpassed $100 billion. Thus do poverty, underdevelopment, and dependency become perpetuated.

The implications of the IMF recommendations in the long run adversely affect not just the underdeveloped countries but the developed ones as well. Constrained to cut imports, debtor nations buy less abroad. Imports from the United States fell drastically during the 1980s. That drop in sales may have cost a net loss of more than 800,000 jobs in the United States. The IMF recommendations that nations export but reduce their imports if carried to its conclusion raises the question "How can everyone sell if nobody buys?" No nation will be able simultaneously to repay its debt, grow economically, and maintain its political and social equilibrium. A solution to this threatening problem lies partly in reducing the interest rates while stretching out the length of time for repayment. However, the main solution to the debt crisis, like the solution to all the economic problems bedeviling Latin America, requires economic development. The debt crisis is but one more symptom of underdevelopment.

Underdevelopment manifests itself in a tragedy of far greater proportions than the debt: growing hunger. Today, a majority of Latin Americans literally starve. The austerity measures of the IMF deepen this unnecessary tragedy.

In 1985, about two-thirds of a Latin American population of 380 million, increasing at a rate of nearly 2.5 percent a year, were physically undernourished in one form or another. United Nations statistics reveal that fully a quarter of all Brazilian children under four years of age suffer a protein-energy deficiency, while one-third of Guatemala's children under four do. In Mexico in 1979, 100,000 children under five years of age died of malnutrition. Fifty percent of the babies are born into conditions inadequate for proper growth. Mexican children are sick an average of 55 days a year as compared to the 15 days a year an average child is sick in a developed country. The social and economic statistics readily reveal the reasons for the poor health of Mexican children. For example, in 1982, Mexico produced 5 million liters of milk less than in 1978, or sufficient milk for only 23 percent of the population. Fully 48 percent of the rural and 33 percent of the urban population in southern Brazil receive fewer than 2,250 calories per day; the figures are 75 and 63 percent respectively in northeastern Brazil. About half of Peru's children are malnourished. In Honduras, 50 percent of the rural children die before they reach their fifth birthday. Poor nourishment directly or indirectly accounts for most of those deaths. The grim reality of hunger goes beyond death to curse the living. The social toll of these alarming statistics is a population stunted in growth, with low resistence to infectious diseases, a poor physical constitution, and unsatisfactory mental development.

The tragedy of hunger is as unnecessary as it is irrational. After a visit to El Salvador in 1977, Father Timothy S. Healy, president of Georgetown University, noted the arresting contradiction: "An agricultural people . . . starve to death on rich land while they farm it." The tragedy is explicable. The land continued to be used inefficiently. For example, in the El Salvador Father Healy visited, 50 percent of the land on farms over 100 acres either lay fallow or was used as a pasture. The production of export crops rose, while basic food staples declined. As we have seen elsewhere in this book, roughly 90 percent of the land belongs to 10 percent of the landowners, a degree of concentration far greater than in any other region of comparable size. The pattern of land tenure determines the use made of land (an emphasis on export over subsistence crops) and a complexity of economic and social relations, all beneficial to the landowners.

The agrarian sector of the Latin American economy is less and less able to satisfy the needs of the population. Although it has been estimated that in the 1970s population increase and agricultural production kept pace with each other, the statistics deceive. Large amounts of agriculture went into export. A growing proportion of the cereal crop became cattle feed. In 1961–63, Latin America utilized 32 percent of the cereal grains to feed cattle; in 1972–74, the figure rose to 40 percent. In other words, the amount of grain available to feed people decreased. At the same time, one must remember that beef feeds only the wealthy, so that the majority benefited in no way from increased cattle feeding. In Brazil throughout the late 1970s and into the 1980s, ever larger amounts of land grew grains used to make an alcohol substitute for petroleum. Such production did not feed the legions of the hungry but rather propelled the automobiles of the middle class. The consequences are obvious for the poor: as more land is devoted to grain alcohol production and less to food production, food prices rise and the poor face even leaner years.

The distressing reality is that Latin Americans do not feed themselves, and none of the prescriptions of the IMF or the bankers addresses this fundamental reality. At the end of the 1970s, the United Nations Food and Agriculture Organization observed, "No Latin American nation has foregone food imports in the past eight years. . . . The maintenance of, and increase in, their food supplies is one of the main problems of most Latin American countries." With relatively limited foreign exchange reserves and low nutritional levels, El Salvador, Guatemala, Guyana, Haiti, and Honduras suffered the most difficult food shortages. Food shipments to those nations quadrupled between 1971 and 1978. During the same period, four oil-exporting nations, Ecuador, Mexico, Trinidad, and Venezuela, used their newly acquired wealth to import an ever larger percentage of their food supplies. Latin America expended 60 percent more for the importation of food in 1978 ($6.4 billion) than it had in 1971 ($4 billion). In the 1980s, the Caribbean islands imported more than $1 billion worth of food annually, spending minimally about 10 percent of income from exports to import food. Under present conditions in Latin America, there exists no justification to predict a decline or even a stabilization of these mounting food imports. If there is to be an improvement in diet and nutrition, food production will have to double. With existing institutional structures, no possibility of that increase exists.

It is a measure of Latin America's underdevelopment—its traditional propensity to grow rather than to develop—that this vast region, which must spend its hard-earned international currencies to import food to feed the population, is in reality a "net" exporter of foods, the primary exports. Latin America continues to export grains, meats, sugar, bananas, coffee, cocoa, and soybeans because the large landowners, foreign as well as domestic, earn handsome profits from such exports, more than they might earn selling food on the domestic market. It is a further measure of Latin America's underdevelopment that most of the arable land lies unused or underused.

This text must stress that Latin America is fully capable not only of feeding its own population well but also of contributing significantly to world food supplies. One must recall, as a point of comparison, that the vast and relatively populous Incan empire fed its inhabitants well and maintained large food surplus to compensate for lean years and natural disasters. That same area has been unable to do so since the Spanish conquest in the sixteenth century. In this particular case, we are challenged to understand why Incan technology, efficiency, and productivity surpassed Western technology, efficiency, and productivity, or why the Incan empire of the fifteenth century was more developed than Peru, Ecuador, and Bolivia of the twentieth century.

One probable solution to the staggering agrarian problems of contemporary Latin America is to put the unused and underused lands into the hands of the unemployed and underemployed.

The newly created peasant class could feed itself and provide surpluses for the local marketplaces. Furthermore, access to land might reduce the flow of migrants from the countryside into the already overcrowded cities. The answer sounds easy; its implementation would be difficult. The middle class and particularly the elite, who own the land partly for speculative and investment purposes, partly for profit, and partly to control the labor supply, have no intention of divesting themselves of it for the benefit of the impoverished rural masses, national development, or any other reason. It will take all the force of a strong government to alter the landholding structure in Latin America and then to sustain the new peasants with the agrarian reforms they will need. But until that agrarian reform takes place, no amount of investment, certainly no amount of rhetoric, will fundamentally alter the unjust institutions inherited from the past.

As Latin America moves through the decade of the 1990s, little evidence emerges of greater agricultural efficiency; and where the efficiency manifests itself, it usually produces for export rather than national consumption. Those oases of efficiency are capital intensive, supplanting people with machinery. Besides forcing hundreds of thousands of would-be peasants to trek to the cities, that machinery consumes gasoline, whose price has skyrocketed in all but a few privileged regions. The high cost of oil imports already has burdened Latin America with a unprecedented debt that threatens some nations with bankruptcy. Thus, mechanized agriculture is a risky and possibly even a negative answer to rural deficiencies of production.

In a few regions of Latin America, Peru and Bolivia for example, land reform has taken place in recent times. But a land reform that does not give people access to water, credit, and/or services has not been the correct answer either. It becomes increasingly clear that land reform and agrarian reform are not synonymous. The former constitutes changes in ownership; the latter includes changes in production and service structures as well, a much deeper institutional change.

The Nicaraguan land reform, with its emphasis on food production, illustrates what could be done. By 1982, corn and bean production had climbed 10 and 45 percent respectively, while rice production doubled compared to figures for 1977–78. Nicaragua stood on the threshold of food self-sufficiency. Unfortunately, attacks by counterrevolutionaries under the direction of the CIA have diverted funds from farming to defense, and farmers who should have been in the fields have had to go to the war front, thus postponing further agrarian achievements.

Current land ownership and use exemplify perfectly the prevalence of the past institutions. Furthermore, they illustrate a basic theme running the course of nearly half a millenium of Latin American history: the historical institutions contribute significantly to the creation and perpetuation of mass poverty. There seems little doubt that so long as those historical institutions predominate, poverty will remain a major characteristic of Latin America. To bring about development, basic institutional changes will be needed; although, it must be emphasized, basic institutional changes, legislated but not enforced, in law but without spirit, will not produce development.

THE CRISIS OF UNDERDEVELOPMENT: CENTRAL AMERICA

Central America serves as an exaggerated example of the crisis of underdevelopment besetting late twentieth-century Latin America. The region can be described by the classic dependent growth model, an emphasis on exports rathern than internal production, on profits rather than on wages. The economies grew but could not develop. Growth depended on highly cyclical external demand for its primary products: coffee, bananas, cotton, and beef. Any benefits from periodic growth accrued to a small portion of the population; the majority remained marginalized and voiceless in a society that was run neither by nor for them. Conservative estimates place 60 percent of the population in the impoverished category. No amount of ecnomic growth could help—or had helped—that majority achieve a satisfactory standard of living. In late 1986, in a homily during Mass at the cathedral in San Salvador, Archbishop Arturo Rivera Damas stated, "The real cause of underdevelopment is the ideological, economic, and political dependence of our countries."

With the notable exception of Costa Rica, the Central Americans have had little or no experience with democracy. Occasionally the elite and, much later, the middle class exercised the formalities of democracy for

Central America

their own enhancement, but the military always kept a sharp eye on such rare experiences and readily intervened if the ballot box suggested even a hint of social, economic, or political change in the offing. The electoral farces in Guatemala, El Salvador, Honduras, and Nicaragua in the 1960s and 1970s confirmed the traditional forces in power or served as excuses for further military intervention. To those who wanted to challenge underdevelopment, poverty, dependency, authoritarian rule, and a long catalog of social iniquities, the ballot box offered no opportunity, a realization that gave form to the guerrilla movements in Guatemala and the formation of the Sandinista Front for National Liberation in Nicaragua in the 1960s.

The economic collapse of the region in the mid-1970s detonated a social explosion. Since the end of the nineteenth century, the local economies remained intimately linked with those of the North Atlantic marketplaces. Economic recessions in the metropolises destroyed the fragile export-oriented economies of Central America. The most severe examples occurred in the 1930s and again after 1975. Prices for primary exports declined, while the need for ever more expensive imports rose. The governments borrowed abroad to bridge the gap. The economic disaster further threatened an already unstable industrialization.

The creation of a Central American Common Market in 1960 had opened a regional market able to sustain some import-substitution industries that no single Central American nation could support. Admittedly the Market had problems and weaknesses from the start. Industrialization proved to be capital intensive, therefore creating few jobs. Heavy expenditures for machinery and technology drained hard currencies. Many of the plants assembled rather than manufactured, importing component parts, putting them together, and then exporting the finished product. Such assembly plants did little for the local economy except employ a few workers at modest salaries. Foreign capital predominated. About 62 percent of all industries were in the hands of non-nationals. Unequal industrial growth characterized the Market, igniting local rivalries and jealousies. Guatemala and El Salvador boasted of the lion's share of the industrialization, to the annoyance and economic disadvantage of Honduras, Nicaragua, and Costa Rica. The 1969 "Soccer War" between El Salvador and Honduras, whose immediate cause was rivalry and riot on the soccer field but whose more fundamental causes included the Honduran fear of rising numbers of illegal Salvadoran immigrants and El Salvador's economic supremacy, destroyed the Common Market. Defeated in the "One-Hundred Hours War," Honduras refused to allow shipments of goods to or from El Salvador to cross its territory. The Common Market had not recovered from the disruptions caused by the war when the world recession of the mid-1970s sent the prices for Central America's exports into a tailspin.

Economic reverses sparked political unrest. A nervous alliance of landowners, commercial bourgeoisie, and the military forcefully repressed the protest when and where it occurred. To do so, they turned increasingly to the United States for military support to thwart rebellion.

In 1979, the revolution triumphed in Nicaragua, guerrilla warfare accelerated in Guatemala, and a coup d'etat brought liberal officers and reformers to power in El Salvador. In the official eyes of Washington, Central America had burst into the flames of subversion. Always suspicious of change in Central America, the United States viewed the new trends as a threat to both hemispheric stability and U.S. security. Disturbed by Iran's holding of U.S. hostages in 1980, the U.S. government showed no tolerance for any perceived security threat in Central America. El Salvador felt the full brunt of U.S. suspicions.

That small Central American nation represents one of the few examples in Latin America of true overpopulation. More than 6.5 million people inhabit 8,260 square miles. Thus, El Salvador has twice the population of Nicaragua packed into less than one-sixth the area. A few families traditionally owned most of the best land (roughly 2 percent of the population owned 60 percent of the 4 million acres of arable land). That minority dominated the nation's coffee and cotton economy and maintained an intimate alliance with the army. In 1932, after one of Latin America's most dramatic peasant uprisings under the intellectual inspiration of Farabundo Martí, the military dominated the Salvadoran government. Like their counterparts elsewhere, the military ruled in the name of the elites. When years of frustration came to a head over the military's rigging of the 1977 presidential elections, the nation disintegrated into civil war. A military coup staged by junior officers forced General-President Carlos Humberto Romero from power on October 15, 1979, retired senior officers, and turned the government over to a civilian-military junta.

In early 1980, the junta, even though it had become more conservative in its composition, made some serious efforts to institute reforms. It nationalized the banking system and the sale of coffee. Most significantly, on March 8, 1980 the junta promulgated Decree 153, a thorough land reform. In the first phase of the reform, the government nationalized estates exceeding 1,250 acres and turned them into cooperatives run by the workers themselves. The government promised payment in bonds to former owners. Those estates grew mainly cotton and sugar cane, although some produced coffee and raised cattle. A second phase was to have nationalized estates exceeding 375 acres, later raised to 612 acres. A third phase was intended to benefit the peasants directly. That "Land to the Tiller" phase was to have transformed renters of small plots into owners. Over 80 percent of such plots measured fewer than five acres each.

The land reform sounded good on paper, and efforts were made to implement it, but unfortunately it was not successful. Some landowners distributed their large estates among relatives and friends so that the acreages fell below the minimum affected by the reform law. Phase two never went into effect. Part of the bureaucracy, much of the military, and virtually all of the landowners obstructed the reform. Money and technicians— and, some suspect, willingness—were in short supply. Nor did the landlords meekly accept the reform decrees. They sponsored vigilante groups that received the cooperation and participation of the army in their intimidation and murder of the peasantry. Jorge Villacorta, a former undersecretary of the Ministry of Agriculture, observed, "In reality, from the first moment that the implementation of the agrarian reform began, what we saw was a sharp increase in official violence against the very peasants who were the supposed 'beneficiaries' of the process." No one has better described that brutal violence than the Salvadoran novelist Manlio Argueta in his riveting novels, *One Day of Life* and *Cuzcatlan*.

Analyses of the progress of the land reform were first cautious, then pessimistic. Perhaps a *New York Times* headline (August 3, 1981), "Salvador Land Program Aids Few," summed up the conclusions of those disappointed with the reform record. Corruption, inefficiency, financial deficits, lack of peasant participation, and a shortage of technical and agricultural skills plagued the program. In December 1981, the Salvadoran Peasants Union, claiming to speak for about 110,000 peasants, denounced the failure of the land reform program. They blamed the death squads, the military, and a slow, "frequently hostile" bureaucracy for the failure. Very few "permanent titles" were ever granted to individuals or, for that matter, to the peasant cooperatives. The legal and psychological ramifications of this failure for both the peasants and former landlords have been significant. The peasants remain fearful, while the landlords maintain hopes of repossession. In August 1982, Roy Prosterman, the U.S. legal expert who prepared the land reform law for South Vietnam and then repeated his exercise for El Salvador, declared in a bitter essay in *The New Republic* that the land reform had been gutted. José Napoleón Duarte, chief of the Salvadoran government between 1980 and 1982, and elected president in March 1984, concluded in early 1984, "The land reform is dead." In fact, in June 1984, the National Assembly terminated phase three of the reform. Not surprisingly, the collapse of agrarian reform coincided with the mounting intensity of civil war.

In 1980, after the junta of reformers had been pushed aside by more traditional figures, the advocates of change formed a political alliance, the FDR (*Frente Democrático Revolucionario*, the Revolutionary Democratic Front), and a united military front, the FMLN (*Frente Farabundo Martí para la Liberación Nacional*, the Farabundo Martí Front for National Liberation). The FDR issued a broad program of its objectives, called for (1) national independence, priority to Salvadoran needs, and subservience to no foreign country; (2) profound political, economic, and social reforms to guarantee human dignity, welfare, liberty, and progress; (3) nonalignment in international affairs; (4) democratic government; (5) a new national army; (6) support for private enterprise; and (7) religious freedom. Obviously the implementation of this program would revolutionize El Salvador. In the process it would eliminate the army and reduce the influence of the agrarian-industrial elite. The lines were clearly drawn between the beneficiaries of the traditional society and the advocates of change. A smoldering struggle between the army and the guerrillas erupted into a full-scale civil war as the rebel ranks expanded. The civil war reduced the governing junta's role to an effort to maintain some semblance of order. In March of 1980, the situation fell to a desperate low with the assassination of Archbishop Oscar Romero, a gentle spokesman for political moderation and social justice. In another blow to the civilized mind, soldiers raped and killed three U.S. nuns and a lay missionary later that same year.

Until 1979, the military and the elite had been capable of dealing effectively with any challenge to their authority. The events of 1979–80 demonstrated they could no longer frighten their opponents, regardless of how violent their death squads became. For the first time, they had to reach out to the United States for direct support. Their tactic was a simple one that had already proven effective in many parts of the hemisphere. The Latin American elites identified any longing for change, no matter how modest, with communism. They fully appreciated the Pavlovian response of U.S. officials to any charge that communism was afoot in the Western

Hemisphere. Once the alert to a "communist threat" in El Salvador had been sounded, military aid from Washington cascaded over the nation. In the 1980s, such aid reached $3 billion, or at least that was the officially acknowledged figure.

By 1989, the FMLN forces, estimated to number 10,000 fought in all parts of the nation; they collected their own taxes along the national highways; their attacks and sabotage pretty nearly destroyed the national economy. Successful again in penetrating the largest cities, they were attacking military and other targets in San Salvador by early 1989. Pentagon officials concluded that the demoralized army could not fight without U.S. support. With more than 60,000 people killed in eight years—many of them civilian victims of right-wing death squads—El Salvador suffered one of the bloodiest civil wars in Latin American history. The tragic history of modern El Salvador illustrates the lengths to which those who hold power will go to keep it and to prevent change.

The contemporary histories of Guatemala, Costa Rica, and Honduras are shaped largely by reactions to the civil war in El Salvador and the revolution in Nicaragua. All three experience the severe economic problems of underdevelopment: high and rising trade deficits, crippling debts, stagnant or declining prices for exports, growing land concentration accompanied by peasant protests, and mounting unemployment. Those very problems incline some, perhaps large numbers, to examine the programs for change advocated by the Sandinistas and the Salvadoran rebels. The attraction of revolutionary solutions to old problems worries the moderate and conservative elements.

Guatemala and Costa Rica, the extreme northern and southern flanks of Central America, tried to remain as aloof as possible from the isthmian conflicts. Sporadic guerrilla challenges, on occasion verging on civil war, have kept the Guatemalan military busy at home. Since the CIA toppled Arbenz in 1954, the military of Guatemala has firmly held the reins of political power, first reversing the revolutionary changes that had been introduced and then preserving the traditional institutions that were resurrected. In doing so, the generals earned an unsavory international reputation for violations of human rights. Some sources estimate that as many as 100,000 Guatemalans have been killed in the struggles since the fall of Arbenz, most of them by death squads, while another 250,000, mainly Indians, have fled across the border into Mexico to escape the holocaust. The internal crises occupy the military and inhibit Guatemala from playing a significant role in the rest of Central America.

Costa Rica, for its part, wants to be isolated from the turmoil. The presence of Nicaraguan exiles, particularly the counterrevolutionary forces that operated until 1986 from the uninhabited Costa Rican side of the border with Nicaragua, involved Costa Ricans in Nicaragua's revolution more than they would like. The United States exerted considerable pres-

sure on Costa Rica both to support the counterrevolutionaries and to oppose the Sandinistas. Confronting a faltering economy, which could not be
addressed let alone solved in a war-ravaged Central America, President
Oscar Arias seized the diplomatic initiative after his inauguration in 1986,
calling for a broad, peaceful settlement by Central Americans of their region's political problems. He won the Nobel Peace prize in 1987 for his
imagination and energy. Carrying out his broad proposals for peace challenged him and the Central Americans, partially because the United States
gave only lip service to the plans.

More than Guatemala and Costa Rica, Honduras became completely
involved in the crises. It has the uncomfortable geographic distinction of
being bordered by three nations in the throes of change or challenge:
simmering guerrilla warfare in Guatemala, a civil war in El Salvador, and a
revolutionary government in Nicaragua. At the same time, monumental
economic problems challenge Honduras, the poorest of the Central American states and the second most impoverished nation of Latin America, after
Haiti. Its population of 5.1 million grows at an annual rate of 3.5 percent,
one of the highest in the world. All of its economic statistics indicate widespread social injustice. Approximately 53 percent of the population is illiterate; infant mortality is 118 per 1,000 live births. Nearly 90 percent of the
rural population and 66 percent of the urban population live below the
poverty level. The economy rides a roller coaster of rising fiscal deficits and
foreign debts and falling export income and foreign reserves.

Honduras exemplifies the classic enclave economy. In the first half of
the twentieth century, three companies—United Fruit, Standard Fruit, and
Rosario Mining—dominated the economy. The first two grew and exported
bananas, and the third extracted gold and silver. Foreigners owned those
companies; they shipped their products abroad from specific locales. Only
an insignificant residue of the wealth generated remained in Honduras.
Those companies owned and operated the railroads as well as several of the
principal ports. The banana companies controlled the oil, beer, and tobacco
industries. In 1950, the three companies earned sums equal to the entire
Honduran budget. Occasionally Hondurans made efforts to regulate the
companies. A major strike against the banana companies in 1954 strengthened the unions and increased salaries and benefits for the workers. The
victory instilled a better sense of nationalism among the Hondurans and
made the unions a new social and economic force. President Ramón Villeda
Morales (1958–64) tried to further curb the fruit companies as well as to
institute a modest land reform and social security program.

The victorious strike and the reforms of Villeda Morales unnerved
the landowners and military. The generals overthrew Villeda Morales during his final days in office and, with a brief exception in 1971–72, ruled
Honduras directly until 1982. Corruption and ever greater conservatism
characterized the military governments. When the military turned the gov-

ernment over to an elected civilian in early 1982 the economy was in a shambles from which it has failed to recover.

At that moment, the administration of President Ronald Reagan discovered the strategical location of Honduras and resolved to use it in order to destabilize Nicaragua and contain the Salvadoran rebels. Consequently, U.S. military aid to Honduras jumped impressively. The United States held joint military exercises with Honduras throughout the 1980s. Honduras provided ample opportunity for the United States to construct air bases and strips, a sea port, radar sites, military encampments, and tank traps. During those exercises, the U.S. military forces operated close to both the Nicaraguan and Salvadoran frontiers. After 1983, Honduras was for all intents and purposes an "occupied country."

Much was being done to militarize Honduras under the rationale that the military would guarantee democracy. Yet, no example exists in Honduran history (or in Central American history for that matter) in which the military contributed to the strengthening of democracy. To the contrary, examples abound of the military's consistent hostility to democracy. Efraín Díaz Arrivillaga, Honduras's sole Christian Democratic congressman in 1983, worried aloud, "The country has not been democratized. State powers are not dependent. The people have no effective participation. The government has been acting and legislating behind the people's backs. A further cause for concern is the growing violation of human rights and the lack of guarantees for individuals." While the Honduran government poured money into joint military maneuvers with the United States, it halted desperately needed public-works projects for lack of funds. While the economy disintegrated, Honduras boasted of the most modern air force in Central America.

In a close working alliance with the United States, Honduras actively supports the government of El Salvador against the FDR/FMLN. It permits the Nicaraguan counterrevolutionaries to train on its territory and to launch repeated attacks into Nicaragua. It willfully meddles in the affairs of its neighbors; some say it is fulfilling an historic role, since Honduras contributed to the CIA invasions of Guatemala (1954) and Cuba (1961) and to the U.S. intervention in the Dominican Republic (1965). In every way possible, the Honduran governments have sabotaged peace efforts in Central America, including those of President Arias. Most observers accuse the weak and dependent governments of Honduras of being the surrogate of Washington. In such a role, Honduras intensifies the Central American crises and probably in the long run its own internal conflicts as well. Accelerated militarism in an impoverished nation undermines democracy and delays development. The international dimension of that militarism has made Honduras the center of the Central American crises of the 1980s.

The forces in Central America that want to diminish the region's dependency and substitute development for periodic growth are locked in battle with those fearful of change, the beneficiaries of traditional institutions and relationships. This crisis of underdevelopment also intertwines with a related crisis of decolonization as many Central Americans challenge the hegemony the United States has exercised over the region for the past century. The Central American crisis also reflects broader dramas visible throughout all of Latin America. The Brazilian poet Romano de Sant'Anna caught the essense of those dramas in his poem "What Kind of Nation Is This?": "I live in the twentieth century. I'm off to the twenty-first still the nineteenth's prisoner. . . ." Latin Americans, like Central Americans, do not want to enter the twenty-first century shackled to the institutions of the nineteenth.

UNITED STATES OPTIONS

Never friendly toward revolution in Latin America, the United States regarded the boldness of the Cuban experience as threatening to its security. The popular response Fidel Castro received from millions of Latin Americans awoke the government of President John F. Kennedy to the reality that the majority of the Latin Americans wanted change. Fearful that the formula they might choose would be communistic, Kennedy and his advisors devised an imaginative plan to encourage but channel change along a democratic path.

In 1961, President Kennedy, always extremely popular among Latin Americans of all political suasions and socioeconomic levels, launched his Alliance for Progress, a program to encourage economic development, to promote the growth of democracy, and to urge social justice. It was an optimistic, if unrealistic, program that if carried out would have altered much of Latin America. It is doubtful whether Kennedy or his advisors understood the full implications of the program they professed to support. Too theoretical and vague on one level, too revolutionary on another, the Alliance for Progress thus contained the seeds of its own destruction. It failed, for the traditional oligarchy had no intention of freely volunteering to give away or sell its lands, to tax itself more heavily, or to share power with a broader base of the population. A decade after the Alliance's creation, there were more military dictatorships and less evidence of democracy than at any time in recent memory. In a ten-year span, military rule replaced thirteen constitutional governments, with the United States supporting the Latin American military lavishly. In truth, over two-thirds of Alliance for Progress funds went to military dictators or to military-controlled civilian governments, despite the intention that funds would be used to buttress democracy. Economically, the area's condition was certainly more precarious in 1971 than it was in 1961. The rate of economic growth per capita over the decade averaged a pitiful 1.8 percent, lower than it was in the years before the

Alliance for Progress and far from the minimal goal of 2.5 percent set by the Alliance. In November of 1968, President Richard Nixon concluded that the alliance had "done nothing to reduce the ominous difference which exists between North and South America." Disappointment, almost disbelief, in the meager results of the Alliance—after funneling nearly $10 billion into Latin America—was widespread both there and in the United States. Senator Frank Church, chairman of the Senate's Subcommittee on Western Hemisphere Affairs, voices that dismay when he mused, "We thought we were seeding the resurgence of democratic governments; instead, we have seen a relentless slide toward militarism. We thought we could remodel Latin societies, but the reforms we prescribed have largely eluded us." On March 13, 1971, the tenth anniversay of the Alliance for Progress passed unnoticed, unmentioned in Washington. In theory, the Alliance for Progress was a positive foreign policy, but Washington never insisted on the implementation of its own best wisdom.

A disconcerting cynicism seems to have pervaded the original conception and the advocacy of the Alliance for Progress. In the mid-1970s myriad investigations, journalistic probes, and frank exposés revealed the shallowness in U.S. government circles of the rhetoric encouraging the "democrative alternative" for Latin America. The State Department, the CIA, and the Pentagon, in tune with the wishes of the multinational corporations, favored the status quo and suspected even the most toothless reforms of communist influence. So long as the "democratic alternative" frustrated

U.S. influence spread quickly and deeply into Latin America after the opening of the twentieth century. The walls of this building in a small Nicaraguan town advertise "Chiclets" gum and "Chesterfield" cigarettes in 1927.

Montgomery Ward offered the middle class of Montevideo, Uruguay,
all the modern gadgetry it sought by the second decade of the
twentieth century.

change in the South, it received U.S. support, but every time it threatened
to institute real reforms, the United States acted in alliance with the Latin
American middle class and elits to subvert it. Indeed, the list of U.S. interventions thwarting the popular will of Latin Americans, 1954 to the present, is a long one. Declassified documents and published first-person accounts abundantly detail the mischief. William Blum's *The CIA: A Forgotten
History* (1986) catalogs and discusses the interventions. *The Tower Commission
Report* (1987) and *The Chronology. The Documented Day-by-Day Account of the
Secret Military Assistance to Iran and the Contras* (1987) both provide the details
of the Iran-Contra scandal that rocked the foundations of the Reagan
presidency. They reveal the extent of U.S. participation in the wars and
crises of Central America, particularly in the nearly decade-long obsession
of Washington with the overthrow of the Nicaraguan government.

Phillip B. F. Agee, a former CIA deep-cover agent in Latin America in
the 1960s, has written in his book *Inside the Company: CIA Diary* (1975) that
the agency's main task was to check the drive toward independent action
and change in Latin America. That effort, he concluded, "has the result of
strengthening minority governments which perpetuate great wealth for a
few and widespread poverty. It has the result of strengthening injustice."
The sad truth, emerging in abundant detail, is that U.S. foreign policy
toward Latin America has represented the interests of large multinational
corporations and evinced no interest, other than occasional rhetorical plati-
tudes, in either the development or democratization of that region. The
CIA apparently found eager collaborators among the Latin Americans
themselves who, sharing the "company's disdain for democracy and development," facilitated its operations.

The governments of presidents Lyndon Johnson, Richard Nixon, and Gerald Ford uninhibitedly cooperated with the Western Hemisphere's bumper crop of dictators, apparently oblivious to the torture, imprisonment, and summary executions that bloodied many of the military regimes in power. Washington remained tolerant so long as the Latin American governments professed anticommunism, provided no cause for concern over hemispheric security, and welcomed business, banking, industry, imports, and investments from abroad. The status quo enlivened with growth in Latin America was much easier for the Department of State to deal with than the more fluid situations that spawned reform, requiring an imaginative creativity diplomats often seem devoid of.

The long preoccupation of Washington with communism and its determination to cast every effort at change within the framework of the East-West conflict, long ago exhausted the patience of those Latin Americans seeking to alter their societies. They believe Washington's policies insist on maintaining Latin America's dependency. The Mexican intellectual Leopoldo Zea framed their belief in these words:

> The Cold War, much more than an effort to make sure that the non-Western nations do not become communist, has been a pretext to make certain that these peoples do not achieve within the system any status other than as the

This astonishing poster from Patzcuro, Mexico, shows a curious blend of modern commercial influence with established religious practice in the mid-1960s. The poster reads, "September 8. A pilgrimage of the entire town of Patzcuro to the Basilica. The Most Holy Virgin of Health awaits all the inhabitants of Patzcuro, her favorite children. At 6:30 in the afternoon everyone should meet in the Guadalupe Sanctuary before proceeding to the Basilica where we will arrive at 7:00. Everything tastes better with Pepsi."

Burger Boy of Mexico City, 1980, illustrates again the pervasive United States culture and commercialism visible everywhere in Latin America.

dependencies they have been since they were incorporated into Western history. From that point of view, the nationalism embraced by the peoples of the Third World is seen as synonymous with communism. Those very values which the Western World has prized as its own are also seen as the negation of that World when demanded by non-Western peoples. The Western World refuses to allow these other peoples to play any but a subservient role in the system.

Such a conclusion receives a sympathetic hearing in Latin America.

To his credit, President Jimmy Carter began his administration with a willingness to try new approaches toward Latin America. As a measure of his announced flexibility, he dispatched the personable Andrew Young to the Caribbean and northern South America as his ambassador of good will, the herald of a new diplomacy. Young impressed and delighted the Latin Americans. He proclaimed an end to the era of interventions; the United States extended respect in a search for friendly cooperation. The president attempted to reduce old tensions with Cuba by reestablishing the U.S. diplomatic presence there, in the form of the earlier-mentioned Havana "interest section." He disturbed the oligarchs and the military with his talk of human rights. He even administered a few well-deserved verbal slaps to the grossest offenders. Of greatest significance, Carter rectified an old injustice by signing new treaties with Panama.

On September 7, 1977, Panama's General Omar Torrijos Herrera and President Jimmy Carter signed treaties to return the Panama Canal Zone to Panamanian control and to put the canal itself under eventual Panamanian operation. The two treaties, will reunify Panama and return to that nation its primary resource, a vital and unique piece of geography. The treaties, which symbolize an important effort to eliminate one of the most glaring reminders of United States imperialism, came close to meeting the demands of the Panamanians as well as promising to safeguard United States interests and security. Both sides recognized that the new treaties were not perfect, but they responded to a pragmatism that made them acceptable to the diverse demands of two different peoples. One of the two treaties will terminate U.S. control of the canal on December 31, 1999, and calls for joint U.S.–Panamanian management, protection, and defense of the canal until then. Meanwhile Panama increasingly assumes responsibility for public services and for the operation of the canal. A second emphasizes the neutrality of the canal both in times of peace and war, requiring that it remain open to transit by the vessels of all nations. The Panamanian people approved the treaties by the plebiscite on October 23, 1977. The ratification debate in the U.S. Senate aroused a lively national discussion, unusual for bringing U.S. attention to bear on Latin America. Opponents spoke of threats to U.S. security, emphasized the role of the canal for U.S. international commerce, and resented turning over to Panama a masterpiece of U.S. engineering. Those favoring the treaties felt that the United States would achieve greater security through a friendly working relationship with Panama, pointed out the declining importance of the canal in a new age of supertankers and huge aircraft carriers that no longer fit the restricted locks or the depths of the canal, and warned that claims the Canal Zone was U.S. territory rested on shaky ground. Following a lengthy and heated debate, the Senate ratified the treaties on March 16 and April 18, 1978. The majority decided that the interests of U.S. diplomacy, security, commerce, and investment would best be served by creating a new partnership with Panama based on equality and cooperation. The other Latin American nations applauded.

Carter's positive policy toward Latin America reached its zenith with the ratification of the treaties. The old temptations to cast Latin American events simplistically in the East-West molds of the Cold War quickly returned, hastened in part by the close relationship between Havana and Moscow. As Cuba's interests in Africa warmed, Washington cooled toward its island neighbor. The United States denounced Cuba's expanding role in Africa and expressed equal apprehension about the stronger role Castro played in the Caribbean. Both Jamaica and Grenada maintained close relations with Havana. Cuba became the champion of Puerto Rican independence.

President Carter regarded both the triumph of the Nicaraguan revolution and the coup of the reformers in El Salvador with suspicion. Assistant Secretary of State for Inter-American Affairs Viron P. Vaky defined the cautious new policy of the Carter administration in late 1979. Speaking of the violence in Central America, he stated, "The central issue is not whether change is to occur, but whether that change is to be violent and radical or peaceful and evolutionary and preserving individual rights and democratic values. . . . Our task, therefore, is how to work with our friends and to guide and influence change, how to use our influence to promote justice, freedom and equity to mutual benefit—and thereby avoid insurgency and communism." The statement demonstrated little contact with historical realities. Wishful thinking would neither bring about the necessary reforms nor stem the tides of violence. In both Nicaragua and El Salvador, Washington hoped to strengthen the "forces of moderation." This hope that moderate change would take place without offending anyone characterized U.S. policy toward Latin America as the decade of the 1980s opened. Historical precedent offered little cause for optimism.

Under the administration of President Ronald Reagan, the official view of global events returned to the concept, widely held in the United States in the early 1950s, that the world was divided between East and West and that every struggle, no matter how remote or isolated, reflected the broader conflict between capitalism and communism. Such an interpretation took a dim view of social change, more often that not classifying it as communistic or at least Communist-inspired. Not surprisingly the Reagan administration considered Nicaragua to be a "Communist menace" to Central America and the rebels in El Salvador equally threatening. For that reason, Washington militarized Honduras and generously supplied aid and arms to the Salvadoran army, all in the name of a crusade to contain communism.

The policy of U.S. military pressure on Nicaragua evoked world condemnation, as well as congressional and domestic protest. The United States armed, trained, and financed the Nicaraguan counterrevolutionaries, many of whom were mercenaries or former soldiers and officers under Somoza, while others were citizens disgruntled with the revolution. In early 1984, the CIA mined Nicaraguan harbors. In classic Agent 007 style, commandos from a CIA "mother ship" slipped into the harbors of Corinto, Puerto Sandino, and El Bluff to lay the mines under the protection of U.S.–piloted attack helicopters. Five international ships and at least eleven Nicaraguan patrol boats and fishing boats hit the mines. World opinion condemned the aggression.

Nicaragua took the United States to the International Court of Justice. The United States refused to go. Laurence H. Tribe, professor of constitutional law at Harvard University, summarized much of the concern raised by the mining and subsequent court case when he wrote:

President Reagan rightly invokes international law to denounce terrorism, but when other nations attempt to judge his foreign policy by the same set of rules, he prefers to pick up his marbles and go home. . . . Government under law is no mere game that we can quit whenever we don't like the rules. By stalking out of World Court, the Reagan Administration derailed progress toward a world in which nations are governed by something other than the law of the jungle.

On June 27, 1986, the World Court ruled that U.S. support of the counter-revolutionaries broke international law.

The U.S. intervention in the tiny island-nation of Grenada (289 square miles, with a population of 100,000), in October of 1983 fed fears of a new era of armed interventions. When Maurice Bishop came to power in 1979, his government emphasized health and educational projects. To rescue a moribund economy, the government sought to construct an airport large enough to accommodate wide-bodied passenger planes as an encouragement to tourism. Bishop first approached the United States, Great Britain, and Canada for funds to build the 9,000-foot runway. They refused. The Cubans then agreed to build the airport, much to the annoyance of the United States. Officials in Washington, critical of Bishop's friendship with Castro, claimed the new airport had strategic value, a potential landing strip for Cuban and Soviet planes. Disputes over policy and leadership within the New Jewel Movement, the governing party, led to violence in October 1983, and the murder of the popular Bishop by his rivals. The confusion and unrest that followed provided the pretext for a massive U.S. invasion on October 25, 1983. In so doing, the United States violated the Montevideo Treaty (1934), the Buenos Aires Protocol (1937), and the United Nations and Organization of American States charters, to which it subscribes, that prohibit signatory nations from intervention, direct or indirect, in the affairs of others. With the exception of six small Caribbean islands, Israel, and El Salvador, international opinion condemned the intervention as morally and legally wrong. The invasion damaged the reputation of the United States. Apparently the intervention brought few benefits to the "rescued" Grenadians. The *Los Angeles Times* reported in 1986: "Grenada's economy has not improved. Unemployment is up. Two factories built with U.S. economic aid, and much publicity, have gone broke." The intervention also established a dangerous precedent, as the United States escalated its military presence in Central America.

Desiring a wider public consensus for his Central American policies, President Reagan appointed a special commission under the chairmanship of Henry Kissinger to formulate a plan for future U.S. relations with Central America. In early 1983, the Kissinger Commission issued a report calling for increased military spending accompanied by a program of economic aid. It reasoned that the military could bring peace to Central America and then guarantee both democracy and development. Critics doubted that even with lavish funding the military could restore peace. Anyway, pointing to the long military record of subverting democracy and ignoring development, they labeled the military as part of the problem rather than of the solution. The economic aid portion of the report repeated the prescriptions of the Alliance for Progress, whose failure has already been noted. At any rate, the Kissinger Plan collected dust on the shelf. Washington pursued military goals.

At the beginning of 1983, four Latin American nations, Venezuela, Colombia, Panama, and Mexico, met on La Contadora Island off the coast of Panama to prepare a peace plan for Central America. Among other things, the Contadora plan called for reductions in arms and troops, the removal of all foreign military advisors, the closing of foreign military bases, the end of attempts to subvert governments, and democratic elections. In July 1985, the governments of Argentina, Brazil, Uruguay, and Peru announced the formation of the Contadora Support group. The eight nations, in their Declaration of Cartagena, cautioned, "If a peaceful and negotiated solution is not found for the Central American conflict, this will affect the political and social stability of all Latin America." The United States virtually ignored the Contadora Peace Plan.

An historical preference for the military and the elites has cast the United States in the role of defending Central America's existing institutions. Any attack on those institutions disturbs Washington, which has long equated change with a threat to U.S. security in the Western Hemisphere. Certainly, because of its past support of and association with those institutions, Washington correctly perceives a challenge to its hegemony. Central Americans want greater control over their own destiny; they want to reduce their dependency. To accomplish those goals they have to reduce U.S. predominance.

Questions of security are certainly legitimate concerns for any nation. It seems only natural that discussions in Washington would focus on how U.S. security interests in Latin America are best served. The formula for hemispheric security resulting from such discussions will vary. Basically the policy makers face two alternatives. A policy that tends to endorse the status quo but also perpetuates the obvious iniquities and breeds violence might complement present U.S. interests—but does it serve them well in the long run? Or, would U.S. security be enhanced by a radically changed Latin America in which the majority enjoy a reasonable quality of life, share in the benefits their nations can afford, and feel an identification with their governments? Those who select the latter must expect some fundamental changes affecting land structures, political institutions, foreign investments, and profit remittances. The option for the long-term policy would annoy U.S. investors, disturb those sensitive to the sometimes shrill rhetoric of reform and revolution, and raise questions initially of security risk, although it would harmonize with North American idealism and sense of "fair play." In the long run it would ease hemispheric tensions, probably increase trade (the United States sells more to developed nations than to impoverished ones), and certainly strengthened hemispheric security. The catch is that there must be a short-term period of tolerance for the long-term gain. The second alternative would require the United States to place less emphasis on a negative anticommunist policy and place more on a positive policy favoring reform. This option is not an easy one to take, especially in view of myths and misunderstandings about Latin America current in the United States. Risks clearly are involved. Hopefully, this book has made it clear that change is inevitable and that there is more to gain from encouraging than from discouraging it.

Besides its importance to the security of the United States, Latin America remained a significant market and area of foreign investment. By the end of 1980, the Latin Americans had purchased $29 billion worth of exports from the United States, approximately one-sixth of all U.S. exports. At the same time, U.S. companies and citizens had invested $35 billion in the area, just about 80 percent of all U.S. private investments in the developing world.

Senator Robert F. Kennedy seems to have understood both the challenge and the opportunity before the United States in Latin America when he stated,

> A better life for the people of Latin America can only come out of the progress toward a better, more democratic political and social structure. If we allow ourselves to become allied with those to whom the cry of "communism" is only an excuse for the perpetuation of privilege, if we assist, with military materials and other aid, governments which use that aid to prevent reform for the people, then we will give the Communists a strength which they cannot attain by anything they themselves might do. . . . The responsibility of our time is nothing less than to lead a revolution. A revolution which will be peaceful if we are wise enough, human if we care, successful if we are fortunate enough, but a revolution which will come whether we will it or not.

Such dynamic leadership will require the establishment of a negotiated peace in Central America and a positive policy of cooperation with those Latin American governments actively addressing the need for agrarian, tax, and political reforms, regional economic cooperation, and public works. There are many reasons to believe that a positive foreign policy encouraging peace and development will enjoy the support of large numbers of Latin Americans, strengthen their traditional friendship with the United States, bring greater stability and prosperity to the Western Hemisphere, and enhance hemispheric security. In a provocative historical survey, *The Rise and Fall of the Great Powers. Economic Change and Military Conflict from 1500 to 2000,* Professor Paul Kennedy, an historian at Yale University, concluded that the

United States at the end of the twentieth century must adapt its policies to reflect a changing world or lose its international leadership: "The only serious threat to the real interests of the United States can come from a failure to adjust to the newer world order."

THE ENIGMA

Change always occurs. Change has taken place in Latin America. Latin America in the 1990s differs markedly from Latin America in the 1880s. Perhaps most noticeable among the changes is the presence of a significant middle class exercising a dominant role in the social, economic, and political life of each nation. Many of the most vigorous political parties spring from that class. Leaders from that class direct the potent force of nationalism, encourage industrialization and progress, and contribute to the vitality of the cities. Urban unionized laborers constitute a relatively new and important group as well. Some of them enjoy a reasonable wage and impressive social benefits. On occasion they have exerted political influence. Transportation and communication networks now cover large parts of most of the nations, giving them a greater cohesion than ever before. Increasingly Latin Americans use their own natural resources to promote national growth.

In the past two decades, the Roman Catholic Church, or significant individuals within it, has played an active leadership role in encouraging change, belying the Church's long identification with the status quo. In the most brutal dictatorships of contemporary Latin America, the Church, often the only audible voice of criticism, has issued the most piercing cry for justice.

The Church increased its social concerns in the mid-1960s. The Second Vatican Council (1962–65) addressed some of the pressing worldly problems, revealing a greater attention to matters of secular welfare. Pope Paul VI called for an observance of human rights in his encyclical *On the Progress of Peoples*. The 1968 bishops' hemispheric conference in Colombia took up the cause of social justice, and a decade later (1979), at their Mexico meeting, the bishops reaffirmed their position, urging priests and nuns to work on behalf of the poor and politically oppressed. Interesting statistics demonstrate that wherever the clergy supported the cause of social justice, whether it was Chile, Paraguay, Nicaragua, Brazil, or elsewhere, church attendance rose, as did applications for the priesthood. At the same time, the Church paid dearly for its outspoken protests. During the 1970s approximately 850 bishops, priests, and nuns were murdered, arrested, and/or tortured. The vicious assassination of Archbishop Oscar Romero in March of 1980, while he was offering mass in San Salvador, outraged all civilized people.

Brazil's Paulo Evaristo Cardinal Arns set the tone for the Church's social concerns in the 1980s in his *Suggestions for a Social Policy*. He condemned the social iniquities exaggerated by industrial growth and denounced "decreased autonomy and growing dependence on the economies of the industrialized world." The Vatican supported that call for social justice during the visit of Pope John Paul II to Brazil in July 1980. During his twelve-day visit, the pope emphasized that the Church must not become directly involved in political parties and ideologies. He condemned the use of violence to achieve social justice. Nonetheless, he firmly stated that the Church must "serve the cause of justice" by using its voice to "summon consciences, guard people and their liberty and demand the necessary remedies." John Paul warned, "The persistence of injustice threatens the existence of society from within. This menace from within really exists when the distribution of goods is grounded only in the economic laws of growth and bigger profit, when the results of progress reach only superficially the huge levels of the population, when there persists a large gap between a minority of the rich on the one hand and the majority of those who live in want and misery on the other." More than 120,000 workers in the stadium of Sõa Paulo city cheered those words. While a persuasive force for change, the Church is by no means united on these issues. Further, a concrete program for change does not accompany the sharp criticism.

To balance this assessment of change we must return to a familiar theme: despite pockets of change, a veneer of progress, and apparent modernity, much of Latin America retains the flavor of the distant past. In short, the change and modernization that have occurred in the last century have had little positive effect, particularly on the quality of life of the majority.

A major reason for this constancy is that one characteristic still dominates—and enervates—Latin America: the economies grow but do not develop. The most dynamic part of each economy remains linked to exports. The economic policies and performance strengthen institutions nurturing dependency. It is those institutional structures, minimally altered by time, that create the ever-present enigma of widespread poverty amid potential wealth.

As Latin America moves through the final decade of the twentieth century, the problems created by the remarkable continuity of those institutions weigh as heavily, perhaps more heavily, than ever. They beg for a solution. No reason exists to believe that time alone will solve these problems. To the contrary, it seems to have strengthened them. The level of frustration felt by the majority certainly seems higher. It will require some imaginative restructuring of institutions to solve the problems and to relieve the frustration.

The human dimension of these problems staggers the mind. Probably the most terrifying reality is that most of the population is hungry, malnourished, and sick. The overall illiteracy rate still hovers at 40 percent. The work force grows at a faster rate than the creation of new jobs. The annual per capita income remains low, about one-tenth that of the United States. In the mid-1980s, per capita income dropped 10 percent in Latin America. However, in reality even that income is highly unbalanced, with a few receiving most of it.

Capitalism in Latin America has concentrated income. Economist David Felix concluded, "The overriding conclusion I draw . . . is that capitalistic economic growth in the Latin American institutional and cultural complex is strongly biased toward income concentration and minimal rates of improvement in the quality of life of the lowest 60 percent." The abundant wealth does not diffuse. In Brazil, the share of national income claimed by the poorest 50 percent declined from 17.7 percent in 1960, to 15.6 in 1970, to 14.6 in 1980; while the share for the richest 10 percent rose from 39.7 percent in 1960, to 46.4 in 1970, to 47.7 in 1980. Mexico experienced the same trend: the poorest 20 percent received 7.8 percent of the national income in 1950 but only 1.9 in 1975, while the top 10 percent increased its share from 38.6 to 43.5 percent. World Bank economist Marcelo Selowsky concludes that prevalent and persistent Latin American poverty "is, and will increasingly be, a purely distributive problem rather than the result of a lack of aggregate resources." In their sobering study, *Economic Growth and Social Equity in Developing Countries,* economists Irma Adelman and Cynthia Taft Morris assert, "Our findings strongly suggest that there is no automatic, or even likely, trickling down of the benefits of economic growth to the poorest segments of the population in low-income countries. On the contrary, the absolute position of the poor tends to deteriorate as a consequence of economic growth. . . . The only hope of significantly improving the income distribution in these countries in a transformation of the institutional setting." The dispossessed majority is not the only victim. The United Nations Economic and Social Council reported in the mid-1980s that "part of the middle class is falling back into poverty." In sum, the quality of life for the majority remains abysmally low, while the middle class fails to realize the economic benefits it seeks.

Disproportionately high international debts with crippling interest rates, a nervousness among investors and bankers about future investments and loans, penurious prices for the primary exports of Latin America, runaway inflation, high unemployment with ever increasing numbers of young people entering the job market, and insufficient food production for local consumption are among the factors threatening economic growth at the end of the twentieth century. This threat might hold some promise for Latin America if the governments, deprived of economic growth, would turn their attention to development.

No area is more challenged to change than Latin America. Voices are raised everywhere advocating change. Some hoped to bring about that change through reform, such as President Salvador Allende of Chile, who stated, "Our task is to change the system. . . . Only by changing the system, by putting it at the service of the people, can we solve the problems that have grown over the many years. We must build a new state, with new politics, a new economy, a new culture." Others elsewhere call for change through revolution. One Tupamaro guerrilla, known only as El Eco, concluded,

> We are not satisfied with conditions as they are today. Things are not going right in Uruguay and therefore we need change. I do not know the final form, but it must be clearly different from what we have today . . . a complete restructuring of our society so that there is a better distribution of wealth, so that all segments of society are heard on political matters, and so that Uruguay is not made the tool of foreigners.

These fervent hopes of revolutionaries and reformers remain unrealized, with the exceptions of the continuing revolutions in Cuba and Nicaragua. Reforms, revolutions, democracy, populism, and military governments of varied types have failed. They have not provided a satisfactory quality of life for the majority. The formidable force of continuity proves to be stronger than all previous efforts to produce change.

Possibly the solution to the prevalent poverty in the midst of potential plenty lies not in exotic foreign formulas eagerly imported into or imposed upon Latin America by the left and right and all political hues in between. Unfaltering loyalty to imported solutions for domestic problems has reaped few rewards for the Latin Americans. That a solution might lie within Latin America itself, within the pragmatic communal approach of the majority, is a possibility governments shun. Yet, solutions to old problems might well be found in local values and experiences. Given access to land, seeds, tools and water, the rural masses conceivably could make Latin America flourish. They could feed themselves, supply the local marketplace, and minimize dependency. Such a solution entails the restructuring of power because it will remove land from the monopoly of the few and distribute it to the many, thereby diminishing the former's wealth, prestige, and power while enhancing the latter's position; the luxuries and privileges of the few might diminish as the basic welfare of the many improves. Accompanying that fundamental shift in land ownership and productivity there must be a centrally administered national plan for development. Massive public works projects will alleviate urban unemployment and underemployment while providing the housing, schools, and hospitals needed. Industry will be directed to meet the basic needs of the many, not the exotic tastes of the few. A rational manufacturing program will produce trucks to transport food, not sportscars for the privileged; pasteurized milk for school children, not carbonated soft drinks; sturdy sandals for the barefooted, not expensive leather shoes for export. Such a government must reflect the desires of the majority; it must lean upon and be supported by the majority. Identification between people and government must be complete. Through that identification the local culture will triumph. The challenge for change will have been met.

Well-defined institutions from the past, enshrined by the elites and middle classes and which rely on the strength of the military, still prevail. Brazil, Uruguay, Chile, Nicaragua, and El Salvador have given us proof in the last two decades that those who enjoy privileges and benefits from society will not freely give up their positions. If history does in fact suggest "lessons" on which we can draw, then it teaches that change of any fundamental nature will not be achieved easily. Eventually it will probably result from the dialectic of violence so long a characteristic of Latin America—the violence expressed by those who feel oppressed, who desire to share in the benefits of society, and who seek change and the violence imposed by those who enjoy power, who benefit from the status quo, and who desire to perpetuate their domination. As we have seen, it is much easier to maintain the present system than to bring about authentic change. While the Latin Americans are perfectly capable of solving their own historical problems, they can attend to them best only if left alone. Only they can pursue the hope of José Martí of an economically viable and politically independent Latin America in which all people can live in dignity, and the vision of José Vasconcelos of the emergence of a "new race," characterized by beauty, peace, and well-being.

The Latin American experience indicates that change will require strong, determined, and well-led governments to break with the past and pursue an innovative course. Until such governments appear, Latin America, with few exceptions, manifests all the signs of an underdeveloped area: low per capita income, unequal distribution of wealth, economic dependency, high birth and death rates, endemic diseases, undernourishment, and illiteracy. The enigma remains: poor people inhabit rich lands.

A Chronology
of Significant Dates
in Latin American History

1492	Columbus reaches the New World.
1494	The Treaty of Tordesillas divides the world between Spain and Portugal.
1500	Cabral discovers Brazil.
1503	Spain legalizes the encomienda in the New World; Casa de Contratación created.
1512	The Laws of Burgos regulate the treatment of the Indians.
1513	Balboa discovers the Pacific Ocean.
1521	Hernán Cortés completes the conquest of the Aztec empire.
1524	Creation of the Council of the Indies.
1532	First permanent settlements in Brazil.
1535	Francisco Pizarro completes the conquest of the Incan empire; the first viceroy arrives in Mexico.
1542	The New Laws call for an end of the encomiendas.
1543	The first viceroy arrives in Peru.
1545	The Spaniards discover silver at Potosí.
1630–54	The Dutch control as much as one-third of Brazil.
1695	The Luso-Brazilians discover gold in the Brazilian interior.
1763	The capital of the Viceroyalty of Brazil is moved to Rio de Janeiro.
1776	Creation of the Viceroyalty of the Plata.
1804	Haiti declares its independence.
1808	The royal family of Portugal arrives in Brazil.
1810	Padre Miguel Hidalgo initiates Mexico's struggle for independence.
1811	Paraguay and Venezuela declare their independence.
1814–40	José Gaspar Rodríguez de Francia, the populist caudillo, dominates Paraguay.
1816	Argentina declares its independence.
1818–43	Jean-Pierre Boyer, a populist caudillo, rules Haiti.
1819	Brazil puts a steamship into service, the first in South America.
1821	Mexico, Peru, and Central America declare their independence.

1821–23	Emperor Agustín I rules the Mexican empire.
1822	Prince Pedro declares Brazil's independence and receives the title of emperor.
1823	President James Monroe promulgates the Monroe Doctrine.
1824	The Battle of Ayacucho marks the final defeat of the Spaniards in South America.
1824–38	The United Provinces of Central America in existence.
1825	Bolivia declares its independence.
1825–28	The Cisplatine War between Brazil and Argentina to possess Uruguay results in a stalemate and Uruguayan independence.
1829–52	The populist caudillo Juan Manuel de Rosas rules Argentina.
1830	The political union of Gran Colombia dissolves, leaving Colombia, Venezuela, and Ecuador to go their independent ways.
1838	The first railroad in Latin America is inaugurated in Cuba.
1839–65	The populist caudillo Rafael Carrera governs Guatemala.
1846–48	The United States and Mexico fight. The United States gains California, New Mexico, and Arizona from its victory.
1847–1903	The Cruzob rebellion in Yucatan and Mayan self-government.
1848–55	The popular caudillo Manuel Belzu governs Bolivia.
1850	The United States and Great Britain sign the Clayton-Bulwer Treaty to check the expansion of each in Central America. Unionization of workers slowly begins in the largest Latin American nations.
1852	Chile inaugurates the first railroad in South America. Chile and Brazil initiate telegraphic systems.
1864–67	Archduke Maximilian of Austria rules Mexico under French protection.
1865–70	In the War of the Triple Alliance, Argentina, Brazil, and Uruguay fight and eventually defeat Paraguay.
1876	The first refrigerator ship carries beef from Buenos Aires to Europe.
1876–1911	Profirio Díaz governs Mexico.
1879–84	The War of the Pacific pits Chile against Peru and Bolivia.
1886	The University of Chile awards the first medical degree to a woman in Latin America.
1888	Brazil abolishes slavery.
1889	The military dethrones Emperor Pedro II of Brazil; Brazil becomes a republic; the coffee planters begin their domination of Brazil.
1889–90	The first Inter-American Conference meets in Washington, D.C.
1898	As a result of the Spanish-American War, Cuba gains its independence from Spain and the United States takes possession of Puerto Rico.
1901	In the Hay-Pauncefote Treaty, Great Britain acknowledges U.S. supremacy in Central America.
1903	Panama gains its independence and signs a treaty with the United States for the construction of an interoceanic canal.
1903–29	José Batlle dominates Uruguayan politics, bringing stability and economic growth as well as the middle class to power.
1909–33	U.S. intervention and occupation of Nicaragua.

1910–40	The Mexican Revolution.
1911	Emiliano Zapata advocates agrarian reform in his Plan of Ayala.
1914	The Panama Canal opens.
1915–34	The United States occupies Haiti.
1916–22	Hipólito Irigoyen governs Argentina as its first middle-class president.
1916–24	The United States occupies the Dominican Republic.
1917	Promulgation of the Mexican constitution, the blueprint for the Revolution.
1919	Promulgation of the Uruguayan constitution, the blueprint for middle-class democracy.
1920–24	Arturo Alessandri, a representative of middle-class interests, governs Chile.
1927–33	Augusto César Sandino leads the guerrilla struggle in Nicaragua to expel the U.S. Marines.
1929	The world financial collapse reduced Latin American exports but encourages import-substitution industrialization. Ecuador grants the vote to women, the first in Latin America.
1932–35	Bolivia and Paraguay fight the Chaco War.
1934–40	The Mexican Revolution reaches its apogee under President Lázaro Cárdenas.
1937	Bolivia nationalizes foreign oil companies.
1938	Mexico nationalizes foreign oil companies.
1940	Promulgation of the Cuban constitution, a middle-class and nationalist blueprint for change.
1944–54	The Guatemalan revolution.
1945	Gabriela Mistral, Chilean poet, is the first Latin American to receive the Nobel Prize in literature.
1952	Guatemala promulgates its land reform.
1952–64	The Bolivian revolution.
1953	Bolivia puts into effect its land reform.
1954	The CIA overthrows President Jacobo Arbenz of Guatemala.
1959	Triumph of the Cuban revolution and the advent of Fidel Castro to power. Cuba issues its Agrarian Reform Law.
1961	Washington breaks diplomatic relations with Cuba. The CIA sponsors the Bay of Pigs invasion in an attempt to overthrow Castro. President John F. Kennedy announces the Alliance for Progress.
1964	The Brazilian military deposes President João Goulart and establishes a dictatorship.
1965	The United States invades and occupies the Dominican Republic.
1970	For the first time, urban Latin Americans equal in number their rural counterparts.
1970–73	President Salvador Allende sets in motion profound reforms to peacefully and democratically change Chile.
1973	The Chilean military overthrows President Allende, who dies in the attack on the presidential palace. The Uruguayan military terminates their nation's twentieth-century experiment with democracy.

1974–76   Isabel Perón serves as president of Argentina, the first female chief of state in the Western Hemisphere.

1977   Panama and the United States sign a treaty returning the Canal Zone to Panamanian control and putting the canal under Panamanian direction by 1999.

1979   Triumph of the Nicaraguan revolution. Young military reformers stage a coup d'etat in El Salvador.

1981   Nicaragua promulgates its agrarian reform law. Latin America enters a severe economic crisis.

1982   Argentina invades the Falkland Islands and is defeated by Great Britain.

1983   The United States invades Grenada and overthrows government. Economic reverses highlight Latin America's increasing difficulty in making international debt payments.

1984   The CIA mines the harbors of Nicaragua. Latin America's foreign debt reaches an unmanageable $350 billion. Contadora Group presents its Peace Plan for Central America.

1985   Brazil returns to democracy and civilian rule. Latin American population surpasses the 400 million mark.

1987   At Esquipulas, the five Central American presidents sign a regional peace plan. President Oscar Arias wins the Nobel Peace prize.

1988   Effective political plurality characterizes the Mexican presidential election for the first time since the Revolution began.

Statistics on the Nations of Latin America and the Caribbean

COUNTRY	AREA (SQ. MILES)	POPULATION (1986)	CAPITAL	PRINCIPAL PRODUCTS
Argentina	1,072,749	32,900,000	Buenos Aires	Meats, grains, wool, hides, dairy, meat byproducts, minerals
Bahamas	4,400	245,000	Nassau	Rum, fruits, vegetables
Barbados	166	254,000	Bridgetown	Sugar, molasses, rum
Bolivia	424,163	7,000,000	La Paz	Tin, tungsten, lead, zinc
Brazil	3,287,195	151,400,000	Brasilia	Coffee, cotton, cacao, beans, manganese, iron ore
Chile	286,396	13,100,000	Santiago	Copper, nitrate, wheat, iron, wines
Colombia	439,519	31,800,000	Bogotá	Coffee, petroleum, cattle, bananas, rice, cacao
Costa Rica	19,575	2,700,000	San José	Coffee, cacao, bananas
Cuba	44,218	10,500,000	Havana	Sugar, tobacco, fruits, nickel
Dominican Republic	18,703	7,000,000	Santo Domingo	Cacao, sugar, coffee, bananas, rice
Ecuador	104,506	10,900,000	Quito	Bananas, cacao, coffee, sugar, gold, balsa wood, petroleum
El Salvador	8,061	6,500,000	San Salvador	Coffee, cotton, oils, balsam
Granada	133	10,000	St. George's	Rum, sugar, bananas
Guatemala	42,042	9,700,000	Guatemala City	Coffee, bananas, chicle, cotton
Guyana	83,000	850,000	Georgetown	Bauxite, sugar, rice, coconuts
Haiti	10,714	7,500,000	Port-au-Prince	Sisal, sugar, textiles
Honduras	44,480	5,100,000	Tegucigalpa	Bananas, coffee, lumber, silver, gold

COUNTRY	AREA (SQ. MILES)	POPULATION (1986)	CAPITAL	PRINCIPAL PRODUCTS
Jamaica	4,411	2,400,000	Kingston	Bauxite, alumina, sugar, bananas, mineral fuels, rum, citrus fruits
Mexico	760,000	89,000,000	Mexico City	Cotton, petroleum, coffee, sugar, wheat, lead, zinc, corn, silver
Nicaragua	54,864	3,900,000	Managua	Coffee, cotton, sugar
Panama	29,306	2,200,000	Panama City	Bananas, abaca, cacao, fish
Paraguay	157,047	4,200,000	Asunción	Lumber, tannin, livestock, corn, cotton
Peru	496,223	22,300,000	Lima	Cotton, sugar, lead, copper, petroleum, gold
Surinam	63,251	415,000	Paramaribo	Aluminum, rice, sugar
Trinidad and Tobago	1,980	1,200,000	Port-of-Spain	Petroleum, sugar, asphalt, rum, cacao, coffee, citrus, fruits, cement
Uruguay	72,172	3,100,000	Montevideo	Wool, meat, hides
Venezuela	352,146	21,200,000	Caracas	Petroleum, iron ore, canned fish, coffee, cocoa, sugar

A Glossary of Spanish and Portuguese Terms

Adelantado   An individual in colonial Spanish American authorized by the crown to explore, conquer, and hold new territory. He pushed back the frontier and extended Spanish claims and control of the New World.

Alcaldes mayores   In colonial Spanish America, appointed officials who held administrative and judicial responsibility on local or district level.

Aldeia   An Indian village or settlement in Portuguese America administered by the religious orders until the mid-eighteenth century and then by secular officials thereafter.

Audiencia   The highest royal court and consultative council in colonial Spanish America.

Ayllu   A communal unit in the Incan empire that worked the land in common, part for themselves and part for the Incan ruler and priestly elite.

Bandeirante   Particularly active during the 1650–1750 period, these individuals penetrated the interior of Brazil to explore, to capture Indian slaves, or to search for gold.

Cabildo   The municipal government in Spanish America.

Cabildo abierto   The municipal council in Spanish America, which expanded under special circumstances to include most of the principal citizens of the municipality.

Campesino   A farmer or peasant.

Capitão-mor   (plural, *capitães-mor*) A military rank given to commanders of the local militia in colonial Portuguese America.

Capitulación   A contract between monarch and *adelantado* stating the duties and rewards of the latter.

Casa da Suplicação   The highest court in the Portuguese empire and therefore the supreme court for judicial disputes in colonial Brazil.

Casa de Contratación   The Board of Trade established in Spain in 1503 to organize, regulate, and develop trade with the New World.

Caudillo   (Portuguese, *caudilho*) A strong leader who wields complete power over subordinates.

Cédula   A royal edict from the Spanish monarch.

Científico   A high administrator in the government of President Porfirio Díaz of Mexico (1876–1911), infused with Positivist ideas, who believed national problems could be solved by scientific solutions. Such men were prominent during the last two decades of his administration.

Compadrio   A godparent relationship.

Composición   A Spanish legal device for claiming land through surveys.

Comunero   A participant in the Comunero Revolt that occurred in New Granada in 1781.

Congregación   The Spanish policy of concentrating Indians into villages.

Consejo de las Indias   The Council of the Indies established in Spain in 1524 to advise the monarch on American affairs.

Conselho geral   In Portuguese America, a municipal council expanded under special circumstances to include most of the principal citizens of the municipality.

Conselho Ultramarino   The Overseas Council established in Lisbon in 1642 to advise the crown on matters relating to the empire and its administration.

Consulado   In colonial Spanish America, a guild of merchants acting as a sort of chamber of commerce.

Coronel   (plural, *coroneis*) A civilian political boss of a Brazilian municipality. The system of political control founded on the local bosses came to be known as *coronelismo*.

Corregidor   An official in colonial Spanish America who was assigned to Spanish as well as Indian communities as tax collector, police officer, magistrate, and administrator.

Creole   A white born in the Spanish American empire.

Cumbe   A settlement of runaway slaves in Spanish America.

Denuncia   Under Spanish law, the process of claiming land that does not have legally recognized owners.

Ejido   The common land held by Indian communities and used for agriculture in Mexico.

Encomendero   The person who received an *encomienda*.

Encomienda   A tribute institution used in Spanish America in the sixteenth century. The Spaniard received Indians as an entrustment, *encomienda,* to protect and to Christianize, but in return he could demand tribute including labor.

Fazenda   A large estate or plantation in Brazil.

Fazendiero   The owner of a large estate or planation in Brazil.

Finca   A large estate in Spanish America.

Fuero militar   A special military privilege in Spanish America that exempted officers from civil legal juridsiction.

Gaucho   The cowboy of the Pampas.

Hacendado   A large estate in Spanish America.

Homens bons   In Portuguese, literally the "good men," those who belonged to the upper echelon of Brazilian colonial society. They voted for members of the municipal council.

Inquilino   A Chilean peasant.

Jefe   Chief or leader; boss. In Spanish America, it is often used as synonymous with *caudillo.*

Latifundia   The system of large landholdings in Latin America.

Mandamiento   A forced labor system.

Mascarada   A public festivity in which all or part of the participants wear costumes and masks.

Mazombo   In Portuguese America, a white born in the New World.

Mestizo   A person of mixed parentage. Usually it refers to a European-Indian mixture.

Mita   A forced labor system in which the Indian was required to labor for the state. It is most often associated with Indian labor in the Andean mines.

Oidor   A judge on the *audiencias* of Spanish America.

Palenque   A settlement of runaway slaves in Spanish America.

Patrón   In Spanish America, the owner or boss or one in a superior position.

Peninsular   In Spanish America, a white born in Europe who later came to the New World.

Porfiristas   Those in Mexico who supported Porfirio Díaz or his policies.

Porteño   An inhabitant of the city of Buenos Aires.

Presidencia A subdivision of the viceroyalties of Spanish America, having a president as the chief executive officer.

Pueblo A town, but it can also mean "people."

Quilombo A settlement of runaway slaves in Portuguese America.

Ranchos Squatter settlements in Venezuela.

Regidor Municipal councilman in Spanish America.

Reinol (plural, *reinóis*) In Portuguese America, a white born in Europe who later came to the New World.

Relação The high court in Portuguese America.

Repartimiento A labor institution in colonial Spanish America in which a royal judge made a temporary allotment of Indians for a given task.

Residencia In both the Spanish and Portuguese American empires, a formal inquiry into the conduct of a public official at the end of his term of office.

Sambo A person of mixed Indian and African parentage.

Senado da Câmara In Brazil, the municipal government, in particular the town council.

Sertão The interior, backlands, or hinterlands of Brazil. The term refers particularly to the hinterland region of northeastern Brazil.

Sesmaria A land grant in colonial Brazil.

Soldadera During the Mexican Revolution, a woman who was attached to a soldier. The *soldaderas* cooked for the soldiers, tended the ill and wounded, and fought.

Tenente In Brazil, an army lieutenant. The word is often used to denote those junior army officers during the 1920s and early 1930s who favored social, economic, and political reforms.

Vecindad Literally "neighborhood" in Spanish, but in Mexico City it can refer to a "tenement" dwelling.

Visita In both the Spanish and Portuguese American empires, an on-the-spot administrative investigation of a public employee ordered by the monarch.

Visitador In colonial Spanish and Portuguese America, an official in charge of making a special investigation for the monarch in the New World.

A Glossary of Concepts and Terms

Scattered throughout this text are a series of concepts and terms, some of which are defined—"reform" and "revolution," for example—and some of which are not—"capitalism," "socialism," and "Enlightenment," for example. The purpose of this glossary is to provide brief working definitions for the concepts and terms frequently encountered in the text. Definitions very widely. They can be slippery. I have attempted to define the words in accordance with their use in the text, but I realize these definitions will neither satisfy everyone nor be universally applicable.

Capitalism   An economic system characterized by private ownership and investment, economic competition, and profit incentive.

Centralism   A high concentration of political power in the capital city.

Communism   Communism really denotes a future society, one yet to be achieved. Societies often termed Communist are really at best in a transitional phase whose goal is a form of community living free from hierarchical controls and enjoying common property. This book uses the term within a contemporary context to mean a government ruling in the name of the workers and peasants to best serve their ends and an economic system controlled by that government. The government owns the means of production in the name of the workers and peasants. This text distinguishes socialism from communism by the degree of state ownership, by the degree of democracy, and the existence of a plurality of political parties.

Conservatism   The term is generally associated with nineteenth-century political parties whose disposition was to preserve things much as they were, exercising caution in the acceptance of change.

Democracy   A system of government in which all or most of the citizenry participate in the decision-making process. Western democracy stresses equality of all citizens before the law, a government responsive to the majority, regular elections, civil liberties, and plural political parties.

Dependency   Dependency describes a situation in which the economic well-being, or lack of it, of one nation, colony, or area results from the consequences of decisions made elsewhere. Latin America was first dependent on the Iberian mother-lands, then in the nineteenth century on England, and in the twentieth on the United States, whose decisions and policies directly influenced, or influence, its economic prosperity or poverty. Obviously to the degree a nation is dependent, it will lack "independence" of action.

Development   The maximum use of a nation's potential for the greatest benefit of the largest number of inhabitants.

Elites   Those persons who occupy the highest or most eminent positions in society.

Enlightenment   Broadly identified with eighteenth-century Europe, the Enlightenment introduced a series of ideas associated with the forms of democracy and capitalism of the nineteenth century. The Enlightenment believed in human social evolution and thus became a kind of philosophy of progress and perfectability. The ideas of the Enlightenment exerted a profound influence on the writing of the U.S. Constitution and on the ideology of the Latin American elites.

Federalism   In a feudal political system, political power is divided and/or shared between a central government and regional or local governments.

Feudalism   Strictly speaking, this term refers to a form of social organization prevalent in Europe from the time of the dissolution of Charlemagne's empire until the rise of the absolute monarchies, roughly from the ninth to the fifteenth centuries. Its general characteristics were strict class division, private jurisdiction based on local custom, and a landowning system in which the owner, the lord, allowed the serf to work land in return for services and/or payments. By extension, the term is used in Latin America to designate a system in which a few own the land and control the lives of the many who work the land for them. Those few enjoy comfortable lives, while the workers live in misery largely dependent on the whims of the land-owners. The term today has connotations much more emotional than legal.

Growth   Growth indicates numerical accumulation in a country or region's economy and generally does not reveal who, if anyone, benefits from it.

Institutions   This book's most frequently used term and its most difficult to define, "institutions" represent the recognized usages governing relations between people, an entire complex of such usages and the principles governing it, and the formal organizations supporting such a complex. Perhaps Webster's unabridged dictionary offers a more satisfactory and comprehensive definition: "A significant and persistent element (as a practice, a relationship, an organization) in the life of a culture that centers on a fundamental human need, activity, or value, occupies an enduring and cardinal position within a society, and is usually maintained and stabilized through social regulatory agencies." Examples range from patriarchal families to the military, from village social structure to land division.

Liberalism   This term is generally associated with nineteenth-century political parties whose disposition was to relax governmental control, to expand individual freedom, and to innovate.

Luso-Brazilian   This term encompasses both Portugal and Brazil. In Roman times, the area we now associate with Portugal bore the name Lusitania, the adjective being Luso.

Mercantilism A term coined in the eighteenth century, it is a belief that the nation's economic welfare can best be ensured by governmental regulation of a nationalist character. The policy as imposed by the Iberian nations meant that the welfare of the motherlands received preferential treatment to those of the Latin American colonies, generally considered to exist for the enrichment of Spain and Portugal.

Metropolis This term refers to that country exerting direct or indirect control over another. For Spanish America, the metropolis in the colonial period was Spain; for Brazil, Portugal. During the nineteenth century, the metropolis for Latin America was England; in the twentieth century it has been the United States.

Modernization In Latin America, modernization consisted largely of copying and adopting, rarely adapting, the styles, ideas, technology, and patterns of Northern Europe in the nineteenth century and the United States in the twentieth.

Nationalism This term refers to a group consciousness that attributes great value to the nation-state, to which total loyalty is pledged. Members of the group agree to maintain the unity, independence, and sovereignty of the nation-state as well as to pursue certain broad and mutually acceptable goals.

Nation-state This term, implying more than the area encompassed by the geographic boundaries of a country, signifies that a central authority effectively exercises political power over that entire area.

Neofeudalism *Neo*, from the Greek, signifies "new" or "recent." See the entry "feudalism."

Oligarchy These privileged few rule for their own benefit, demonstrating little or no responsibility toward the many.

Patriarchal, Patriarchy This term refers to a type of family arrangement, or government, in which the father or an elderly male rules.

Patrimonialism A system in which the landowner exerts authority over his followers as one aspect of property ownership. Those living on his land fall under his control. He rules the estate at will and controls all contact with the outside world. The term describes the hacienda system.

Physiocrat Doctrine This concept originating in the eighteenth century urges society to survey scientifically its resources and, once knowing them, to exploit them. Maximum profit results from the exploitation and international sale of those resources.

Populist Political movements or governments that seem at least outwardly opposed to the status quo are in some cases termed "populist." They advocate a system appealing to and supported by large numbers of the ordinary citizens, generally the urban working class. In practice, they often provide temporary relief or benefits without actually reforming basic social structures.

Positivism This nineteenth-century ideology originated in France. Its principal philosopher was Auguste Comte. Positivism affirmed the inevitability of social revolution and progress. According to Comte, that progress was attainable through the acceptance of scientific social laws codified by Positivism.

Reform   To reform is to gradually change or modify established economic, political, or social institutions.

Revolution   Revolution denotes the sudden, forceful, and violent overturn of a previously stable society and the substitution of other institutions for those discredited.

Socialism   As used in this text, socialism denotes a democratic society in which the community owns or controls the major means of production, adminstering them for the benefit of all.

Readings
to Supplement the Text

An impressive number of paperback books are in print in English that make excellent supplementary readings for this text. The following brief guide to the paperback literature on or about Latin American history is divided into three parts: National Histories, Topics, and Novels. As of 1988, all of these books were in print. Unfortunately, paperback editions have the tendency of going out of print quickly. However, some of them enjoy a longevity in print that speaks well of their quality and assures their avilability, and it is a selection of those books I have attempted to compile in this bibliography.

For those who might wish to acquaint themselves with a long and inclusive guide to hardcover works, as well as essays and articles, on Latin American history, I recommend they begin by consulting Charles C. Griffin, ed., *Latin America: A Guide to Historical Literature* (Austin: University of Texas Press, 1971). *The Handbook of Latin American Studies,* prepared by an array of scholars for the Library of Congress and published annually since 1936, surveys the current bibliography, complementing the Griffin work as well as supplying the bibliography since 1971.

NATIONAL HISTORIES

Excellent national histories exist in paperback. These books tend to emphasize themes rather than present a simple narrative flow of the past. Thomas E. Skidmore and Peter H. Smith emphasize economic history after 1880 with six country and one regional (Central America) studies; *Modern Latin America* (New York: Oxford University Press, 1984). Frederick B. Pike offers a study of comtemporary Spanish-speaking Latin America in his *Spanish America, 1900–1970: Tradition and Social Innovation* (New York: Norton, 1973). For specific nations, there are David Rock, *Argentina, 1516–1987. From Spanish*

Colonization to Alfonsin (Berkeley and Los Angeles: University of California Press, 1987); Herbert S. Klein, *Bolovia: The Evolution of a Multi-Ethnic Society* (New York: Oxford University Press, 1982); E. Bradford Burns, *A History of Brazil* (New York: Columbia University Press, 1980); Franklin W. Knight, *The Caribbean: The Genesis of a Fragmented Nationalism* (New York: Oxford University Press, 1978); Ralph Lee Woodward, Jr., *Central America: A Nation Divided* (New York: Oxford Univerisity Press, 1985); Brian Loveman, *Chile: The Legacy of Hispanic Capitalism* (New York: Oxford University Press, 1988); Jim Handy, *Gift of the Devil. A History of Guatemala* (Boston: South End Press, 1984); Michael C. Meyer and William L. Sherman, *The Course of Mexican History* (New York: Oxford University Press, 1979); Eric Wolf, *Sons of the Shaking Earth: The People of Mexico and Guatemala; Their Land, History and Culture* (Chicago: University of Chicago Press, 1970); José Carlos Mariátegui, *Seven Interpretive Essays on Peruvian Reality* (Austin: University of Texas Press, 1974); and John V. Lombardi, *Venezuela. The Search for Order, The Dream of Progress* (New York: Oxford University Press, 1982).

TOPICS

For colonial Latin American history, there are a variety of outstanding syntheses and specific studies. The masterpiece of sophisticated synthesis remains Stanley J. Stein and Barbara H. Stein, *The Colonial Heritage of Latin America* (New York: Oxford University Press, 1970). James Lockhart and Stuart B. Schwartz provide a mature, masterful study of the colonial past, *Early Latin America. A History of Colonial Spanish America and Brazil* (New York: Cambridge University Press, 1983). In *The Forging of the Cosmic Race. A Reinterpretation of Colonial Mexico* (Berkeley and Los Angeles: University of California Press, 1981), Colin M. MacLachlan and Jaime E. Rodriguez offer new perspectives on the Mexican colonial past as the cradle of a new nation and "race." As an introduction to colonial Brazil and the Portuguese empire in the New World, C. R. Box has written the lively *The Golden Age of Brazil, 1696–1750* (Berkeley and Los Angeles: University of California Press, 1975). Leslie Bethell has edited three collections of tight, interpretive scholarly essays: *Colonial Spanish America, Colonial Brazil,* and *The Independence of Latin America* (New York: Cambridge University Press, 1987). Richard Graham provides a thoughtful summary of the independence period in his *Independence in Latin America* (New York: Knopf, 1972).

Two general essays and six country or area studies provide academic insight into the first half-century of national history in Leslie Bethell, ed., *Spanish America after Independence. c. 1820–c. 1870* (New York: Cambridge University Press, 1987). In *The Poverty of Progress. Latin America in the Nineteenth Century* (Berkeley and Los Angeles: University of California Press, 1983), E. Bradford Burns offers an interpretation of the nineteenth century as a period of intense struggle between the folk and the elite over the iplementation of modernization. It is impossible to understand the mentality of the nineteenth-century elite without reading Domingo F. Sarmiento, *Life in the Argentine Republic in the Days of the Tyrants, or Civilization and Barbarism* (New York: Hafner, 1960) and Euclydes da Cunha, *Rebellion in the Backlands* (Chicago: University of Chicago Press, 1970). As the da Cunha book points out, not all Latin Americans favored modernization. Another superb example of people's resistance to the imposition of European ideas and ways is Nelson Reed, *The Caste War in Yucatan* (Stanford: Stanford University Press, 1964). A meaty introduction to theory and examples of peasant rebellion in Peru and Bolivia will be found in Steve J. Stern, ed., *Resistance, Rebellion, and Consciousness in the Andean Peasant World, 18th to 20th Centuries* (Madison: University of Wisconsin Press, 1987).

The important questions of development and change are discussed in Fernando Henrique Cardoso and Enzo Faletto, *Dependency and Development in Latin America* (Berkeley and Los Angeles: University of California Press, 1979); Fidel Castro, *The World Economic and Social Crisis* (New York: Ediciones Vitral, 1983); Jeanine Swift, *Economic Development in Latin America* (New York: St. Martin's Press, 1978); Andre Gunder Frank, *Lumpenbourgeoisie, Lumpendevelopment: Dependence, Class, and Politics in Latin America* (New York: Monthly Review Press, 1974); and Shelton H. Davis, *Victims of the Miracle: Development and the Indians of Brazil* (New York: Cambridge University Press, 1977). The major tragedies of underdevelopment, hunger, and the importance of agrarian reform are the subjects of three very important books: Alain de Janvry, *The Agrarian Question and Reformism in Latin America* (Baltimore: Johns Hopkins University Press, 1985); George W. Schuyler, *Hunger in a Land of Plenty* (Cambridge, Mass.: Schenkman, 1980); Jospeh' Collins, *What Difference Could a Revolution Make? Food and Farming in the New Nicaragua* (San Francisco: Institute for Food and Development Policy, 1986); and Medea Benjamin, *No Free Lunch. Food & Revolution in Cuba Today* (San Francisco: Institute for Food and Development Policy, 1984).

A fuller understanding of how the ordinary people live, are influenced by national institutions, and react to those institutions emerges from the pages of Eric R. Wolf and Edward C. Hansen, *The Human Condition in Latin America* (New York: Oxford University Press, 1974). Carolina Maria de Jesus, a black woman who inhabited the slums of São Paulo, left us a diary of her experiences and thoughts: *Child of the Dark* (New York: New American Library, 1962). *Don't Be Afraid, Gringo. A Honduran Woman Speaks from the Heart. The Story of Elvia Alvarado*, translated and edited by Medea Benjamin (San Francisco: Institute for Food and Development Policy, 1987) relates in first-person the courageous story of a savvy, impoverished woman who became an outspoken peasant leader. In *The Human Tradition in Latin America. The Twentieth Century* (Wilmington, Del.: Scholarly Resources, 1987), editors William H. Beezley and Judith Ewell offer a unique perspective, twenty-three biographies of "ordinary people," a human face on the recent past.

Three classical interpretations of Latin American cultures by Latin Americans are José Enrique Rodó, *Ariel* (Austin: University of Texas Press, 1988); José Vasconcelos, *The Cosmic Race* (Los Angeles: Department of Chicano Studies, California State University, 1979); and Gilberto Freyre, *The Masters and the Slaves. A Study in the Development of Brazilian Civilization* (Berkeley and Los Angeles: University of California Press, 1986).

For a thoughtful study of race relations in a comparative dimension, read Carl N. Degler, *Neither Black nor White: Slavery and Race Relations in Brazil and the United States* (New York: Macmillan, 1971). Katia M. de Queirós Mattoso adopts the viewpoint of the slaves from capture in Africa to manumission in Brazil in her overview, *To Be a Slave in Brazil, 1550–1888* (New Brunswick, N.J.: Rutgers University Press, 1986). For Spanish America, Leslie B. Rout, Jr., has written a sweeping account, *The African Experience in Spanish America. 1502 to the Present Day* (New York: Cambridge University Press, 1976). One of Haiti's major intellectuals, Jean Price-Mars, discusses the duality, French and African, of his nation's culture in his 1928 classic, *So Spoke the Uncle* (Washington, D.C.: Three Continents Press, 1983), providing insights into the rich cultural diversity of Latin America.

The Latin American and Caribbean Women's Collective offers fourteen studies, mainly economic, of the roles women have played in *Slaves of Slaves. The Challenge of Latin American Women* (London: Zed Press, 1980). For a psychological study of the most politically powerful women in Latin American history, consult the challenging *Eva Perón. The Myths of a Woman* (Chicago: University of Chicago Press, 1979) by J.M. Taylor. For a more individualized understanding of the role of women in one society there is Mary Lindsay Elmendorf, *Nine Mayan Women: A Village Faces Change* (New York: John Wiley, 1976). For Brazil of the 1890–1930 period, two women provide us with valuable insights into their views of their society: Elizabeth Bishop, ed., *The Diary of "Helena Morley"* (New York: Eco Press, 1977), and Rachel de Queiroz, *The Three Marias* (Austin: University of Texas Press, 1963).

In *Mexico 1910–1976: Reform or Revolution* (London: Zed Press, 1979), Donald Hodges and Ross Gandy discuss the revolution, its meaning, and its impact on Latin America. To provide an intelligent background to the crises in Central America, Tom Barry cultivates the *Roots of Rebellion. Land & Hunger in Central America* (Boston: South End Press, 1987). Jonathan L. Fried, et al. compiled an informative reader, *Guatemala in Rebellion. Unfinished History* (New York: Grove Press, 1983), on revolution and counterrevolution. The paperback literature on Nicaragua and El Salvador grows monthly. It is enormous. Particularly useful because they provide a broad background and understanding are John A. Booth, *The End and the Beginning. The Nicaraguan Revolution* (Boulder, Colo.: Westview Press, 1985); Thomas W. Walker, *Nicaragua. The Land of Sandino* (Boulder: Westview

Press, 1982); Tomás Borge, et al., *Sandinistas Speak. Speeches, Writings, and Interviews with Leaders of Nicaragua's Revolution* (New York: Pathfinder Press, 1982); Tommie Sue Montgomery, *Revolution in El Salvador. Origins and Evolution* (Boulder: Westview Press, 1982); and Enrique A. Baloyra, *El Salvador in Transition* (Chapel Hill: University of North Carolina Press, 1982). Penny Lernoux reviews the drama and dilemmas of contemporary Latin America in her highly readable *Cry of the People. The Struggle for Human Rights in Latin America—The Catholic Church in Conflict with U.S. Policy* (New York: Penguin Books, 1982).

Studying Latin American history is also learning about U.S. foreign policy, since the United States has played such an important role, particularly in the twentieth century. For an introduction to the material available, the following three paperbacks offer insight and clear style: Cole Blasier, *The Hovering Giant. U.S. Responses to Revolutionary Change in Latin America* (Pittsburgh: University of Pittsburgh Press, 1976); Richard Newfarmer, ed., *From Gunboats to Diplomacy. New U.S. Policies for Latin America* (Baltimore: John Hopkins University Press, 1984); and Harold Molineu, *U.S. Policy Toward Latin America. From Regionalism to Globalism* (Boulder, Colo.: Westview Press, 1986).

The role played by the CIA in Latin America is well outlined by William Blum, *The CIA. A Forgotten History* (Atlantic Heights N.J.: Zed, 1986). Specific case studies are illuminated and documented in James Petras and Morris Morley, *The United States and Chile: Imperialism and the Overthrow of the Allende Government* (New York: Monthly Review Press, 1975); Peter Wyden, *Bay of Pigs: The Untold Story* (New York: Touchstone Books, 1980); Richard H. Immerman, *The CIA in Guatemala. The Foreign Policy of Intervention* (Austin: University of Texas Press, 1982); and Stephen Schlesinger and Stephen Kinzer, *Bitter Fruit. The Untold Story of the American Coup in Guatemala* (Garden City, N.Y.: Doubleday, 1983).

NOVELS

Fortunately, a wide variety of Latin America's authors have been translated into English. Their works are available in relatively inexpensive paperback editions. They provide an insight into their society through the fictional documentary. I particularly recommend novels by these socially conscious authors: Jorge Amado (Brazil), Manlio Argueta (El Salvador), Miguel Angel Asturias (Guatemala), Mariano Azuela (Mexico), Alejo Carpentier (Cuba), Carlos Fuentes (Mexico), Carlos Gagini (Costa Rica), Gregorio López y Fuentes (Mexico), Gabriel García Márquez (Colombia), Graciliano Ramos (Brazil), Mario Vargas Llosa (Peru), and Agustín Yáñez (Mexico).

Index

Betancourt, Rómulo, 259
Bishop, Maurice, 337
Blacks, 23–26, 212–19. *See also* Slaves
    Caribbean, 217–19
Blaine, James G., 172
Bogotá, 19
Bolívar, Simón, 73, 76, 84, 85, 98
Bolivia, 103, 104, 112, 138, 273–79, 307, 318
    agriculture, 276–77
    under Belzu (1848–1855), 125–27
    Indians, 166, 273, 276
    land ownership, 276
    land reform, 276
    the military in, 277
    nationalization, 274–76
    under Paz Estenssoro, 275–76
    railroads, 145–46
    revolution of 1952, 275, 278, 298, 299
    silver, 29, 30
    tin mines, 275–76
    women, 254
Bonifácio de Andrada e Silva, José, 86
Bosch, Juan, 302–3, 306
Boyer, Jean-Pierre, 79, 121
Brasilia, 244
Brazil, 23, 99, 102, 110, 112, 121, 132, 133,
    139, 146, 147, 342
    abolition of slavery, 132, 133, 212–13
    agriculture, 114, 154, 229, 309–11
    aldeia system, 35
    Amazon rain forest, 311
    Argentina and, 104–5
    Bahian Conspiracy (1798), 75–76
    bandits, 167
    blacks in, 24–25, 215–17
    the Church in, 56–58, 133, 260, 310, 311
    coffee interests, 180–81
    colonial, 19–20, 40–48, 65–67, 70–72
        captaincies, 40, 45
        the Church, 56–58
        courts, 44–45
        governors-general later called viceroys),
            44–45
        municipal governments, 45–47
        plantation families, 47
        regions of settlement, 48
    democracy, 256–58, 260, 261, 301, 311,
        312
    discovery and early history, 15, 16
    economic growth under military regimes,
        309–10
    economy, 109
    film industry, 203–4
    foreign debt, 311, 318
    foreign investment, 237
    gold in, 29–31
    government, 95–97
    immigration, 158
    independence, 86–87
        transfer and legitimization of power af-
        ter, 95–97

    Indians, 11–12, 35–36, 66, 211–12
    industrialization, 140–41, 309–10
    industry, 66–67, 236, 237
    inflation, 311
    land ownership, 37–38, 114–17, 160, 228
    maintenance of unity in 19th century,
        103–4
    middle class, 179–82
    military dictatorship, 308–12, 314–15
    the military in, 133, 180–82, 261, 303,
        307
    monarchy, 132, 133, 179, 180
    nationalism, 200–204, 208
    northeastern, 230–32
    oil industry, 208
    oligarchy, 181
    political stability (19th century), 131–33
    population, 48
    Positivism and progress in, 142–43
    Quebra-Quilo Revolt, 164–65
    rural masses, 230–32
    slave resistance and revolts, 164
    slaves, 35–36, 180
    trade, 111, 114–15, 138, 177
    urbanization, 155
    women, 247, 250–52, 254–55
    workers and unions, 239–40
British Honduras, 163. *See also* Belize
Buenos Aires, 19, 90, 101, 135, 155, 158,
    238
    colonial era, 52–53
Bulnes, Manuel, 140
Bunau-Varilla, Philippe, 176
Bureaucracy, 41–42

Cabildo, 50–51
Cabral, Pedro Alvares, 15
Calderón, Rafael, 239
Calderón de la Barca, Frances, 102, 115–16,
    247
California, 53, 103
Calles, Plutarco Elías, 191, 193–94
Caminha, Pero Vaz de, 12
Cámpora, Héctor, 242
Capitalism, 92, 109, 342
    defined, 355
    Positivism and, 142
Cárdenas, Lázaro, 195–97, 212, 239, 240
Caribbean region, 16, 20
    encomiendas, 31
    independence, 217–20
Carranza, Venustiano, 191–93
Carrera, Rafael, 122–25
Carter, Jimmy, 334–36
Casa de Contratación, 17, 48, 62, 63
Castilla, Ramón, 136
Castillo, Bernal Diaz del, 11
Castillo, Otto Rene, 272–73
Castillo Armas, Carlos, 270
Castro, Fidel, 209, 233, 280–82, 284–85,
    287

Development, 210, 222, 356. *See also* Indus-
trialization; Modernization
growth and, 95
Diaz, Porfirio, 161, 135–36, 139, 142, 144,
190–91
Dictatorship. *See also* Caudillos
military. *See* Military dictatorship
populist, 303
Dollar Diplomacy, 173
Dominican Republic, 101, 171, 302–3, 317
Dominicans, 32
Drug trafficking, 277, 318
Duarte, José Napoleón, 326
Dulles, Allen, 268
Dulles, John Foster, 268, 270
Durant, Will and Ariel, 301
Dutch colonists, 19–20

Echeverría, Esteban, 90
Economic dependency. *See* Dependency
Economic development. *See* Development
Economic growth, 112
development and, 95
Economic nationalism, 206–10
Economic prosperity. *See* Prosperity
Economic Societies of the Friends of the
Country, 71–72
Economy. *See also specific topics and specific
countries*
in 19th century, 108–17
Ecuador, 103, 112, 147, 307, 318
Education and schools, 89–90, 156–57,
178–79. *See also specific countries*
folk culture and, 94
women, 250
Eisenhower, Dwight D., 270, 278
Elites:
caudillos and, 118–19
defined, 130–31
after independence, 95–100
El Salvador, 319, 324–27
civil war, 326–27, 329
export economy, 149–52
institutional conformity, 149–53
land reform, 325–26
Encomiendas, 31–34
Enlightenment, the, 69–72, 81, 111
consequences of, 89–95
defined, 356
Española, 29
Export economy, 154, 229, 230, 235, 318,
320–21. *See also* Trade; *specific countries*

Falkland Islands, 170, 316
Federalism, 98, 103, 356
Ferdinand VII, King of Spain, 32–34, 77,
106
Ferreyra, José Augustin, 205–6
Feudalism, 38, 160, 312
defined, 356

neofeudalism, 161
Figueiredo, João Baptista, 311, 312
Films, 203–6, 307
Cuban, 283–84
Folk cultures (or societies), 94–95
caudillos and, 119–20
Fonseca, Carlos, 294
Fonseca, Deodoro da, 180
Food exports, 320–21. *See also* Export econ-
omy; *specific crops and countries*
Food imports, 229–30, 320
Food production, 229–30. *See also* Agricul-
ture
Foreign debt, 2, 146, 316–22. *See also specific
countries*
International Monetary Fund (IMF) and,
317–19
Foreign intervention, 100–101, 146, 170–
72. *See also* United States, military in-
terventions by
by France in Mexico, 108
Foreign investment, 139–40, 209
in 19th century, 111
United States, 176–77, 209–10, 237–38
after World War II, 237–38
Foreign trade. *See* Trade
France, 19, 77–78, 101, 140, 170, 211
Haitian independence and, 78–79
intervention in Mexico, 108
Francia, José Gaspar Rodríguez de, 79–81,
120
Free trade, 126
Frei, Eduardo, 259, 304
Freyre, Gilberto, 216
Friedman, Milton, 315
Fuentes, Carlos, 3, 198

Gama, Vasco da, 15
Gauchos, 122
Geisel, Ernesto, 311, 312
Generation of 1837, 90–92
Geography of Latin America, 3–7
Germany, 140, 146
Goiás, 29
Gold, 17–21, 28–29
Gómez Farías, Valentín, 107
Goulart, João, 308
Government, after independence, 95–100
Gran Colombia. *See* Colombia
Great Britain, 74, 85–86, 140, 143, 170, 171,
176, 218, 316
Caribbean colonies, 20
economic relations with Latin America,
110–11
investments in Latin America, 139–40
trade, 138
Grenada, 218, 335
U.S. intervention, 337
Guadeloupe, 20
Guatemala, 9, 144, 179, 218, 264–73, 301–2
agriculture, 267–68

Guatemala (*cont.*)
  under Arévalo, 266–67
  under Carrera (1839–1865), 122–25
  cultural nationalism, 269
  Indians, 34, 123–24
  land reform, 267, 269, 271
  the military in, 327
  quality of life, 272
  U.S. interventions, 270–72
Guayaquil, 147
Guerrilla movements, 2, 301–2. *See also spe-
  cific countries*
Guianas, 20
Guipúzcoa Company, 73–74
Guyana, 218, 219
Guzmán Blanco, Antonio, 142

Haiti, 25, 104, 174, 214–15, 219, 230
  Boyer's rule (1818–43), 121
  independence, 78–79
Havana, 19
Hay, John, 176
Hay-Pauncefote Treaty, 176
Health, 32. *See also* Quality of life
  Spanish conquest and, 18
Henry "the Navigator," Prince of Portugal,
  13–14
Hernández, José, 156
Herndon, William Lewis, 6
Hidalgo, Father Miguel, 81–82
Hispaniola, 16, 17, 56
Holy Alliance, 100, 106
Honduras, 307, 324, 328–29
Housing, 246
Huerta, Victoriano, 191
Humboldt, Alexander von, 55, 65, 70, 105
Hunger and malnutrition, 2, 229, 230, 319
Hunt, E. Howard, 270, 285–86

Illiteracy, 156–57
  Mexico, 193
Immigration, 93, 158–59, 218
Incas, 10, 18. *See also* Peru, Indians
Income distribution, 342
  Chile, 225
Independence, 69, 77–78. *See also specific
  countries*
  Caribbean nations, 217–20
  elitist leadership of movements for, 83–
    87, 89
  transfer and legitimation of power after,
    95–100
Indians, 15–16, 20–22, 31–37, 161. *See also
  specific countries*
  Argentina, 227–28
  Bolivia, 125–27, 166, 273, 276
  Brazil, 11–12, 35–36, 66, 211–12
  the Church and, in colonial era, 32, 53–
    56
  encomiendas and, 31–32
  in labor force, 22, 31–36

landownership and, 36, 37
Mexico, 162–63, 166–67, 212
nationalism and, 211–12
Peru, 35, 75, 212, 312, 313
rebellions by, 162–63
repartimiento system, 34–35
Spain and, 31–35
women, 21
Industrialization, 140–41, 153, 170, 178,
  207, 234–38
Industry, 112, 113
  Brazil, 66–67, 236, 237
  dependency of, 235–36, 238
  Mexico, 236
Infant mortality, 2–3
Inflation, 2
Inquisition, 57
Institutional conformity, 148–53
Institutions, defined, 356
Intellectuals, 156. *See also* Enlightenment,
  the; Literature
  cultural nationalism and, 201–6
  the Enlightenment and, 69–72
  racial theories, 211
  women, 252
Intendancy system, 63
International Monetary Fund (IMF), 317–18
Intervention. *See* Foreign intervention
Iran-Contra scandal, 332
Irigoyen, Hipólito, 183
Isabel, Queen of Spain, 31–32
Iturbide, Augustin de, 97–98

Jamaica, 218–19, 335
Jesuits, 35, 56, 58, 66
John III, King of Portugal, 40
John Paul II, Pope, 341
Johnson, Lyndon, 262, 302
John V, King of Portugal, 66
John VI, King of Portugal and Brazil (for-
  merly Prince Regent), 77, 86, 95
Juárez, Benito, 101, 107, 108
Judicial system, colonial era, 44–45, 50

Kennedy, John F., 302, 330
Kennedy, Robert F., 339
Kissinger, Henry, 337
Kissinger Commission report, 337–38

Labor (work force), 179, 223. *See also* Proletariat; Unions
  Argentina, 240–42
  colonial era, 31–36
  encomiendas and, 31–34
  Indian, 22, 31–36
  Mexico, 239, 240
  in 19th century, 112–13
  repartimiento system, 34–35
  slave. *See* Slaves
  Uruguay, 239
  women in, 255

Poverty, 245–46
Progress, 130, 141–42. *See also* Modernization
    ideology of, 90–93
    institutional conformity and, 148–53
Proletariat, 179. *See also* Labor
    rural, 230–32
    urban, 238–42, 245
Prosperity, 130, 136–41
Prussia, 100
Puerto Rico, 56, 173, 212, 220

Quality of life, 162. *See also specific countries*
    Caribbean nations, 218, 219
Quebra-Quilo Revolt, 164–65
Querino, Manuel Raimundo, 24, 215
Quesada, Gonzalo Jiménez de, 19
Quito, 19, 147, 245

Racial attitudes, 210–17
Racism, 91
Railroads, 143–46
Ramos, Graciliano, 230–31
Reagan, Ronald, 297–98, 329, 336–38
Rebellions, in 19th century, 162–65
Recife, 20
Regionalism, 103
Religion, 25
Repartimiento system, 34–35
Revolution, 343. *See also* Independence; *specific countries*
    defined, 189–90, 358
    phases of, 264
Rio de Janeiro, 44, 77, 102
Río de la Plata, 6–7, 19
River networks, 6–7
Rodrigues, Raimundo Nina, 215
Roman Catholic Church, 28, 40. *See also specific countries*
    change encouraged by, 340–41
    colonial era, 53–59
    democracy and, 259–60
    Indians and, in colonial era, 32, 53–56
    land ownership by, 105, 107–8
    in 19th century, 105–8, 115, 119
Romanticism, 156
Roosevelt, Franklin D., 197
Rosas, Juan Manuel de, 90, 91, 101, 122, 200
Russia, 100

Saint Domingue, 78. *See also* Haiti
Salvador da Bahia, 23, 25, 44, 61
Sandinista Front for National Liberation (FSLN), 292–93
Sandino, Augusto César, 174–75, 292
San Gabriel Mission, 53
San Martín, José de, 84, 85, 98
Santa Anna, Antonio López de, 107
Santiago de Chile, 155
Santos Zelaya, José, 174

São Paulo, 155
Sarmiento, Domingo Faustino, 90–92, 156, 178–79
Schools. *See* Education and schools
Sendero Luminoso (Shining Path), 314
Sepúlveda, Juan Ginés de, 34
Silver, 19, 21, 29
Slave revolts, 25
Slaves (slavery), 23–25, 161
    abolition of, 85, 112, 212–13
    Brazil, 35–36, 180
    Indian, 32–34
    Saint Domingue (Haiti), 78
Slave trade, 23
Soccer War, 324
Socialism, defined, 358
Somoza, Anastasio, 175
Somoza, Anastasio, Jr., 293
Soviet Union, Cuba and, 282
Spain (Spaniards), 101, 171
    abolition of slavery, 212
    Caribbean colonies, 20
    the Church and, 54
    colonial administration, 40, 41, 48–53, 62–65, 101
        mercantilism, 62
        the military, 63–65
    conquest and settlement by, 16–19
    exploration and discoveries, 14–15
    gold and silver and, 28–30
    independence of colonies from. *See* Independence
    Indians and, 31–35
    Napoleon and, 77
Spanish-American War, 173
Squatter settlements (shantytowns), 246
Stability. *See* Political stability
Standard Oil Company of Bolivia, 274–75
Steamships, 110, 147
Strong, Rev. Josiah, 172–73
Sucre, 98
Sugar, 16–17, 20, 38, 39

Taft, William Howard, 173–74
Tariffs, 112, 140
Tejada, Lidia Gueiler, 254
Telegraph, 146–47
Texas, 103, 107, 171
Tobago, 218
Toledo, Francisco de, 49
Tordesillas treaty, 15
Toro, David, 274–75
Torres, Camilo, 302
Torrijos Herrera, Omar, 335
Toussaint L'Ouverture, 78–79
Trade, 28. *See also* Export economy; Mercantilism; *specific countries*
    1930, 206–7
    African, 22–23
    colonial era, 17, 19–20, 65–67, 72–74
    free, 126